ERASMUS ON LITERATURE

His *Ratio* or 'System' of 1518/1519

Edited by Mark Vessey from the translation and notes by Robert D. Sider

None of the works included among Erasmus' 'Literary and Educational Writings' in the Collected Works of Erasmus captures his most adventurous thinking about how texts signify in – and thereby make or remake – worlds of thought, feeling, and action. The one that comes closest to doing so, the *Ratio verae theologiae* ('A System of True Theology'), was first published separately in 1518 and 1519, then appeared in the preliminaries to the New Testament in Erasmus' revised 1519 edition.

This handy *Ratio* or compendious 'System' gave advice on how to interpret complex texts and develop persuasive arguments based upon them. Its lessons were applied to the canonical Scriptures as source discourse, and to everyday Christian theology as target discourse. They unfold in response to the special difficulties and incitements of the biblical text in Latin and Greek, within a framework provided by classical grammar and rhetoric, adjusted to the examples of the Church Fathers as exemplary interpreters of the Bible. At every turn, the *Ratio* reveals the instincts and intuitions of an exceptional theorist and practitioner of the cognitive, social, and political arts of written language. This student edition, the first of its kind in any language, is based on the translation and notes by Robert D. Sider in the Collected Works of Erasmus volume 41. It has been designed to make it easier to estimate the long-term value of this particular work and of Erasmus' works more generally, and to allow for a multidisciplinary understanding of the lives of human beings as symbol-using creatures in worlds constructed partly by texts.

MARK VESSEY is Principal of Green College and Professor of English Literature at the University of British Columbia.

ROBERT D. SIDER is General Editor of the New Testament Scholarship for the Collected Works of Erasmus.

ANTHONY GRAFTON is Henry Putnam University Professor of History at Princeton University.

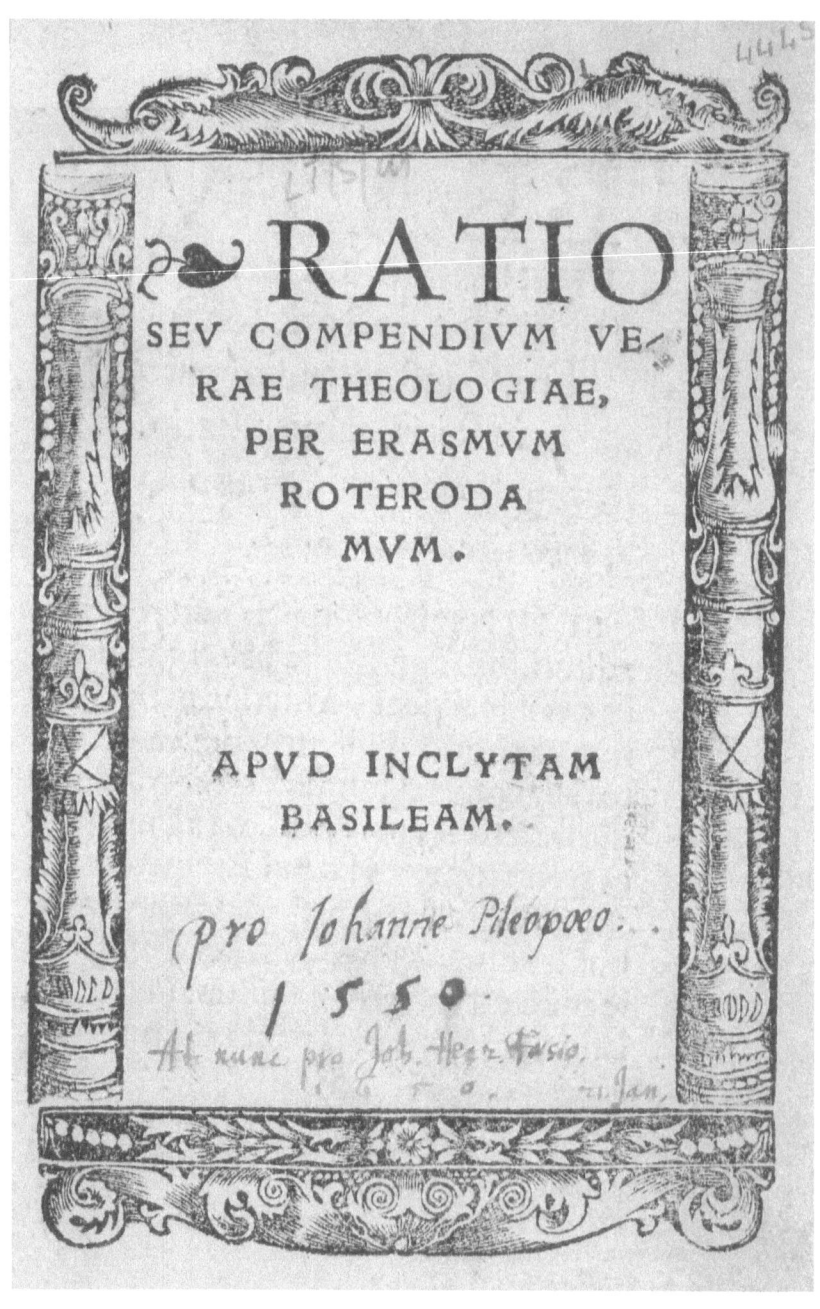

Figure 1. Title page of the *Ratio seu compendium verae theologiae*, published by Johann Froben at Basel, January 1519

The Bodleian Libraries, University of Oxford (Shelf mark Vet D1 f. 78)

Erasmus on Literature

His *Ratio* or 'System' of 1518/1519
(The *Ratio verae theologiae*)

Edited by MARK VESSEY from
the Translation and Notes
by ROBERT D. SIDER

With a foreword by Anthony Grafton and essays
by Brian Cummings, Kathy Eden, Riemer Faber,
and Christopher Ocker

UNIVERSITY OF TORONTO PRESS
Toronto Buffalo London

© University of Toronto Press 2021
Toronto Buffalo London
utorontopress.com

ISBN 978-1-4875-0269-0 (cloth)   ISBN 978-1-4875-1583-6 (EPUB)
ISBN 978-1-4875-2210-0 (paper)   ISBN 978-1-4875-1582-9 (PDF)

Erasmus Studies

The translation of the *Ratio verae theologiae* used here is that of Robert D. Sider from the Collected Works of Erasmus: volume 41, *The New Testament Scholarship of Erasmus: An Introduction with Erasmus' Prefaces and Ancillary Writings*, edited by Robert D. Sider. The notes to the *Ratio* were abbreviated and adapted from those by Robert D. Sider (in the same volume) by Mark Vessey, who assembled and arranged the contents of the present edition.

Library and Archives Canada Cataloguing in Publication

Title: Erasmus on literature : his Ratio or 'System' of 1518/1519 : (The Ratio verae theologiae) / edited by Mark Vessey from the translation and notes by Robert D. Sider ; with a foreword by Anthony Grafton and essays by Brian Cummings, Kathy Eden, Riemer Faber, and Christopher Ocker.
Names: Vessey, Mark, editor. | Container of (expression): Erasmus, Desiderius, –1536. Ratio verae theologiae. English. | Sider, Robert D. (Robert Dick), translator.
Series: Erasmus studies.
Description: Series statement: Erasmus studies | The translation of the Ratio verae theologiae used here is that of Robert D. Sider from the Collected Works of Erasmus: volume 41, The New Testament Scholarship of Erasmus: An Introduction with Erasmus' Prefaces and Ancillary Writings, edited by Robert D. Sider. The notes to the Ratio were abbreviated and adapted from those by Robert D. Sider (in the same volume) by Mark Vessey, who assembled and arranged the contents of the present edition. | Includes bibliographical references and indexes.
Identifiers: Canadiana (print) 20200410121 | Canadiana (ebook) 20200410318 | ISBN 9781487522100 (paper) | ISBN 9781487502690 (cloth) | ISBN 9781487515836 (EPUB) | ISBN 9781487515829 (PDF)
Subjects: LCSH: Erasmus, Desiderius, –1536. Ratio verae theologiae. | LCSH: Erasmus, Desiderius, –1536 – Translations into English. | LCSH: Erasmus, Desiderius, –1536 – Criticism and interpretation.
Classification: LCC PA8502.E5 S53 2021 | DDC 480 | 199/.492–dc23

University of Toronto Press acknowledges the financial assistance to its publishing program of the Canada Council for the Arts and the Ontario Arts Council, an agency of the Government of Ontario.

Canada Council   Conseil des Arts
for the Arts   du Canada

ONTARIO ARTS COUNCIL
CONSEIL DES ARTS DE L'ONTARIO
an Ontario government agency
un organisme du gouvernement de l'Ontario

Funded by the   Financé par le
Government   gouvernement
of Canada   du Canada

Canadä

Contents

Illustrations	vii
Foreword by Anthony Grafton	ix
Notes on Contributors	xv
Abbreviations and Works Frequently Cited	xvii
Abbreviations of Biblical Books Used in Explanatory Notes	xix
Editor's Introduction	3
Chronology of Erasmus' Life and Works	17
Part 1: APPROACHES TO ERASMUS' *RATIO* OR 'SYSTEM' OF 1518/1519	19
The *Ratio* in Erasmus' Life and Work to 1519 Mark Vessey	21
Erasmus, Sacred Literature, and Literary Theory Brian Cummings	48
Biblical Poetics in Scholasticism and the *Ratio* Christopher Ocker	63
The *Ratio* and *Annotations* as Theory and Practice of Biblical Interpretation Riemer Faber	80
The Parable of Sincere and Sophistical Discourse in the *Ratio* Kathy Eden	93

Part 2: THE *RATIO VERAE THEOLOGIAE* — 109

Scheme of Contents of the *Ratio verae theologiae* — 111
Note on the Text — 113

RATIO VERAE THEOLOGIAE OR 'SYSTEM OF TRUE THEOLOGY'

Preface: Purpose of the *Ratio* — 114
Elements of a Method for the Study of Scripture — 115
The Unity in Variety of the Gospel — 131
'The Wonderful Circle and Harmony of the Entire Drama of Christ' — 146
The Figurative Character of the Language of 'Sacred Literature' — 197
Elements of a Method for the Study of Scripture *(concluded)* — 223

Explanatory Notes — 247
Conspectus of Church Fathers Cited in the *Ratio* — 329

Bibliography — 335

Concordance of Editions of the Ratio — 343

Index of Rhetorical Terms and Literary-Critical Concepts — 351

General Index — 353

Illustrations

1 Title page of the *Ratio seu compendium verae theologiae*, published by Johann Froben at Basel, January 1519
  frontispiece   ii
2 List of contents for the fifth class of Erasmus' works, from the *Catalogus novus omnium Lucubrationum Erasmi Roterodami*, published by Johann Froben at Basel, September 1524   29
3 Title page of Erasmus' *Lucubrationes*, published by Mathias Schürer at Strasbourg, September 1515   40
4 Title page of the *Novum instrumentum*, published by Johann Froben at Basel, February 1516   43

For James K. McConica

Foreword

ANTHONY GRAFTON

Erasmus had strong views about how to read texts, as he did about many other things, from warfare to justice. But he never went to war or administered justice, and he spent his life arguing about and practising interpretation. At the start of his literary career, he addressed the best way to read Scripture in the *Enchiridion*. He explained how to approach classical literature in his *Adagia* of 1508 and in his treatises on education, the *De ratione studii* of 1511 and the *De copia* of 1512.[1] By the time he returned to the subject in his prefaces to his 1516 New Testament and developed it in the *Ratio verae theologiae*, published and republished in 1518–19, he drew on decades of reflection and argument.

Unlike some other specialists in hermeneutics, moreover, Erasmus put his theories into practice, everywhere from the comments on classical aphorisms in the *Adagia* to his *Annotations* on and *Paraphrases* of the New Testament – not to mention his scholia on the letters of Jerome, which took shape in the same years as his New Testament commentaries. He was still thinking hard about precepts and practices in later years, when he wrote his polemical dialogue on style, the *Ciceronianus*, and compiled his immense manual on preaching, the *Ecclesiastes* – both key documents for his ways of reading secular and sacred literature.

The present volume makes the *Ratio verae theologiae* available in a precise and readable English version. Notes explicate Erasmus' terminology and identify his sources. The accompanying essays trace the book's development and set it into its multiple contexts. They show that Erasmus' manual on how to read and his commentaries and paraphrases

---

1 For the versions of commentary theorized and practised in the Renaissance, see Céard 'Theory and Practices of Commentary in the Renaissance.'

were parts of a single, organic enterprise, which was at the core of his life's work.

Erasmus' theories and practices were partly shaped by his inheritances. The *De doctrina Christiana* of Augustine buttressed his claims that one should apply the same literary tools to the Bible and imaginative literature. Jerome's works supported his argument that the New Testament must be studied in every witness to its oldest form, including the Greek and Old Latin texts – even though doing so revealed that neither Jerome's Vulgate nor Erasmus' own protean Latin rendering of the text could claim authoritative status, word by word. Some medieval exegetes had emphasized highly technical questions that Erasmus dismissed as pointless pedantry, unrelated to the real meaning of the New Testament. His mockery of the scholastics led to bitter controversies. But other medieval commentators had insisted on the importance of the literal sense and the usefulness of patristic scholarship, and Erasmus learned from them. The medieval *Glossa ordinaria* supplied him with dozens of samples of older commentary, which he regularly drew on even as he rendered the compilation obsolete by exposing its errors and insufficiencies.[2]

Ancient writers on grammar, rhetoric, and literature, above all Quintilian, gave him the tools, such as constant comparison of passages, which he applied on every page of textbook and commentaries alike. Above all, the Netherlandish meditative traditions he knew in his youth and the classical rhetorical tradition that judged all utterances by their impact came together in his approach to scriptural reading. Working from this foundation, he argued with compulsive eloquence that the New Testament, properly approached, would transform its readers. Read the text as it should be read, and it would pull you into the scenes of Jesus' life, ground you in the mysteries of Christian belief, and make you, passage by passage, into as good imitators of Christ as humans could be. Pagan texts – Plato's account of the *Sileni* of Alcibiades – could also work wonders. But they could not compare to the New Testament revelation of the living Jesus.

No single work – not even the *Ratio* – fully represents the moving target that was Erasmus' theory and practice of interpretation. Some tools served him in many contexts, over the long term. In the *Ratio* he argued that the reader of Scripture must set the text into history. Doing so helped make the text spring to vivid life: 'Now if we will learn from historical literature not only the setting, but also the origin, customs,

---

2 de Jonge 'Erasmus und die Glossa Ordinaria zum Neuen Testament'

institutions, culture, and character of the peoples whose history is being narrated or to whom the apostles write, it is remarkable how much more light and, if I may use the expression, life will come to the reading' [**19**]. Reading historically enabled the reader to penetrate to the true sense of allegories, which remained opaque to those who could not identify the stones and plants, animals and customs that served as their outer shell. Above all, reading historically made clear that certain commands and practices of the early Christians were responses to the particular conditions they had faced in a rapidly changing world, and should not bind the modern church: 'There are many other things of this kind that were instituted for use in those times but have later been consigned to oblivion or changed; for example, many sacramental ceremonies. Many rites were then not observed that we are now told to observe; for example, feast days and perhaps the private confession of sins – would that at the present time we might use it as profitably as we use it indiscriminately!' [**48**]. The same sensitivity to change in culture and language later underpinned Erasmus' argument, in the *Ciceronianus*, that modern Christians could not adopt the language of Cicero without making it impossible to discuss their own religion – not to mention the many other customs and technologies that set their world apart from the ancient one.

Yet building a method was the work of decades. Erasmus forged and reforged many of his tools in the course of a lifelong confrontation with ancient and modern models, in the course of which his positions changed with new experiences of editing, commenting, and revision. In the *Ratio* he uses the example of Aelius Donatus, the fourth-century commentator on Terence and Virgil with whom Jerome had studied, to clarify the way in which Origen had applied secular learning to the exegesis of Scripture: '[Origen] does for the divine books exactly what Donatus does for the comedies of Terence in laying bare the intent of the poet' [**27**]. As a younger man, Erasmus had sharply criticized the old master. In 1508, commenting on a line from Terence's *Phormio* in the *Adagia*, he noted with asperity that Donatus had offered three conflicting interpretations of it without choosing one of them. He dismissed this approach as 'guesswork,' the result of 'variable and uncertain conjectures.'[3] Erasmus was right to point out that Donatus had deliberately compiled variorum commentaries.[4] But not everyone agreed with

---

3 *Adagia* I v 3; CWE 31 386. His reference is to *Aeli Donati quod fertur Commentum Terenti*, ed. Paul Wessner, 2 vols. (Leipzig: Teubner, 1902–5), II 473.
4 For Donatus' working method, see now Zetzel *Critics, Compilers and Commentators* 122, 132–6.

him that this approach was pointless. When Jerome defended himself against Rufinus, who had denounced him for including heretical material in his commentary on Ephesians, he argued that compilation was the central task of the commentator: 'they quote the opinions of many individuals and they say "Some interpret the passage in this sense, some in another sense."' The decision lay, as it should, with the 'prudent reader,' who, 'like an expert money-changer, will reject the falsely minted coin.'[5] This striking image caught the attention of many Renaissance interpreters, including Azariah de' Rossi, who used it to describe the task of the prudent reader in his massive work on the interpretation of the Hebrew Bible, the works of Philo and many other texts, the *Light of the Eyes*.[6] The Erasmus who saw the value of Donatus's commentaries had realized that the endless cycles of questioning and speculation in Origen's *Homilies on Genesis* focused the reader's mind on the essential elements of such biblical dramas as the sacrifice of Isaac. He had also supervised the 1516 Froben edition of Jerome's works, and learned to see Jerome's teacher as an exemplary figure in the history of commentary.

Over time, Erasmus included more materials from the tradition of exegesis in his editions of the New Testament, and engaged more intensively with them in his *Annotationes*. The 1519 edition, for example, contains the Greek Canon Tables of Eusebius, with their preface, also in Greek: an ingenious system for lining up the passages in the Gospels that were parallel in content without disturbing the order of the texts themselves. One of the central forms of literary interpretation since the ancient world had been bio-bibliography: the provision of basic information about the author of a text and the rest of his or her writings, as an introduction – called an *accessus* in the Middle Ages – to the work itself.[7] Drawing on Eusebius and others, Jerome had compiled a stately series of bio-bibliographical notices in his *De viris illustribus*. Erasmus incorporated Jerome's notices on the four evangelists into the 1519 and later editions of his New Testament, putting them at the beginnings of the Gospels. He also engaged with Jerome in the *Annotations*, making clear that he saw Luke, for example, as a human writer, whose work had a particular context and intention.[8] Tracing the origins of each ingredient in Erasmus' mighty work does not yield an interpretation of it, as

---

5 Jerome *Contra Rufinum* 1.16; PL 23 cols 428–9; translation by J.N. Hritzu in Jerome, *Dogmatic and Polemical Works* (Washington, DC: Catholic University of America Press, 1965), 79–80
6 See Veltri *Alienated Wisdom* 51–2.
7 Clark 'Reading the Life Cycle'
8 Vessey 'The Actor in the Story' 62–9

Mark Vessey points out in his introductory essay below. But as he has also shown, it makes clear as no other approach can the full complexity and richness of what Erasmus wrought.

This potent brew found many eager consumers. Most histories of hermeneutics say little about Renaissance humanism – except to acknowledge its new emphasis on historical interpretation – and pass directly to the Reformation, when elaborate manuals were written and the term itself was coined. Yet the Reformation's theorists of hermeneutics, Philipp Melanchthon and Matthias Flacius Illyricus, hatched the egg that Erasmus had laid. One task, for Erasmus, confronted every interpreter: identifying the *scopus*, translated below as 'target point,' of the text. The best way to help tyros learn to read the Scriptures, he argued, would be to provide them not with a training in scholastic argumentation but with the *scopi* to look for as they worked their way through the text. These would enable them to harvest its central lessons as they read: 'It would be more to the point, in my opinion, to hand down to our young tyro doctrines reduced to a compendium and to their chief particulars, and this above all from the Gospel sources, then from the apostolic Epistles, so that everywhere he might have clearly defined target points with which to set in line his reading' [35]. Protestants did not agree that Erasmus had found the true *scopi*: he concentrated on the conduct and virtue of the first Christians rather than on their doctrines, which all Protestants saw as the core of the Scriptures. But they took over his method eagerly, and used it for everything from scriptural exegesis to church history. Flacius, for example, taught generations of young Protestant readers to believe that every text had a single *scopus*, or goal. The reader must strip each book down to its central point as a surgeon strips the flesh from a human body to reveal the structure of its bones (the analogy was Flacius's own).[9] The young men who compiled the patristic and medieval sources for the Protestant church history that Flacius organized, the *Magdeburg Centuries*, organized their notebooks around the *scopi* of their sources, which they used to organize the excerpts from which the history was drawn.[10] Erasmus would not have used the analogy to anatomy, which was characteristic of the interdisciplinary culture at Wittenberg.[11] But he might have felt

---

9 See Matthias Flacius Illyricus, *De ratione cognoscendi sacras literas: Über den Erkenntnisgrund der Heiligen Schrift*, ed. and trans. Lutz Geldsetzer (Düsseldorf: Stern-Verlag Janssen, 1968).
10 See Lyon 'Baudouin, Flacius, and the Plan for the Magdeburg Centuries.'
11 See Ross 'Anthropologia.'

an ironic pleasure, had he lived long enough, in seeing the leader of the rigorously scripturalist Gnesiolutherans apply to Scripture and the world of the early church a method of analysis that he had first devised for schoolboys reading the classics.[12] Catholic preachers, especially in France, found inspiration in Erasmus' demonstrations of how to read Scripture for homiletic purposes, even if his *Ecclesiastes* was too cumbersome and repetitive – and suspect – to be very useful at the level of the ordinary mendicant.[13]

'Books that show in detail how humanists worked are few.' So wrote Arnaldo Momigliano, a great historian of scholarship, in 1949.[14] Recent studies of Renaissance humanism have made this one of the rare sentences in Momigliano's work that are now obsolete. But no group of scholars has done more to show modern readers how a humanist worked than the world's specialists in Erasmus – especially those who have translated and explicated so much of his interpretative writing for the University of Toronto Press's Collected Works of Erasmus. And no book adds more to our knowledge of humanism as a living practice than this rich combination of text and commentary, which enables us to watch over Erasmus' shoulder as he urges readers to join him in transforming the study of the Scriptures and being transformed by them.

---

12 On the notebook method that Erasmus took over from fifteenth-century educators and publicized with great success, see the pioneering treatment in Bolgar *The Classical Heritage and Its Beneficiaries* 265–75, 431–4, and also Moss *Renaissance Truth and the Latin Language Turn* 157–88; for its impact especially in Protestant theology, see more generally Christ-von Wedel *Erasmus of Rotterdam*.
13 Worcester 'The Catholic Sermon'; Michelson *The Pulpit and the Press in Reformation Italy* 52
14 Arnaldo Momigliano, review of José Ruysschaert, *Juste Lipse et les Annales de Tacite: une méthode de critique textuelle au xvie siècle*, *Journal of Roman Studies* 39 (1949): 190–2 at 190

Notes on Contributors

Brian Cummings is Anniversary Professor of English and Related Literatures, University of York

Kathy Eden is Chavkin Family Professor of English and Professor of Classics, Columbia University

Riemer Faber is Professor of Classical Studies, University of Waterloo

Anthony Grafton is Henry Putnam University Professor of History, Princeton University

Christopher Ocker is Director of the Program in Medieval and Early Modern Studies at the Institute for Religion and Critical Inquiry, Australian Catholic University in Melbourne

Robert D. Sider is General Editor of the New Testament Scholarship for the Collected Works of Erasmus

Mark Vessey is Principal of Green College and Professor of English Literature at the University of British Columbia

Abbreviations and Works Frequently Cited

Allen	*Opus epistolarum Des. Erasmi Roterodami* ed P.S. Allen, H.M. Allen, and H.W. Garrod (Oxford 1906–58) 11 vols and Index
ASD	*Opera omnia Desiderii Erasmi* (Amsterdam 1969–)
CEBR	*Contemporaries of Erasmus: A Biographical Register of the Renaissance and Reformation* ed P.G. Bietenholz and T.B. Deutscher (Toronto 1985–7) 3 vols
CWE	Collected Works of Erasmus (Toronto 1974–). References are to volume, page, and (where available and necessary) line number.
Ep	Epistle of Erasmus from CWE, when translated, or from Allen. References in all cases are by letter number in Allen (also used by CWE) and line numbers. Line numbers are those of CWE, with additional reference to numbering in Allen as needed.
ERSY	*Erasmus of Rotterdam Society Yearbook* (1980–2007)
ES	*Erasmus Studies* (2008–, continuing ERSY)
Holborn	*Desiderius Erasmus Roterodamus: Ausgewählte Werke* ed Hajo Holborn and Annemarie Holborn (Munich 1933; repr 1964)
LB	*Desiderii Erasmi Roterodami opera omnia* ed J. Leclerc (Leiden 1703–6; repr Hildesheim 1961) 10 vols
PG	*Patrologiae cursus completus ... series Graeca* ed J.-P. Migne. Patrologia Latina Database, electronic version representing the first edition (Paris 1844–65; ProQuest Learning Company 1996–2020)
PL	*Patrologiae cursus completus ... series Latina* ed J.-P. Migne. Patrologia Latina Database, electronic version representing the first edition (Paris 1844–65; ProQuest Learning Company 1996–2020)

Abbreviations of Biblical Books Used in Explanatory Notes

Old Testament

Gen	Genesis
Exod	Exodus
Lev	Leviticus
Num	Numbers
Deut	Deuteronomy
Josh	Joshua
Judg	Judges
Ruth	Ruth
1 Sam	1 Samuel
2 Sam	2 Samuel
1 Kings	1 Kings
2 Kings	2 Kings
1 Chron	1 Chronicles
2 Chron	2 Chronicles
Ezra	Ezra
Nehemiah	Nehemiah
Esther	Esther
Job	Job
Ps (*pl* Pss)	Psalms
Prov	Proverbs
Eccles	Ecclesiastes
Song of Sol	Song of Solomon
Isa	Isaiah
Jer	Jeremiah
Lam	Lamentations
Ezek	Ezekiel
Dan	Daniel

Hos	Hosea
Joel	Joel
Amos	Amos
Obad	Obadiah
Jon	Jonah
Mic	Micah
Nah	Nahum
Hab	Habbakuk
Zeph	Zephaniah
Hag	Haggai
Zec	Zechariah
Mal	Malachi

New Testament

Matt	Matthew
Mark	Mark
Luke	Luke
John	John
Acts	Acts of the Apostles
Rom	Romans
1 Cor	1 Corinthians
2 Cor	2 Corinthians
Gal	Galatians
Eph	Ephesians
Phil	Philippians
Col	Colossians
1 Thess	1 Thessalonians
2 Thess	2 Thessalonians
1 Tim	1 Timothy
2 Tim	2 Timothy
Titus	Titus
Philem	Philemon
Heb	Hebrews
James	James
1 Pet	1 Peter
2 Pet	2 Peter
1 John	1 John
2 John	2 John
3 John	3 John
Jude	Jude
Rev	Revelation

ERASMUS ON LITERATURE

His *Ratio* or 'System' of 1518/1519
(The *Ratio verae theologiae*)

Editor's Introduction

For an author whose books were once a staple of the academic textbook market, Erasmus cuts a slim figure on Anglophone syllabuses today. Alone of his works, the *Moria* or *Praise of Folly* can now be found whole in more than one classroom edition, the sign of a continuing popularity that would have tickled Dame Folly herself. His once bestselling *Adages* and *Colloquies* have been widely excerpted and anthologized. When his other 'Literary and Educational Writings,' as they are styled in Volumes 23 to 29 of the Collected Works of Erasmus (CWE), appear outside those library volumes and their online equivalents, it is usually piecemeal. While the name of Erasmus may have gained fresh currency as a badge of student mobility in pre-Brexit Europe, Erasmian texts and ideas that were once indispensable elements of a Europe-wide, Latinophone 'Republic of Letters' are probably no more familiar nowadays to English-reading students of the humanities than they were before the launch of CWE in 1974.

Is it possible that Erasmus, for all his protean fluency across genres and publishing formats, fatally hurt his chances of a lasting curricular presence by failing ever to encapsulate his most deeply felt convictions? After the early, experimental *Enchiridion militis christiani* or *Handbook of the Christian Soldier*, where does one look for the mature Erasmus' 'Handbook of Erasmianism'? It is not necessary to read far in this author to recognize that he would be a difficult thinker ever to tie down in writing. His contemporary detractors were quick to seize upon what they perceived to be his slipperiness. Yet clarity and pungency of discourse were as dear to Erasmus as obliquity and abundance, and few teachers of any subject at any time have been more sedulous than he of their students' convenience. How could this most practical and practised of communicators have completed a career that yielded nine bulky folio volumes of collected *opera*, without spinning off anything like a student's guide to his leading ideas and most firmly held principles?

Erasmus did in fact provide such a guide. The compact work in question has for five hundred years lain hidden, if not always in plain sight, then in a prominent place amid the contents of his oeuvre as he organized them. It here appears once more – as it did for the first time in Latin towards the end of 1518 and under another imprint early in 1519[1] – as a self-contained handbook for students, now in an English translation, with notes and other supporting material designed to bring it so far as possible within an early twenty-first-century intellectual horizon.

Erasmus' *Ratio* or 'System' (1518/1519)

Erasmus had thrown together a miniature prototype of this book in time for it to be inserted among the preliminaries of his edition of the New Testament – the *Novum instrumentum*, as it was then entitled – in the spring of 1516. There the text was headed simply *Erasmi Roterodami methodus*, 'The Method of Erasmus of Rotterdam,' leaving the application of the method to be inferred from its publishing context. When a hugely expanded version of the Erasmian 'system or method' (*ratio seu methodus*) appeared separately in 1518, its purpose was signalled in the title as to show a way 'for arriving by a short cut at true theology': *Ratio seu methodus compendio perveniendi ad veram theologiam*.[2] Long before a university publisher in our time hit upon the idea of a series of 'Very Short Introductions,' Erasmus and his printers had correctly foreseen the appeal to students in theirs of 'A Fairly Short Introduction to Theology.' It was largely shock appeal. The ideal user of this handbook was not just going to learn something *about* theology; he or she was going to learn to *do* it. An online course leading in six weeks to a qualification to practise neurosurgery would be less scandalous today than the offer of this Erasmian *Ratio* or short course was then.

No art, science, or field of study was ever more forbiddingly professional than theology, in Europe, ca 1518. It was the monopoly of graduates and professors of the subject – men like Martin Luther, whose name and opinions were then just coming to notice beyond the circles of his colleagues and students at the University of Wittenberg, to the consternation of some. And was *Erasmus*, the same Erasmus who in his youth

---

1 For details of these and other early editions, see CWE 41 481–5 and below 45–6, with the Note on the Text (113).
2 Comparing the *Methodus* of 1516 with the *Ratio* of 1518/1519, Sider describes the latter as 'essentially a new work' (CWE 41 482).

had given up studying for a degree in theology at the University of Paris out of disgust at the curriculum and teaching methods, who had set up instead as a freelance instructor of grammar and rhetoric, and since acquired a reputation as an elegant promoter in print of styles of eloquence and erudition based on ancient Latin and Greek models – was *this* man now offering virtual course-credit for a subject in which he could show no solid credentials of his own? That was what critics among the professional theologians, including Luther, would soon charge him with doing, even as some of them tried to tar him with Lutheranism.

What, precisely, was the scope or ambition of Erasmus' *Ratio* or 'System'?

The evidence of its early titling is equivocal. The long form, quoted above, emphasized the instrumental quality of what was on offer, setting 'true theology' as the point of arrival at the end of a process. In the same spirit, and already anticipating criticism, Erasmus in the 1516 *Erasmi Roterodami methodus* assimilated his function as guide to that of the 'many-headed statues of Mercury that were once customarily placed at crossroads, and from time to time by their direction conduct the traveller to a place where they themselves will never arrive' [3].[3] On the strength of that analogy, we could think of the *Ratio* as laying out a course with theology as its final destination. It would then be something like a course of *pre*-theology, comparable to courses for premedical students now, and Erasmus would have had his defence in place against charges of encroaching on the experts' turf.

It is unlikely, however, that Erasmus ever meant to concede so much or claim so little. As early as the first sentence of the *Ratio* of 1518/1519, describing what he had done in 1516 as to have provided 'a sort of method and system for the study of theology' (*methodum quandam ac rationem theologici studii* [1]), he implied that such study was the matter of the text already in hand, and not something to which his readers would proceed only upon becoming 'candidates of a most venerable theology' [2]. Their theological candidacy was already being enacted under his tutelage, in those pages. Granting that, could we still draw a line between the *study* and the *practice* of theology, and say that Erasmus prudently avoided crossing it? Not unless we read against the grain of his discourse. 'Let this be your first and only goal,' he wrote, 'that

---

3 Bold numerals in square brackets refer to paragraphs in the text of the 1518/1519 *Ratio* in this edition, which includes extensive passages taken over verbatim or almost verbatim from the 1516 *Methodus*; see below, 14, 247, and endnote on 1/9–10.

you be changed, be swept away, be inspired, be transformed into what you are learning' [10]. The language of 'goals' or 'target-points' (*scopi*) would become more insistent in the *Ratio*. Yet already in this initial formulation, dating from 1516, the ideal topography of pathway and destination risked being short-circuited. By sleight of hand in the *Ratio* Erasmus would go on to suggest that the process he had in mind was similar to that obtaining in disciplines like rhetoric and logic [10]. We may suspect, however, that he was partly redescribing those disciplines to make them fit his counter-institutional model of theological study. Whereas Quintilian had needed all twelve books of his *Institutio oratoria* to set out a course of rhetorical training, upon completion of which a young Roman might be ready to begin pleading in court, Erasmus launched his handbook by positing an ideal student on the brink of a radical change of life and being, if not already caught up in such change. The 'short way' or 'short cut' (*compendium*) advertised in longer forms of the title of the work could thus appear more sudden than some curious readers and would-be theologians might have been expecting.[4] The Erasmian method does not look forward to graduation; its beginning, middle, and end *is* personal transformation. It is not a syllabus, but a model for living. And it is all about life-changing discourse in action. The abbreviated form of the title used when this text of Erasmus appeared among the preliminaries of the second (1519) edition of his New Testament, namely *Ratio seu compendium verae theologiae* ('A System or Compendium of True Theology'), was perfectly fitting. Despite the disarming talk of Mercury statues and the like, the initial address of this *Ratio* to the reader was as immodest as Folly's at the beginning of the *Moria*. 'Look,' it says, '*this* is how to do theology. Ready or not?'[5]

Therein lay the shock value of the book, and its original market appeal. Five centuries later, it is unlikely that any publisher specializing in Christian theology would reissue the *Ratio* as a freestanding work. To say that is not to diminish its historical significance. The continuing interest and importance of the Erasmian *Ratio* or 'System' of 1518/1519 for the history of European and worldwide religious

---

4 We should note, however, that between the *Methodus* of 1516 and the *Ratio* of 1518/1519 Erasmus inserted a phrase to mitigate that appearance of suddenness: 'You may conclude that you have made progress ... if you sense that *little by little* you are becoming a different person' [10]. See below, 59.
5 For convenience, the text in hand will usually be referred to in the following pages as the *Ratio verae theologiae* or simply as the *Ratio*. Robert D. Sider points out that 'in many early editions the upper margin of the pages of the text carried only the very short and simple title, *Ratio verae theologiae*' (CWE 41 484).

formations and re-formations, for the long history of Christian theology, and for the history of biblical exegesis and hermeneutics are all beyond question. Thanks to work done in recent decades on Erasmus' New Testament scholarship, in particular, there has probably never been a better time than the present to reconsider his place and role in those histories. For such purposes, the annotated translation of the *Ratio* provided by Robert D. Sider in CWE 41: *The New Testament Scholarship of Erasmus: An Introduction with Erasmus' Prefaces and Ancillary Writings* is indispensable. Sider's English presentation of the *Ratio* and the precursor *Methodus* situates these works in Erasmus' career as a student, editor, and expositor of the Bible, tracks his engagement with Christian exegetical traditions, and flags the many places where his statements in the 1518/1519 and later editions fuelled debates in progress among his contemporaries or sparked new theological controversy. Despite its modest subtitle ('An Introduction'), Sider's essay on 'The New Testament Scholarship of Erasmus' (1–388) is now the definitive treatment of its subject. His edition of the *Methodus* (423–54) and *Ratio* (479–713) in English will in due course be complemented by the annotated edition of the Latin texts that are in preparation for the Amsterdam *Opera omnia Desiderii Erasmi* (ASD).

This paperback edition of the *Ratio* reprints Sider's translation, modified only by the insertion of paragraph numbers and (non-authorial) section headings for ease of reading and cross-reference. For all areas of coverage, except two, it reproduces, abridged and with occasional minor adjustments, the substance of his annotation. The exceptions concern (1) variant Latin versions of the biblical texts cited by Erasmus, and (2) most matters of theological controversy. For guidance on those points the reader is advised to refer to the full documentation in CWE 41.

This is not an edition of the *Ratio* with the theology left out; without the theology there would be no *Ratio*. This is, however, an edition of the *Ratio* that does not provide a dedicated channel for what can now fairly be considered the background noise of sixteenth-century theological contestation. More positively: this edition of the *Ratio* grants Erasmus a premise that his contemporary critics were extremely reluctant to allow him, namely that the best way to do theology was to take the New Testament itself as the supremely expressive, affective, persuasive medium of the personally and socially transformative teaching of Jesus Christ as ultimate author of those and other canonical books, through the action of the 'divine spirit.' That is a theological premise. But it is also, without prejudice to any theology, a *literary* premise, in that it makes an assumption about the possibilities of interaction between (A) human minds-in-bodies and (B) 'texts' or artefacts of written language.

Formulating the project of the *Ratio* in those terms reminds us of the myriad ways in which Erasmus appears in history as an exponent of what has been called the 'textual condition' or, in more traditional terms, as a 'man of letters.' The sequencing and publishing history of his works in CWE reinforce the point. Volumes 1–22 comprise his 'Letters' (ie correspondence) in the *epistolary* sense, a sense developed and refined by him into something like a new 'literary' sensibility. Next come the 'Literary and Educational Writings' (CWE 23–9), which he called works 'regarding instruction in letters' (*qui spectant ad institutionem literarum*), where the immediate referents of his term *literae* were the arts of discourse known since antiquity as grammar and rhetoric. In his personal scheme of works, the *Colloquies* (39–40) belonged to the same category, as in principle did the *Adages* (30–6) and *Apophthegmata* (37–8), wherever they might fall in practice. In fact, the whole of the monumental structure of Erasmian 'Letters' and 'Literary and Educational Writings' constituted by CWE 1–40, with the sole exception of a few volumes of correspondence dating from after 1519, was in place in print in that modern series before the *Ratio* appeared as part of the volume of New Testament prolegomena. The publication of CWE 41 in 2019 provided the opportunity for this paperback edition. To contemplate Erasmus' *Ratio* or 'System' of 1518/1519 as a sequel to the 'literary' contents of CWE 1–40, while recognizing its utility as a key to the 'New Testament Scholarship' in CWE 42–60, is to begin the thought experiment of *Erasmus on Literature*.

The publishing history of CWE foregrounds an effect that could in any case have been felt by readers of the *Ratio* in late 1518 or early 1519. The purported 'System' was the newest production of a writer who had by then proved himself extraordinarily alert to the cognitive and affective potentials of written and printed texts. If so accomplished a textualist were to expound the nature and powers of a text or 'scripture' as uniquely important to his culture as the Latin Bible, what difference might that make – not only to theology at the time but also, over time and in our time, to what has since come to be known as 'literature'?

While a question of that order may seem in retrospect to have been shaping itself in the minds of literary critics and historians for more than a century now, it is only in the last few decades that it has taken clear form.

Erasmus on Literature

Erasmus has been a figure in literary history for as long as that modern genre has existed. Placing him as a theorist of literature, or as a practitioner who could have influenced theories or ideas of 'literature' held by others, has been a harder task. In the historical anthologies of literary criticism and theory that began to circulate in English-speaking academic milieux at the beginning of the last century, and that were still a standard feature of curricula in university English and Comparative Literature programs at the beginning of this one, the sections devoted to the late medieval and early modern periods typically moved the student along at a brisk clip from Dante and Boccaccio to Sir Philip Sidney, with perhaps a glance at the Italian theorists of poetry whom Sidney laid under contribution in his *Defence of Poesy*. One of the first to compile such an anthology, G.E.B. Saintsbury, afraid of failing in his task as a literary historian if he did not 'set forth at some length ... the critical position of Erasmus,' confessed to finding less to his purpose in that writer's works than he had expected. '[I]t is almost enough to read the *Adagia* and *Apophthegmata*,' he glumly remarked, 'to see how much there is left out which a literary critic *pur sang* could not but have said.' To complicate matters, as he explained in a footnote, Erasmus was at the time (ca 1900) 'still only readable as a whole, or in combination of his really important literary work, in the folios of Beatus Rhenanus or Le Clerc,' by which he meant the *Opera omnia* issued at Basel soon after the author's death and the edition published at Leiden (in Latin, *Lugdunum Batavorum*) at the beginning of the eighteenth century (LB). It was 'a thousand pities,' Saintsbury went on, 'that this more important literary work has not been re-edited together accessibly and cheaply.'[6] Exactly where Saintsbury would have located that 'more important literary work' within the works of Erasmus, had they then been more easily accessible to him, we can only guess. Now that a convenient English edition is to hand, it may be time to ask again after the missing Erasmian *loci critici*.

If the term 'literature' in wider discourse stands for something distinctive, where does Erasmus stand in relation to it?

Saintsbury belonged to only the second or third generation of public critics and university teachers who could have taken a thing called 'literature' for the subject of a distinct academic field. It was essential that 'literature' in that understanding not be subject to any regime of knowledge or experience other than the one reputedly its own. That is why it could then seem so unfortunate that Erasmus had allowed his attention to stray as often as it had from 'the strictly literary side of the Art' of criticism; that he had, as Saintsbury put it, devoted so much of his energy

---

6 Saintsbury *History of Criticism* II 10–11. His own anthology, *Loci Critici*, had no place for Erasmus. Further discussion in Vessey '"Nothing If Not Critical"' 435–9.

to matters 'textual and exegetical' and to 'forms of Biblical and patristic text-criticism.' These were not just temporary strictures of Saintsbury's. No less hard or fast would be the quasi-institutional bounds of 'literature' fenced and policed by literary critics against intrusions from Christian theology and all strains of biblical exegesis until at least the middle of the twentieth century. Where, in those days, were the Bible and the Church Fathers in 'literary' curricula? Or the vast enterprises of medieval Jewish and Christian biblical interpretation? Or their successive reconfigurations down to the time of the so-called Higher Criticism and the Romantic reaction to an Enlightenment philosophy that in its more sceptical moods threatened to dispel all mysteries, including those of the divinely inspired texts or scriptures beginning for Christians with Genesis and ending with Revelation?[7]

Defective as the old literary-critical anthologies were for the period from Dante to Sidney, their omissions in that zone were as nothing compared with the blanks that they left between between Pseudo-Longinus *On the Sublime* in the first (?) century AD and the author of the *Commedia* in the thirteenth. (Dante, we should note, was then usually summoned as a champion of poetry in the *lingua volgare*, not as any kind of theologian.) Historically imagined, 'literature' in the modern understanding was seen to take its first rise from Dark Age, indigenous, vernacular, pagan, originally oral traditions of future European nations – traditions *not* abounding in explicitly literary-critical doctrine – and its second from an elusive and inarticulable mingling of Arab and troubador 'romance' spirits in the eleventh century. Classical Greek and Latin precedents were referenced only warily, when they could be made to conform to Romantic canons of taste. Post-classical, ecclesiastical, theological, and biblical-exegetical writing in Latin, though constituting by far the largest part of the written legacy of the western Middle Ages, was ignored on principle as a kind of *anti*-literature. If Sidney's first 'unelected vocation' was as poet, his second, we could think, was as protomodern literary theorist. A double distinction akin to his separation of the practice of 'right poetry' (whether in verse or prose) from the poetry of the Bible, on the one hand, and from competing arts and professions, including theology, on the other, would in any case be normal in academic literary study for a long time. It took the large-scale, anti-disciplinary, hermeneutic and semiological upheavals of the 1950s, 1960s, and 1970s – the movements

---

7 It is to such a reaction that most historians now look for the genesis of the (late) modern idea of Literature as a *sui generis* discursive force and cultural form, separable from other forms of written discourse.

of thought that we now associate with a 'linguistic' or 'textual turn' in the humanities and social sciences – to trigger the tidal waves of enthusiasm for 'the Bible and Literature,' 'Christianity and Literature,' 'Literature and Theology,' 'Literature and Religion,' and so on, that have since relandscaped large tracts of academic terrain and, in the process, resituated the project of CWE (along with others of its time).

Even before the late twentieth-century semio-textual revolution took hold, signals were being picked up from the previously silent universe of medieval theorizing about *literae*, writing or 'texts.' In 1958, a year after Craig R. Thompson's selection of Erasmus' *Colloquies* appeared in a modern publisher's Library of the Liberal Arts, the American Chaucer scholar D.W. Robertson Jr produced for the same series a translation of Augustine's *De doctrina christiana* ('On Christian Teaching'), the earliest and most influential of all handbooks for Christian students of the Bible. The case argued by Robertson for the role of Augustine's ideas in subsequent western literary aesthetics and interpretive practices ensured that sections of *De doctrina christiana* soon began to be incorporated in historical anthologies of *loci critici*. Robertson cited Erasmus' late-career treatise on preaching, the *Ecclesiastes*, for its praise of Augustine's skill in explaining the obscurity of Scripture, and his early *Handbook of the Christian Soldier* for the idea, derived from Augustine, 'that it is more profitable to read a single verse of a Psalm spiritually than to read the whole Psalter literally.'[8] Had it come to hand, he might have mentioned Erasmus' *Ratio* or 'System,' which (like the *Methodus*) began by pointing to 'the four books' of the *De doctrina christiana* where Augustine 'discussed virtually this very subject both fully and with exacting care' [4]. The work of a professional grammarian and rhetorician who unexpectedly became a bishop, *De doctrina christiana* has been called 'a classic of western culture.'[9] It is the place where the language and textual arts taught by such Roman masters as Cicero and Quintilian were first consequentially confronted with the reality of the Bible in Latin. Tellingly, one of the first products of the new Erasmian research that began to appear in the 1960s was a dissertation on Erasmus' use of *De doctrina christiana*, from his earliest perusal of the work ca 1490 to the composition of the *Ecclesiastes* in the last decade of his life.[10] At the centre of that dissertation were 'Les préfaces de la Bible,' including, pre-eminently, the *Ratio* or 'System' as one of the paratexts of Erasmus' second (1519) edition of the New Testament. The scholarly reconstruction of Erasmus' working

---

8 Augustine *On Christian Doctrine* trans Robertson xii–xiii; for Erasmus' *Ecclesiastes* or *The Evangelical Preacher*, see CWE 67–8.
9 Arnold and Bright *De doctrina christiana: A Classic of Western Culture*
10 Béné *Érasme et saint Augustin*

relationship with the Church Fathers – not only Augustine, but also Jerome, Origen, Chrysostom, and others too – would be a major factor in the revision of narratives of his cultural-historical significance that can be dated from the festivities of the long quincentenary of his birth (1967–70) and that was to be carried forward by the Amsterdam (ASD, 1969–) and Toronto (CWE, 1974–) editions of his works in Latin and in English.[11]

The invitation to think again about 'Erasmus on literature' was issued in due form in the inaugural address by Sem Dresden, one of the founding editors of ASD, at the quincentenary conference held in 1969 in Rotterdam. His title was 'Presence of Erasmus.' That presence, he underlined, was 'first and foremost bookish (*livresque*) and, as it were, verbal.' Already with those words his listeners were put in mind of Erasmus' claims, made in his prefatory pieces for the New Testament edition, for the 'presence' of Christ in Scripture. 'From remote antiquity onwards,' Dresden pointed out, 'people had been alert to the curious presence rendered by books, and by texts in general.' Some had been especially attracted by the 'presence of a totality' that book or text could seem to afford. (Jacques Derrida's *Of Grammatology*, critiquing a western 'metaphysics of presence' and playing up 'the idea of the book' as 'the idea of a totality,' was published in 1967.) Although Erasmus, as Dresden saw him, was not of the party of Ficino, Pico, Reuchlin, Agrippa of Nettesheim, and Paracelsus, whose ideas would feed into the book mysticism of 'German romanticism, in particular Novalis, and also of Mallarmé,' he was in his way the votary of a 'cult of book and text.'[12] Returning to the subject in another inaugural address – for the 450th anniversary of Erasmus' death in 1986, and so in the midst of a general explosion of 'literary theory' – Dresden took the opportunity to sketch some of the groundwork for a future study of 'Erasmus and texts.'[13] He was minded, he said, to take 'text' in the sense of 'literary text.' Yet immediately with that ascription of the 'literary,' difficulties arose:

> Although I may well have an idea, however vague and incomplete, of what *literature* is supposed to mean in our time, I am completely ignorant of what conceptions were held of it at the time of humanism and the Renaissance. As soon as I put the question, an unexpected answer looms. Were I to say that no such notion was then current, I would probably

---

11 Mansfield *Erasmus in the Twentieth Century*; Den Boeft 'Erasmus and the Church Fathers'; Vessey '"Vera et Aeterna Monumenta"'; CWE 41 77–9.
12 Dresden 'Présence d'Erasme' 1, 6–7 (my translations here and below)
13 Dresden 'Érasme et les belles-lettres' 4

startle you. Do we not, as a matter of course, speak of the literature of the fifteenth or sixteenth century? Do there not exist, from that period, works of the finest poetry and of magnificent prose? I would be the last to deny it but I would submit, even while granting as much, that I still do not know what conception Erasmus and his contemporaries had of *literature*. It is entirely possible that we are projecting our own conception on phenomena of a wholly different era that had quite other notions in this matter. And that indeed is what appears to be the case.[14]

Rather than settle for this aporia, Dresden argued that even 'if the word *literature* does not exist [in the time of Erasmus] in the sense that we are now accustomed to give it, that does not mean that the phenomenon itself of *literature* is absent.'[15] Then he resumed his analysis of Erasmian ideas of the special power of texts to make absent persons present, paying particular attention to Erasmus' use of the category of *bonae lit(t)erae*. Without ever translating *bonae literae* as 'literature,' he detected an affinity between Erasmus' sense of the ideal function of what he called 'good letters' and a certain modern understanding of the 'literary' text:

> The text that renders something absent present is close to what we like to understand by 'literary' text. Without lingering over the difficulties that lurk here, I simply note that for Erasmus, who only recognizes *bonae litterae*, there would be no problem with such an identification. The reason is that for him there exists a text that lifts itself far above all others and differs from them in a radical and essential way: *bonae litterae* become the Good News [ie the Gospel].[16]

Provisional as these statements were meant to be, elliptical as they are at many points, Dresden's twin anniversary orations marked out with some boldness and clarity a field of study that other scholarship on Erasmus since the 1970s has done much to fill in, without yet producing anything like an overall consensus, let alone an orthodoxy.[17]

---

14 Dresden 'Érasme et les belles-lettres' 5
15 Dresden 'Érasme et les belles-lettres' 6
16 Dresden 'Érasme et les belles-lettres' 14
17 See also eg Boyle *Erasmus on Language and Method in Theology* (1977); Cave *Cornucopian Text* (1979) esp 17–34, 39–53, 82–94, 138–41, 158–67; Chomarat *Grammaire et rhétorique chez Erasme* (1981); Grafton and Jardine *From Humanism to the Humanities* (1986); Waswo *Language and Meaning in the Renaissance* (1987) esp 213–35 ('Erasmus and Literature'); Jardine *Erasmus, Man of Letters* (1993); Hoffmann *Rhetoric and Theology: The Hermeneutic of Erasmus* (1994) esp 61–94 ('Language, Literature,

How did Erasmus' exceptional performance as *un homme de textes* (Dresden) influence the long-term history of ideas and practices of the ('literary') text and of what has come to be known as 'literature'? How, if at all, did his working assumptions differ from those of his predecessors and contemporaries, 'humanist' or 'scholastic'? How was his thinking about the New Testament, object of the most intense and sustained of all his philological engagements, related to his other endeavours as an educator in the new medium of print and as publicist of new or revived styles of cognitive and affective response by readers to books? The relevance of these questions for an understanding of Erasmus' life's work and for larger intellectual and cultural histories has been sufficiently shown by scholarship. Until now, however, one of the most critically important Erasmian texts for research in this field has been familiar only to connoisseurs of Erasmus' New Testament scholarship, and inaccessible to readers lacking a good command of Latin. As Augustine's *De doctrina christiana* was long invisible to students of 'literature,' so Erasmus' *Ratio* or 'System' of 1518/1519 has until now been a closed book to most of them. The purpose of this volume is to lay it open again.[18]

The essays in Part 1 offer an array of historical and interpretive contexts in which to view the *Ratio verae theologiae*. Part 2 presents the *Ratio* in Robert Sider's translation, with the portions of text carried over from the 1516 *Methodus* set in italic (as in CWE 41). New with this edition, and strictly *non*-authorial, are sectional headings inserted in the text to point up the often loose but still discernible articulations of Erasmus' discourse in the work of 1518/19, as revised and expanded in its later editions (1520, 1522, 1523).[19] Significant textual variants between editions are recorded in footnotes to the text. Explanatory endnotes

---

and Scripture'); Moss *Printed Commonplace-Books and the Structuring of Renaissance Thought* (1996); Eden *Hermeneutics and the Rhetorical Tradition* (1997) 64–78 ('Erasmian Hermeneutics: The Road to *sola scriptura*'); Cummings *Literary Culture of the Reformation* (2002) esp 102–18; Ocker *Biblical Poetics before Humanism and Reformation* (2002) esp 184–219; Moss *Renaissance Truth and the Latin Language Turn* (2003) with ERSY 26 (2006): 89–101; Vessey 'Erasmus' Lucubrations and the Renaissance Life of Texts' (2004); Eden *Renaissance Rediscovery of Intimacy* (2012) 73–95; Cummings 'Erasmus and the End of Grammar' (2009), 'Erasmus and the Invention of Literature' (2013), 'Encyclopaedic Erasmus' (2014), 'Erasmus on Literature and Knowledge' (2018).

18 At Ep 145:179, writing from Paris at the beginning of 1501, Erasmus spoke of a project of his for a work, *De literis*, which might now be translated, 'On Literature.' This is usually taken for a reference to his *Antibarbari*, no part of which appeared in print until 1520.

19 For an overview of the inserted section headings see 'Scheme of Contents of the *Ratio verae theologiae*,' below 111–12, and for basic information on the early editions, 'Note on the Text,' below 113.

are keyed by line-number within paragraphs, the paragraph numbering – in bold type – being another novelty of this edition, intended to facilitate cross-reference by temporarily averting the necessity, hitherto felt by all students of the *Ratio*, to multiply citations of the source-text according to edition(s) used. The reader wishing to locate a paragraph from this edition in another need only run an eye across the 'Concordance of Editions.'[20] In view of the special status accorded by Erasmus to the examples of the Church Fathers as interpreters of Scripture and model theologians, it was thought useful to add a 'Conspectus of Church Fathers Cited in the *Ratio*' as a guide to his choices and range of reference.[21] Those patristic citations are included again in their place in the general index. There is a separate index of rhetorical terms and other concepts critical for Erasmus' thinking about the interpretation of texts. The bibliography includes all secondary works cited in the introductory materials and explanatory notes, along with the most heavily cited primary sources from beyond CWE. Whenever reference is made to a primary source that is not readily accessible in a standard series of editions or translations, as also sometimes when it is, a full citation will be found at the point of reference.

   The idea for this book was born several years ago at a meeting of the editorial board of the Collected Works of Erasmus. It has come about through the goodwill of Robert Sider, whom no words of gratitude can repay. As often in Erasmian studies, James McConica has been a driving force. So from the first has Anthony Grafton. To Erasmus' credit, my fellow essayists stepped up unhesitatingly; sharing this project with them has been a pleasure as well as a privilege. Suzanne Rancourt and Barb Porter at the University of Toronto Press saw what was needed and delivered it with a grace now rare in scholarly publishing. Judy Williams, as copy editor, and Dania Sheldon, in indexing, displayed such acumen as our author, had he witnessed it, would have praised to the skies. All these I thank wholeheartedly. Since, shape-shifter that he was, Erasmus will always be a writer's writer, it may be fitting also to record that it was a writer – one that 'chose the living world for text,' more gladly than Yeats's friend did – who brought home to me, for the *Ratio*, the truth of an art that would make more 'passionate and simple' human beings of us.

M.V.
Vancouver, September 2020

---

20 Below, 343–50.
21 Below, 329–33.

Chronology of Erasmus' Life and Works

1469	27 Oct: Erasmus' birth (or 1466, as has also been supposed)
c 1478–83	Attends school of the Brethren of the Common Life at Deventer
c 1483–6	Attends school at 'sHertogenbosch
1486	Enters the Augustinian monastery at Steyn, near Gouda, as a novice
1492 (?)	Ordained priest
1492/3	Enters the service of Hendrik van Bergen, bishop of Cambrai
1495–9	First stay in Paris, studying theology
1499	First visit to England, where he meets Thomas More and John Colet
1500–2	Second stay in Paris; in 1500, short collection of *Adages* (= *Collectanea*) published there
1502–4	First stay in Louvain; refuses offer to teach at university
1503	*Lucubratiunculae aliquot* ('A Few Short Nightworks'), including *Enchiridion militis Christiani* or *Handbook of the Christian Soldier*, published at Antwerp
1504–5	Third stay in Paris
1505?–6	Second visit to England, staying in the house of More
1506–9	Travels to Italy; in 1507?–8 working in Venice with Aldo Manuzio, who in 1508 publishes the first expanded edition of *Adages* (= *Chiliades*) with 3260 proverbs
1509–14	Third stay in England; visit to Paris 1511 to see his printer there, Josse Bade; lecturing in Cambridge 1511–14, working on Seneca, Jerome, and New Testament; *Moria* or *Praise of Folly* (1511); *Copia: Foundations of the Abundant Style* (1512)
1514–16	First visit to Basel; begins association with Johann Froben, who prints second edition of *Adages* (1515) and, in 1516, first edition of New Testament (*Novum instrumentum*) and

	the works of St Jerome; included among the preliminaries of the *Novum instrumentum* are the *Paraclesis* and *Methodus* (precursor to the *Ratio verae theologiae*); trips to England (1515) and Netherlands (1516); made councillor to Emperor Charles V
1517	In Antwerp, with Pieter Gillis; visit to England; move to Louvain
1517–21	Second stay in Louvain; *Paraphrase on Paul's Epistles to the Romans* (1517) inaugurates series of New Testament paraphrases; various trips, including Basel (1518), to supervise second edition of New Testament (published 1519, including *Ratio verae theologiae*); becomes associated with the faculty of theology at Louvain; early version of the *Colloquies* (1518); from this time onwards, Erasmus heavily involved in religious controversies
1521–9	Move to Basel; attempts to mediate between Protestants and Catholics
1529–35	Basel turns Protestant; Erasmus moves to Catholic Freiburg im Breisgau
1535	Final move back to Basel
1536	12 July: death of Erasmus; collected works published in Basel in nine volumes (1538–40), volume 5 containing the *Ratio verae theologiae* with other works 'that teach piety' (*quae instituunt ad pietatem*)

PART ONE

APPROACHES TO ERASMUS' *RATIO* OR 'SYSTEM' OF 1518/1519

The *Ratio* in Erasmus' Life and Work to 1519

MARK VESSEY

'The name of Erasmus shall never perish,' wrote the Englishman John Colet in 1516, and he has been right so far.¹ Erasmus was one of the first literary celebrities of the print era, a man who made his name as a publishing writer at a time when most people thought of an 'author' as someone long dead. In the mixed manuscript and printed book culture of the early sixteenth century, dead authors' names still counted for more than lively titles. The conventions of book titling evolved slowly, and Erasmus' printers were no trailblazers in that regard. Of the dozens of books authored by him and issued between 1500 and 1520, just one – the *Moria* or *Praise of Folly* (1511) – had a title that still sounds catchy today, and its title word in the original Greek (*moria*, 'folly') was a pun on the name of its dedicatee, another Englishman, Thomas More. With its irrepressible female speaker, satirical sketches of contemporary society, playful-ironic tone, and flights of theatrical fancy, *Praise of Folly* falls more comfortably than most of Erasmus' other compositions within the scope of what has counted since the nineteenth century as 'literature.' The work was a *jeu d'esprit*, composed – Erasmus tells us in his prefatory letter to More – in holiday mood, for a coterie of friends who shared his opinions on controversial topics and got his jokes.² He slipped it into print almost surreptitiously. Yet within a few years he was ready to cite this bravura piece of clowning as proof of the steadfastness of his purposes as a theologian.³ Almost accidental in appearance, but wholly

---

1 In Erasmus' correspondence, Ep 243:49. The occasion was the appearance of the *Novum instrumentum*, the New Testament edited by Erasmus, in 1516. For biographical information on persons associated with Erasmus, consult *CEBR*. Trapp *Erasmus, Colet and More*.
2 CWE 27 83
3 Below, n45

characteristic of Erasmus, the *Praise of Folly* offers a suitably shifting viewpoint from which to bring into focus the still more adventurous composition that would be the *Ratio verae theologiae*, or 'System of True Theology.'

The Author of the *Ratio* or 'System' of 1518/1519

What public figure was Erasmus cutting, or about to cut, when he rode over the Alps on his way from Italy to England in the summer of 1509, trying out voices of Folly as he went? He name-checks himself towards the end of *Praise of Folly*, during a moment's pause by his heroine after she delivers a swingeing attack on the manners of the clergy. Like other mortals, she reminds her listeners, those persons thrive on foolishness. As if to underline the point, she reels off a series of supposedly popular sayings, then interrupts herself: 'But enough of quoting proverbs; I don't want you to imagine I've been plundering the notebooks of my friend Erasmus.'[4] The indirect but unmistakable allusion is to the *Adages*, a printed collection of annotated proverbs compiled by Erasmus.[5] In later years, Erasmus would become adept at cross-referencing his own publications in this way. He and his collaborators would also learn to use printed anthologies of his letters to publicize his projects and boost sales of his books. Folly's vanity on behalf of her 'friend Erasmus,' author of the fast-selling *Adages*, points the way to such tricks of print-based marketing. It is also a reminder to us that, as late as 1509 and even 1511, the reputation that Erasmus enjoyed beyond the circles of his friends in England and elsewhere was due mainly to one book.

Like *Folly*, the *Adages* was originally the accident of a journey, in that case an ill-fated return passage from England to France in January of 1500. One of Erasmus' well-born English students in Paris, William Blount, had invited him to England, where he had spent several pleasant months in the company of learned and influential men, including More and Colet. The stay had ended badly, however. On passing through the port of Dover on his way back to Paris, Erasmus had been forced to hand over most of his ready money to customs officials. The little anthology of Latin proverbs entitled simply *Adagiorum collectanea* ('A Collection of Proverbs'), published in Paris in the summer of 1500,

---

4 CWE 27 141
5 Selection in *Adages of Erasmus* ed Barker; full text in CWE 31–6, with introduction in CWE 30. See Mann Phillips '*Adages*'; Eden *Friends Hold All Things in Common*.

was put together hastily in the hope of a quick financial return. While not quite the first thing by Erasmus to appear in print, it was the first thing of his that could be considered a commercial prospect. And it evidently sold well, both to students and to a wider public of readers looking to pick up the patter of smoothly turned Latin phrases, redolent of a deep 'classical' culture (the 'new learning' of the day), that was then becoming a marker for elite social status in northern Europe. Erasmus already had his eye on that constituency before he was mulcted at Dover, and his daily work as a private tutor had given him plenty of opportunities to try out likely instructional formats for it. In the course of the decade after *Folly*, he and his printers would corner a substantial part of the textbook market with products that now come mainly under the heading of 'Literary and Educational Writings' in the English edition of the Collected Works of Erasmus (CWE 23–9). By the time Erasmus himself began devising the scheme for a future edition of his collected works, in the early 1520s, such textbooks formed an obvious first class in it, ahead of the *Adages*, which by then bulked large enough to make a second class by themselves.[6] Of course, no one could have foreseen those contours of a life's literary work as early as 1500. At that stage, as Marshall McLuhan remarked, Erasmus had forsaken a socially sanctioned role – that of Augustinian monk – and not yet found a steady job.[7] Having left his monastery to serve a bishop and given up that service, begun studying theology in Paris and dropped out of his degree course, built up a clientele as a private tutor and then gone on extended vacation, Erasmus on his return from England in 1500 had little to show, apart from some fine friends, for his years of industrious freelancing outside the cloister. No wonder, therefore, that we detect a note of vicarious smugness in Folly's later mention of his well-stocked and highly sought-after notebooks.

The Erasmus who started writing up *Praise of Folly* upon arrival in England in 1509 had reason to be pleased with himself. The Italian trip had been a success. Most notably, it had yielded a greatly expanded edition of the *Adages*, published at Venice towards the end of the previous year by Aldus Manutius, doyen of printers to the new learning, whose books were known for the beauty of their typographic design and especially for the elegance of their Greek fonts. (These greater *Adages* were heavy with Greek, which Erasmus took pains to translate into Latin,

---

6 Ep 1341A in CWE (from 1523/4); revised scheme (1530) in Ep 2283. Summaries of both catalogues: CWE 24 694–702.
7 McLuhan 'Erasmus'

since the majority of his readers would have had little or no knowledge of the other ancient classical language.) An earlier, modest expansion of the *Adages*, in 1506, had consolidated the achievement of the original slender volume of 1500, but the Venetian edition was a quantum leap forward, and not only for the number of proverbs on sale. Erasmus' annotations on individual adages were now in many cases taking on a life of their own, turning into miniature essays in social criticism, providing him with a soap-box in print. With the *Adages* of 1508 – full title: *Adagiorum chiliades*, 'Thousands of Proverbs' – Erasmus found a public voice. We could even say that he extemporized the voice of the modern editorial column: familiar, authoritative, opinionated, wise.

The extempore quality of the annotations in the 1508 *Adages* is most apparent in the transitional passages that introduce each new chiliad or section of a thousand proverbs, of which there were three in all. The lines in praise of Aldus Manutius' editions of ancient texts, at the start of the second chiliad – in a digression on the proverb *Festina lente*, 'Make haste slowly' (the motto of the Aldine press) – are famous. There Erasmus imagines a coming miraculous restoration of the texts of 'good authors' in Latin, Greek, Hebrew, and Chaldaean (by which he meant Aramaic):

> A labour indeed worthy of Hercules, fit for the spirit of a king, to give back to the world something so heavenly, when it was in a state of almost complete collapse; to trace out what lies hid, to dig up what is buried, to call back the dead, to repair what is mutilated, to correct what is corrupted ... And another point: however loudly you may sing the praises of those men who by their valour protect or even extend the boundaries of their country, they are active at best in worldly things and constrained within narrow limits. But he who restores a literature in ruins (almost a harder task than to create one) is engaged on a thing sacred and immortal, and works for the benefit not of one province only but of all nations everywhere and of all succeeding ages. Last but not least, this was in old days the privilege of princes, among whom Ptolemy won special glory, although his library was contained within the narrow walls of his own palace. Aldus is building a library which knows no walls save those of the world itself.[8]

Grateful as Erasmus no doubt was to Aldus, such prophecy was hyperbolic. Nor was it yet clear how Erasmus himself would contribute to the collective work of humanist scholars and printers engaged in publishing

---

8 *Adages* II i 1 CWE 33 10

more correct *texts* of ancient writers.⁹ At first glance, the *Adages* was a project of a different order. Far from restoring any ruined 'literature' to its original architectural dimensions, the compilation provided hands-on access to the most readily recyclable remains of Greek and Latin writers of antiquity.

To head off this and other possible criticisms of his book, Erasmus offered a lengthy apology for it in a development on the proverb *Herculei labores*, 'The labours of Hercules,' which begins the third and final chiliad. His strategy is twofold. He enlarges the metaphor already used to compliment Aldus, now arguing for the utility of the *Adages* as part of a more general project for 'rebuilding the republic of letters.' And he archly confesses his own limitations. 'I was not unaware,' he states, 'that what this work needed was not someone basically a theologian (*theologum hominem*).' To execute it properly would be a lifetime's work for a person with a different preparation and different priorities from his:

> I saw that the nature of the enterprise was such as in itself would have no limits and therefore felt it essential to measure the scale of it not by the logic of the task but by my own commitments, spending on it not the labour it required but as much as I thought could be spared without doing wrong from my own researches. I have therefore finished my task in rather too much of a hurry, partly because in this field I felt myself to be, as it were, off my beat; partly so as to be able when this was finished to return with my whole heart to the subjects proper to my profession, which I had interrupted for some months in compliance with the wishes of a friend rather than with my own judgment.¹⁰

By this account, the immense travail of the *Adagiorum chiliades* of 1508, to say nothing of its further expansions in later years, was a short cut by a man in a hurry to get back to doing something else. Erasmus would always be a man of the short cut (in Latin, *compendium*), at all scales. Proverbs appealed to him, in the first place, as a punchy way of grasping and expressing ideas. The sentence just quoted makes its own short cut between the period in 1500 during which, on his telling, Erasmus compiled the original collection of *Adages* at the urging of his friend

---

9 A sense of Aldus' enterprise can be got from the prefaces to classical and humanistic Latin works, including Erasmus' *Adages*, issued by his press, handily edited and translated by Grant *Aldus Manutius*.
10 *Adages* III i 1 = CWE 34 179

and patron William Blount, and the more sustained labours in Italy that had brought the present, greater work to its (temporary) completion. Erasmus was bragging. In just a few months he had all but carried off a task that could have detained a more qualified person for a lifetime; now others could easily perfect what he had left! That was not the sum of his apology for the *Adages*, however. Behind the braggadocio was the new self-consciousness of one who could now disarmingly profess himself a *theologus homo* or 'basically a theologian.'

Erasmus was less likely to have made such a profession before 1506, when he obtained a doctorate in theology – by a short cut – from the University of Turin.[11] That had been the first stop on his Italian tour. Repelled by the theology curriculum of the University of Paris, where he had been a student in the 1490s, he had not hitherto earned or otherwise obtained any academic degree. Having now made up for lost time and acquired the right to the doctor's cap that would be one of his standard accessories in later portraits, he began to sport the title of theologian. His pretended self-disqualification in 'The labours of Hercules' is of a piece with the affected concern of the author of *Praise of Folly* that some might consider that 'bit of nonsense [to be] too frivolous' for one of his theological profession. Those who did, he suggested, should consider the example of St Jerome, who showed a similar taste for satire in off-duty moments.[12]

Erasmus had been practising such alibis since going into print with the *Adagiorum collectanea*. In order to publish that collection, he had been obliged, he told his friend Blount in the preface, to 'put aside [his] nightly labours over a more serious work.'[13] The expression translated there as 'nightly labours,' *lucubrationes*, was Erasmus' term of choice for his own writerly undertakings, including those of the 'more serious' kind that he was already planning by the time he left England at the end of 1499. He had given further hints of them in a volume of *Lucubratiunculae* ('Lesser Nightworks') published at Antwerp in 1503. 'Christ alone is my Apollo, the source of my vein; his mystic words are my Helicon,' sang the verses prefacing the contents of that volume.[14] They consisted

---

11 Grendler 'How to Get a Degree'
12 CWE 27 84. Erasmus' self-styling after Jerome: Jardine, *Erasmus, Man of Letters*. In the 1517 portrait by Quinten Metsys, Erasmus in his doctor's cap appears beside a bookshelf holding copies of the New Testament and of Jerome ('HIERONYMUS'), both published in 1516 in editions overseen and largely undertaken by him; see below 41–2 and the cover of this edition.
13 Ep 126:19–20 = Allen Ep 126:15–16: *intermissis gravioris operae lucubrationibus*
14 CWE 85 75 #36. Vessey 'Erasmus's *Lucubrationes*'

of a clutch of prayers, poems, and other short devotional pieces, an exhortation to a young man on cultivating virtue, the transcript of a debate between Erasmus and Colet on Christ's agony in the Garden of Gethsemane, and, nestling inconspicuously among these other items, a far more ambitious and substantial work entitled *Enchiridion militis Christiani*, 'Handbook [or Dagger] of the Christian Soldier.'

Unlike the *Adages*, the *Lucubratiunculae* does not seem to have excited much interest at first. As evidence of the slant of its author's thinking at the time, however, it is now priceless. In Erasmus' later plans for his complete oeuvre,[15] the exhortation to the young man on the pursuit of virtue would jostle with the *Praise of Folly* in the fourth class, comprising works of moral instruction. (The third class was to consist of his many letters and dedicatory prefaces.) Otherwise, the contents of the *Lucubratiunculae* – together with items added to make a larger volume of *Lucubrationes* brought out in 1515 – fell squarely in the fifth class, made up of works 'teaching piety' (*quae instituunt ad pietatem*). By his own testimony at all periods, the inculcation of piety was at the very heart of Erasmus' writerly endeavour.[16] As he came to see things by the early 1520s, the most important expressions of his project for 'godliness, holiness, charitable living, [and] virtuous or devout life' were the annotated edition of the New Testament (1516–; sixth class) and the *Paraphrases on the New Testament* (1517–; seventh class). Beyond those productions lay his apologetic or controversial writings, most of them in defence of the New Testament edition and exegesis (1515–; eighth class), and his editions of the early Christian authors known as 'Church Fathers,' making up an essential complement of the same (1516–; ninth class).

In this perspective, Erasmus' labours as a publishing *theologus homo* unfolded over two or three decades with a consistency of purpose and design that is all the more impressive when we make allowance for the detours that he claimed were forced upon him by the needs of the moment or the solicitations of his friends and collaborators. While not altogether illusory – Erasmus (personal motto: *Concedo nulli*, 'I yield to no one') was extraordinarily tenacious in his intellectual pursuits – this appearance of consistency was at least partly contrived after the fact. Pivotal for it is the sequencing of texts at the beginning of the central (fifth) section of his eventual total oeuvre, the class containing works conducing to piety. First in line there stood the *Enchiridion*, originally

---

15 See above, n6.
16 For the sense of *pietas* in Erasmus' use, see John W. O'Malley's introduction to CWE 66; the phrase cited in the next sentence above is his (xi).

published in the *Lucubratiunculae* of 1503 and to be accompanied in the author's ideal scheme of republication by a lengthy preface to the Benedictine monk Paul Volz that he wrote for its reissue as a stand-alone treatise in 1518. Following that came the work presented here, the *Ratio verae theologiae*, and – closely related to it, as we will see – the *Paraclesis* or 'Exhortation to the Pious Reader.'[17]

After the *Praise of Folly*, the *Enchiridion* and *Paraclesis* were and are probably the two best known of Erasmus' writings, the former widely appreciated as a primer in piety or what Erasmus also called the 'philosophy of Christ,' the latter famous as an appeal, launched with his edition of the New Testament in 1516 – before the name of Luther had resounded outside Wittenberg – for the text of the Holy Scriptures to be made directly available to all.[18] Both these manifestos, along with his *Folly*, appeared in print in English translations in the sixteenth century.[19] Not so the *Ratio verae theologiae* of 1518/1519 and later editions, despite its continuing popularity in Latin and its clear importance as an articulation of its author's working assumptions as a biblical theologian and verbal artist.[20] By resituating the *Ratio* between the *Enchiridion* and the *Paraclesis*, we have a chance to read Erasmus as he implicitly asked to be read – from the imaginative centre of his collected works.

Before coming to the *Paraclesis* and the *Ratio*, we should remind ourselves of how the *Enchiridion* ended. Erasmus addressed his 'small extempore treatise' on Christian living to a friend, he said, confident that the latter would learn all that he needed from 'the reading of Scripture' (*sacra lectio*) but anxious lest he be coerced into joining a monastic order. Being a monk was not in itself a state of holiness (*monachatus non est pietas*). Erasmus would not speak either for or against a monastic lifestyle:

> I merely advise you [he wrote] to identify piety not with diet, or dress, or any visible thing, but with what I have taught here. Associate with those in whom you have seen Christ's true image; otherwise, where there are none whose society can improve you, then withdraw from human intercourse

---

17 *Paraclesis*: CWE 41 404–22
18 For the impact of Luther's reforms on Erasmus' project for popularizing the Scriptures, see Seidel Menchi, 'How to Domesticate the New Testament.'
19 Devereux *Renaissance English Translations* ##16, 25, 23. Modern translation of the *Enchiridion* (with prefatory letter to Paul Volz) in CWE 66 8–127, of *Folly* in CWE 27 83–153; for the *Paraclesis*, see above, n17.
20 Devereux #29 records an English translation of the *Ratio* 'made about 1530' by John Caius (1510–73) but 'probably never printed.' No copy is known to have survived.

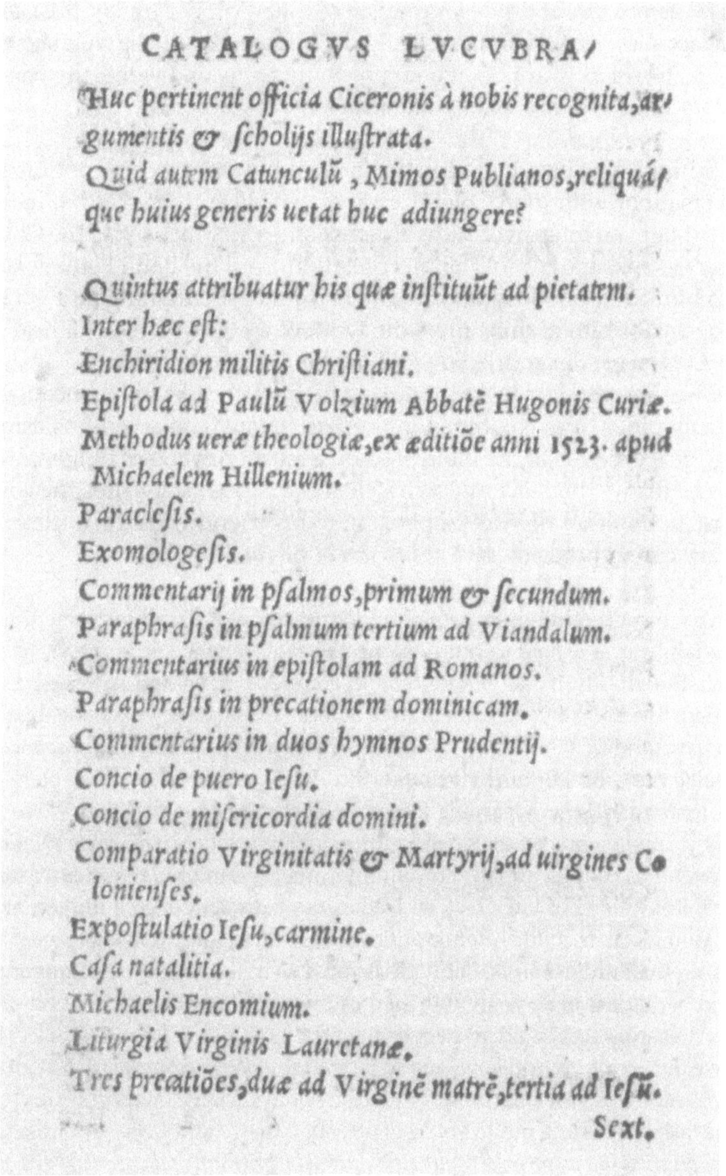

> CATALOGVS LVCVBRA/
>
> Huc pertinent officia Ciceronis à nobis recognita, ar/
> gumentis & fcholijs illuſtrata.
> Quid autem Catunculũ, Mimos Publianos, reliquá/
> que huius generis uetat huc adiungere?
>
> Quintus attribuatur his quæ inſtituũt ad pietatem.
> Inter hæc eſt:
> Enchiridion militis Chriſtiani.
> Epiſtola ad Paulũ Volzium Abbatẽ Hugonis Curiæ.
> Methodus ueræ theologiæ, ex æditiõe anni 1523. apud
>   Michaelem Hillenium.
> Paraclefis.
> Exomologefis.
> Commentarij in pfalmos, primum & fecundum.
> Paraphrafis in pfalmum tertium ad Viandalum.
> Commentarius in epiſtolam ad Romanos.
> Paraphrafis in precationem dominicam.
> Commentarius in duos hymnos Prudentij.
> Concio de puero Iefu.
> Concio de mifericordia domini.
> Comparatio Virginitatis & Martyrij, ad uirgines Co
>   lonienfes.
> Expoſtulatio Iefu, carmine.
> Cafa natalitia.
> Michaelis Encomium.
> Liturgia Virginis Lauretanæ.
> Tres precatiões, duæ ad Virginẽ matrẽ, tertia ad Iefũ.
>
> Sext.

Figure 2. List of contents for the fifth class of Erasmus' works, from the *Catalogus novus omnium Lucubrationum Erasmi Roterodami*, published by Johann Froben at Basel, September 1524.

Universitätsbibliothek Basel (Shelf mark VD16 E 2124)

as far as you can, and take for company the holy prophets and Christ and the apostles. Above all make Paul your special friend; him you should keep always in your pocket and 'ply with nightly and with daily hand' [Horace, *Art of Poetry*, 268–9] and finally learn by heart.[21]

The (re)turn to St Paul had been the most important outcome of Erasmus' conversations with John Colet during his first visit to England. It had led him to begin an intensive study of Greek and sent him back to the Church Fathers as masters of biblical interpretation, both the Latin Fathers familiar to him from his early upbringing and monastic training and – a new discovery for him at this time – the work of the great Greek biblical exegete, Origen of Alexandria.[22] A zeal like Paul's for preaching Christ, as the latter was represented in Scripture and in the daily talk and demeanour of the truly pious, was combined in the *Enchiridion* with an enthusiasm for allegorical exegesis of the Bible fired by a recent reading of Origen.

As he draws the *Enchiridion* to a close, Erasmus overwrites the course of instruction that he was dispensing to his friend with the outline of a literary career of his own:

> I have been carefully preparing an interpretation of [Paul] for some time. Certainly it is a bold venture. None the less, relying on heaven's help, I shall earnestly try to ensure that, even after Origen and Ambrose and Augustine and all the commentators of more recent date, I may not appear to have undertaken this task without any justification or profit. Second, I shall try to cause certain malicious critics, who think it the height of piety to be ignorant of sound learning (*bonarum litterarum*), to realize that, when in my youth I embraced the finer literature of the ancients (*politiorem veterum litteraturam*) and acquired, not without much midnight labour, a reasonable knowledge of the Greek as well as the Latin language, I did not aim at vain glory or childish self-gratification, but had long ago determined to adorn the Lord's temple, badly desecrated as it has been by the ignorance and barbarism of some, with treasures from other realms, as far as in me lay; treasures that could, moreover, inspire men even of superior intellect to love the Scriptures (*ad divinarum scripturarum amorem inflammari*). But, putting aside this vast enterprise for just a few days, I have taken upon myself the task of pointing out to you, as with my finger, a short way to Christ (*ut tibi veluti digito viam, quae compendio ducit ad Christum, indicaremus*).[23]

---

21 CWE 66 127
22 Godin *Érasme lecteur d'Origène* 12–118; McConica *Erasmus* 36–7; and see below 56.
23 CWE 66 127

The Greek word *enchiridion* means a 'hand-held device,' hence 'handbook' or 'dagger' as used in the title of this *Enchiridion* for a Christian soldier. The pocket St Paul that Erasmus imagined in his reader's hands was another such device, like an Aldine edition of one of the Greek poets that Horace (in the passage of the *Ars poetica* remembered at that point by Erasmus) wanted to put in the hands of *his* ideal reader. All books published in Erasmus' name before 1516, apart from some editions and translations of classical authors and the *Adagiorum chiliades*, which were in-folio, appeared in the more handy quarto or octavo formats.[24] Seasoned traveller that he was, Erasmus was an adept of portable books that would set their readers on the most direct path to an aimed-for state of mind or heart.

Neither of the two greater works of Erasmus outlined in the passage above would ever appear in print as a big book. The tenth division of his oeuvre later assigned to the commentary on Paul's Epistles went unfilled,[25] while the task of justifying the study of ancient (ie Greek and Latin) languages and literatures as a resource for present-day Christian teaching was one that he would discharge over the years in a variety of different genres and formats. Probably no one but Erasmus ever meant to hold Erasmus to those early commitments anyway. Had a sharp-sighted contemporary kept track of his literary output between the 1503 *Lucubratiunculae* and 1508 *Adagiorum chiliades*, he or she would have seen only scattered hints of evolving major works: on the one hand, Latin translations of texts by Euripides and Lucian, which helped perfect the translator's command of Greek at the same time as they popularized those classical authors; on the other, an edition of the critical notes (*annotationes*, Erasmus calls them) on the Latin text of the New Testament made by the fifteeenth-century Italian humanist Lorenzo Valla, an intervention that in Erasmus' eyes offered both a model and a sanction for a more thoroughgoing attempt to transmit the force of the Greek text of Paul and other New Testament writers effectively to a Latin readership.[26]

This, then, was the man who came back to England in 1509, lured by his friend Blount's promise of patronage from the new king, Henry VIII, and who sat down at More's house in London to compose the *Praise of Folly*. How, in the course of the next decade, 'Desiderius Erasmus'

---

24 Vanautgaerden *Érasme typographe* 499–527 provides a conspectus of Erasmus' most important publications, including basic bibliographical data.
25 For the history of this abortive project, see now CWE 41 26n141.
26 Rummel *Erasmus' Annotations* 13–14; Christ-von Wedel *Erasmus* 55–9; CWE 41 18–20.

became the name of the most influential living writer in Europe is a story worth briefly retelling here. For it is also the story of the genesis of the *Ratio verae theologiae*.

Genesis of the *Ratio*

Aside from the *Praise of Folly* and one other publication, Erasmus' stay in England from 1509 to 1514 was not distinguished by the appearance of major new works of his. London, Oxford, and Cambridge were not at that time important centres for the printing and dissemination of Latin books. Nor did Erasmus ever find in England a scholarly and commercial milieu to match the one that he had briefly known while living at the house of Aldus Manutius in Venice. Our best biographical source for this period is his correspondence with Henry VIII's Latin secretary, Andrea Ammonio, published several years later and mainly informative about the day-to-day realities of Erasmus' English life, which were those of a freelance scholar still in search of an adequate salary.[27] Although his friends continued to exert themselves for him, Erasmus' expectations of royal and ecclesiastical patronage in England were never fully satisfied. The one real job that came his way – a lectureship in Greek at Cambridge University, which he held between 1511 and 1514 – does not seem to have particularly suited him. Still, Cambridge had well-stocked libraries, and Erasmus, who never took a proper holiday, found ways of pressing ahead with projects that answered in his mind to the long-promised *lucubrationes*. Meanwhile, *parerga* or spin-off compositions came into print when he needed the money and his printers were ready.

So it was with the one substantial book of his published during this English sojourn, a volume issued in 1512 by his regular Paris printer Josse Bade, containing several works dedicated to Colet for the school that he had set up in the precincts of St Paul's Cathedral in London. Two of those works have a bearing on the future *Ratio verae theologiae*. One of them was itself a *Ratio* – full title: *De ratione studii*, 'On the Method of Study' – for the schoolboys of St Paul's, with tips for their teacher too. Like the *Adages* and most of the rest of Erasmus' eventual 'literary and educational' production, this *Ratio* aimed at inculcating personal fluency in persuasive discourse, in writing or speech, of the kind made

---

27 Erasmus' correspondence for these years is conveniently collected and translated in Thomson and Porter *Erasmus and Cambridge*, and in CWE 2.

possible by the student's assimilation of 'words and things' transmitted by texts surviving from ancient Greece and Rome and ancient Christianity. Respecting the early Christian material, Erasmus advised the teacher:

> Among theological writers, after the Scriptures, no one writes better than Origen, no one more subtly or attractively than Chrysostom, no one more devoutly than Basil. Among the Latin Fathers, two at least are outstanding in this field: Ambrose who is wonderfully rich in metaphors, and Jerome who is immensely learned in the sacred Scriptures. If you lack the time to dwell on them individually, I nonetheless recommend that they all be savoured. But for the present it is not my intention to compile a comprehensive list.[28]

We recognize the characteristically Erasmian notes of economy and deferral. The author of the *Ratio* is measuring the resources available to him and the tasks that he himself might one day accomplish, along with the capacity of his readers and their students.

A similar calculation appears in the main work of the 1512 volume, which would quickly gain a currency like that of the *Adages*, as part of the equipment of the performance-ready speaker and writer of Latin. This was the *De copia* or 'Foundations of the Abundant Style,' published at that moment, Erasmus says, 'to open up the way for teachers and students and to provide the raw material for future work,' albeit at the cost of temporarily distracting its author from 'more serious studies.'[29] Divided into sections on 'Abundance of Expression' and 'Abundance of Subject-Matter' – that is, of words (*verba*) and things (*res*) – the *Copia* culminates in a set of guidelines for creating a customized stock of telling examples and turns of thought or phrase derived from one's reading across, as it were, 'the whole field of literature' (*per omne genus autorum*) by entering them into a notebook under systematically arranged topical headings (*loci communes*, 'commonplaces').[30] In the accompanying *Method of Study*, Erasmus recommended that the student devise a system of penmarks with which to flag promising passages in the course of reading.[31] The man whose notebooks had helped launch his writerly

---

28 CWE 24 673:7–14
29 CWE 24 295:28–9, 297:2 (ASD 1–6 26:23 *gravioribus studiis*)
30 CWE 24 635–48; ASD I–6 258:517. On the method in general, see Moss *Printed Commonplace-Books* and *Renaissance Truth* 157–88.
31 CWE 24 670:15–18

career with the *Adages* was now teaching a whole class of readers how to make their way in the rapidly expanding cognitive and discursive world of *print* on paper. That lesson would be well learned and often retaught. It was the *ratio* or 'system' underlying much of the 'literature' of the later European Renaissance. The heavily marked and annotated copies of early printed books in modern research libraries and antiquarian booksellers' catalogues are the residual archive of a multigenerational quest, inspired and enabled by Erasmus and others, for practical agility in the idioms of Latin-born, print-borne learning or 'letters' (*literae*).

Had Erasmus succumbed to plague in Cambridge in the summer of 1513, as false report claimed at the time, he would still be remembered for a roller-coaster of a satire (*Folly*) and for two of the formative works of early modern European 'literary' culture (*Adages, Copia*). In fact, by accident or providence, he was then about to embark upon an astoundingly productive phase of publishing activity. The accident, if such it was, concerned the reissue of the *Adagiorum chiliades*. With the Aldine press temporarily closed, Erasmus looked first to Josse Bade in Paris, who would no doubt have liked to market the *Adages* and *Copia* together. But could Bade come anywhere near Aldus' production values, particularly in the printing of Greek characters? Before the matter was settled, something unexpected happened. Another printer, Johann Froben, successor to the Amerbach business in Basel, brought out an unauthorized reprint of the *Adages* that not only matched the appearance of the Aldine edition but was also – thanks to the work of one of the press-correctors, young Bruno Amerbach – more correct in its Greek. Within weeks of Erasmus' seeing that reprint, a copy of the Aldine text marked up by him for a revised edition was placed by his agent in Froben's hands.

No one was more easily detoured than Erasmus by the prospect of more elegant short cuts to wisdom and eloquence. Early in 1514, he left Cambridge for London. By the end of August he was in Basel. As the euphoria of the Aldine *Adages* had propelled a late-graduating *theologus homo* over the Alps towards England in 1509, the lure of an even greater *Adages* drew him in the opposite direction five years later. The Erasmus feted by scholars and literary men in town after town as he made his way up the Rhine Valley in the spring of 1514 was known for more now than his prodigious notebooks. There was the madcap *Folly*, of course, as well as the *Copia*, and various editions and translations of classical authors. There was also a buzz of prepublicity for something bigger. In his conversations on the way to Basel, Erasmus spoke of going on to Rome. And he talked up – and, in his letters of the time, numbered off – works (*lucubrationes*) that the world could soon expect from him, and that even the pope might want to sponsor.³²

One letter, to the prior of the house of Augustinian canons at Steyn near Gouda that was still his official religious home, even though he would never return to it, cast this publicity in the form of an apology for the alternative, freelance, 'literary' lifestyle that he had fashioned for himself since leaving there twenty years earlier. He wrote it upon landing at Calais, though not before checking that the bag holding his work-in-progress had come safely ashore too. Not surprisingly, given the addressee, there is no mention in this letter of *Folly* or of Greek and Latin classics. Instead, Erasmus references the still little known *Enchiridion*, the *Adages* ('a profane work ... but most helpful for the whole business of education'), the *Copia* ('a useful handbook for future preachers'), and his checked luggage:

> In the course of the last two years [he writes] I have, among many other things, revised St. Jerome's epistles ... I have also revised the whole of the New Testament from a collation of Greek manuscripts and ancient manuscripts and have annotated over a thousand places, with some benefit to theologians. I have begun a series of commentaries on Paul's epistles, which I will finish when I have published this other work. For I have made up my mind to give up my life to sacred literature (*sacris litteris*).³³

What were these works in hand? The 'commentaries on Paul' had been announced long before in the *Enchiridion*,³⁴ the latter being the only publication by Erasmus that his prior was likely to have seen; though never to be issued as such, they would, as we shall see, play a part in the unfolding story of his *lucubrationes*. The other two projects advertised here would not come to wide notice for a few more months, though their origins and development can be conjecturally tracked in earlier correspondence of his that was printed after 1514. The scheme for 'revising' the letters and epistolary treatises of Jerome had grown out of an idea for unscrambling the miscopied Greek and other obscure passages in that Church Father's work, conceived around 1500 in the

---

32 Reflecting the use made of many of them soon afterwards as printed publicity for Erasmus' commercial projects, the frequency of his extant letters rises sharply after his return to the Continent in the summer of 1514. The story told above and below is, for the most part, a highly selective abridgment of materials in CWE 3 and 4.
33 Ep 296:161–9
34 Above, nn23, 25

course of the compilation of the original *Adages*.³⁵ The one for 'revising' the New Testament – by which Erasmus meant proposing emendations to the Latin text wherever it did not accurately or adequately represent the supposed Greek original – had been encouraged, if not directly inspired, by his discovery in 1504 of Valla's *Annotations on the New Testament*.³⁶ By 1514, it appears, Erasmus had a set of his own critical notes ready to publish, each keyed to a lemma in the standard ('Vulgate') edition of the Latin text.³⁷ Having seen the job Froben had made of the 1513 *Adages*, he now saw him as a likely printer for the 'revisions' (*castigationes*) of Jerome and the New Testament, both of which would require generous sprinklings of Greek type. In the letter to his prior, he made this out to be the work of a few months. The first fruits of his critical activity on biblical and patristic Christian texts once safely gathered in, he would then settle down to the remainder of a lifetime devoted to 'sacred literature' – whatever that might entail, besides (presumably) his continued absence from the Augustinian monastery at Steyn.

By accident or providence, the moment when Erasmus walked into Froben's print shop in Basel can now be seen as marking the end of his career as a serial improviser of 'literary' vocations and the beginning of a destiny – the 'Erasmus' of history – fashioned in a range of media, but chiefly in print, by him, his fellow-workers, and his detractors.³⁸ While no single narrative line can capture the ensuing process in all its complexity, an episodic account of Erasmus' publications and publicity over the period from 1514 to 1519 will reveal the importance of the *Ratio verae theologiae* for the whole.

November 1514

Publication of an expanded edition of *Folly* (Strasbourg: Matthias Schürer), in which the walk-on character 'Erasmus' appears a second time, now as one of the leaders in a company of 'Greeklings' (*Graeculi*) intent, according to Folly, on 'catching out the many theologians of today by blinding them with the smokescreen of their *annotationes*.'³⁹

---

35 Rice *Saint Jerome* 116–36; Jardine *Erasmus, Man of Letters* 55–82; Pabel *Herculean Labours* 50–77. Selected texts in CWE 61: *The Edition of St Jerome*.
36 Above, n26
37 Rummel *Erasmus' Annotations* 21–6
38 See further Vessey 'Basel 1514'
39 CWE 27 144, translation adjusted. Screech *Ecstasy* 242–4 provides some back-story; see also CWE 41 24–5.

For the first time, Erasmus' self-styling *in print* associates him, if only obliquely here, with a theological project grounded on the study of Greek, issuing in notes or scholia on a biblical text, directly contesting the scholastic, professional theological establishment of his time.

December 1514

Publication of a revised edition of *Copia*, with a (new) complementary work of rhetorical instruction, the *Parabolae* ('Parallels') (Strasbourg: Schürer).[40] The volume also contains a letter from Erasmus, dated 21 September, to the humanist and theologian Jakob Wimpfeling, who had hosted him in Strasbourg earlier in the year. There Erasmus listed his works in hand, which now included an 'edition' of Jerome's letters and, more startlingly, 'the New Testament translated by me (*Novum Testamentum a me versum*), with the Greek facing, and notes on it by me.'[41] Since his arrival in Basel at the end of August, his biblical-theological venture had assumed new dimensions. No longer just a set of textual notes on selected passages in the Vulgate, it was to present a continuous Latin translation that differed at many points from the Vulgate, and a parallel printing of the Greek.[42]

February 1515

Revised edition of the *Adages* (Basel: Froben), including additional comment on the proverb *Illotis manibus* ('With unwashed hands'), criticizing those who attempt to 'interpret Holy Scripture untaught and unpractised in Greek, Latin, and Hebrew and indeed in the whole of Antiquity,' and holding up Jerome as a model 'theologian.'[43]

---

40 For Erasmus' understanding of the rhetorical device of *parabola*, also translatable as 'parable,' and its importance for the *Ratio*, see the essay by Eden in this volume.
41 Ep 305:228–32
42 The possibility that Erasmus prepared a revised Latin translation of the New Testament in England as early as 1506/9 was decisively excluded by Brown 'Date' (but see now Monfasani 'In Defense'). Also essential for an understanding of his eventual project is de Jonge 'Novum Testamentum.' On the translation itself: Botley *Latin Translation* 115–63. As Sider concludes, 'it is unlikely that [Erasmus] had formulated any clear plan for what became the New Testament much before its actual publication' (CWE 41 4). See further CWE 41 25–32.
43 *Adages* I ix 55 CWE 32 212

March 1515

Reissue of *Folly* (Basel: Froben) with explanatory notes co-authored by Erasmus and Gerardus Listrius, one of Froben's scholarly press-correctors. Passages directed against scholastic theologians – including the programmatic additions of November 1514 (see above) – are pointed up.

June 1515

First issue of the *Enchiridion* as a separate work (Louvain: Dirk Martens). Martens had published the original *Lucubratiunculae* (1503) and reissued it in 1509, from Antwerp. Having recently set up in Louvain, where members of the theology faculty were alert to Erasmus' newest initiatives (see below), he was well placed to influence perceptions of the latter's emergent oeuvre.

August 1515

A booklet printed by Froben at Basel, with an unrelated poem on a recent military campaign for its title-piece, also presents three promotional items by Erasmus: (1) revised texts of letters that he had sent a little earlier to Pope Leo X and two Roman cardinals, praising Jerome for his Christian learning, eloquence, and mastery of Scripture, advertising the coming Erasmus-Froben edition of the saint's work, and soliciting papal patronage for it; (2) the revised text of a recent letter of his to Martin Dorp (Maarten van Dorp), a Louvain-based humanist and theologian (and occasional collaborator of Erasmus'), in which Erasmus replied to protests about *Folly* and doubts about the propriety of emending the Vulgate, conveyed to him by Dorp on behalf of colleagues in the Louvain theology faculty.[44] The mainstay of the defence of *Folly* was the claim that it was meant, like the *Enchiridion*, to teach a Christian lifestyle: 'the *Folly* is concerned in a playful spirit with the same subject as the *Enchiridion*.'[45] In favour of his New Testament project, Erasmus urged the examples of the Church Fathers and Valla. (This

---

44 Epp 335, 334, 333, and 337. On the Dorp-Erasmus exchange: CEBR 'Maarten van Dorp'; Rummel *Erasmus and His Catholic Critics* I 2–13; Jardine *Erasmus, Man of Letters* 111–22.
45 Ep 337:98–9

letter to Dorp would be routinely reprinted as an adjunct to later editions of *Folly*.)

September 1515

While work goes forward on the New Testament and Jerome in Basel, an enlarged edition of the former *Lucubratiunculae* (1503, 1509) is now published as Erasmus' *Lucubrationes* (Strasbourg: Schürer), though it includes none of the 'more serious' work that he has been promising for a decade.[46] In keeping with the author's 'theological' self-styling at this time, the *Enchiridion* was moved up to first place in the order of contents. Among the added items was an allegorical commentary on Psalm 1 ('Beatus vir'), punningly dedicated to Erasmus' collaborator on the New Testament, Beatus Rhenanus (Beat Bild). Drawing heavily on commentaries by Jerome, Augustine, and other Church Fathers, this was the first piece of sustained, line-by-line biblical exegesis that Erasmus had published. (He had spoken in the *Copia* of devoting a work to scriptural allegories, and the future *Ratio* would cover some of that ground.)[47] Two features of the preliminaries of the 1515 *Lucubrationes* are noteworthy in this connection. The title-page border composes a portrait gallery of the four Latin 'Doctors of the Church' (Jerome, Ambrose, Augustine, Gregory) and of four high-profile, stylistically distinctive biblical 'authors' (David, Isaiah, Paul, John); the graphic model may have been the frieze of classical writers and King Solomon on the title page of the 1515 *Adages*. Turning the page, the reader came next upon a preface by Nikolaus Gerbel, a press-corrector for the Erasmus-Froben New Testament and well briefed by Erasmus. Gerbel unhesitatingly ranks Erasmus with the Church Fathers as a biblical exegete and, before signing off ahead of the *Enchiridion*, pledges that the same author would before long 'set out a pattern for students, showing by what route and short cut (*compendio*) lovers of sacred letters may arrive at the true theology (*ad veram illam Theologiam*), at a pure and faultless understanding of Holy Scripture, [and] at Christ the summit of all Christian studies.'[48] The birth certificate for an Erasmian theological *Ratio* had been made out. It only lacked a date.

---

46 Vessey 'Erasmus's *Lucubrationes*' 250–5; 'Erasmus (1515)' 142–6.
47 CWE 24 635:11–12: 'I shall deal at greater length and in more detail with this subject in a short work I have in hand on scriptural allegories.' See below, 100 n24 and CWE 41 21–2.
48 Erasmus *Lucubrationes* sig 4

Figure 3. Title page of Erasmus' *Lucubrationes*, published by Mathias Schürer at Strasbourg, September 1515.

Centre for Reformation and Renaissance Studies, University of Toronto (Shelf mark PA 8501 1515)

February 1516

After frenzied labours, the Erasmus-Froben team completes the printing of the *Novum instrumentum* (ie New Testament) in time for the spring book fair at Frankfurt.[49] The edition (in a single volume) presents a Greek text with a facing Latin version that is intermittently different from the Vulgate, reflecting critical choices made by Erasmus and justified by him in the endnotes (*Annotationes*) that follow in a separate sequence, still keyed to Vulgate lemmata. The title page announces that the Latin text has been 'revised and corrected' against the Greek, in the light of the oldest and best manuscripts, and according to the citations, corrections, and interpretations offered by the 'most approved authors,' the chief of whom are listed by name – the majority Greek and Latin Church Fathers, beginning with Origen. The 'title' modulates after that into an invitation: 'If you love true theology (*veram Theologiam*), then read, take notice, and finally decide ... ' This, then, was to be a 'study' edition of the New Testament: the reader who knew Latin – and perhaps some Greek too – would be able to make up his or her own mind about the text at each doubtful point. Ahead of the edition proper there were several prefatory pieces by Erasmus: (1) a dedicatory letter to Pope Leo X, (2) an exhortation to 'pious readers' to let themselves be transformed by the 'philosophy' taught by Christ's uniquely persuasive acting and speaking presence in the New Testament (the *Paraclesis*), (3) a short disquisition headed 'The Method of Erasmus of Rotterdam,' and (4) a rationale for the editorial work as a whole (the *Apologia*). The opening sentences of the 'Method' (*Methodus*) imagine a reader coming fresh from the preceding *Paraclesis*:

> But perhaps some reader will say to me, 'Why do you urge me on when I am already listening?' ... 'Point out rather the way and the manner in which anyone at all can arrive by a short cut (*compendio*), as it were, at that philosophy you so greatly praise ...'[50]

Beyond this opening gesture, there is nothing in the *Methodus* to tie it to its place among the preliminaries of the *Novum instrumentum*. It is the guide that Gerbel had previewed a few months earlier (in his preface to the *Lucubrationes*), the latest product of Erasmus' proliferating work as – what, now, if not some kind of (biblical) theologian? In 1516, this

---

49 CWE 41 32–58
50 CWE 41 424

'Method' was 'of Erasmus of Rotterdam' but had no discipline or pursuit for explicit object. The object had, however, been specified by Gerbel and also on the title page of the book in hand: 'true theology,' *vera theologia*. Produced in haste after the sudden change in scope (in late 1514) of Erasmus' New Testament text-critical project, the 1516 *Novum instrumentum* immediately drew both applause and negative comment. Following the earlier letter to Dorp, the writings by Erasmus in defence of his own positions – the future contents of the eighth class of his collected works – begin as early as 1517.[51] Meanwhile, he and his associates would be busy revising his New Testament for a second edition: correcting errors, bringing more of the Latin version in line with the *Annotations*, increasing the documentation (mainly from the Church Fathers) provided in the notes.

June 1516

Publication of the complete works of St Jerome (Basel: Froben), in nine volumes. Erasmus took direct editorial responsibility for the first three, containing letters and other *opuscula* in epistolary form and (in the second) texts traditionally ascribed to Jerome but rejected by Erasmus as spurious.[52] The whole is preceded by a *Life of Jerome* composed by Erasmus on the basis of contemporary documents – chiefly Jerome's own writings – in which the saint appears as a tireless and embattled biblical theologian, almost in the style of his biographer.

October 1516

First published selection of letters to and from Erasmus (Louvain: Martens).[53] Responsibility for the initiative was assumed by his friend Pieter Gillis, but Erasmus clearly had a hand in it. An expanded edition of this 'Selected Letters' (*Aliquot epistolae*) would appear under the same auspices in April 1517. Around the same time, at Gillis' instigation, the painter Quinten Metsys completed a double portrait of Gillis and Erasmus as a gift for Thomas More, in which Erasmus is pictured in front of a bookshelf on which are displayed copies of his New Testament, Jerome, translations from Lucian, and *Folly*. He is shown in the act of

---

51 Rummel *Erasmus and His Catholic Critics*; CWE 41 256–86
52 See above, n35.
53 Early publishing history of Erasmus' correspondence: CWE 3 347–53; Jardine *Erasmus, Man of Letters* 147–74.

NOVVM IN

ſtrumentū omne, diligenter ab ERASMO ROTERODAMO
recognitum & emendatum, nõ ſolum ad græcam ueritatem, ue-
rumetiam ad multorum utriuſq; linguæ codicum, eorumq; ue-
terum ſimul & emendatorum fidem, poſtremo ad pro-
batiſſimorum autorum citationem, emendationem
& interpretationem, præcipue, Origenis, Chry
ſoſtomi, Cyrilli, Vulgarij, Hieronymi, Cy-
priani, Ambroſij, Hilarij, Auguſti/
ni, una cū Annotationibus, quæ
lectorem doceant, quid qua
ratione mutatum ſit.
Quiſquis igitur
amas ue-
ram
Theolo/
giam, lege, cogno
ſce, ac deinde iudica.
Neq; ſtatim offendere, ſi
quid mutatum offenderis, ſed
expende, num in melius mutatum ſit.

APVD INCLYTAM
GERMANIAE BASILAEAM.

CVM PRIVILEGIO
MAXIMILIANI CAESARIS AVGVSTI,
NE QVIS ALIVS IN SACRA ROMA-
NI IMPERII DITIONE, INTRA QVATV
OR ANNOS EXCVDAT, AVT ALIBI
EXCVSVM IMPORTET.

Figure 4. Title page of the *Novum instrumentum*, published by Johann Froben at Basel, February 1516.

Centre for Reformation and Renaissance Studies, University of Toronto (Shelf mark BS 1990 1516)

writing out the first few lines of his paraphrase of St Paul's Epistle to the Romans.⁵⁴

November 1517

Erasmus' *Paraphrase on Paul's Epistle to the Romans* (Louvain: Martens) appears shortly after Erasmus' arrival in Louvain, where he was associated with the theology faculty of which Dorp was a member. 'Suppose I had expounded all the sacred books by way of a paraphrase, and made it possible to keep the sense inviolate and yet to read them without stumbling and understand them more easily? Would they [ie critics of his New Testament] quarrel with me then?,' he had asked a friend in a letter that was quickly printed in the (October) 1516 selected correspondence.⁵⁵ Following the publication of the *Novum instrumentum*, Erasmus had meant to return to work on his (never to be completed) commentary on Paul, 'but somehow,' as John Bateman observes, 'that intention was transformed into the idea of elucidating [his Epistles] through a paraphrase.'⁵⁶ In the coming years, Erasmus would compose paraphrases on all the New Testament books except Revelation.⁵⁷

August 1518

New edition of the *Enchiridion* (Basel: Froben), 'virtually reborn in Froben's types,'⁵⁸ with a lengthy preface by Erasmus addressed to the Benedictine monk and theologian Paul Volz. 'A man who has really learnt the way has a good part of a complicated journey already behind him,' Erasmus wrote. It would be helpful, he then suggested, if a committee of suitably learned and saintly men could be struck and charged with 'the task of reducing into brief compass the whole philosophy of Christ, out of its purest sources in evangelists and apostles and its

---

54 See above, n12. A detail of this portrait appears on the cover of the present edition of the *Ratio*.
55 Ep 456:93–6
56 Bateman 'Textual Travail' 216. For the commentary on Paul, see above, nn23, 35, 34.
57 English translations of the Paraphrases in CWE 42–50. For the genre as practised by Erasmus, see Cottier 'Erasmus's Paraphrases,' essays in Pabel and Vessey eds *Holy Scripture Speaks*, and ES 36.2 (2016), a special issue on the Paraphrases, and Bloemendal, 'Erasmus and His Paraphrases'; and on the relation of the Paraphrases to Erasmus' edition of the New Testament, CWE 41 149–82, 212–55.
58 CWE 66 23

most generally accepted expositors [ie the Church Fathers], in a simple but none the less scholarly fashion, short but clear.'[59] The volume also included a translation by Erasmus of a commentary on Isaiah by the Greek Church Father Basil of Caesarea.

November 1518

Publication of the *Ratio seu methodus compendio perveniendi ad veram theologiam* (Louvain: Martens), the first appearance of the *Ratio* or 'System' translated in the present volume. The work incorporated material from the *Methodus Erasmi Roterodami* of 1516 but had now been enlarged by a factor of ten. It would be published again under a slightly different title, by Froben at Basel, in January 1519, before being included in the second edition (March 1519) of the Froben-Erasmus New Testament; see further below. Erasmus instigated the separate publication of the *Ratio* by Martens at Louvain, and there are no substantial differences between the forms of the text issued in Louvain in 1518 and in Basel in 1519, which can therefore be considered as together representing a single 'first edition' of the work. (The present translation is based on that 1518/1519 edition, and also takes account of additions and other authorial changes made in later [1520, 1522, 1523] editions, as indicated in the footnotes.)[60]

Meanwhile, at Basel in November 1518, and in this case without Erasmus' authorization, Froben and Beatus Rhenanus brought out a small volume of 'Patterns for Everyday Conversation' (*Familiarium colloquiorum formulae*), derived from teaching materials that Erasmus had put together for his own use in Paris in the late 1490s. The same work, now approved by Erasmus and with corrections to its text, would be reissued by Martens in March 1519 and by Froben in May of that year. As many as thirty editions of these *Colloquia* would be issued by various printers before March 1522, when Froben published an expanded set of dialogues by Erasmus under the same title.[61] Later editions by Froben at intervals down to 1533 would contain further supplements, as the *Colloquies* became a Europe-wide primer of conversational Latin, and,

---

59 CWE 66 8, 11
60 For publishing details of the early editions, see the Note on the Text below (113), and CWE 41 481–5; for the additions and other changes made in the editions of 1520, 1522, and 1523, CWE 41 185–90.
61 CWE 39 xx–xxvii

not incidentally, another vehicle for the propagation of Erasmus' views on all subjects.[62]

January 1519

Froben publishes the *Ratio seu compendium verae theologiae* at Basel.

March 1519

Froben publishes the second edition of the Erasmian New Testament, now more conventionally entitled *Novum Testamentum*, in two volumes (with the *Annotations* in the second volume), and including the *Ratio seu compendium verae theologiae* in the place formerly occupied by the *Methodus Erasmi Roterodami*, as well as an essay in which Erasmus replied to critics of the first edition.[63] This would be the only time the *Ratio* appeared among the preliminaries of an edition of the New Testament overseen by Erasmus.

The *Ratio verae theologiae* is the most condensed and accessible expression that we have of an Erasmian theory and practice of expounding 'literary' texts. Like other declamatory and didactic pieces of his, including the *Praise of Folly*, his *Ratio* or 'System' of 1518/1519 is simultaneously hard-hitting and insinuating. Propulsive in its rhythms, it turns out on inspection to have a fairly straightforward underlying structure, wherein key elements of the list-like presentation in the earlier *Methodus* are worked up afresh with a wealth of examples and with the insertion in later editions (most notably in 1520) of further corroborative instances either elicited by current events and controversy or suggested by the author's advancing paraphrases of the New Testament.[64]

The *Ratio* sets forth Erasmus' recommendations on how to interpret and respond to complex written verbal artefacts and on how to develop a facility in presenting effective arguments based upon them. It does so within a framework derived from the routines of classical grammar and rhetoric, adjusted to the examples of the Church Fathers as exemplary if by no means infallible expositors of Christian Scripture, and at every turn it reveals Erasmus' well-honed instincts as an instructor in the social and political arts of language across a variety of discursive genres

---

62 See below, 48–52.
63 CWE 41 96–113
64 Summaries of the contents of the *Ratio* in Hoffmann *Rhetoric and Theology* 32–9 and below, 111–12

and publishing formats. Like its nearest precedent in terms of content, Augustine's essay *De doctrina Christiana* or 'On Christian Teaching,'[65] the *Ratio* aspires to a certain generality of application while being inextricably enmeshed in the debates of its moment and milieu. Recent scholarship, summed up in CWE 41 and the series of volumes devoted to Erasmus' New Testament (CWE 42–70) and controversial writings (CWE 71–84), has gone a long way in teasing out the work's immediate contextual relationships. The foregoing paragraphs have aimed to show how closely its genesis was connected with other aspects of Erasmus' book-based, print-borne pedagogical and theological enterprise, as that enterprise evolved and assumed its determining forms in the decade opened by the *Praise of Folly*. Specialized research on Erasmus can take us that far. Larger historical questions – as, for example, about the long-term impact and influence of the ideas and principles set forth by him in the text in hand, and about their place in the story of human theorizing and application of the cognitive, affective, and kinesic potentials or affordances of 'literary' texts and 'literature' in general – remain open.[66] This essay and the four that follow here will, we hope, make it easier for such large literary- and cultural-historical questions to be meaningfully put, and answered, by future readers of the Erasmian *Ratio* or 'System' of 1518/1519.

---

65 See above, 11.
66 For the kinesic and other affordances of literary texts, see Cave *Thinking with Literature*, an essay that – without mentioning Erasmus – invites us to rethink the Erasmian premises of the same scholar's groundbreaking *Cornucopian Text*.

Erasmus, Sacred Literature, and Literary Theory

BRIAN CUMMINGS

In Erasmus' colloquy *Confabulatio pia* ('The Whole Duty of Youth'), the young scholar Gasparus, a sixteen-year-old from John Colet's school of St Paul's in London, describes his daily routine. He is a pious little fellow, possibly modelled on Thomas Lupset, one of Colet's earliest and most favoured pupils. 'What is learned best is learned from earliest childhood,' he says.[1] He goes to church all the time, and prays that he will never do anything that he might have to confide to a priest in confession. He resolves not to commit himself to marriage or the monastic life too early, since he has heard many stories of monks and husbands complaining of their bondage. Instead, he dedicates himself to improving his conduct and maintaining his innocence. Otherwise, he says, 'I apply myself to literature and other branches of study (*bonas literas ac disciplinas*) that will be useful in whatever career I may follow.'[2] Gasparus sums up the Erasmian lifestyle in a nutshell, sly jokes included.

The whole colloquy extemporizes on the question of what literature is, and how to read it. One issue is whether *bonae literae* should include the poets. Gasparus is happy to read the purest of them (*castissimos*); anything indecent he will skip, 'as Ulysses sailed past the Sirens with ears stopped.'[3] It is a delightful Erasmian irony: because of course you have to read Homer to find out how to get past the Sirens. What discipline will he dedicate himself to, since literary study can lead on to just about anything? Here, the author lays another trap for the reader. Gasparus is attracted to theology, except that it is so prone to bad-tempered quarrels. Erasmius, his interlocutor (based on Erasmus' godson, the son

---

1 CWE 39 91
2 CWE 39 98:32–4 (ASD I-3 180:1796–7)
3 CWE 39 98:37–8 (ASD I-3 180:1800–1)

of his printer and publisher Johannes Froben, although in later editions the identity is changed to Erasmus himself), replies that theology is now shunned by many, 'since they see there is nothing that is not called into question.'[4] The word here translated as 'question' (*quaestio*) explicitly refers to the theological schools. Right on cue, the faculty of theology at Paris subsequently condemned this sentence as erroneous. In replying to them, Erasmus can scarcely believe his luck.[5] The theologians respond to his colloquies like a ventriloquist's dummies.

Gasparus resolves to stick to *quod lego in sacris literis* ('what I read in the sacred texts'), and to allow theology to range as it pleases elsewhere, disputing and defining as it goes. Erasmius marvels at this principle, and wonders which Thales could have taught him. The answer, quick as a flash, is naturally Colet, although meanwhile some readers are chasing through their *Adages* to twig the reference to Thales. Erasmus, as ever, is two steps ahead. Buried in the pleasantries is an argument about how to read the Bible. Gasparus' frame of reference is liturgical and monastic. He is taught to imbibe *sacrae literae* in church, by attending mass, saying the Creed (*Symbolum*), taking in the Gospel and Epistle of the day, or listening to sermons. *Lectio divina* – the divine office of the medieval church – is as a mother to him, nurturing the precocious (perhaps, Craig Thompson suggests, 'even a little priggish') child.[6] But sometimes, Gasparus admits, he is let down by the preacher, or cannot hear the priest. Here he is left to his own wits, and must 'provide myself with a little book containing the Gospel and Epistle for the day, and then I recite or read it myself (*aut pronuncio aut oculis lego*).'[7] Very deliberately, he refers to silent reading, or reading by the book:

> GASPARUS: I pass the time with sacred reading (*sacra lectione*); I read the Gospel and Epistle with commentary (*cum interpretatione*) by Chrysostom or Jerome or any other holy and learned interpreter I happen to meet.[8]

Erasmius is a little shocked: isn't the living voice of a preacher better (*viua vox*)? Gasparus has interrupted the vision of liturgical experience with another kind of reading: one that happens *cum oculis*, and also

---

4 CWE 39 99:9–10 (ASD I-3 180:1811–12)
5 Erasmus replied in his *Clarifications Concerning the Censures Published at Paris in the Name of the Faculty of Theology There* (1532), CWE 82 277–8.
6 CWE 39 88; Thompson compares Gasparus to a later pupil of St Paul's School, John Milton.
7 CWE 39 95:34–6 (ASD I-3 176:1688–90)
8 CWE 39 96:23–6 (ASD I-3 177:1717–19), translation modified

cum interpretatione. The interpreter may come from any text that he has to hand, but his favourites are late classical and patristic (ie Church Fathers such as Chrysostom or Jerome). In this little reading lesson is contained the complete argument of Erasmus' colloquy. The whole thing is done so lightly we may not even notice what has happened. Gasparus is reading, thinking, interpreting, and perhaps even believing, for himself. That is why the theologians at Paris are getting so worried. However, Erasmus notes with pleasure at the end of the colloquy, *extra iocum*, joking aside, the dialogue has uncovered a system worthy of imitation, *imitari rationem istam*.[9]

Sacrae literae and bonae literae

Confabulatio pia was first published in the *Familiaria colloquia* of March 1522. By this time, Erasmus had published a *ratio* all of his own, containing an outline theory of imitation (*imitatio*). *Ratio verae theologiae* was published separately in 1518, and at least ten further editions appeared by the time the final edition of the *Colloquies* was published in 1533. Meantime, 'The Whole Duty of Youth' was a self-fulfilling prophecy. In some editions it was called *Pietas puerilis* ('Boyish piety'). By 1534, Gregory, the son of Thomas Cromwell, at the time Henry VIII's most trusted councillor, was being taught from it at the very school in which the dialogue is set.[10] The Spanish humanist and reformer Juan de Valdés borrowed from it in his *Diálogo de doctrina cristiana* (1529) – and was promptly taken as a Lutheran for doing so.[11] Reading is a dangerous activity.

The *Ratio* sets out exactly to achieve the purpose desired in the colloquy: how to read Scripture for yourself. Within this straightforward intention lies a controversial suggestion. Erasmus proposes a reading method *outside the schools*, whether in the guise of schoolroom, monastery, or university. To do so, he has to construct a theory of literature as much as a theory of theological method. His rationale becomes apparent in amiable prefatory remarks, which explain how the *Ratio* grew out of the *Methodus* attached to his New Testament. In providing a 'system for

---

9 CWE 39 99:29 (ASD I-3 181:1829)
10 According to a report made to Thomas Cromwell by Gregory's tutor, Henry Dowes, in 1534; see *Letters and Papers, Foreign and Domestic, of the Reign of Henry VIII* ed J.S. Brewer, J. Gairdner, and R.H Brodie (London: HMSO, 1862–1932) VII 446 #1135.
11 Bataillon *Erasmo y España* 535

the study of theology' [1] he provided a text that was 'indeed brief' but also *satis copiosa* ('sufficiently copious'). Now he is redoing this work over again, 'somewhat more expansively.' These epithets are from the heart of the Erasmian literary strategy.[12] At one level he is merely playing with the clichés of prefaces; he will be just loquacious enough to be brief enough. But *copiosa* is of course also a reference to his major work of rhetorical theory, *De duplici copia rerum ac verborum commentarii duo* (1512).[13] The *Copia* is the beginning of everything in Erasmus. It was reprinted at least 150 times in the sixteenth century, becoming the foundation for pedagogical practices on composition and style for generations. Light of touch, but grand in appearance, it taught theory *and* practice.

The word *copia* refers not only to the elegance that knows when enough is enough, but also to the fount of words from which eloquence finds its source. *Copia* is a personal code for Cicero's figure of the *universum flumen* or 'universal river.'[14] Erasmus adopts this metaphor at the opening of his work, to demonstrate the *copia argumentorum* which could embrace all possible arguments, the universe which comprises language itself as a medium, in practice as well as in theory.[15] A universe of words is balanced by the universe of things. This justifies Erasmus' claim to be a Quintilian for today, a comprehensive handbook to reading and writing. Yet Erasmus' book *Copia* is very easy to misunderstand, whether as a manual for good writing, or as a textbook explaining figures of speech (both of which it is, providing the model for an explosion of such books for a century and beyond). For it is also something else, and much bigger (Erasmus would say, more copious). It is a meditation on language, even on philosophy, interpreted as *both* the sum of all the possible ways of saying anything, and the best way of saying just *this*.

The original edition of Erasmus' colloquies, the *Familiarium colloquiorum formulae* of 1518, is clearly an extension of *Copia* to provide a literary model for ways of making dialogue. *Copia* also explains the theological method in the *Ratio*:

> It is indeed a great thing to arouse in human hearts a burning desire for the study of theology, but it takes a more expert practitioner to expound the way and the method of this heavenly study. [2]

---

12 Cave *Cornucopian Text* 18
13 See above, 33–4.
14 Cicero *De oratore* 2.38.162 (trans Sutton and Rackham *On the Orator*)
15 CWE 24 295

Whether Erasmus departs from medieval reading practices has been carefully disputed by Christopher Ocker.[16] But he certainly claims something new. *Non minima negotii pars est adeundi negotii viam nosse*, 'Not the least part of a task is to know how to set about it' [3]. The way at hand will have deviations and digressions, he says; once again, literary signals to the initiate of the rhetorical byways of *copia*. Like the many-headed statues of Mercury placed at crossroads to forewarn wary travellers and guide them to unexpected places, Erasmus promises to mark out the unknown territory of Scripture. He will, though, make use of previous guides, principally Augustine's *On Christian Doctrine*, and the *Mystical Theology* of Pseudo-Dionysius. To these he will bring his own talents, like a bargain-basement Minerva.

Already, in the opening moves of the preface, Erasmus sets out, without phrasing it as too direct a question, both the central thesis and the controversial stumbling-block of his treatise: How does reading Scripture relate to reading literature in general? Are *sacrae literae* different from *bonae literae*? To this day, Erasmian scholarship and literary studies in general divide in two on this question. Sometimes it is a dialogue of the deaf, so that two Erasmuses exist in parallel. For the classical or rhetorical Erasmus, of the *Adages*, the *Copia*, or the *Colloquies*, it is assumed that the methodology of *bonae literae* comes first, and the theoretical principles of Erasmus' pedagogic project and his literary revival are worked out in a secular and classical sphere before being applied (as and when necessary) to other interests in Scripture or moral theology. Others, who favour Erasmus the Christian philosopher, have downplayed the literary dynamic of Erasmus' theology. Instead, they ask how Erasmus fits in with Reformation or Counter-Reformation theology; with humanism and scholasticism; or with conciliarism or incipient toleration theory. In this, Erasmus scholarship follows the genealogy of modern academic disciplines, in which literature and theology have their distinct histories, values, and priorities.

This is where the significance of the *Ratio* or 'System' of 1518 and later editions comes into focus, because while many readers of the classical Erasmus assume it is a work of theology, it is in fact one of the places where Erasmus considers principles of literary criticism most fully and most philosophically. The genesis of this lies partly in the expansion of the 1518 *Ratio* from the 1516 *Methodus*. Where *Methodus* spoke of the theologian's need for grammar and the liberal arts, the *Ratio* (especially

---

16 See his essay below, and, for fuller argument and documentation, Ocker *Biblical Poetics*.

when revised in 1519) intertwines the interpretation of Scripture meticulously with the figures and tropes of classical rhetoric. While *Methodus* spends a couple of pages on the 'whole course and circle of Christ's life,' the *Ratio* paints a complex portrait of Christ, etching the image with details from the Gospels. In the process, Erasmus constructs a sophisticated theory of representation in literature, making the ideal of *mimesis* a prompt for a revaluation of the presence in the New Testament of the historical Christ as a person living in its pages.

In the midst of this is a small decision which sums up his enterprise. He substitutes for the traditional phrase *sacra scriptura* the mildly novel term *sacrae* or *divinae literae*.[17] Cicero used the term *Graecae literae* to refer to the writings of his Greek models, and *studium literarum* to the study of Roman poets. Cassiodorus, writing in the sixth century AD, transferred the term to describe scriptural writing as *divinae literae*.[18] Erasmus favoured both *literae humanae* and *bonae literae* as terms for the discipline he practised. Johannes Oecolampadius describes Erasmus in his preface to the 1516 *Novum instrumentum* as shining with equal brilliance 'in sacred and humane letters, in both of which he himself is the high priest.'[19] Two things go on in this seemingly tiny philological manoeuvre. One is that *scriptura* is no longer *scriptura*: it is no longer a category *sui generis*, writing like no other writing. The other is that it is made to be no different in principle from other *literae*. This enables Erasmus to be styled, with humanist hyperbole, 'high priest,' even though he is a priest only nominally, and a doctor *honoris causa*.[20] What he is in 1516 by universal consent is a master of letters. How do we translate such a term? 'Literature' is not a word in use in this period, whether in Latin or English (or French or German), and scholarship is very wary of using it for any period before the Romantics. Nonetheless, the attempt by Erasmians such as Jacques Chomarat to replace it with *grammatica* or *rhetorica* is not entirely convincing either.[21] Erasmus never describes what he does within the conventional terminology of either the schoolroom or its textbooks. On the other hand, he uses the word *litera* with abandon. Indeed, the prospectus for an edition of his complete works declares that the first volume will cover texts *quae spectant*

---

17 *Ratio* **19**, translated by Sider as 'divine literature'
18 For the sense and applications of *literae* in Cassiodorus and the relation of his program of Christian readings to those of Augustine and Jerome, see Halporn and Vessey *Cassiodorus: Institutions* 27–37.
19 CWE 41 776
20 See above, 26.
21 Chomarat *Grammaire et rhétorique chez Érasme* I 21–2

ad institutionem literarum.[22] He is determined to mark out for himself and for the followers of his method a territory which is 'literary' even if not exactly 'literature.'

The Literal and Allegorical Senses of Scripture

If Scripture is literary, how do we read it, and how do we know what it means? Here, Erasmus demands a radical redescription of traditional categories of argument. Theology, he says, has in the past dealt in doctrines on which the church is agreed, and over which it has proprietorial rights. As well as the New Testament prefaces (*Paraclesis* along with the *Methodus*), the *Ratio* builds on the *Enchiridion militis Christiani*, one of Erasmus' earliest works from the beginning of the century, but reissued in 1515 and especially frequently after 1518 with a new preface by Paul Volz.[23] Erasmus in the *Ratio* creates a model of theology based on a theory of literary interpretation. This includes a nascent form of textual criticism; a knowledge of the ancient languages; and developing humanist principles of historical philology. Augustine and Aquinas, foremost of the old and the new 'Doctors of the Church,' would have mastered the original languages of the Bible if they could. It is never too late to learn ancient languages, he says encouragingly. Rudolph Agricola, doyen of the first generation of northern humanists, was over forty when he took up Greek; on a personal note, Erasmus adds that he himself is fifty-two, and still intends to work on his Hebrew [17].

As well as philology, Erasmus exhorts the reader to an extensive exploration of territory covered in his rhetorical and literary treatises going back to the *Copia*. Grammar and rhetoric have taken a backward place in relation to dialectic, he avers, but now must be proclaimed as the key to the Scriptures [21]. However, Erasmus also enjoins a more imaginative form of poetics. He goes on to combine a sometimes mystical invocation of allegorical principles with a rigorous attention to figures of speech. God, he says, 'speaks to us in the arcane books more truly and more effectively than he spoke to Moses from the bush, provided we approach the conversation with a pure heart' [6]. What does it mean, then, when Moses has to take off his shoes on Mount Horeb? Freeing the feet is like freeing the heart of the burden of earthly desires.

---

22 Allen I 38:19–20 (CWE 24 694:11–12, 'everything that concerns literature and education'). On Erasmus' division of his own works, see above, 23, 27.
23 See also above, 27–31.

Not only the Old Testament, but also the Gospels and Epistles, are full of poetic figures like these. Figurative language is the stuff of Scripture.

Behind this apparently throwaway remark on a detail of the story of Moses and the burning bush lies a methodological principle which comes to form the heart of the *Ratio*. The humanist – as indeed Augustine recommends in *De doctrina christiana* – has to know not only rhetoric but all the liberal arts, and indeed also have an understanding of the things of nature and of everyday objects, for example the stars, or animals, trees, and jewels.[24] We need, in short, to know all the *loci* (the 'places') spoken about in *divinae literae*. The *loci* are fundamental to Erasmian humanism. They are a feature of Ciceronian rhetoric (indeed *copia* cannot be understood without *loci* to guide the way), and also of the new logic of Agricola.[25] Place logic (based originally on the *topica* of Aristotle) is a sophisticated theory of how the *res* (the 'matter') of the world is to be understood, and arguments about it organized. But *loci* means something else to Erasmus in the context of scriptural writing:

> In truth the prophets often stud their books with the names of places, like lights of a sort, and if anyone tries to investigate the allegory, he will not do so either safely or auspiciously if he has no knowledge of the setting of the places. [19]

In other words, *loci* not only do logical work but are also figuratively intrinsic to the writing of the Scriptures. Even here, Erasmus needs a simile to explain his thinking: the names of the places (*locorum vocabula*) are 'like lights.'

In telling us to look more carefully at 'stars, animals, trees, jewels,' Erasmus is probably alluding to a crucial passage on metaphor in his favourite rhetorical textbook, Quintilian's *Institutio oratoria*. In Book 8, coming to the subject of 'tropes,' Quintilian remarks that we sometimes use words 'properly' and sometimes metaphorically. Indeed metaphor is, he says, 'the most beautiful of tropes,' and its name is itself a trope, since the Greek word *metaphora* is in Latin *translatio*, a carrying away of something from one place to another.[26] Some forms of metaphor are a

---

24 For the scriptural exegete's equipment of liberal learning, see especially Book 2 of the *De doctrina christiana* (trans Green *On Christian Teaching*), and for the interpretation of figural language in Scripture, Book 3. Erasmus' debt to this work of Augustine, in the *Ratio* and elsewhere, is comprehensively studied by Béné *Érasme et saint Augustin*. See also 74–5 below.
25 Mack *Renaissance Argument* 155–7
26 Quintilian *Institutio oratoria* 8.6 (trans Russell *The Orator's Education*)

specialized form of language, what we call ornamental language: this is common in poetry. But there are forms of metaphor which are 'necessary.' It is 'by necessity,' he says, that country people call a vinebud a *gemma*. 'What else could they say?' Quintilian asks disarmingly. Similarly the crops are called 'thirsty,' and the harvest is said to be 'in trouble,' or a man 'hard' or 'rough,' because there is no *proprium nomen*, no literal term by which we could say this. A *gemma* is a rhetorical shorthand, then, for a metaphor for which no literal equivalent exists. When the translator in the Loeb edition of the *Institutio oratoria*, Donald A. Russell, says that 'the true development is probably the reverse: the sense of "jewel" is derived from the similarity of a precious stone to a bud,' he may be correct, but he seems to have missed the point: we cannot tell from nature where the literal sense ends and the figurative begins.[27]

This is all the harder to decipher, Erasmus states, in relation to ancient languages which we no longer speak, which are full of 'dead' metaphors, and most of all ancient Hebrew, where often the citation in Scripture may be the only surviving instance of a word. In that situation, he says, 'often the understanding of the mystery (*intellectus mysterii*) hangs upon the very nature of the thing' [19]. In the past, deprived of a methodology by which to make the right distinctions, using the wrong dictionaries, or misled by their own obstinacy, commentators have made 'a quadruped out of a tree, a fish out of a jewel, a river out of a musician, a shrub out of a town, a bird out of a star, pants out of plants.'

However, there is a further problem, as much philosophical as philological. The key here comes with Erasmus' word *mysterium*. This argument goes back to his *Enchiridion* from years before. In theology we should always prefer the spirit to the flesh, he says there; and so likewise in all literary works 'which are made up of a literal sense and a mysterious sense, body and soul, as it were ... you are to ignore the letter and look rather to the mystery.'[28] This is Erasmus' first statement of his literary preference for the allegorical over the literal in the interpretation of Scripture, a principle he explicitly finds in Origen and in Jerome. Looking for the *mysterium* is for Erasmus always the taste of choice. But in the *Ratio* (as already in the *Methodus*) he has reached a further level of sophistication in his literary theory. When we go to church, he says, it is natural to kiss everything, to reverence everything, 'as though some divine power is everywhere present' [8]. This applies just as much in relation to the 'inner sanctuary' of Scripture. If readers approach the text of the Bible with the

---

27 Quintilian *Orator's Education* trans Russell, III 428
28 CWE 66 67

same reverence as the tabernacle of God, if they come with 'sincere faith,' they will be allowed to see 'certain mysteries.' So Moses taught us 'when he veiled his face so that he might not look upon the Lord speaking to him from the bush' [8]. This is a marvellous Erasmian touch: for of course, Moses is teaching us how to think figuratively, even as he is giving us an example of how to greet God reverently. And so Moses teaches us method (and literary theory) as he goes along. If we encounter something in Scripture which seems out of accord with the divine nature of the teaching of Christ, we are not to blame what is written, but see if it derives from a literary trope concealed in the writing, or else from a corruption in the text. The careful reader, learned in philology, is thus doing nothing more than Moses prophesied or Augustine demanded.

In that sense, it is indeed the case that we read Scripture no differently from the way that we read secular literature: 'it will be useful for the young man destined for theology to be carefully practised in the figures and tropes of the grammarians and rhetoricians' [23]. A significant part of the *Ratio* consists of finding all the tropes in Scripture, whether in the Old Testament or in the Gospels of Christ or in the Epistles of Paul. Quintilian is the best guide here, we are told, although Erasmus is quick to note that Augustine himself was a trained rhetorician in the ancient tradition [23]. And yet it is not at all the case that Erasmus transfers the methods of secular literary criticism over to the divine. Indeed, Erasmus says, deadpan as ever, it seems that Jesus loves figurative speech. Christ clothes almost all his teaching in parables, which is the mark of a poet [29].[29] It is no more than godly to elucidate his figures of speech. The radical nature of Erasmus' argument is not his classicism, however much that has come to be the cliché of the modern history of literary theory. Rather, he saves his most radical intervention in the philosophy of literature for his treatment of the literary in Scripture.

Imitation and the Affections of the Heart

Interpretation and meaning are not the final motivation, however, either of theology or of reading:

> Let this be your first and only goal, this your prayer, attend to this alone, that you be changed, be swept away, be inspired, be transformed into what you are learning. [10]

---

[29] See the essay by Eden, below.

Just as the aim of rhetorical study is to speak well, so the aim of theological study is to be inwardly and outwardly transformed. This passage is left intact from the first version of the *Methodus* in 1516. The language is both strong and specific: *ut muteris, ut rapiaris, ut affleris, ut transformeris.* Erasmus' use of the verb *rapio* for a powerful spiritual experience goes back once again to the *Enchiridion*: 'You will feel inspired, swept away (*rapi*), transfigured in an ineffable manner by the divine power.'[30] *Rapio* is a verb used both in the Vulgate and in Erasmus' edition of the Latin New Testament to convey Paul's Greek for entering into paradise (2 Corinthians 12:2, 4).

Yet it is not only a term for religious feeling. Erasmus means a peculiar literary effect:

> The food of the soul is useful not if it remains in the memory as in the stomach, but only if it penetrates into the very affections and into the very viscera of the mind. [10]

Scripture works not only in the *memoria* but on the *affectus*. This is one of the most complex words in the ancient lexicon. The modern equivalent is 'emotions,' but this conveys almost nothing of the controversies that the word inspired. The Greek word *pathe*, better translated as 'passions,' expressed a sense that such feelings are difficult to control and perhaps inimical to reason. Plato described the passions as those parts of human nature that are closest to the instincts of the body, and as such 'burdensome and heavy and earthly and visible.'[31] The Stoics took up Plato's argument in routinely condemning the passions, and in making the greatest challenge of moral philosophy the attempt to place them under control. Erasmus is at his most Platonic in the *Enchiridion*, and there shows something of the same equivocation. In the *Ratio*, he recommends instead the more practical treatment of the passions in Aristotle [23]. Indeed, by the time of his *Annotations* on the New Testament, Erasmus had undergone something of a change of heart. At Romans 8:27 he suggested changing the reading in the Vulgate (*quid desideret spiritus*, 'what the spirit desires') to *affectus spiritus* ('the feeling of the spirit'). Lorenzo Valla had made a similar suggestion in his *Adnotationes*, where he referred to the *sensus* ('the feeling' or 'the sentiments') of the spirit.[32]

---

30 CWE 66 34
31 Plato *Phaedo* 81c
32 CWE 56 222–3 with refs. The CWE translators render Erasmus' *affectus* here as 'disposition.'

This annotation later got Erasmus into trouble when Frans Titelmans in his *Collationes super Epistolam ad Romanos* (1529) argued that *sensus* and *affectus* were too coarse to be applied to the spirit, which has no part in the passions of the body.[33] Erasmus responded at length to this critique in a letter to Pieter Gillis, one of his most trusted humanist collaborators. While the Stoics, and Cicero, he says, often refer to *perturbationes animi* ('disturbances of the soul'), later Latin writers also translate the Greek *pathe* by a range of other words, such as *affectus, motus, cupiditates,* and *morbi*.[34] This reflects the ambiguity of the concept itself. In any case, Christian writing must reject the paradoxes of the Stoics, which, even if true in principle, are impossible to achieve. The *affectus*, he concludes, cover many experiences which are acknowledged by men and women living by the spirit, such as joy, grief, hope, fear, love, hate, benevolence, and pity. These are all unquestionably 'feelings,' he says, and furthermore, they are used by Christ of himself, and even in reference to the divine nature.

This discussion a few years later provides a powerful commentary on the *Ratio*. It can also be used to show the central place of the *affectus* in Erasmus' literary theory. The way to find out if you have learned from reading Scripture is 'if you sense that little by little you are becoming a different person' [10]. The expression 'little by little' (*paulatim*, not in the *Methodus*) is added to show that the effects of affective reading are gradual, not a matter of instant conversion. Reading Scripture is a kind of emotional training. By way of preliminary example, Erasmus draws attention to the way in which the story of Abraham and Isaac is recounted. Using Origen's homily on Genesis, Erasmus enumerates 'with how many devices the father's mind is assailed again and again.' He lists the terms of endearment in the passage, in a vivid piece of literary criticism: 'so that for a long time the mind of the father was vexed with changing thoughts, human affection drawing him one way, the divine command urging him another' [25]. The key terms in the analysis are *affectu humano* and *patriae caritatis* ('fatherly love,' translating Origen's term *philostorgos*). This feature of *divinae literae* should always be mirrored in our method of theology.

---

33 See Erasmus' *Response to the Discussions of a Certain 'Youth Who Would Teach His Elders'*, CWE 73 224–5, where *affectus* is translated 'desire.' On this altercation and, more generally, Erasmus' understanding of *affectus* and cognate terms, see Essary 'Annotating the Affections.'

34 Ep 2260:160–87 (Allen lines 174–201)

Erasmus treats the sacrifice of Isaac as a prime case of *enargeia*, the rhetorical figure where a speaker describes an event so vividly, in such detail, that it seems as though the event is happening right in front of us. Furthermore, Erasmus' literary criticism is also an example of *enargeia*: it imitates the very figure it describes. In this way, we begin to apprehend the full sophistication of his rhetorical theory, and of the philosophical basis of his analysis, however much he eschews the formal methods and vocabulary of traditional philosophy. Indeed at this point Erasmus introduces the term the 'philosophy of Christ' [32] even while trotting out a critique of the scholastic masters such as Robert Holcot. Part of this philosophy consists in moral commands [35]. But as Erasmus expands the point, he emphasizes a different feature of the Gospels, in which Christ 'seems to have taken upon himself the feeling of the members' [42]. That is, he imitates human passions, or as we might say, impersonates them. Indeed Erasmus specifically says of Jesus that he takes on a *persona* in his giving of the keys to Peter (Matthew 16:18–19) and that Paul, too, in Romans 7:24 'speaks rather with the voice of some other person' [43].

The 'method of taking personae' [44] is expanded later in the *Ratio* into an exposition of what Erasmus calls (with conscious daring) the 'drama of Christ,' *fabula Christi* [67]. *Fabula* is a complex Latin word, combining a sense of story, fiction, and also drama (Cicero uses it in all three ways). Christ's life, Erasmus says, is 'acted out' for our benefit. Predictably, this phrasing earned him the opprobrium of opponents as diverse as Noël Béda and Martin Luther.[35] Yet underlying the radical phrasing is a theory of *imitatio* in which the whole of the life of Christ is an example. By this Erasmus means not only the conventional theory of moral imitation, but a literary theory of representation reaching back to the ancient tradition of *mimesis*. Christ does not teach humility by preaching, but by washing the disciples' feet [68]. Some things in the life of Socrates or other virtuous men accord with the life of Christ. In the writings of the prophets such as Moses there are many precepts to follow. But this is nothing in comparison to the way that Christ's example completes the circle. 'Everything to this point is to be revered; the rest is to be read or even to be imitated' [70]. In Christ alone we find everything congruent with everything else.

This is followed by an extraordinary argument in which Christ is described as the embodiment of *copia*. Erasmus calls it the 'diversity in Christ,' *varietas Christi*. Christ contains in himself all the different voices

---

35 References at CWE 41 546 n287

in the world, not only that are, but that could ever come into being. 'He became all things to all people but without ever compromising himself (*ut nusquam tamen sui dissimilis esset*)' [**72**]. This translation does not quite catch the Latin. Unlike any human being, Christ can never be unlike himself: he is always himself. This recalls an odd phrase earlier in which it is said that Christ sometimes 'dissimulates' (*dissimulat*) the voices of others [**39**]. To understand the apparent discrepancy, we have to consider the theory of *mimesis*. In drama the actor impersonates another human in the sense of acting *like* her. Christ does this in adopting the voice of the woman taken in adultery: he 'dissimulates her.' But Christ, unlike an actor, remains always himself even as he does this, he is *nusquam sui dissimilis*, never unlike himself.

While Aristotle's *Poetics*, the key ancient text on *mimesis*, was known to Erasmus, it is not thought that he studied it in detail. However, Cicero's dialogue *De oratore* contains a passage on the imitation of Socrates which would give Erasmus a foundation for his treatment of the subject here.[36] Yet Cicero does not explain Erasmus' urgent originality as he attempts to account for Christ's investment in *imitatio*. Sometimes Christ represents the divine, at other times he 'plays the part of a human being' [**72**]. Sometimes he speaks, at others he is just as effective in using silence. Sometimes he performs a miracle without any trouble, at others he emphasizes its difficulty. In one case, the raising of Lazarus, he manifests his emotions, 'sheds tears, groans in the spirit,' cries out with a piercing cry [**75**]. In another case, in the hiring of the labourers in the vineyard, Jesus shows the benefits of a complex narrative in which a whole variety of emotional reactions are required [**88**]. In this way the Gospels are a continuous experience of *enargeia*, and at the same time fulfil the perfect condition of *copia* itself. Christ's variety is like the variety of the world in its entirety.

The theoretical framework of the *Ratio* thus builds on the biblical poetics of medieval Latin *imitatio*, but also moves the rhetorical analysis of biblical figures of speech within a theory of affect. Christ 'wanted us to return his love by loving him as a true man, who truly suffered for us' [**80**]. We may without exaggeration call this the affective turn in Erasmus, one which he identifies in the Epistles of Paul almost as much as he does in the Gospels. That is, *imitatio Christi* is not confined to the life of Christ but is also displayed everywhere in *divinae literae*. Reading Scripture is like an education of the emotions, teaching us everything

---

36 Cicero *De oratore* 1.54 (trans Sutton and Rackham *On the Orator*)

from trust in ourselves to shame and remorse [116–17]. Yet the ultimate lesson is that of love:

> For what else does Christ teach, what else does he inculcate by his whole life except the most consummate love? This was the one thing he had come to teach us. [125]

God *is* love, after all, as Erasmus confirms via 1 John 4:16: 'Those who abide in love abide in God, and God abides in them.' Once again, though, Erasmus reframes the theology of Scripture by reference to the theory of imitation: 'Be imitators of God,' he quotes Paul from Ephesians 5:1–2, 'as very dear children, and walk in love as Christ also has loved us' [137]. How he means the phrase *imitatores dei* is shown by a phrase he has just embedded in his definition of love: 'love makes all things common to all' [133].[37] The letters of friends (what Cicero called *epistolae familiares*) bind all together: Erasmus was renewing precisely this tradition with editions of his own letters even as he alludes to those of Cicero before him.[38] *Ama et fac quod vis*, he cites from one of the most famous places in all of Augustine, 'love and do what you will' [138]. Nonetheless, it is a translation out of theology into literary theory, via an understanding of literature as the place where emotions are educated so that we *can* love what we will. The *Ratio* is a contribution not only to a reappraisal of the significance of literary interpretation to theology, but to literary theory in general. It is in this way a resounding manifesto concerning the status of Scripture as a kind of literature, one which expands the territory of *literae* rather than simply borrows from it.

---

37 See Eden *Friends Hold All Things in Common* 142–63.
38 See Eden *Renaissance Rediscovery of Intimacy*.

Biblical Poetics in Scholasticism and the *Ratio*

CHRISTOPHER OCKER

Erasmus against Scholasticism

Erasmus ridiculed scholastic theologians, accusing them of vainglorious sophistry. He casually mentioned the offenders by name: Peter Lombard, Hugh of St Cher, Alexander of Hales, Albert the Great, Thomas Aquinas, John Duns Scotus, William of Paris, William Ockham, Durand of St Porçain, Giles of Rome, Robert Holcot, Pierre d'Ally, Gabriel Biel, Nicholas of Lyra, and even occasionally the pious Jean Gerson; and he dismissed whole categories of professors – Scotists, nominalists, scholastics, and sophists.[1] The schoolmen were counterpoints to Erasmus' own intellectual program, his 'multigeneric, ultimately theological enterprise of textual instruction, conducted chiefly through print and largely in prose.'[2] He believed that his work imitated the example of St Jerome, translator-commentator, holy-man scholar of late antiquity.[3] He intended to reproduce 'an eloquence already shared by the biblical poets, prophets, and evangelists, and their patristic successors.'[4] He meant to correct an inarticulate, degraded state of mind.

Erasmus planned to develop a distinctly textual theology by the time he published his *Lucubratiunculae* in 1503. The plan unfolded after he arrived at Basel in 1514, building on an enterprise begun in Lorenzo Valla's *Collatio Novi Testamenti* and *Repastinatio dialectice*, and continued

---

1 In his *Ecclesiastes* or 'Evangelical Preacher': CWE 68 495–6, 539–40; in the *Apology against a Dialogue of Jacobus Latomus*: CWE 71 78.
2 Vessey 'Erasmus's *Lucubrationes*' 250
3 Ep 141. See above, 26 n12, 42.
4 Margolin 'Duns Scot et Érasme' 98

for the rest of his life.⁵ Accompanying the effort all along the way was the scholastic theologian, who proved the need for his editions, treatises, and annotations. They needed him, Erasmus said in effect, because scholastic theology was so prevalent and bad.

For the most part, Erasmus portrayed scholasticism with pitiless economy, in dismissive phrases and generalizations.⁶ 'Once Alexander of Hales ruled. Thomas came after. Then came Scotus. Albert had his century. Gerson had his. At one time the faction of realists flourished, as they are called. Now the faction of nominalists almost rule.'⁷ Send the dialecticians eastward and utterly confound the Turks, he recommended in the *Praise of Folly*.⁸ Nicholas of Lyra, Thomas Aquinas, and Jean Gerson put on sophistical airs and introduced pointless distinctions, he said in the *Ecclesiastes*, a year before he died.⁹ And yet, despite a clear preference for the 'mummified authors' of antiquity and his belief that ancient learning had been grossly compromised by theologians since the rise of universities, Erasmus also argued for specific continuities between his own Christian philosophy and a general theological consensus (most famously, on the subject of free will), especially in the last two decades of his life. He thought he, his humanist and Lutheran contemporaries, and medieval theologians could all be improved upon.¹⁰

When Jacob Latomus (or, to give him his vernacular name, Jacques Masson), professor of theology at Louvain, complained that Erasmus' *Ratio verae theologiae* set the new humanism against medieval learning, Erasmus balked.¹¹ In a riposte that would prove emblematic of his mature stance towards scholasticism, he countered that his purpose was constructive, 'to link linguistic skills, elegant expression, and a

---

5 See the essay by Vessey in this volume, with Epp 93, 108; Vanautgaerden *Érasme typographe* 279–84; Charles Trinkaus 'Introduction,' CWE 76 xx–xxi and n23; Nauta 'Lorenzo Valla.'
6 Craig Thompson's four-page footnote on a line spoken in Erasmus' colloquy 'The Godly Feast' by the character Eusebius – 'I would much rather let all of Scotus and others of his sort perish than the books of a single Cicero of Plutarch' – summarizes his complaints against speculative theologians: CWE 39 192:21–3, with 227–31 (n190).
7 Ep 1581:653–7, translation adjusted; Margolin 'Duns Scot et Érasme' 99
8 CWE 27 129
9 CWE 68 539
10 Bejczy *Erasmus and the Middle Ages* 157, 170–2, 186–7, and passim.
11 Jacobus Latomus *De trium linguarum et studii theologici ratione dialogus* (Antwerp: Michael Hillenius Hoochstratanus, 1519), esp sig Biiij(v) to the end (signature numbers end at sig Eiii[r]). For this controversy, see Rummel *Erasmus and His Catholic Critics* I 63–93.

knowledge of ancient authors with the traditional methods of study.' There was, he said, no 'single passage even in some comical work of mine where I have written that time spent on authors like Scotus is time wasted.'[12] Defending the *Ratio* in his *Apology against a Dialogue of Jacobus Latomus*, Erasmus argued that patristic literature encouraged scholars to say better what really mattered in the writings of the schoolmen, not to reject scholasticism out of hand.[13] 'There are passages in my works where I have given Aquinas the highest place among modern theologians,' he said. 'But I do not think there is one where I have said that he is the only modern theologian who is worth reading.'[14] In fact, not long before composing this self-defence against Latomus, he had written from Louvain to the Parisian humanist and jurist Nicolas Bérault that it was neither his aim nor within his power to drive 'Thomas or Scotus from the universities in disgrace or ... out of their ancient inheritance,' nor was he 'sure that it would be desirable, unless we could see some school of thought ready to hand which would be better than they ... Enough for me if theology gets more sensible treatment than it has hitherto, and if we now and again fetch from its fountain-head in the Gospels what most people hitherto have been content to draw from pools that are not altogether clear.'[15] Could Luther's have become the replacement school of thought?

No. A year after writing to Latomus, while Luther's condemnation for heresy unfolded, Erasmus praised the rector of the University of Erfurt for recalling a 'frigid and quarrelsome' scholastic theology that 'had sunk to such a pitch of futility ... to the fountain-head,' but not destroying it, as Luther seemed to threaten to do: 'Luther has rendered a great service by pointing out so many abuses, but I wish he had done so in more civil language ... yet it would be quite wrong, where he has said what wanted saying, to leave him quite without support, or in the future no one will dare to speak the truth.'[16] The next day he wrote a commiserating letter to Luther himself, recounting his own mistreatment at the hands of a Spanish Franciscan who had attacked his annotation on John 1:1, *In principio erat sermo*, in the presence of Henry VIII and Catherine of Aragon, about the time of Edward Lee's more famous attack on Erasmus' translation of the verse; and he recounted other attacks on the

---

12 CWE 71 38–9. See also the pertinent remarks of Denis L. Drysdall in his introduction to Erasmus' controversial writings, CWE 73 xl.
13 CWE 71 39
14 CWE 71 78
15 Ep 1002:11–24 (9 August 1518)
16 Ep 1127:16–29

new learning, expressing his sympathy and appreciation for Luther's situation, while admonishing the German reformer to back away from controversial writing and focus on biblical commentary alone.[17] This, of course, Luther did not do, and he could never become a new alternative to the old theologians, not to Erasmus.

Erasmus continued to be accused of attacking the old theologians for the rest of his life. He always considered the accusation unjust. His criticism of the Vulgate, he wrote to Noël Béda in 1525, when the distance between him and Luther had become unmistakable, was not to replace Jerome but to improve the old translation. Did not commentators favoured by scholastics (Thomas Aquinas, Bede, Nicholas of Lyra) do the same, perhaps more quietly?[18] Monks were irritated by 'the fact that in my writings I sometimes disagree with Scotus, Thomas, Lyra, and Hugh [of St Cher], and that I repeatedly stress the nature of true religion ... Yet I nowhere condemn them totally, though I place them second to better men.'[19] He could describe schoolmen as moderates.[20] He could say that, in sacred matters, the style of Thomas Aquinas or John Duns Scotus easily surpassed the imitators of Cicero.[21] Erasmus, in short, tried to frame his criticism of scholastic theology as a judicious and constructive form of engagement with the past.

How much medieval theology did he really know? To answer this question, we must look closely at his use of medieval sources *and* consider his medievalism against the grain of its prevailing rhetoric. There seem to be only four exceptions to Erasmus' practice of dismissive generalization in his entire *Opera*, where he chose to reveal explicit, technical knowledge of scholastic debate.[22] These passages amount to a few lines of the *Praise of Folly*;[23] scattered remarks added to the 1519 edition of the *Ratio verae theologiae*; an interesting passage of the *Hyperaspistes* (comparing debates among Luther and his supporters to scholastic arguments);[24] and a lengthy addition to his own annotation on a verse in one of St Paul's letters, namely 1 Timothy 1:6, added in the 1519

---

17 Ep 1128A (1 August 1520)
18 Ep 1571 (28 April 1525)
19 Ep 1747:101–5, to Mercurino Gattinara (3 September 1526)
20 Erasmus *Apologia de 'omnes quidem'* CWE 73 61
21 Bejczy *Erasmus and the Middle Ages* 168
22 They are listed by M.L. van Poll-van de Lisdonck, ASD VI-10 12–13 note to lines 93–231.
23 ASD IV-3 146–8 (lines 394–416) = CWE 27 126–7, where he lists several technical scholastic positions
24 CWE 76 260–1

edition of the New Testament. This last passage, by far the most substantial, is especially instructive.

The annotation is attached to Erasmus' Latin translation of 1 Timothy 1:6, printed alongside the Greek original in his New Testament of 1516. His translation slightly modifies the Vulgate's Latin:

> The end of the law is love from a pure heart, a good conscience, an authentic faith. From these things certain people stray, diverted to vain speech (*vaniloquium*), wanting to be teachers of the law, not understanding what they say, nor what they insist upon.[25]

In his earliest annotation to the verse, Erasmus explains that the Greek word for 'vain speech,' *mataiologia* (*vaniloquium* in Latin), describes theologians who argue about things among themselves: 'As far as pronunciation goes, *mataiologia* does not differ much from *theologia*.'[26] The similarity goes beyond sound and rhyme to theological practice. Practice has drifted from the gospel into vain speech. 'Instead, we should discuss the things that transform us into Christ and render us worthy of heaven.'[27] To illustrate the metaeology-theology problem, he briefly reviews a scholastic debate over sin. Is sin a privation (a position that was in fact defended by Anselm, Scotus, Ockham, and Gregory of Rimini, none of whom he mentions), or is sin a stain inhering in the soul (a position that was defended by Alexander of Hales, Bonaventure, Aquinas, and Biel, again unmentioned)?[28] Erasmus says, 'Here a theologian should rather proceed so that everyone will abhor and hate sin.'[29] Theological descriptions of sin that distract people from resisting evil are wrong. In this manner, the 1516 annotation contrasts a Christian philosophy with scholastic debate in just a few lines.

Three years later, in the 1519 edition of the *Annotations*, Erasmus expanded this annotation with the longest catalogue of scholastic opinions that he ever produced. Subsequent editions in 1522 and 1527 added a few more items to the expanded text of 1519, yielding altogether a grocery list of about fifty-five technical arguments in theology, metaphysics,

---

25 ASD VI-4 116
26 ASD VI-10 10, 12 (lines 89–90)
27 ASD VI-10 12 (lines 92–3)
28 Scholastic positions on this issue were catalogued by Gabriel Biel, II Sent. D. 30 q. 2 a. 1: Biel *Collectorium circa quattuor libros Sententiarum*, ed Wilfrid Werbeck and Udo Hofmann (Tübingen: Mohr Siebeck, 1984) II 562–8.
29 ASD VI-10 12 (lines 94–5)

and logic.³⁰ The tireless editor of the critical edition, Miekske van Poll-van de Lisdonck, and a German 'inaugural dissertation' published in 1936, identified sources for the vast majority of these opinions.³¹

John Duns Scotus clearly dominated this catalogue of opinions, along with Aquinas and Albertus Magnus, and together they dominated the Erasmian image of scholasticism for the rest of the humanist's life. Aquinas and Scotus were paired, but Scotus was the most frequent example of dialectical obscurity.³² William Ockham does *not* dominate, reminding us that Scotus' voice was often louder in late medieval metaphysics and theology than some twentieth-century scholars have appreciated.³³ Gregory of Rimini, once emphasized by Heiko Oberman as the generator of a late medieval *via Augustiniana*, is entirely absent. Gabriel Biel seldom appears. Scotus may owe his prominence to an obscure Franciscan named Jean Grillot, if Grillot is, as James Farge argued, the Scotist whose lectures Erasmus endured as a student in Paris, when he came to study theology there, and this may have been the most sustained series of lectures in theology Erasmus ever heard.³⁴ The (unnamed) Scotist, Erasmus said in another place, induced a slumber as deep as the sleep of Epimenides, the shepherd boy who slept in a cave for forty years, contemplating quiddities, Erasmus said, alluding to Scotus' theory of abstractive cognition.³⁵ The city of Paris, he once joked, was a place of special Epimenidean devotion, where they venerate a relic of Epimenides' skin tattooed with mysterious glyphs.³⁶ It may have been the same boring Scotist who, according to a 1527 annotation, 'denied that nine years sufficed to understand what Scotus wrote on the mere preface of Peter Lombard.' The joke could allude to the common late medieval practice of lecturing on only parts of Lombard's *Four Books of Sentences*. 'I heard about another guy,' Erasmus continued, 'who declared that it was impossible that a person could understand a single proposition in

---

30 In some instances, more than one related doctrine or problem is combined with another, which why I say *about* fifty-five. ASD VI-10 12–30 (lines 173–231)
31 See the passage cited in the previous note and Dolfen *Stellung des Erasmus*.
32 ASD VI-10 12–30 (lines 173–231)
33 Ocker *Biblical Poetics* 119–20 with nn38–40 there
34 See Farge 'Erasmus, the University of Paris' 26 for the identification of Grillot; Bejczy *Erasmus and the Middle Ages* 73.
35 Epimenides was the Cretan who allegedly authored the Liar's Paradox, saying 'all Cretans are liars.' To Scotus, grasping the quiddity or 'whatness' of an entity was necessary to grasp the essence of things. See Erasmus' commentary on the adage 'You sleep longer than Epimenides' (*Ultra Epimenidem dormis*), *Adagia* I ix 64 CWE 32 217–18.
36 Ep 64

all of Scotus, unless one memorized his entire metaphysics.'[37] By implication, if it took nine years to get through Scotus' commentary on the mere preface, it was surely impossible to understand him in a single lifetime. Chastened by many years of controversy, in the *Ecclesiastes* of 1534 Erasmus paid Scotus a direct, but qualified, compliment: 'Scotus and those like him are useful for understanding *things* (*res*), but useless for speaking'; Aquinas, by contrast, would have been a great speaker if he had got more practice.[38] If Scotus was not entirely bad, Aquinas had been limited by opportunity.

The catalogue of scholastic doctrines, added to the annotation on 1 Timothy 1:6, suggests that Erasmus had more than casual knowledge of scholastic debate. And schoolmen had value. They taught students how to conduct disputations, but could never substitute for the articles of faith, said Erasmus in the *Ratio verae theologiae* [57]. A remarkably gifted student might excel at both disputation and biblical study, but only the latter was indispensable: 'I should prefer to be a godly theologian with Chrysostom, than to be undefeated [in debate] with Scotus' [273]. Ten years after writing these words, in the 1526 defence of his *Colloquies*, responding to the criticism and censorship of Louvain and Paris theologians, Erasmus equalized scholastics and ancient Christian classicizers, ranking the despised Scotus and the late medieval logician Peter of Spain, influential teacher of 'speculative grammar,' with Thomas Aquinas, Augustine, Hilary of Poitiers, Prudentius, Arator, and Juvencus:

> There is diversity of gifts and tastes; men are drawn to godliness by a thousand means. Juvencus is praised for his zeal in putting the gospel story into verse. Nor is Arator without his due praise for doing the same with the Acts of the Apostles. Hilary thunders against heretics, Augustine disputes, Jerome contends in dialogues, Prudentius wars in various forms of verse, Thomas and Scotus fight with the help of dialectic and philosophy. All have the same purpose, but each uses a different method. Variety is not condemned so long as the same goal is sought. Peter of Spain is taught to boys to prepare them the more readily for proceeding to Aristotle. One who instils a liking for something does much.[39]

Scholastic authors could also lead students 'to poetry, rhetoric, physics, ethics and finally to matters of Christian piety.' That same year,

---

37 ASD VI-10 28 (lines 212–15) with VI-10 29–30, note to lines 213–15
38 CWE 68 496:495–6
39 'The Usefulness of the Colloquies' CWE 40 1105–6

answering Luther, Erasmus observed, 'Not all questions are sophistical; some are useful and necessary, as long as they are judicious and are not pursued beyond the proper limits.'[40] Scholastic theology had problems but was not a monolith.

Erasmus' invective and his qualifications presupposed the fact that theologians were still using late medieval textbooks to explore both technical and general problems in logic, metaphysics, and religious doctrine.[41] His rehearsal of scholastic arguments in the annotation to 1 Timothy 1:6 is more than enough to convince the student of medieval theology, along with the editor of the critical edition of the *Annotationes*, that Erasmus actually knew what he was talking about. How, then, were medieval theologians part of his multigeneric approach to a textual theology?

To answer this question adequately, we must expand our notion of scholasticism to include an internal scholastic critique.

Biblical Scholasticism

It has been rightly said that 'dialectic was the mainstay of the scholastic system.'[42] It is true that Erasmus criticized deductive, logic-driven approaches to theology. But in its basic content, his criticism of scholasticism was unoriginal. Complaints against rationalist vanity were well known from the writings and reputation of Jean Gerson (d 1429) and endorsed by the Erasmus-promoter Jakob Wimpfeling, whose celebratory defence of the Parisian chancellor as a mystical-pastoral alternative to speculative theology epitomizes Gerson's prestige among humanists like Erasmus.[43] The complaints reached further back to a line of critics that included the Benedictine biblical commentator (and defender of church autonomy) Bruno of Segni (d 1123); the Benedictine abbot, friend of Thomas à Becket, and supporter of church autonomy Peter of Celle (d 1183); the Parisian scholar and bishop of Tournai Stephen of Tournai (d 1203); and the lawyer-pope Ugolino da Segni, alias Pope Gregory IX (d 1241) – that is, back to scholars reacting to the very beginnings of

---

40 CWE 76 135
41 Nauta 'Lorenzo Valla' 193–4
42 Rummel 'Scholasticism and Biblical Humanism' 1
43 Jakob Wimpfeling, *De vita et miraculis Joannis Gerson defensio* (Strasbourg: no publisher, no date [1506]) sig Aii(v). For Erasmus' acquisition of Gerson's works, see Van Gulik *Erasmus and His Books* 33 n123, 144, 196, 315 #169.

dialectical theology in the late twelfth century right into the generation of Richard Rufus of Cornwall (d c 1260), whose Parisian commentaries on Aristotle helped establish the place of Aristotelian metaphysics and natural philosophy in theological lectures for the rest of the Middle Ages.[44]

It continued from there. The Carmelite John Baconthorpe (d c 1348), exact contemporary of William Ockham, along with several fourteenth-century popes and the general chapters of the Dominican, Augustinian, and Carmelite orders, said *sophismata* (speculative exercises in propositional logic) had no place in theology.[45] They knew what they were talking about. The most influential theologians of the four mendicant orders ranked among the most expert dialecticians – men such as Robert Holcot, Adam Wodeham, Gregory of Rimini, and Guibert de Tournai. Reactions to speculation in theology also slipped into the critique of mendicant friars, familiar to us from Erasmus, other northern humanists, and the early Protestants, who freely ridiculed them for hypocritically practising a false poverty, and for their schismatic theological divisions. In sum, late medieval theology was not so speculative, some of the time.

Speculation seemed to contradict a patristic concept of biblical language familiar to Bible commentators in late medieval schools from St Jerome's letter to the priest Paulinus.[46] The letter to Paulinus could be found at the beginning of most medieval manuscripts of the Bible as a first prologue. It offered brief instructions for Bible study, rehearsing the patristic concept of biblical speech as *sermo humilis*, the humble, unphilosophical dialect of Greek used by the simple fishermen who were believed to have written the New Testament. Obviously, simplicity need not contradict deductive theology. William Ockham, among others, took simplicity as a characteristic of good logic applied to practical ends. Simplicity was also a characteristic of holiness, and Jerome modelled both erudition and piety for late medieval theologians. A great deal of monastic literature promoted simplicity in life and verbal expression, which nurtured the humanism of Renaissance cloisters in northern Europe. Medieval biblical scholars noted and reiterated the theme of the Bible's simplicity in commentaries on Jerome's preface to the Bible and in other places. These included the Dominican Nicholas of

---

44 Dolfen *Stellung des Erasmus* 14–18; Wood 'Richard Rufus' Significance'
45 Margolin 'Duns Scot et Érasme' 106; Ocker *Biblical Poetics* 114–20
46 Jerome Ep 53, esp the section numbered 3 in modern editions; English trans of the letter with Erasmus' comments in CWE 61 207–27

Gorran, a contemporary of Scotus, and the Cistercian Jacques Fournier and the Franciscan Nicholas of Lyra in the next generation.[47] To be sure, worry over William Ockham's logic at Paris in the 1340s coincided with a growing chorus of voices fretting over vainglorious sophistry.[48] The complaints against sophistry were so common that Jeremy Catto, surveying theological writing in fifteenth-century Oxford, could wonder about whom they were actually complaining.[49] And the voices would include Erasmus' in the *Ratio verae theologiae*: 'The language of truth is simple ... but nothing is either simpler or truer than Christ' [227].

In addition to the critique of intellectual vanity there is also the fact that the theological curriculum continued to require Bible lectures all through the fourteenth and fifteenth centuries, in every university faculty of theology, and in the very numerous schools of the Augustinian, Carmelite, and Franciscan Orders. In Dominican schools, Bible lectures were less routine, but they also occurred. European collections of medieval manuscripts are brimming with biblical commentaries copied on paper in the miscellany volumes compiled by students working their way through fifteenth-century schools. Historians have barely begun to study this literature. The idea that late medieval scholasticism was a quagmire of logical speculation, suggested by a naive reading of humanistic and early Protestant polemics, is undermined by these sources. Erasmus observed in the *Ratio verae theologiae*, 'people who have relied on dialectic alone ... attribute so much to this discipline that they suppose the Christian faith is finished and done for if it is not secured by ... dialectic, though meanwhile they disdain grammar and rhetoric as utterly superfluous' [21]. But not all late medieval theologians, whatever their shortcomings, disdained grammar and rhetoric or neglected textual study.

Erasmus used medieval biblical scholarship. We know from 1536 booklists prepared for the transfer of his library to Jan Łaski near the time of Erasmus' death that Erasmus had a few medieval writers in his personal library. They shared space with biblical commentaries by Luther, Philip Melanchthon, Oecolampadius, Frans Titelmans, Jacques Lefèvre d'Etaples, and Tommaso de Vio Cajetan; polemical writings from both sides of the Reformation; a great many grammatical and rhetorical works; parts of the *Corpus Iuris Canonici* and the *Corpus Iuris Civilis*; and various classical and patristic works, writers related to the Reuchlin

---

47 Ocker *Biblical Poetics* 24, 45, 222
48 Ocker *Biblical Poetics* 118–20
49 Catto 'Theology after Wycliffism' 264–5

affair, and Erasmus' own writings and editions.[50] There were the works of Bede, which included Bede's biblical writings, Aquinas on the letters of the apostle Paul and the Gospels, and the works of Jean Gerson, Peter Lombard's *Four Books of Sentences*, Durand de St Porçain's commentary on Lombard, and two parts of Aquinas' *Summa theologica*.[51] Erasmus also owned an edition of the Ordinary Gloss with the Postilla of Nicholas of Lyra. It has been identified as the six-volume edition published by Johannes Froben and Johannes Petri at Basel between 1506 and 1508, well before Erasmus moved there.[52] It included an alphabetical index and a marginal concordance to Gratian's *Decretum*, integrating a tool often used by late medieval Bible scholars to find authoritative opinions on relevant topics. The Gloss with Lyra was actually a small library of medieval biblical scholarship. It complemented the most influential medieval scholastic commentary, the Gloss, with Lyra's literal comments, his moral commentary, Paul of Burgos' replies to Lyra, and Matthew Döring's rebuttals to those replies. Accordingly, Erasmus thought it snobbery to write off works like the Ordinary Gloss or the influential Dominican commentaries by Hugh of St Cher (d 1263), which were also published by Johannes Froben at Basel in six volumes in 1504.[53] Erasmus meant to build upon a scholastic-exegetical legacy, he argued in 1522, responding to the Louvain Carmelite Nicolaas Baechem, when Baechem attacked Erasmus' Latin rendition of the Greek text of 1 Corinthians 15:51. His rendition, Erasmus replied, was orthodox because it was consistent with ancient Greek Christian commentators, and the variableness of readings was acknowledged by Jerome, the Pseudo-Jerome commentaries on the Pauline Letters (unknown to him, by Pelagius), the Ordinary Gloss, and Hugh of St Cher, writers whose authority Baechem easily recognized.[54] A similar point was made *to* Erasmus by the Zurich Hebraist Konrad Pellikan (Conradus Pellicanus) in defence of Martin Luther in 1525, suggesting the Hebraist's investment in an argument for scholastic continuity. Luther's departures from 'the schoolmen and our learned friends in Paris,' Pellikan said, could be

---

50 Van Gulik *Erasmus and His Books* 92–110, 207–450
51 Van Gulik *Erasmus and His Books* ##160, 161, 162, 163, 165, 168, 169, and 170
52 Van Gulik *Erasmus and His Books* 306 #154 (the Gloss edition is VD 16 B 2583). The marginal concordance to Gratian's *Decretum* appears to have been copied from the edition produced by Froben and Petri at Basel in 1498. Van Gulik points to evidence that Erasmus used the earlier edition, too.
53 Erasmus *Apologia de 'sermo'* (1520b) CWE 73 26. Erasmus had access to a Bible edition with Hugh of St Cher's *Postilla*: van Gulik *Erasmus and His Books* 306 #154.
54 Erasmus *Apologia de 'omnes quidem'* CWE 73 48, 55

traced not only to 'the good Fathers of the church' but also to 'what they call the *Glossa ordinaria*,' which 'the sophists of the Sorbonne ... wrapped up as they were in their texts of Aristotle, and satisfied with Peter Lombard and his articles of belief,' simply did not read.[55] Another admirer of Erasmus, Wolfgang Capito, cathedral preacher in Basel, soon to become a leading Strasbourg Protestant, could say that Erasmus' biblical scholarship superseded his predecessors Lyra, Hugh of St Cher, 'and other commentators of that kidney.'[56] Erasmus, of course, encouraged this interpretation of his work. According to the dedicatory preface to his 1516 edition of Jerome, it was a barbarian conspiracy that used scholastic authors ('Occam, Durandus, Capreolus, Lyra, Burgensis, and even poorer stuff than that') to perform 'the holocaust of humane literature and good authors.'[57] But in 1529, he told the Louvain Franciscan Frans Titelmans, in self-defence, that it was fair to use Lyra judiciously, critically.[58] To be a critic was not to destroy but to redeem. Seasoned by a decade of theologians censuring him, and by the Luther affair, Erasmus chose to be a renovator, not demolisher, of medieval Bible study.

He meant to be *seriously* critical of scholasticism. Erasmus vaguely referred to his use of medieval books in the *Ratio verae theologiae*, when he recommended 'our predecessors' for possible solutions to the inconsistencies between the four Gospels [79]. Theology led students of the Bible astray, rendering them, Erasmus complained, 'sometimes more uncouth than rustics, more vain, more irritable, more poisonous in tongue and absolutely more disagreeable ... even than they themselves normally are, so that, in the eyes of some, theology itself seems to have made them what they are' [11]. But still, a medievalist might see vaguely familiar terrain in Erasmus' programmatic outline for a theology based on biblical reading, such as we find in the *Ratio verae theologiae*.

The *Ratio verae theologiae* singled out ancient Christian writings that had helped scholars since Carolingian times to consider rhetorical aspects of biblical interpretation: Augustine's *De doctrina christiana* (correcting the eccentric use of rhetorical terms in the rules of Tyconius, among other things), Pseudo-Dionysius' *Divine Names*, and his *Mystical Theology* [4, 233]. The *De doctrina christiana* argued that the liberal arts and natural philosophy were prerequisites for Bible study, that the

---

55 Pellikan, Ep 1639:192–7 in Erasmus' correspondence, CWE 11 362:192–7
56 Capito, Ep 459:77–82 in Erasmus' correspondence, CWE 4 61:80–1
57 Erasmus, Ep 396:99–105
58 *A Response by Desiderius Erasmus to the Discussions of a Certain 'Youth Who Would Teach His Elders'* (1529) CWE 73 258–9

articles of faith measured valid interpretation, and that clear Bible passages interpret the obscure – all points adapted, codified, and propagated by scholars of the monastery of St Victor at Paris in the twelfth century, in the formative years of what one might call a biblical scholasticism.[59] Dionysius helped medieval scholars conceptualize mystical interpretation. Like Erasmus, medieval scholars believed that the figurative quality of biblical language, the Bible's peculiar rhetoric, reflected a kind of divine strategy, to captivate and penetrate human minds with 'the fragrance of heavenly mysteries.'[60] Like Erasmus, they insisted that proper interpretation required a subjective readiness on the part of readers, and some, like Henry of Langenstein, first rector of the University of Vienna, who wrote one of the two largest hermeneutical treatises of the fourteenth century, described a reader's aptitude as a kind of extension of prophetic inspiration, which in turn reflected a reader's moral aptitude, another Erasmian theme.[61] Hugh of St Victor named six 'circumstances' that impinge on the meaning of a passage, drawing on twelfth-century adaptations of Cicero's *Topics*.[62] Erasmus names six, too, emphasizing textual over natural qualities.[63] They both lean on classical rhetoric. Like Erasmus, medieval interpreters associated allegory with a Christian 'supersessionist' view of Judaism, believing that a pattern of shadow and revelation was carved into historical time.[64] Although Bible commentaries before Erasmus tended not to stress the reader's personal identification with Christ as Erasmus emphasized it in the *Ratio*, a growing body of late medieval parabiblical literature did just that.[65] Erasmus saw prevalent themes in the entire Bible giving order to the interpretation of individual passages, emphasizing the collection of commonplaces familiar in biblical humanism.[66] Like Erasmus, late medieval Bible scholars emphasized the thematic structure

---

59 Ocker *Biblical Poetics* 33–4; *Ratio* **19, 237, 248**
60 The quoted words are Henry of Langenstein's: Ocker *Biblical Poetics* 103, 105, 107–8; see *Ratio* **185–98**.
61 *Ratio* **6–7**; Ocker *Biblical Poetics* 50, 149–61
62 The six are: physical objects as such and their properties, persons who signify mysteries in their deeds and experiences, numbers in their various arrangements and computations (he names nine), places, times (such as seasons), and events; Hugh of St Victor, *De scripturis et scriptoribus sacris praenotatiunculae* xiv–xvi, in PL175 cols 20–4. See Copeland *Rhetoric, Hermeneutics, and Translation* 70–2.
63 Addressee, time, occasion, what precedes, what follows, *persona* (speaker's role): *Ratio* **41**.
64 *Ratio* **83–91**; Ocker *Biblical Poetics* 26–8, 49–51, 57–9, 64–5, 179–83
65 Ocker 'Bible in the Fifteenth Century'
66 *Ratio* **35**; Ocker *Biblical Poetics* 185–213

of the Bible as a whole and within individual books.⁶⁷ Both Erasmus and late medieval commentators might have taken issue with Henri de Lubac, a key figure in the *nouvelle théologie* in post-war France, when he elevated the famous *quadriga* of literal, allegorical, tropological, and anagogical senses to an axiomatic position.⁶⁸ Like Erasmus, late medieval commentators used the *quadriga* as a way to approach the polyvalence of language, not as a strict method for distinguishing meanings, because historical and figurative meanings overlap all the time.⁶⁹ Like very many Bible readers since the Ostrogoths and the Visigoths, late medieval commentators identified Greek and Hebrew idioms and rhetorical figures of speech, which they found listed by Boethius, Isidore, Donatus, and any number of grammarians – but not by the Quintilian rediscovered by Poggio Bracciolini and adored by Erasmus.⁷⁰

Erasmus critically engaged medieval biblical scholarship. In the 1519 *Ratio verae theologiae*, he complained that scholars relied on handbooks attributed to Jerome (such as *De nominibus Hebraeorum*), the twelfth-century grammarian Everard of Bethune, Isidore of Seville, and Donatus, the late antique grammarian who had been Jerome's teacher.⁷¹ These tools, on which medieval commentators relied, had been surpassed in Erasmus' day, yet they were still being used. So, in the 1520 edition of the *Ratio verae theologiae*, Erasmus told a story that he repeated several more times in his life, to illustrate how the tropes of *synecdoche* and *hyperbaton* could clarify discrepancies between the three Gospels. A clever Scotist once ridiculed this method, Erasmus recalled, boasting that he had learned to read the same way from the grammar of Alexander de Villa Dei.⁷² A Scotist, or anyone else, easily could have. Alexander de Villa Dei was available in eighty-six editions, with and without commentary, whole or in part, published from 1501 to 1524 alone.⁷³ Erasmus' argument with the Scotist was over quality and refinement: his own works were better for identifying idiomatic expressions peculiar to Latin, Greek, and Hebrew and for exploring the significations embedded in

---

67 Ocker *Biblical Poetics* 24–9
68 De Lubac *Medieval Exegesis*
69 *Ratio* 217, 233; Ocker *Biblical Poetics* 142–8 and 'Four Senses of Scripture'
70 *Ratio* 15, 23, 29, 42, 185, 201–15; Ocker *Biblical Poetics* 98
71 *Ratio* 22, 210, 234, 253. Everard lists 103 tropes in the *Graecismus*. Alexander of Villa Dei listed 80. Donatus listed 33.
72 *Ratio* 201
73 Data from a search of the *Verzeichnis der im deutschen Sprachbereich erschienenen Drucke des 16. Jahrhunderts*, accessible online. Interestingly, no edition was published in the German-speaking lands between 1525 and 1553.

rhetorical figures of speech.⁷⁴ He recommended Origen for allegories, Chrysostom for *loci communes*, which is to say, authors that he would eventually edit for commercial editions; he disliked allegories of chess and numerology, preferring a more sober figurative exegesis.⁷⁵ Against Latomus in 1518, he noted that his New Testament annotations correcting Augustine, Aquinas, Hugh of St Victor, and Nicholas of Lyra were meant to show the need for a corrected New Testament text.⁷⁶ His translation was meant to go beyond medieval glosses.⁷⁷ He thought he could make medieval exegesis better.

Biblical Scholasticism and Textual Theology

The difference between Erasmus and his predecessors was thus a matter of quality and degree, not of kind – except at one crucial point. Erasmus drew a sharp contrast between biblical reading and theological dialectic, separating his textual theology from any notion of a deductive science. By contrast, late medieval theologians did not perceive any significant tension between rhetorical and dialectical treatments of biblical language and ideas. This was probably due to the inferiority of their knowledge of classical rhetoric, which limited their ability to explain literature by its communicative strategies.⁷⁸ Yet it is worth remembering that many of Erasmus' readers leaned towards the medieval theologians on this very point, preferring to use an Erasmian textual method to identify, collect, and arrange specific, vitally important theological distinctions, commonplaces, as Erasmus recommended in the *Ratio verae theologiae*, while perceiving no conflict between a textual theology and finely tuned doctrinal polemic.

A recent dissertation offers an example. It closely examines a commentary on St Paul's First Letter to the Corinthians by Zurich's Heinrich Bullinger, published in 1534 and written over the previous year, when Erasmus was arguably at the height of his influence.⁷⁹ Erasmus, along with Quintilian and Agricola, helped Bullinger identify and discuss thirty-two rhetorical figures in the letter, allowing Bullinger to build an

---

74 *Ratio* 12, 16–17, 199–200, 208–10
75 *Ratio* 23, 28, 227, 231
76 Erasmus *Apologia contra Latomi Dialogum* CWE 71 58; see also CWE 71 49.
77 Erasmus *Apologia contra Latomi Dialogum* CWE 71 70
78 Ocker *Biblical Poetics* 112–83
79 Kim 'Humanistic Commentary on Scripture in Zurich'

image of a text that transparently portrayed the gospel while resolving theological debates in favour of positions Zurich took against Anabaptists, papists, and Lutherans. In other words, Erasmus helped Bullinger demonstrate Zwinglian doctrine in opposition to every going alternative. Melanchthon, Calvin, a forgotten Johann Philonius Dugo, even John Eck, composers of *Loci communes* and *Institutiones christianae*, took a decidedly more systematic approach to biblical commonplaces than Bullinger ever did. Calvin, in particular, thought his *Institutes* merely 'set in order' the teachings of Scripture.[80] In each successive edition of the *Institutes*, he expanded arguments against opposing positions, just to help the rest of us see the clarity of his arrangement of biblical commonplaces, which an Erasmian might dismiss as a distinction-making cancer. What is striking about Bullinger, Calvin, or any number of Erasmus' younger Protestant contemporaries is that one could have done at least part of this philological spade-work using medieval sources, such as Donatus, Alexander de Villa Dei, and Evrard of Bethune, the handbooks of Jerome and Pseudo-Jerome, Bede, or Isidore. But this body of scholarship was closely associated with a medieval deductive science. They needed tools that let their theological distinctions pose as commonplaces in a textual theology, and Erasmus provided them.

This was precisely what Erasmus disliked about Luther. He identified Protestant polemicists with theologians of the recent past, an opinion confirmed for him by Luther's bitter polemic in *De servo arbitrio* (1525), even if Luther depended heavily on the confidence inspired in readers by the method Erasmus described in the *Ratio verae theologiae*. Luther rejected scholasticism when it was convenient, but posed 'another sophistical argument no less sophistical than the previous one.'[81] Erasmus was right, in his way. The new theologians – not only Luther, but Zwingli, Melanchthon, Bucer, Bullinger, Oecolampadius, Osiander, and a small army of young monks, students, and priests reading their books – were making distinctions with the tools of an Erasmian textual theology.

The vast majority of commentary-writing 'theologasts' kept doing just that, producing their own handbooks with Erasmian tools: making distinctions, believing that their distinctions were fluent, reliable, learned, humanistic readings of biblical ideas. This lasted a few decades more. It has been said that 'humanism opened up new ways of reading and composing texts, built partly on the precepts of ancient dialectic

---

80 See Muller *Unaccommodated Calvin* ch 2.
81 Erasmus *Hyperaspistes* CWE 76 260–1

and rhetoric, partly on [the humanists'] own imaginative and creative interpretations of these old texts. This move towards a new hermeneutics, a new approach to texts, arguments, and meaning is perhaps the most significant contribution of humanism.'[82] But partly contrary to Erasmus' wishes, his new textual theology seems to have reinvigorated narrow theological distinction-making during and after the bipolar religious controversy that developed in his later years.[83]

---

82 Nauta 'Lorenzo Valla' 207
83 I thank Dr Miekske van Poll-van de Lisdonck for her corrections and suggestions.

The *Ratio* and *Annotations* as Theory and Practice of Biblical Interpretation

RIEMER FABER

The publication of the *Novum instrumentum* in 1516 signalled the launch of what became a 'huge New Testament Project' destined to occupy Erasmus for the remainder of his career.[1] Given the opportunity to publish the notes he had been gathering on the New Testament books, together with a Greek text and a Latin version, Erasmus soon would be drawn into an ecclesiastical and theological whirlpool at the centre of which was the Bible. Keenly aware of the imperfections in the hastily prepared edition, he commenced work on a new and improved version even before the first was lifted from the presses. Indeed, the Herculean labours he was expending upon New Testament scholarship propelled him forward in his vast enterprise of reformulating the entire Christian experience as the *philosophia Christi* or 'philosophy of Christ.' This phrase, appearing in the 'Exhortation to the Reader' (*Paraclesis*) prefatory to the 1516 New Testament,[2] is more than a summary of Erasmus' understanding of the Christian faith. It expresses an entire program of making the Scriptures directly accessible to believers in order that they may be transformed into the image of Christ.

The New Testament project embraced three components of biblical scholarship in particular. The first was Erasmus' theory of biblical interpretation, initially sketched out in the *Methodus* (1516) and augmented in the *Ratio verae theologiae*. The *Ratio* appeared first as a separate publication in 1518 and as part of the *Novum Testamentum* in 1519. Containing entirely new sections, such as the portrayal of Christ as model for the exegete [72–96], a fuller discussion of parables and allegories

---

[1] Bloemendal 'Erasmus' *Paraphrases on the New Testament*' 107; Nellen and Bloemendal 'Erasmus' Biblical Project'
[2] CWE 41 407

[186–97, 216–33], and a much-expanded treatment of literary and rhetorical figures and tropes [199–215], the *Ratio verae theologiae* presents a well-rounded introduction to biblical exegesis.

The second component was the *Paraphrases*, running commentaries on the New Testament which Erasmus began to publish in 1517 with his paraphrase on Paul's Letter to the Romans. That was followed with paraphrases on the other books of the New Testament (except the Apocalypse) between 1518 and 1524.[3] In composing these treatises, Erasmus' aim was to equip believers with the spiritual weapons needed in service to God, and to cultivate lives of piety and devotion.

The third and largest component in Erasmus' project were the endnotes, called *Annotations*, which had been included as a sort of appendix in the 1516 *Novum instrumentum*.[4] Between 1516 and 1519 these *Annotations* were overhauled and augmented, and with every edition thereafter they increased even more, so that by 1535 they required 783 folio pages instead of 300 in 1516.[5] The expanded *Annotations* allowed Erasmus to present new exegetical material drawn from the Church Fathers and to respond to the critics of the first edition. But they also gave him the opportunity to put into practice his theories of biblical interpretation through their detailed discussion of obscure or difficult passages and their engagement with the readings of earlier exegetes. It is the purpose of this essay to illustrate the nature of Erasmus' hermeneutics by demonstrating how several key principles articulated in the *Ratio* are implemented in the *Annotations*.

Given the concurrent expansion of the *Methodus* into the *Ratio* and of the *Annotations*, it is not surprising that in the treatise on hermeneutics Erasmus should direct his reader to the commentary. On five occasions Erasmus corroborates observations about scriptural interpretation in the *Ratio* with explicit reference to the *Annotations*. In fact, in the words of Robert Sider, '[t]he expansion of the 1516 *Methodus* into the 1519 *Ratio* enabled the latter to serve effectively as a preface to the enlarged edition of the New Testament of 1519, particularly with the *Annotations* in

---

3 On the nature of the *Paraphrases*, see the General Introduction to the New Testament Scholarship by R.D. Sider, CWE 41 9–11 and relevant chapters there; also Pabel and Vessey *Holy Scripture Speaks* and essays in ES 36.2 (2016).
4 For the place of the *Annotations*, see now CWE 41 78–97 and van Poll-van de Lisdonck 'Die Annotationes,' with Rummel *Erasmus' Annotations on the New Testament*.
5 Sider in his General Introduction to CWE 41 describes how the *Annotations* evolved with each successive edition: 1516 (78–129), 1519 (181–3), 1522 (269–78), 1527 (394–419), and 1535 (487–511).

view.'[6] To give only one example, when dealing with the literary figure of exaggeration, or *hyperbole*, Erasmus directs the reader to consult his commentary: 'In the annotations that I have written on the New Testament I have in scattered fashion pointed out cases of this kind' [200]. Such references reinforce the coherence between the introductory material, the translation, and the commentary; they also express the unity of theory and practice within the larger project of the *philosophia Christi*.

As he reworked and expanded the *Methodus/Ratio* together with the *Annotations*, Erasmus was also pursuing the goal of arranging the entire Bible project in such a way that it would facilitate the moral and social reform of the Christian believer. In his tripartite New Testament scholarship, as described above, Erasmus developed a discourse that united the principles of biblical exegesis with the implementation of biblical teaching in the life of every Christian. In the *Ratio* this discourse concerns three aspects of interpretation in particular:

For a right understanding of Scripture and its meaning, the exegete must (1) become an imitator of Christ, the incarnate Word, as he is portrayed in Scripture. God's compassion for fallen humanity and his desire to redeem it find clearest expression in the manifestation of his only son, in whom God himself came down to earth: 'The Word became flesh and dwelt among us' (John 1:14 RSV). Through his incarnation, Christ mediates the words and thoughts of the Father. It is Christ who has established a new order upon earth, a heavenly kingdom of reborn, reformed citizens who have been taught by his example. Thus the interpreter must seek to grasp Christ's thoughts and his words, and to be conformed to his image.

Having rightly embraced Christ, the exegete must (2) learn how to incorporate the teachings of Christ in his or her own reading of Scripture. Being incapable of understanding God's revelation in all its richness and depth, the fallible human interpreter must trust that, in his Word, God accommodates himself to the human intellect. As the recorded words and actions of Christ himself reveal, God's behaviour and speech are adjusted to the limitations of the human intellect and will. In other words, the principle of accommodation which operates in the history of the redemption of God's people in the old and new covenants operates also on the level of the written communication preserved in the Bible. Proper theological method, then, applies the principle of God's philanthropic condescension to the interpretation of his Word.

---

6 CWE 41 170

Through the inspired writers of the books of the Bible, God conveys his divine truth in human language. By means of comparisons, likenesses, parables, or allegories, the biblical writings mediate divine thoughts to human understanding. For Erasmus, the primary task of theology (or the study of God) is the interpretation of the text of Scripture. The ideal student must therefore (3) become skilled in the literary and rhetorical devices by means of which divine teaching is communicated in the biblical books. Consequently, Erasmus dedicates considerable space in the *Ratio* and the *Annotations* to explicating unusual or foreign diction, figures of speech, and features of biblical style which strain human language in an effort to convey God's truth.

The following sections of this essay consider each of these aspects of the Erasmian biblical project in turn.

Transformational Reading: The Exegete as Imitator of Christ in Scripture

The fundamental premise of Erasmian hermeneutics presented in the *Ratio* is that the interpreter of Scripture is a devout believer, a genuine follower and disciple of Christ. The ideal exegete has been renewed in Christ's image and transformed into his likeness. 'Let this be your first and only goal,' Erasmus states, 'that you be changed ... be transformed into what you are learning' [10]. The exegete must attend especially to those books of the New Testament in which Christ is portrayed most clearly. Fortunately, Erasmus observes in the *Paraclesis*, the books of the New Testament 'restore Christ to us so completely and so vividly that you would see him less clearly should you behold him standing before your very eyes.'[7] To the modern reader, the idea that Christ reveals himself more fully in the biblical writings than he did while he was in the flesh on earth may seem far fetched. But in the *Annotations* to Paul's Letter to the Galatians, Erasmus demonstrates that the apostle Paul – whom he calls the 'supreme interpreter of our religion'[8] – states in so many words that the Gospel presents a living picture of Christ. The Galatians were sliding back from faith in Christ to their former observance of the Law, and Paul reminds them that before 'their very eyes Jesus Christ was clearly portrayed as crucified' (Galatians 3:1 RSV). In

---

7 CWE 41 422
8 CWE 43 3

a lengthy note added in the *Annotations* of 1519, Erasmus paraphrases Paul's words here: 'as though portrayed hanging on the cross, Christ has been manifested before your eyes.'[9] Of course, Erasmus goes on to clarify, Christ 'had not been crucified among the Galatians, but through faith he was represented to them as crucified.' Noting that the Greek verb which Paul uses here, *proegraphe*, 'was portrayed,' is a term used for representation in writing as well as in painting, Erasmus interprets the apostle to mean that the faith of those who believe in Christ's atoning sacrifice without having seen him is as great as that of those before whose eyes Christ had been crucified. The word of Christ was so preached to the Galatians 'that they knew and believed [his crucifixion] no less than if the act had been performed in their very presence.'[10] In other words, because Christ revealed himself fully in the Gospel, the Galatians are able to perceive him as he truly was.

Just as the Galatians beheld Christ himself in the Gospel that was proclaimed to them, so too the exegete must perceive Christ in the words of Scripture. In the same passage of the 'Exhortation to the Reader' (*Paraclesis*) already quoted above, Erasmus writes: 'These books show you the living image of his holy mind and Christ himself, speaking, healing, dying, rising to life again. In short, they restore Christ to us so completely and so vividly that you would see him less clearly should you behold him standing before your very eyes.'[11] Because Christ is present in the words of the Bible, it is there that the exegete learns who Christ is. One must appropriate Christ in order to interpret his teaching correctly. Only having assumed Christ's spirit of patience, kindness, love, and gentleness, will the Bible interpreter understand correctly what the actions and words of Christ mean. For this reason, Erasmus discourses at length on the exemplary character and behaviour of Christ which the exegete should imitate [**104–29**].

Christocentric Hermeneutics: Accommodation in the History of Redemption and Revelation

In another lengthy section of the *Ratio*, Erasmus elaborates on the idea that God treats people differently according to their place on the timeline of salvation history [**45–50**]. Throughout the ages, and within the

---

9 CWE 58 48
10 CWE 58 49
11 See n7 above.

grand scheme of his plan for redemption, God has made concessions to fallen humanity by adjusting the devotion and piety he demands of his people and also the extent of his self-revelation to them. Three main periods in the history of salvation and revelation are recorded in the Scriptures. The first period is the time which preceded the life of Christ. It is the era of the Old Testament patriarchs, priests, prophets, and kings, and of the people of Israel during and after the exile. Once this period was over, the temporary traditions of circumcision, the sabbath, and the performing of sacrifices disappeared also. The second period is 'when the shadows of the former law were fading as the light of the gospel was near at hand and now approaching' [46]; it was a time of transition from the old covenant to the new as recorded especially in the Gospels and the Acts of the Apostles. The third period is the time when Christ 'was now becoming widely manifest to the world through miracles and teaching, and the evangelical doctrine was being proclaimed – without, however, forbidding the observance of the law' [47]. Certain concessions were made to those Christians for whom the removal of Old Testament traditions formed a stumbling-block. For the reader of the Bible, the hermeneutic division of distinct time periods explains how God accommodates himself to the weaknesses of different people in different circumstances. And for the exegete, appreciation of these varying times serves to explain some of the most difficult passages in Scripture, especially those which treat the function of Jewish customs and traditions in the new covenant.

It will be worthwhile to consider briefly how the principle of theological accommodation operates in Erasmus' exegetical practice. One illustrative example is the so-called Synod of Jerusalem, recorded in Acts 15:19–20. At this synod, held during the third time period, the apostles decided to instruct the newly converted Gentiles 'to abstain from food polluted by idols, from sexual immorality, from the meat of strangled animals and from blood' (Acts 15:23 RSV). This decision challenges the reader of Erasmus' day, for abstinence from what has been strangled and from blood was regarded by the later church as not forbidden, and the prohibition seems to conflict with the contemporary teaching of the church. Erasmus' explanation for these restrictions is that they were imposed during the period of transition from Law to Gospel when the apostles wished to avoid causing offence to those Jewish Christians who followed the traditions of their forefathers [48].

Another text illustrative of theological accommodation is Romans 13:11, where the apostle Paul exhorts his readers to live in holiness, 'since we know what hour it is ... for salvation is nearer now than when we first believed' (RSV). Prompted by the progression in redemptive history which this text implies, Erasmus in 1519 expanded his *Annotation* on the verse with an illuminating note which echoes the *Ratio*: 'All time is divided into various *horae* [periods]: there was a period before the Law; under the Law; under the gospel. The Gentiles lived in darkness, the Jews in shadows, unaware that they were asleep ... But now that the clear light of the gospel has shone forth, it is shameful for anyone still to be asleep.'[12] Here Erasmus applies the hermeneutic key of periodization in salvation history to a particular text.

The incarnate Christ, in whom God's philanthropic condescension takes human form, stands at the centre of the three time periods recorded in Scripture; he is the scope of theology. As the mediator between God and humanity, Christ also embodies the accommodation of God the Father: 'The Word became flesh and dwelt among us' (John 1:14 RSV). In Christ, God's truth is mediated to mankind. This means not only that Christ emptied himself of divine glory by becoming a servant and atoning for sins, but also that while he lived on earth he adjusted his own actions, thoughts, and speech in order to reach fallen human beings. Christ, who 'became all things to all people,' adjusted his actions and words to suit different people at different times and circumstances [72–7].

As imitator of Christ, Paul adapts his behaviour and speech to the circumstances of his readers in order to instruct them in the faith [97]. In defence of his varying behaviour and mode of writing, Paul states: 'To the weak I became weak, that I might win the weak. I have become all things to all men that I might by all means save some' (1 Corinthians 9:22 RSV). Paul adjusted his writing to suit different first readers. In other words, the *theological* doctrine of accommodation is reflected in the hermeneutical principle of *rhetorical* accommodation. As a literary or rhetorical technique, Paul's accommodation is justified by the fact that in his revelation God (and Christ) accommodated himself to the limitations of the human intellect and comprehension.[13]

Theological and rhetorical accommodation concerns not only the differences between Jews and Gentiles or between those living in the old and new dispensations, but also between every people in every time and place. Therefore the practice of placing God's revelation generally within the context of redemptive history extends in detail to the individual books of the Bible. This means that knowledge of the time when each book was written, and by and for whom it was written, will assist

---

12 CWE 56 356
13 Hoffmann *Rhetoric and Theology* 106

greatly in the interpretation of it.[14] For this reason the exegete may consult classical writings which shed light on the culture of the first readers or addressees of a book. Erasmus states: 'If we will learn from historical literature not only the setting, but also the origin, customs, institutions, culture, and character of the peoples whose history is being narrated or to whom the apostles write, it is remarkable how much more light and, if I may use the expression, life will come to the reading' [19]. Passages which appear to contradict others may be explained by taking into account the difference in time, place, readership, and circumstance of the books of the Bible [37–50, 234–6].

The identification of rhetorical accommodation by Erasmus the exegete in interpreting a particular book of the New Testament is illustrated by two passages in Paul's Letter to the Galatians. In the 1519 edition, in the brief preface (*argumentum*) to the letter, Erasmus depicts the distinct character of the Galatian readers. In the words of Jerome as quoted by Erasmus, the Galatians 'resembled their forebears in dullness of wit'; they were a people 'slow to learn,' a 'fickle and foolish' people who had fallen back into Judaism and with whom Paul must 'comply' (the Latin word here is *obtempero*) by using 'sharp speech' in order to cure them 'with wholesome severity and gentle firmness.'[15] As a principle of exegesis applied to the epistle, accommodation explains away the apparently harsh tone of Paul's manner of speaking, as in the cry, 'O foolish Galatians!' (Galatians 3:1). Cursing of this sort, Erasmus acknowledges, is condemned elsewhere in the Bible (eg in Matthew 5:22), but he defends Paul's use of such language here as being appropriate to the Galatians, who 'had set forth from the wilder regions of the Gauls.'[16] In this letter Paul employs a 'simple and unrefined manner of speaking' to suit the character of the Galatian readers.[17]

Elsewhere in his commentary on the same letter, Erasmus invokes the principle of accommodation to explain also the difficult text that Peter 'stood condemned' by Paul for withdrawing from the company of Gentiles in Antioch when members of the circumcision party arrived (Galatians 2:11–14). The text is difficult because it suggests that Peter erred or committed a sin. According to Erasmus in the *Annotations*, Paul only appears to reprimand Peter, and he does so for the sake of instructing the weak Galatians, who needed strengthening in their newly obtained

---

14 On this principle, see CWE 41 92–4.
15 CWE 42 94; LB VII 943–4
16 CWE 58 44
17 CWE 58 71

faith.[18] This passage illustrates the rule expressed in the *Ratio* that in order to understand the relationship between the author of a Bible text and his first readers, the exegete should 'consider not only what is said, but also the words used, by whom and to whom they are spoken, the time, the occasion, what precedes and what follows' [41]. In sum, the full range of interpretive techniques which in ancient times had been employed by rhetoricians may be applied to the reading of Scripture, too.[19] In the *Ratio* and the *Annotations*, therefore, Erasmus promotes a hermeneutic that is *historical* – accounting for the place of recorded events within the history of salvation – and *grammatical* – accounting for the place of the text within the history of revelation.

Interpretive Strategies: Allegories, Parables, and Figures of Speech

The Scriptures must be studied carefully because their deepest meaning is theological and spiritual, not literal. The customs prescribed for the Jewish people in the first dispensation, such as the celebration of Passover and the rite of circumcision (which respectively foreshadowed Christ's atoning sacrifice and the sacrament of baptism), served as allegories for spiritual truths that are more fully revealed in the New Testament. Throughout the history of revelation, God unfolded divine truths hidden within these visible and tangible customs. The theological allegories are paralleled by literary and rhetorical allegories told by the prophets in the Old Testament and by Christ himself in the New. Just as God in his compassion adapts spiritual teaching to the people's capacity for understanding, so too does Christ adjust his revelation, his spoken Word, to limited human intellectual capability. Both theological and literary allegories are concessions to the weaknesses in human reasoning, and encourage it to rise to a higher plane of existence and meaning. In fact, the moral and religious reform entailed in the *philosophia Christi* is founded upon a reading of Scripture which reaches this higher level of meaning.

In the Scriptures God adjusts his discourse to match finite human capacities of comprehension. He employs modes of thought and language through which humans can, at least partially, comprehend

---

18 CWE 58 36
19 Eden *Hermeneutics* 73; Hoffmann *Rhetoric and Theology* 106; Weiss '*Ecclesiastes* and Erasmus'

spiritual truths. The allegories and parables in the Old and New Testaments convey a hidden theological meaning: 'Under this covering there lies hidden some more recondite sense' [219]. Thus the *theological* doctrine of accommodation is reflected in the hermeneutical principle of *rhetorical* accommodation. And allegory as deep religious truth on a spiritual level is mirrored by allegorical expressions on a smaller scale.[20] All Scripture is metaphorical in the strict sense of the word: it leads the exegete from a literal reading to a spiritual understanding of the divine truth.[21] Because the figurative or allegorical meaning supersedes the literal one, the philological exegesis of the text often is accompanied by allegorical and spiritual explanation.

The close relationship between theological and literary allegory explains why Erasmus shifts somewhat abruptly from a treatment of allegory to a discussion of the 'character of the speech in which sacred literature has been handed down to us' [185]. Erasmus broaches the topic of the inner, deeper meaning of the text because Paul always 'refers everything from its normal meaning to its inner meaning, which is always the sense that is truest, and also the most salutary and of the most extensive application' [196]. Similitude, various forms of likeness or comparison, and analogies share in common with allegory the idea that one thing is said and another is meant.[22] Thus Erasmus broaches the topic of small-scale figures of speech [185–98] which make it possible for divine teaching to be 'placed before the eyes as though portrayed in a picture' [191]. What is more, unlike divine discourse, human writers are fallible and cannot express adequately the fullness of divine thought. Moreover, certain modes of expression and figures of speech, in which the literal meaning differs from the figurative one, must be explained to the reader.

Therefore, in a section new to the *Ratio* in 1518/1519, Erasmus embarks on a lengthy treatment of several figures of speech: metaphor, simile, parable, hyperbole, and synecdoche [201–23]. The recurring references in this section of the treatise to the *Annotations* make explicit the link between *Ratio* and *Annotations*. A fundamental hermeneutical issue discussed here is that each literary figure or trope presents a challenge of interpretation, for it is like theological allegory, which seeks to impart a different meaning from what is stated. Each trope presents a straining of language or even inconsistency in grammar which needs

---

20 Bentley 'Erasmus' *Annotationes*' 44
21 See also 55–7 above.
22 See the essay by Eden, below.

to be explained. To make the point that this task belongs to the exegete, Erasmus often notes that there is a precedent in the commentaries of the Church Fathers for seeking to correct linguistic or grammatical obscurities. To lend greater credibility to this aspect of exegesis, Erasmus reminds his readers: 'Just so that no one disdains this part of literary study as philological and trivial, Augustine in his work *On Christian Doctrine* directs that it be carefully learned as being useful for understanding the canonical books' [210].

In the *Ratio* Erasmus chooses representative literary figures to highlight the value of following a grammatical approach to explain expressions which mean something different from what they say: (1) *hyperbaton* [201], which may be defined as the separation of words that naturally belong together; (2) *hyperbole*, which Erasmus defines as 'a statement that goes beyond demonstrable reality' [202] or in which a speaker or writer 'said more than he meant' [204]; (3) ambiguity, which is 'a fault in discourse, but one that often cannot be avoided' [211]; (4) *abutio*, or the special use of a word that 'sometimes makes the discourse ambiguous' [212]; and (5) *emphasis*, when, as Quintilian says, 'words mean more than they say'[23] or when a special significance is attached to them [214]. These grammatical and literary constructions, composed by inspired but fallible human authors, were seen since the time of the Church Fathers not only as attempts to express something more than human language is able to convey, but also as grammatical infelicities. To demonstrate this point, in his annotation on Romans 1:7 Erasmus alludes to Origen's complaint that Paul sometimes employs confusing and unclear expressions, and Origen attributes these to Paul's Cilician, non-Greek background.[24] Elsewhere Erasmus notes that on many occasions 'Chrysostom and Jerome and Augustine scatter the obscurity of meaning by unravelling the intricacies' of *hyperbaton* and similarly strained language [201]. He cites the Church Fathers on *hyperbata* in his *Annotations* and in the *Ratio* not merely to defend himself against the charge of impious Bible criticism, but especially to show from the history of exegesis that it is the theologian's task to clarify the difficult passages in Scripture.

A similar process of interpretation may be observed regarding *hyperbole*, or exaggeration [202–7], and *emphasis* [212–15]. In the *Ratio*, Erasmus points to Origen, Chrysostom, Augustine, and Jerome as his precursors

---

23 Quintilian *Institutio oratoria* 8.2.11
24 CWE 56 30

in commenting on the figure of *hyperbole*,[25] and he also directs the reader to consult his own *Annotations*.[26] In the *Annotations* on the Epistles to the Galatians and Ephesians, Erasmus twice discusses *hyperbole*, and quotes from the earlier commentaries of Theophylact and Jerome.[27] An implicit appeal to the Church Fathers as justification for explaining unusual grammatical constructions occurs also for the figure of *emphasis*: the five appearances of the term in Erasmus' commentary on the epistles to the Galatians and Ephesians date to 1519 or later, and four of them are linked to references to the *patres*.[28]

Erasmus' treatment of ambiguity, 'a fault in discourse' [211], also exhibits the correlation between the *Ratio* and the *Annotations*. In the *Annotations* on the four synoptic Gospels, Erasmus identifies twenty-eight instances of ambiguity, of which the majority (eighteen) were added in 1519, or later. Ambiguity results from a variety of reasons: Greek words with more than one meaning; ambivalent constructions of the syntax; lack of punctuation. Erasmus explicitly directs the reader of the *Ratio* to consult the *Annotations* for clarifications of ambiguous expressions: 'I have in many places noted it and, where I could, I have eliminated it' by 'a change in the order of the words if the difficulty arises from word placement' [211]. And he underscores the exegete's duty to explain *abutio*, by defining it as 'the special use of a word' that 'sometimes makes the discourse ambiguous' [212]. Erasmus' diction here is telling: faults in discourse must be eliminated; ambiguous language must be removed. Whereas his critics viewed this aspect of Erasmus' grammatical exegesis as subversive of apostolic infallibility, for Erasmus these figures frequently hide the true meaning; the explanation of them facilitates access to the spiritual sense of the text.[29]

This essay has made a case for reading the *Ratio* in conjunction with the *Annotations*. In writing his commentaries on the text of the New Testament, Erasmus frequently was driven by the theoretical assumptions

---

25 *Ratio* **202**: 'And no one should think it absurd to point out hyperboles in the divine books, for Origen does so, as does Chrysostom, and so do Augustine and Jerome.'
26 *Ratio* **205**: 'In the annotations with which I have clarified the New Testament I have pointed out some examples of this type, too.' Erasmus had not commented on *hyperbole* anywhere in the 1516 edition of the *Annotations*; all nine such comments on instances of it in the synoptic Gospels date to the 1519 edition or later.
27 See *Annotations* on Gal 1:6 (1519) CWE 58 6, and on 3:1 (1519) CWE 58 48.
28 Gal 5:12 (1519) CWE 58 88, Gal 6:2 (1535, Chrysostom) CWE 58 99, Eph 3:20 (1519, Chrysostom, Theophylact) CWE 58 165, Eph 4:29 (1519, Theophylact) CWE 58 189, Eph 5:31 (1527) CWE 58 208
29 So Payne 'Toward the Hermeneutics of Erasmus' 28, including allegory among the figures of speech in question.

which he posits in the *Ratio*. The interrelationship is exhibited especially by three interpretive principles which receive extensive treatment in the *Ratio*: the fundamental importance of the exegete's appropriation of Christ as embodied in Scripture; the exegetical value of historical and literary accommodation; and the basic function of literary figures in the exegetical process. Reading the *Ratio* in concert with the *Annotations* reveals a deliberate effort by Erasmus to situate theory in practice. By establishing a framework of classical literary and rhetorical analysis for the interpretation of Scripture, Erasmus sought not only to explain difficult texts but also to lead the reader from an understanding of inspired literature to an appropriation of divine thought.

Borrowing an image from the Church Fathers, Erasmus repeatedly portrays God's discourse with humanity as that of a loving mother with her infant child. In the *Enchiridion* or *Handbook of the Christian Soldier*, an instructional and devotional treatise to serve the Christian on the road to perfection, Erasmus writes: 'Divine wisdom speaks to us in baby talk and like a loving mother accommodates its words to our state of infancy.'[30] In his compassion and love, God has come down to earth in Scripture and in Christ in order to show fallen human beings the way to salvation and the perfect contemplation of the divine. 'Scripture by lisping indistinctly with the words of men so that it may be understood in a less forbidding way, accommodates itself to men's weakness, like a nurse or a mother using baby language to her child to make herself understood,' he writes in his *Explanation of Psalm 85*.[31] At the heart of this condescension is the incarnate Christ, in whom the godhead deigned to dwell in human form. By being transformed into the image of Christ who is fully revealed in the biblical Word, the reader of the Bible is empowered to attain a higher level of spiritual meaning, and so to grow to maturity in a life of piety and devotion to God.

---

30 CWE 66 35
31 CWE 64 20–1

The Parable of Sincere and Sophistical Discourse in the *Ratio*

KATHY EDEN

Designed to turn the new recruit, the *tiro theologiae*, into a devout reader of Scripture, the *Ratio verae theologiae*, destined to become Erasmus' most important hermeneutical work, was published as a companion to his New Testament of 1519.[1] Despite its status as a manual for the inexperienced reader, twenty-first-century readers can be forgiven for finding some irony in this design. For the *Ratio* is not at all easy to read. One of its most astute twentieth-century readers, in fact, called its design into question, judging the *Ratio* 'too diffuse a work to invite structural analysis.'[2] Without providing the kind of analysis this astute reader probably had in mind, the essay that follows offers something of an argument about how the *Ratio* is structured – an argument that takes as its point of departure Erasmus' assertion that true theology, the subject of his manual, breaks down into two fundamental agendas: what he calls prudently explaining divine literature (*sapienter enarrare divinas litteras*) and rendering an account of faith (*de fide ... rationem reddere*) [34]. In the course of the *Ratio*, I want to argue, Erasmus not only integrates these two agendas, but he does so by tethering them to his master trope, the comparison. Whatever structure the *Ratio* has, as I hope to show, it owes to Erasmus' penchant for comparing this to that.[3]

But Erasmus' understanding of this trope, theorized at length in his wildly popular educational manuals, requires some explanation. Following his favourite ancient theorists, and especially Quintilian in his

---

1 On the publication history of the *Ratio* as part of the New Testament of 1519, see the translator's introduction, CWE 41 108–26; for its omission from the edition of 1522, CWE 41 199–200.
2 Boyle *Erasmus on Language* 62
3 For Erasmus' mastery of the comparison in his literary, theological, and educational works, see Eden 'Erasmus on Dogs and Baths.'

Institutio oratoria or 'Orator's Education,'[4] Erasmus assumes that any attention to similarity, to what two things have in common, raises awareness of dissimilarities. Like love and marriage, comparison and contrast for Erasmus go hand in hand. So in an exercise in the *De copia* designed to refine the students' composition skills, including their skill in constructing comparisons, he illustrates his favourite trope by comparing the Roman general Camillus with the provocative Italian humanist Lorenzo Valla.[5] The basis of this comparison is a shared bravery bent on restoration, and the textbook illustration follows the approved pattern of pairing two clauses: the first begins with some version of 'just as' (Lat. *ut, sicut, quemadmodum, non aliter quam*), while the second answers with 'so' (Lat. *ita, itidem*). 'Just as (*Non aliter quam*) Camillus by his bravery repelled the barbarian foe and rescued Rome when it was hard pressed by the Gauls and brought to the edge of disaster,' Erasmus posits, 'so (*ita*) Lorenzo Valla summoned from the grave and restored to their former splendour Latin letters, corrupted, crushed, and extinguished by barbarian ignorance.'[6] This commonality, however, immediately calls forth a complementary difference. Whereas Camillus' courage was motivated by patriotism, Valla's motivation, in contrast, was personal glory. Following a long line of ancient theorists as far back as Aristotle,[7] Erasmus labels this kind of comparison a *parabola*, acknowledging that it is sometimes called *collatio* and *simile*. With this acknowledgment, he raises the vexed question of specialized terminology.

In the early modern period as in antiquity, there is no single term for comparison. Sometimes Erasmus will use *comparatio* as the generic term;[8] at other times, following Quintilian, he will lump all kinds of comparative strategies under the umbrella of a single term like *exemplum*. 'We include under "examples,"' he writes, 'stories, fables, proverbs, opinions, parallels or comparisons, similitudes, analogies (*et fabulam, et apologum, proverbium, iudicia, parabolam seu collationem, imaginem, et analogiam*), and anything else of the same sort.'[9] Elsewhere, he

---

4 Quintilian *Institutio oratoria* 5.11.1–44 (trans Russell *The Orator's Education*)
5 CWE 24 616. On the singular popularity of *De copia* in schools and universities, see Baldwin *William Shakspere's Small Latine* I 179–96 and Mack *History of Renaissance Rhetoric* 80–8.
6 CWE 24 616 (ASD I-6 240:57–61). On the approved form of the *parabola*, which goes back at least to Plato, see Eden 'Erasmian *Parabola*.' On Erasmus, Valla, and the figure of Camillus, see also Vessey 'Cities of the Mind' 51–5.
7 Aristotle *Rhetoric* 2.20.2–4
8 CWE 24 625 (ASD I-6 248:250–77)
9 CWE 24 607 (ASD I-6 232:843–5). Compare Quintilian *Institutio oratoria* 5.11.2.

lists the comparative strategies as *collationes, similia, dissimilia, imagines, metaphorae,* and *allegoriae.*[10] Also like Quintilian, Erasmus advises against getting too caught up in terminological disputes.[11] The goal is not to master the nomenclature but to learn how to deploy the strategies themselves in order to enliven one's style and sharpen one's arguments; and comparisons of one sort or another, Erasmus assures his readers, contribute a great deal to these two objectives:

> In a speech, the εἰκών is more useful in the cause of vividness or impressiveness or stylistic attractiveness, than for proving any point (*ad probationes*). Examples and parallels (*exemplorum et similium*) also serve these ends, but they often help considerably in generating an attitude of consent (*fidem*) in our hearers, especially when they are combined with induction (*inductionem*), for which the Greek is ἐπαγωγή. Plato's Socrates makes great use of this.[12]

Like the more expansive *eikon* (often Latinized as *imago*), some kinds of comparison, in other words, are more stylistic than probative. Others, like the *simile*, serve both purposes, rendering our writing more vivid and inspiring trust or faith (*fides*) in our proofs, especially when they form part of a Socratic induction.[13] Later in the *De copia*, Erasmus illustrates this winning combination:

> Here is induction combined with a parallel (*simile*): Do you not expect a sailor to talk more knowledgeably about sailing than a doctor? And a doctor more authoritatively about medicine than a painter? And a painter better about the techniques of colour and light and shade and perspective than a cobbler? Will not a charioteer be better at discussing the art of driving a chariot than a sailor? (A number of comparisons like this will make everyone prepared to accept the idea that each person will speak best about the thing he knows best. Then one brings in one's parallel case [*similitudo*]). But what will the orator discuss best, when he professes to be able to talk on any topic?[14]

---

10 CWE 24 579 (ASD I-6 24:217–19)
11 For Quintilian on avoiding arguments over terminology, see *Institutio oratoria* 5.11.30–1. For Erasmus on avoiding these same disputes, see CWE 24 621.
12 CWE 24 623 (ASD I-6 246:219–24)
13 For Quintilian on Socratic induction, see *Institutio oratoria* 5.11.2–5.
14 CWE 24 624 (ASD I-6 247:234–48)

Enthusiastically endorsing this Socratic-style argument, Erasmus here stresses the comparative element that inevitably leads one's interlocutor to the desired conclusion. The comparison itself, as we have seen, he characterizes variously as *parabola, simile, collatio,* and *similitudo.*

This strategy of making comparisons is so pervasive in the writings of Erasmus' favourite ancient authors that he collects them into a separate volume often printed with the *De copia,* entitled *Parabolae sive Similia* – a title that sets in high relief the interchangeability of the terms. In the *Ratio,* which also pairs *similia* and *parabolae* [185], Erasmus mentions this volume twice [23, 223]; and in the volume's prefatory letter, he extends this terminological interchangeability even further:

> For the Greek *parabolê,* which Cicero latinizes as *collatio* ... is nothing more than a metaphor writ large (*explicata metaphora*) ... What gives their spice to adages, their charm (*gratiam*) to fables, their point to historical anecdotes? metaphor, which doubles the native riches of a pithy saying, so that Solomon himself, an inspired author, chose to recommend his wise sayings to the world by calling them *Parabolae.* Deprive the orators of their arsenal of metaphor, and all will be thin and dull. Take ... parable (*parabolas*) away from the Prophets and the Gospels, and you will find that a great part of their charm (*gratiae*) has gone.[15]

Not only does the Ciceronian *collatio* correspond to the Greek *parabole,* which Erasmus routinely transliterates into Latin as *parabola,* but this pervasive form of comparison, Erasmus explains, is an expanded metaphor. Or to put it the other way round, the metaphor is a compressed parable, which, when expanded even further, can grow into an allegory. In the *De copia,* Erasmus defines *allegoria* as a *metaphora perpetua,* a continuous metaphor.[16] In its ability to expand and contract, then, the comparison in its various forms demonstrates the two key compositional strategies featured throughout Erasmus' pedagogical primer.

These two complementary strategies of compression and expansion, in fact, account for not only the main focus of the *De copia* but also its clustering of terms into the lists noted above – a clustering that forms a continuum from metaphor to full-fledged narrative and allegory, from *metaphora* to *fabula* and *allegoria.* With this continuum in mind, Erasmus

---

15 Ep 312:44–5 (Allen 33–4)
16 CWE 24 336 (ASD I-6 66:827). In *Apologia adversus monachos* (LB IX 1077E, quoted in CWE 41 673 n970), Erasmus explains that 'Whenever the grammatical sense, or the common and simple sense, is abandoned, this I call allegory.'

calls Socrates' elaborate story of the cave in the *Republic* a *parabola*.¹⁷ (Plato has Socrates call it an *eikon*.)¹⁸ And with this same continuum in mind, Erasmus understands Jesus' discursive habit of comparing the kingdom of heaven to yeast or a grain of mustard or a pearl of great price [195]. The *parabola* of the *De copia*, then, is none other than the *parabola* of the New Testament – the same parable that figures so prominently in Erasmus' manual for the uninitiated reader of Scripture.¹⁹ 'A parable is effectual,' Erasmus explains to his young readers in the *Ratio* in words recalling his advice to young writers in the *De copia*, 'not only for teaching and persuading, but also for stirring the emotions, for alluring with its charm, for bringing clarity, for implanting one central idea deep within the mind, beyond the possibility of escape' [186]. But Erasmus does more in the *Ratio* than feature the parable and other biblical comparisons on the broad spectrum from metaphor to allegory. He also uses comparison to structure his own advice regarding how to understand the sacred communications, parabolic and otherwise, of the most effective scriptural writers, including Moses, Isaiah, Jesus, and Paul. Like his favourite sacred authors, in other words, Erasmus relies heavily on comparison in the *Ratio* to communicate *his* lessons, implanting them deep within the minds of his readers.

One of his early, direction-setting comparisons concerns the Greek Church Father Origen and the fourth-century grammarian Donatus. This comparison is key because it brings into focus one of the two defining agendas of true theology: explicating the text of Scripture or scriptural exegesis. In Erasmus' estimation, Origen is a master exegete, and his mastery makes him comparable to Donatus, whose commentary on Terence figured in the Latin training of every early modern schoolboy. Erasmus' set-up for this comparison, which gives way to a contrast I will return to shortly, recalls his textbook illustration noted above involving the humanist Valla and the Roman general Camillus. For Origen 'does for the divine books,' Erasmus boldly proclaims,

> exactly what Donatus does for the comedies of Terence in laying bare the intent of the poet (*consilium poetae*). Would anyone see such things who had never applied himself to the more refined literature (*politiores litteras*)? who had scarcely tasted the precepts of grammar (and at that, from

---

17 CWE 24 634–5 (ASD I-6 257:491–258 at 493)
18 Plato *Republic* 515A, 517A
19 For Erasmus on the parables of the Gospels, treated throughout the *Ratio*, see, for instance, 86–7, **104–9, 169–88**.

authors ungrammatical), then, soon hurried off to thorny arguments (*ad spinosas argutias*) and dry and troublesome questions, spent the rest of his life in these? [27]

Literary interpretation as practised by Donatus (what Erasmus, following Quintilian, calls *enarratio poetarum*) and scriptural interpretation as practised by Origen (*enarratio divinarum litterarum*) share not only their ends but their means. Their shared end or aim is to understand authorial intention (whether sacred or profane);[20] and their means are all those instruments of proof and style studied by grammarians and rhetoricians alike.

Chief among these instruments is the comparison, which sacred Scripture, like other kinds of writing, deploys in all its forms, from the most compressed metaphors to full-fledged *fabulae* and *allegoriae*. Christ himself, Erasmus insists, 'clothed almost all his teachings in comparisons' (*Parabolis omnia paene convestivit Christus*) [29]; and he did so on the grounds that no other method better captures the hearts and minds of readers than 'the comparison of similar things' (*per collationem similium*), especially when the similarities drawn involve the most common occurrences, like seed cast to the ground or fishermen casting their nets or the cutting of dried branches [232]. 'Now if someone should say that any good that dwells in us comes to us from Christ, its author,' Erasmus concedes, 'he will be understood, it is true; but if he will apply to the same thought the similitudes (*similitudinem*) of the vine-stock and the vine-branches, of head and members, of root and branches, the idea is at once placed before the eyes (*res oculis subicitur*) as though portrayed in a picture (*velut imagine depicta*)' [191]. This vividness or *enargeia*, discussed in great detail in the *De copia* and elsewhere, effectively sweeps readers away, transforming them into what they are learning [10].[21] And this spiritual transformation, Erasmus affirms, is especially facilitated by Christ's

---

20 For Quintilian on *enarratio poetarum*, see *Institutio oratoria* 1.4.2. For the relation between scriptural exegesis and the *enarratio poetarum* of the grammarians, see Eden *Hermeneutics* 7–40, which also discusses throughout the distinction between what words mean and what authors mean, a distinction rooted in rhetoric and fundamental to the history of hermeneutics, including Erasmus'.
21 On *enargeia*, concerning which Erasmus follows Quintilian (*Institutio oratoria* 4.2.63–5, 6.2.27–35, 8.3.61–6), see *De copia*, CWE 24 577–82 and Eden *Poetic and Legal Fiction* 87–94; for the transformative aim of Erasmus' program, Boyle *Erasmus on Language* 112–27.

comparisons, whether they are called *parabolae, collationes, similia,* or *similitudines.*[22]

But Christ is not alone in the New Testament in his reliance on comparisons. Throughout his apostolic letters, Paul favours highly compressed, metaphorical expression, returning, for instance, in his Letter to the Romans to Christ's similitude of the vines, which he refashions, Erasmus informs his young readers, into a *comparatio* 'of the olive tree and the wild olive grafted into it' [116]. Elsewhere the apostle to the Gentiles figures the faithful metaphorically as the 'unleavened,' the repentant as 'awakened,' their bodies as earthen vessels, garments, and tabernacles [192]. 'Now it would be superfluous,' Erasmus admits,

> to recount the number of times [Paul] introduces a similitude (*similitudinem*) from athletes and soldiers, from stadiums, boxers, war. In the ninth chapter of the same Epistle [1 Corinthians], with how many comparisons (*similitudines*) does he insistently repeat the same idea, that thanks is owed for a kindness provided: 'Who serves as a soldier at any time at his own charge? Who plants a vineyard and does not eat of the fruit thereof? Who feeds a flock and does not take the flock's milk?' [1 Corinthians 9:7] [193]

To implant his lesson about gratitude deep in the minds of *his* readers, Paul fashions his similitudes into a set of parallel questions – a rhetorical practice that Erasmus identifies in the *De copia*, as we have seen, as induction or *epagoge* and associates with Plato's Socrates. In keeping with this association, Erasmus explicitly reminds his inexperienced interpreter in the *Ratio* that Paul's method has its roots in Socratic comparisons, what Erasmus calls *similitudines Socraticae* [185].[23]

Scripture itself, then, routinely deploys precisely the kinds of rhetorically effective comparisons that preoccupy Erasmus in his educational writings. Consequently, the apprenticing exegete must learn how to interpret these often confusing comparisons or *parabolae*; and his interpretations must take into account the limited commonalities shared by the two things being compared. As an illustration of the potential confusion caused by ignoring this limit, Erasmus turns to one of his favourite parables from Luke, the so-called Parable of the False Steward

---

22 Hoffmann *Rhetoric and Theology* emphasizes Erasmus' reliance on similitudes, asserting that he 'abandoned the speculation on metaphysical problems in favour of understanding metaphorical language' (8) and tracing this reliance back to a Platonic *similia similibus* (107–8, 116, 128, 144). For Erasmus' use of similitudes, see also CWE 41 632n745 and 634n753.

23 On Socrates as the master of comparisons, see Eden 'Erasmian *Parabola.*'

(Luke 16), which, if read either naively or too scrupulously (*superstitiose*), would seem to promote fraud rather than faith:

> Likewise, in the parable of the administrator (*parabola de oeconomo*) who, in cheating his master, alleviated his debtors, the analogy (*collatio*) does not in every respect correspond – as though we also ought to attend to our own interests by fraud; rather, what in the parable is fraud against the master is in an allegorical sense (*in sensu allegorico*) faithfulness (*fides*). That steward is said to be unjust because through falsified codicils he harmed the master and helped the debtors, and yet one who generously dispenses God's substance is said to be faithful (*fidelis*). [229]

Conceding on this occasion the need for an allegorical reading (understood as one that looks beyond the grammatical or literal sense of the words), Erasmus cautions in general against an overuse or abuse of this method. Just as he rejects in the *De copia* overly scrupulous attention to specialized terminology, so he rejects in the *Ratio* an approach to parables that interprets each and every detail allegorically, including those that function only to sustain the narrative [252]. '[T]hose who are eager to accommodate scrupulously all the parts of a parable to allegory,' he warns, 'frequently end up with more or less flat and trivial comments' [229].[24]

To avoid misreading these and any other confounding scriptural texts, Erasmus recommends an exegetical method that involves another kind of *collatio* or comparison – the so-called *collatio locorum* or comparison of passages favoured by the most accomplished interpreters of antiquity [247–8]. 'Many times a comparison of passages (*locorum collatio*) unravels the knot of a problem,' Erasmus insists, 'when what is

---

24 Erasmus' position on allegorical interpretation in the *Ratio* is complex and evolves over time. On the one hand, Erasmus insists both that Paul himself practised allegorical interpretation [230] and that the Scriptures are full of allegories [216], while, on the other, he worries about exegetes who find these deeper meanings everywhere, turning even the history of the New Testament into an allegory [224]. On the whole, in the *Ratio* he treats allegory as one of a number of comparative strategies after the fashion of the ancient rhetoricians and avoids getting bogged down in theological debate; and he does so both by sending his reader elsewhere, and especially to Augustine's treatment of the topic in the *De doctrina christiana* [45, 233], and by alluding to his unfinished work on theological allegories that will treat the matter more thoroughly [233] (on which see CWE 41 661 n906). For the increased attention to allegory in the *Ratio* of 1522 and 1523, see CWE 40 189–90. On Erasmus' aim to chart a middle course (*sobria mediocritas*) between the indiscriminate allegorizers and the Judaizing literalists, see Eden, *Hermeneutics* 70–3.

said somewhat obscurely at one point is repeated at another point quite clearly' [41]. But the benefits of this kind of *collatio* go beyond the goal of understanding, Erasmus claims, because by comparing the Pauline Epistles with the Gospels and both with Isaiah, 'these will of their own accord stick in the memory and become fixed there' [252]. Like Christ's comparisons in the form of *parabolae*, in other words, exegetical comparisons are effectively learned because they are deeply planted in the mind.[25]

Erasmus' attention to these exegetical *collationes* figures as well in the comparison discussed earlier between Origen and Donatus. For both are master exegetes, and both practise this method. Indeed, Origen considers the comparison of passages the surest way to interpret divine literature (*optima ratio interpretandi divinas litteras*) [248]. While these two skilled interpreters proceed according to best practices in their effort to disclose what the author meant, as we have already seen, those who lack this grammatical and rhetorical training are distracted by other kinds of inquiry that prompt them to spend their time endlessly debating 'thorny questions,' *spinosae argutiae*. Erasmus tellingly designates this stark contrast between the interpreter and the debater a *collatio* – a *collatio studiorum*, a comparison of studies or disciplines [275].

This disciplinary comparison (or contrast), hardly new to readers of Erasmus, arguably does more than any other to shape the *Ratio*, even though Erasmus in closing makes a gesture to dismiss it [275]; in fact, Erasmus reinforces this comparison by contrasting the aims and methods of the disciplines he favours, including grammar and rhetoric and the interpretive practices they underwrite, with those of the one he rejects, namely dialectic.[26] Like Christ and Paul (and Erasmus himself),

---

25 On the exegetical practice of *collatio locorum*, see Hoffmann *Rhetoric and Theology* 179–82 and Eden *Hermeneutics* 55, 88, 97, 103.

26 For Erasmus' participation in the humanist polemics against scholastic dialectic, see the essay by Ocker above and Rummel *Humanist-Scholastic Debate*, and for Luther's tarring Erasmus with these very brushes, Boyle *Rhetoric and Reform* 67–98. On Erasmus' sharpening his attack on scholasticism in the *Ratio*, and more generally on the *Ratio*'s relation to the *Methodus*, see CWE 41 114–19. In the *Enchiridion*, a work the young tyro is not likely to have read, Erasmus insists that the study of Scripture should begin with a grounding in *bonae litterae*: 'These writings shape and invigorate the child's mind and provide an admirable preparation for the understanding of divine Scriptures, for it is almost an act of sacrilege to rush into these studies without due preparation. Jerome reproaches the impudence of those who dare to expatiate on the sacred Scriptures after just completing their secular studies, but how much more impudent are those who attempt the same thing without even having had a taste of the preparatory study' (CWE 66 33).

the rhetorically trained interpreter embraces comparisons, as we have seen. The dialectician or debater, on the other hand, wields syllogisms and other argumentative subtleties, *argutissimae subtilitates* [232], also called *dialecticorum argutiae* [259]. In fact, the debater does 'nothing else than dispute (*disputare*) – not to say prattle (*argutari*)' [34], in large part because he is 'imbued only with those silly, troublesome, and jejune little rules (*praeceptiunculis*) – those, say, of dialectic (*dialectices*), or, more truly, as it is now generally taught, of sophistry (*sophistices*)' [24]. Later in the *Ratio*, Erasmus reinforces this alignment between dialectic and sophistry, resuming his attack on *sophisticae praeceptiunculae*, those petty rules of sophistic [253]. In stark contrast to the true theologian, who labours to transform his listeners through his readings of sacred Scripture, the disputer, also called a vain theologian or *mataeologos* [267], sets his sights on victory in debate, even if it means distorting the meaning of a text:[27]

> It may well be that such things would be said cleverly (*argute*) and with applause ... but in sacred things one must not trifle; nor is it becoming to be clever (*neque decet argutari*), nor does it help to twist anything (*neque expedit torquere quicquam*), lest we deprive of credit (*fidem*) what is true while defending the false. [227]

Through his clever misreadings, in other words, the debater undermines instead of bolstering the trustworthiness or *fides* of the divine word, thereby mismanaging at once both agendas of true theology: explicating Scripture and encouraging faith.

It is their opposing attitudes towards faith, in fact, that serve more than anything else to widen the divide between the approved interpreter and the debater insofar as the one puts his trust in God while the other has faith in himself.[28] To drive home this contrast, Erasmus, in the spirit of his favourite ancient authors, reaches for a striking comparison – this time from Isaiah (64:6). 'Christ perceived the sickness of a man who was arrogating to himself the praise for his goodness,'

---

27 On Erasmus' objections to the polemical distortions of readers, see his letter to Martin Dorp (above, 38–9), which impugns those who 'take a couple of words out of their context, sometimes a little altered in the process, leaving out everything that softens and explains what sounds harsh otherwise' (Ep 337:479–81). See also Eden, *Hermeneutics* 1–3, 71–6.

28 On Erasmus' increased attention to the dangers of self-confidence in the *Ratio* of 1520, see CWE 41 187; on the complex relation between *fides* and *fiducia*, CWE 41 659 and n895.

Erasmus explains, 'when all of our righteous acts are nothing else in the eyes of God than the rags of a woman that are soaked in her menstrual flow' [**110**].[29] Following here as everywhere in Christ's footsteps, Paul has precisely this self-confidence in mind, according to Erasmus, when he fashions the similitude of the olive branch in his letter to the Romans.[30] For there he warns that the price of unbelief or faithlessness (*incredulitas*), speaking metaphorically in terms of branches, is to suffer the punishment of being cut off rather than the reward of being grafted on. Both the cause and effect of this incredulity is trusting in oneself: *vobis ipsis fidentes* [**116**]. Erasmus goes so far as to summarize Paul's most magisterial letter as an express warning against this very self-confidence – a warning he intensifies by reprising the provocative similitude from Isaiah:

> And yet in this whole Epistle [ie Romans] does Paul aim at anything else than to take away the self-confidence (*sui fiduciam*) of Jews and Gentiles alike, and to invite them to the help offered by Christ, placing no trust whatever in themselves? Our righteous deeds are nothing but a rag polluted with menstrual flow. [**114**]

Whereas the right kind of interpreter compares scriptural texts in the interest of increasing *their* trustworthiness or *fides*, the disputer uses Scripture to support his own arguments in the interest of increasing his own – and others' – faith in himself.

Even the best interpreters, however, can on occasion stoop to misguided interpretations, especially when they are motivated by polemical or partisan aims. Erasmus singles out the esteemed Ambrose, who, clearly disregarding the words of the evangelist, insists that Peter denied only the man in Jesus and not the God. Erasmus strenuously rejects this reading of the notorious denial, holding Ambrose accountable for

---

29 In his letter to Martin Dorp in defence of his *Praise of Folly*, Erasmus invokes this same passage from Isaiah: 'But this same folly of theirs overcomes all the wisdom of the world; just as (*quemadmodum*) the prophet compares (*confert*) all the righteousness of mortals to rags defiled with a woman's monthly discharge, not that the righteousness of good men is something foul, but because the things that are most pure among men are somehow impure when set against (*conferantur*) the inexpressible purity of God' (Ep 337:505–10, 480–5 Allen). For this comparison, handed down in *catenae* and invoked in Erasmus' annotation on 1 Corinthians 1:30, see Sider, 'Just and the Holy' 11.
30 For Paul as the 'man who always imitates Christ' for 'no one resembled the preceptor Christ more than he,' see **196**, **130**.

defending Peter cleverly rather than truly (*magis argute quam vere*) [**225**]. For such a defence, Erasmus worries, undermines the trustworthiness of the narrative, what he calls its *fides narrationis*.

Throughout the *Ratio*, in fact, Erasmus features faith as it pertains not only to certain *parabolae*, like the parable in Luke of the false steward, but also to much more expansive scriptural *fabulae*. These include, not surprisingly, the episodes from Matthew of the Canaanite woman, who was *plena fiduciae*, and the centurion, 'who trusted Christ so completely' (*in tantum fidentis Christo*) [**84–5**]. It also includes from the Old Testament the story of Abraham, especially as explained in the homily of Origen, where the *fides* of not only the Hebrew patriarch but of the divine promise of generation takes centre stage [**24–6**].

But the standard for fidelity – for *fides narrationis* – of these Old and New Testament stories is the *fides* or trustworthiness of Christ himself as represented in the fully expanded story of his life, ministry, and death. Erasmus calls this story the *fabula Christi* or 'drama of Christ' [**67**] and takes his time in the *Ratio* to *enarrate* or explain it, from the prophecies that anticipated it to the miracles that punctuated it to the witnesses who testified to it.[31] Routinely performing these miracles before the witnessing multitudes, Christ himself, according to Erasmus, showed special concern for *fides narrationis*:

> And he [ie Christ] made an unquestionable trustworthiness (*certam fidem*) attend every miracle he performed. He did almost everything before a crowd as witness. He sends the lepers to the priests not to be cleansed but that it might be better established that they had been truly cleansed. A man widely known to be blind is healed, his parents are summoned, he himself is called back, and all these actions have only one objective, to build up the trustworthiness of the miracle (*ut fides astrueretur miraculo*). [**94**]

At stake in the divine narrative as recorded in the Gospels, according to Erasmus, is faith in what Christ did and said. With proper instruction, the young interpreter can in turn read these stories 'with a more certain confidence' (*certiore cum fide*) [**67**]. The *fides* of the *fabula*, in other words, informs the interpreter's own *fides*. By helping the new recruit read in this way, Erasmus effectively merges the two activities of true theology, explaining sacred texts and reinforcing faith.

---

31 On the dramatic structure of the *fabula Christi*, including the tripartite structure of *protasis, epitasis*, and *catastrophe*, see Hoffmann, *Rhetoric and Theology* 142–51.

The Parable of Sincere and Sophistical Discourse in the *Ratio* 105

So far the lessons of the *Ratio* have revolved in no small part around a number of different kinds of *collatio* or comparison, including (1) the rhetorical *collationes* featured in the *De copia*, found everywhere in the Old and New Testaments and referred to in Christ's hands as *collationes similium, similitudines*, and, of course, *parabolae* or parables; (2) exegetical *collationes locorum* that aid in the explication of passages that are obscure by comparing them with those that are more easily understood; and (3) *collatio studiorum*, the comparison of the disciplines that establishes the divide between the self-serving, syllogism-wielding debater or dialectician and the rhetorically and grammatically trained yet deeply devout exegete. At the end of the *Ratio*, Erasmus sets these two disciplines at odds one last time on the basis of their discursive practices, carving out of apostolic language a final contrast of sincere (or faithful) and sophistical discourse, *sermo fidelis* and *sermo sophisticus* [**269**].[32]

Although applied in closing to the one who disputes as well as to the one who truly believes [**263**], the *sermo* of the sophist, despite the economy of the phrasing (*fideli sermone potius quam sophistico*), does not properly qualify as *sermo*, the kind of discourse Erasmus associates with Christ and upholds as the discursive model for all Christians. Once again constructing a rhetorical *collatio* according to the requirements of his composition textbook, Erasmus emphasizes this *sermonic* as well as the *parabolic* dimension of proper Christian discourse: '[J]ust as (*quemadmodum*) Christ imitated the speech (*sermo*) of the prophets, so (*ita*) Paul and the other apostles reflect the speech of Christ (*Christi sermonem*), projecting a theme visually (*rem oculis subicientes*), through parables (*parabolis*), and, by frequent repetition, fastening it upon the mind' [**192**]. Aligned throughout the *Ratio* with a number of tropes and figures, including hyperbole, irony, and synecdoche [**201-2, 209**; see also **41**], *sermo Christi* is most closely identified with comparison, and especially with the comparative strategy of the *parabola*. By the end of the *Ratio*, fully in keeping with this identification, Erasmus has followed his favourite sacred *scriptor* in creating his own parable – one that compares sincere discourse to its sophistical counterpart.

---

32 On the apostolic pedigree of this distinction, see CWE 41 707n1122 and Erasmus' paraphrase of Timothy 6:3: 'As knowledge is a modest thing, so nothing is more haughty or stubborn than ignorance. The person who is possessed by this disease becomes hostile to evangelical sincerity, is obsessed with foolish questions and, neglecting everything else in life, engages in verbal duals which contribute absolutely nothing to Christian godliness but only cause it to perish. For envy arises from just such quarrelsome debates when we create authority for ourselves by deliberately demolishing the authority of others' (CWE 44 35).

In his opening remarks, on the other hand, Erasmus calls this discursive practice not *sermo* but *collatio*, 'conference' or conversation [10], contrasting it on this occasion with *conflictatio*, conflict, and warning the inexperienced exegete that even in the heat of argument he must embrace the one and avoid the other. *Collatio* in this sense, as conversation rather than comparison, derives from the same verb *confero* but belongs to a different cluster of terms that includes not only *sermo* but *colloquium*, which Erasmus uses in the *Ratio* to characterize both Moses' intimate communications with God [6] and Christ's with his disciples [171].[33] Like *colloquium* and *sermo*, *collatio*, as part of this cluster, offers the young exegete another closely related model of Christian discourse – one also set in stark contrast to the sophistical discourse of the debater.

In most cases, Erasmus relies on context to indicate the meaning of *collatio* he has in mind. So when he constructs an elaborate comparison between the true theologians of antiquity, like Origen, and their disputatious modern counterparts, he begins with the invitation to compare (*conferat*) and follows with a set of contrasts punctuated by a repetition of the markers *hic* and *illic*. A portion of this lengthy comparison reads:

> There (*Illic*) you will make for the harbour of evangelical truth by a direct course, here (*hic*) you will be struggling among the tortuous intricacies of human questions, or dashing against the Scylla of pontifical power or upon the Syrtes of scholastic dogmas or upon the Symplegades of divine and human laws – unless you prefer to speak of the Charybdis. There (*Illic*) an edifice resting upon the solid foundation of Scriptures rises aloft, here (*hic*) a frame no less vacuous than vast is raised up to an enormous height, built upon the cunning but unreliable arguments of men (*futtilibus hominum argutiis*), or even upon fawning flattery. [28]

With its recognizable disdain for the *argutiae* of the debater, the comparison here, becoming more copious from one edition to the next, sets the course for Erasmus' parable of sincere and sophistical discourse. Elsewhere Erasmus' call to compare is less clear-cut, either coinciding with or maybe even conceding to a call for conversation.

---

33 On the various interrelated dimensions of Erasmus' *collatio*, see Boyle *Rhetoric and Reform* 433–66 and Hoffmann *Rhetoric and Theology* 178–82, who reminds us that '*collatio* functions either as a literary method to ascertain an original text, or as an exegetical method to understand the divine word in Scripture, or as a heuristic method to arrive at the truth through discussion' (179). On *sermo*, see Boyle *Erasmus on Language* 3–31.

After making the initial claim, noted above, that Christ relies on comparisons (*similia*) to communicate his teachings to the common folk and promising his readers that he will revisit this important point 'a little later' [95], Erasmus turns to a related quality of Christ's speech: its gentle, conversational tone, which has no use for the 'tortured syllogisms' of the dialectician [96]. Erasmus then launches into a digression on apostolic discourse with the words *Iam paucis, si libet*, conferamus, *quemadmodum ad magistri formam apostolorum vita doctrinaque respondeat*, translated in CWE 41 and the present volume as 'Now, if you like, *let us consider in a brief comparison* how the life and teaching of the apostles correspond to the pattern of their teacher' [97]. Several pages later, he concludes his digression with 'now let us pursue what we began' [103]. Given that Erasmus explicitly states his intention to delay his discussion of comparison until a later time, and given that the digression itself goes on to range freely, conversation-like, over a number of topics, including loss of land to the Turks, Erasmus' *iam paucis conferamus* could just as well be translated 'let us talk over (or discuss) for a while.'

That the context supports equally these two translations of the verb *confero* helps to set in high relief just how much the *Ratio* relies on *collatio* not just as a preferred rhetorical figure but also, more broadly, as a preferred discursive practice, highlighting, as it does so, the preferences Erasmus shares with his favourite sacred writers.[34] For the many kinds and manifold instances of *collatio*, including the parable of sincere and sophistical discourse, promote the understanding of Scripture that allows faith to flourish. Without comparing this to that, in other words, Erasmus would be hard pressed to advance either agenda of true theology. Armed with rhetorical, exegetical, disciplinary, and discursive *collationes*, on the other hand, he integrates these two agendas, offering a *ratio* or way to read that is able to reform how the new recruit lives because it fortifies what he believes.

---

34 For a comparable ambiguity in Erasmus' use of *confero* at the end of his diatribe (or *collatio*) on free will, *De libero arbitrio diatribe sive collatio*, see Eden 'Erasmus on Dogs and Baths' 2–3, esp n4.

PART TWO

THE *RATIO VERAE THEOLOGIAE*

Scheme of Contents of the
Ratio verae theologiae

The *Ratio*, like its predecessor the *Methodus*, originally appeared in print as a continuous discourse, without any internal headings or other visible articulations. Nor does Erasmus at any point in the work provide either a detailed prospectus or a recapitulation of its contents. To assist users of the present edition, (non-authorial) section and sub-section headings have therefore been inserted in the text; the higher-level divisions are set out below. The initial and final sections denoted A1 and A2 are those in which the *Ratio* follows closely the course of the *Methodus*. Passages where it does so word for word appear in italics in the text.

Preface: purpose of the *Ratio* [1–4]

A1 Elements of a method for the study of Scripture [5–36]
- Preparing to study Scripture [5–8]
- Precaution: the idioms of Scripture [9]
- The goal of studying Scripture: personal transformation [10–11]
- Means to the goal of personal transformation [12–36]
  - learning the languages of Scripture (Latin, Greek, Hebrew) [12–18]
  - having some knowledge of the liberal disciplines [19–22]
  - recognizing the power of figurative and poetic language, the virtues of the ancient theologians, the deficiencies of their modern counterparts [23–34]
  - keeping sight of the aims of the 'philosophy' of Christ [35–6]

B1 The unity in variety of the gospel [37–66]
- Accounting for the variety in the scriptural expression of Christ's teaching [37–50]
  - difference of things taught [37–41]
  - difference of *personae* [42–4]
  - difference of times: five periods of Christian time [45–50]
- Securing the unity and purity of a scriptural understanding of Christ's teaching [51–66]

- the three circles of Christian society [51–6]
- *sidenote on the critical use of ancient and modern theologians* [57]
  - some points of doctrinal controversy [58–66]

B2a 'The wonderful circle and harmony of the entire drama of Christ' [67–184]
- The unity of the Old and New Testaments [67–70]
- *sidenote on the authority of the sacred writings* [71]
- The harmony in variety of Christ's action and discourse [72–96]
- The conformity of the life and teachings of the apostles to Christ's example [97–103]
- How Christ prepares those who are to preach the gospel: disciplining the affections [104–21]
- Finding a pattern for human life in the Gospels and Epistles, or how to 'philosophize' from Scripture [122–84]

B2b The figurative character of the language of 'sacred literature' [185–233]
- specialized tropes: parables or comparisons, allegories, riddles, and proverbs [186–98]
- idioms of everyday speech, in Hebrew [199–200]
- other everyday tropes: heterosis, synecdoche, hyperbaton, hyperbole, etc [201–7]
- idioms of everyday speech, in Latin [208]
- other everyday tropes: irony, ambiguity, emphasis [209–15]
- specialized tropes again: allegories, parables, and the historical sense; the different levels of sense in Scripture [216–33]

A2 Elements of a method for the study of Scripture (concluded) [234–77]
- Means to the goal of personal transformation through study of Scripture (continued)
  - knowing the 'testimonies' of Scripture first hand, respecting their contexts [234–46]
  - keeping a theological commonplace book, construing obscure passages of Scripture in the light of clearer ones [247–50]
  - having Scripture, especially the New Testament, constantly in hand and mind, committing it to memory, assimilating it inwardly [251–3]
  - reading Scripture in the light of the exegesis of the ancient theologians, becoming like them [254–8]
- Polemical coda: the difference between this practice of theology and the current kind [259–77]

Note on the Text

This translation of the *Ratio verae theologiae*, which is that of Robert D. Sider for CWE 41, presents the text as revised by Erasmus down to 1523. Additions to and other departures from the 1518/1519 Louvain-Basel editions (here *1519*) are indicated in the footnotes. Notations in italics in the footnotes refer to these other editions of the *Ratio*:

Schoeffer 1519   Mainz: Johann Schoeffer
1520   Basel: Johann Froben
1522   Basel: Johann Froben
1523   Cologne: H. Alopecius

For details of these editions, see CWE 41 481–5, and for an overview of the revisions made in 1520, 1522, and 1523, CWE 41 185–90.

Only the more substantial changes in later editions are footnoted below. For a comprehensive account of variants, the reader should refer to the apparatus of CWE 41 488–713 and (for the Latin text) to that in Holborn 177–305.

The standard critical editions of the Latin text of the *Ratio verae theologiae*, until the appearance of a new edition in ASD, are those of LB (vol 5) and of Holborn (see Abbreviations and Works Frequently Cited, above xvii). References to the Latin text of the *Ratio* in scholarship on Erasmus – eg in CWE 41 – thus typically take the form 'LB V [column number and letter]' and/or 'Holborn [page and line numbers].' For ease of reference in the present edition, all citations of the *Ratio* in English are by **paragraph number**, the paragraph divisions being those (unnumbered there) of CWE 41. To find the page or column in LB, Holborn, or CWE corresponding to a particular paragraph below, see the Concordance of Editions of the *Ratio*, 343–50 below.

Ratio verae theologiae

Preface: Purpose of the *Ratio*

[1] When I was first about to publish my revised version of the New Testament, I had taken the trouble to add, as certain friends of mine had requested, a sort of method and system for the study of theology. It was indeed brief, but sufficiently copious, I thought at the time, for the preface of a work, for I was afraid that it should appear to be not a preface but a second work added to the first. Even if this reason had not motivated me, the speed with which the work was already hastening to an end demanded brevity. Now I shall do the same work over again, but somewhat more expansively, and I shall arrange it in such a way that this piece can, if one likes, be added as a preface; otherwise it can be read separately. I shall, no doubt, imitate hosts who, parsimoniously sumptuous and magnificently mean, conceal with a common seasoning the scraps of yesterday's victuals that they mix in with fresh fare.

[2] If only I could provide what is demanded of me! It is indeed a great thing to arouse in human hearts a burning desire for the study of theology, but it takes a more expert practitioner to expound the way and the method of this heavenly study. Not that I do so in a manner worthy of the subject (for what can human effort do to match the divine realities?) but in such a way that this labour of mine might offer some small advantage to candidates of a most venerable theology.

[3] *Not the least part of a task is to know how to set about it*. And one makes speed enough who nowhere strays from the path. One often doubles both the expense and the effort when with frequent deviations and long digressions one arrives at length at his destination – if he succeeds in arriving at all. Moreover, the person who points out a way that is also short helps the eager student with a double kindness: first, the student reaches the end of his course in better time; and second, he achieves his goal with less effort and expense. But I am a little apprehensive that someone who knows my slight competence will here at once cry out, 'Will you then point out a way in which you yourself have never walked, or, at least, have walked with little success – about to act in a manner no less ridiculous than if a blind man should claim to lead the blind, as in the Gospel saying?' [Matthew 15:14, Luke 6:39]. Indeed, I should very much like truly to be able to deny your point. But why should *I* not *imitate* those sailors who, though they themselves have barely escaped with nothing at all when their ship has struck upon a rock, *nevertheless are accustomed to have regard for others who set sail, pointing out to them the dangers?* Or, at least, those many-headed *statues of*

Mercury that were once customarily *placed at crossroads,* and *from time to time by their direction conduct the traveller to a place where they themselves will never arrive. To quote a line or two from the poets, 'I shall do the work of a flintstone, which, though itself incapable of cutting, can sharpen a sword.'* Finally, blind man though he may be, if he shows the way, give him consideration nevertheless.

[4] *Now it is true that St Aurelius Augustine, in the four books to which he gave the title* On Christian Doctrine, *has discussed virtually this very subject both fully and with exacting care,* and before him, I suppose, a certain Dionysius in the work that he entitled *On the Divine Names,* again[1] in the little book to which he gave the title *On Mystical Theology* – and it is probable that he did so in the books of *Theological Institutes,* and, again, in the work *On Symbolic Theology. All the more reason why I shall treat this subject not only more succinctly but also in a plainer and less elegant fashion – with a fatter Minerva, as they say – for I am* certainly *not preparing this for distinguished persons, but am striving with such industry as I have to bring help to unsophisticated folk and to ordinary intellects of a lower order.*

A1 – Elements of a Method for the Study of Scripture

Preparing to study Scripture

[5] *Accordingly, what should have in the first place been taught* is extremely easy *and can be told, as those say, like 1,2,3; but* in practical experience *it is by far the first and greatest thing of all, and just as it requires only the slightest effort to teach, so it takes an enormous effort to manifest in practice.* What I mean is this: *that to this philosophy, which is neither* Platonic nor Stoic nor Peripatetic, *but entirely of heaven, we bring a mind worthy of it, one that is not only free from all the stains of sin* (as far as possible), *but at peace and rest from every tumult of the passions, so that the image of that eternal truth may be reflected more distinctly in us, as in a peaceful river or a* smooth and highly polished *mirror. For if Hippocrates requires of his disciples a blameless and holy character, if Julius Firmicus in the superstitious art does not admit a heart and mind corrupted by* the disease of *gain or glory, if the ancient worshippers of the demons would not receive anyone into their profane mysteries unless they had first been cleansed by many observances, how*

---

1 again ... *Symbolic Theology.*] Added in *1520*

much more is it right for us to approach the school – or, more truly, the temple – of this divine wisdom with minds completely cleansed.

[6] In Exodus[2] the people of God, about to hear the voice of God from afar, are ordered to undergo cleansing during a period of two days. Further, what extraordinary purity do we think is demanded of Moses and Aaron, who climb to the top of the mountain and penetrate that misty and awesome darkness where there is seen what no light either of earth or of heaven can show, where they engage close up in conversation with God? It is of the same import, I think, that when Moses was hastening close to Mount Horeb, running up to see the exceptional wonder of a bush that was burning but was not consumed, he was not admitted to conversation with God until he cast off his shoes from his feet. What are the feet except the affections? What are feet freed from the encumbrance of shoes except the soul that is not weighed down by earthly desires, desires for things that are fleeting? But God speaks to us in the arcane books more truly and more effectively than he spoke to Moses from the bush, provided we approach the conversation with a pure heart. Paul calls the exposition of arcane Scripture not philosophy but prophecy. But prophecy is a gift of that eternal Spirit.

[7] For this, therefore, you should prepare your heart, so that you also may deserve to be called by the prophetic term 'taught by God.' *Let there be in you* an eye of faith that is sound and like that of the dove, an eye that sees nothing but the heavenly things. Add to this *a most ardent desire for learning. This incomparable pearl does not deign either to be loved in any ordinary way, or to be cherished along with others; it demands a thirsting soul, and a soul thirsting for nothing else. Let* all pride now be far away, *all arrogance be far away from those about to approach this sacred threshold*. From things of this sort that Spirit at once recoils, for it takes delight in souls that are gentle and meek. The palace of this queen is majestic if you go all the way into its innermost chambers, but access lies through an extremely low portal; you must bend your neck if you want admittance. Let *the appetite for glory be far away, that plague most pernicious to the truth* and customary companion of indomitable natures; *far away obstinacy, the breeder of brawls, and even more, blind temerity*. What his disciples offered to Pythagoras when he taught them certain magical numbers, you should much more offer to the Spirit, your teacher, and distrusting your own judgment, give yourself to the Spirit to be formed and moulded.

---

2 In Exodus ... pure heart.] Except for the last two sentences this paragraph was added in *1520*.

[8] *When you enter places that are to be venerated with religious devotion, you fondly kiss everything, you reverence everything and as though some divine power is everywhere present you treat everything with religious awe. Remember that you must do this much more scrupulously when you are about to enter this inner sanctuary of the divine Spirit. What is granted to you to see, fall down before it and kiss it; what is not granted to see – this, though concealed, worship nevertheless from afar in sincere faith, and venerate, whatever it is. Let ungodly curiosity be absent. You will deserve to see certain mysteries perhaps for this very reason, that in reverence you withdraw yourself from their sight.* Perhaps[3] Moses taught us this when he veiled his face so that he might not look upon the Lord speaking to him from the bush [Exodus 3:2–6].

Precaution: the idioms of Scripture

[9] In the case of other disciplines, Augustine wants us to apply ourselves to them with caution and prudence; he wants us to read books of human learning with judgment and discrimination. In the Scriptures, if you meet anything that little accords with the divine nature or seems to conflict with the teaching of Christ, do not unfairly blame what is written, but assume rather that you do not grasp what you are reading, or that the words contain a trope, or that the text is corrupt, as for example, when you read that God is angry or is moved to repent, though Christian faith regards it as certain that God is absolutely free from affections of this sort; or when you read that Christ bids his disciples to sell their cloaks and buy themselves swords, though earlier it was he who had forbidden them to resist evil.

The goal of studying Scripture: personal transformation

[10] In the case of the disciplines of human learning, each has its own goal: in the case of an orator you seek to speak with facility and flair; in the case of a logician, to make clever inferences and ensnare your opponent. *Let this be your first and only goal, this your prayer, attend to this alone, that you be changed, be swept away, be inspired, be transformed into what you are learning. The food of the soul is useful not if it remains in the memory as in the stomach, but only if it penetrates into the very affections and into the very*

---

3 Perhaps ... bush] Added in *1520*

viscera of the mind. You may conclude that you have made progress, not if you debate more keenly, but only if you sense that little by little you are becoming a different person, less proud, less irascible, less fond of money or pleasures or of life; if every day some vice disappears and some growth in godliness occurs. In debating you must observe prudence and the greatest self-control so that you seem to be engaged in a conference, not a conflict. Let prayer or thanksgiving frequently interrupt the reading – prayer that seeks the help of the sacred Spirit; thanksgiving that acknowledges the favour whenever you feel that you have made progress.

[11] As a result of the habits of certain people, this most holy study has a bad reputation among some, since those who have climbed to the summit and peak of this profession are sometimes more uncouth than rustics, more vain, more irritable, more poisonous in tongue and absolutely more disagreeable in all the familiar intercourse of our lives not only than the uneducated, but even than they themselves normally are, so that, in the eyes of some, theology itself seems to have made them what they are. St James admonishes that the one who has achieved true wisdom should exhibit and show it not by arrogance and obstinacy in debate, but by gentleness and an upright character. He says, moreover, that the knowledge that brings with it a somewhat bitter jealousy and obstinate contention does not come from above; rather, he calls it earthly and unspiritual and devilish. For the wisdom that is truly theological is, he says, first pure, then modest, peaceable, pliant, full of mercy, and good fruits, knowing nothing of partiality, nothing of hypocrisy.

Means to the goal of personal transformation: learning the languages of Scripture (Latin, Greek, Hebrew)

[12] *Now, in regard to that literature by whose support we more easily attain this,* without question *our first concern should be to learn well the three languages – Latin, Greek, and Hebrew – since it is clear that all of mystic Scripture has been handed down in these.* Of these languages St Augustine was genuinely skilled only in Latin, had some small acquaintance with Greek, but neither knew nor hoped to know Hebrew; nevertheless, in On Christian Doctrine book 2 he does not hesitate to declare that the knowledge of these languages is essential whether to understand the sacred books or to restore them. For just as no one reads a text written with an alphabet he does not know, so without a knowledge of the languages no one understands what he reads. *And do not, dear reader, I pray you, here forthwith recoil, beaten back, as though with a club, by the difficulty*

of the task. If you have the intent, if you have a suitable *teacher, these three languages will be learned with almost less trouble than one learns the pitiful stammering of a single 'half-language' today – no doubt because of both the ignorance and the lack of teachers.*

[13] On this count especially it is right that the memory of the most distinguished Jérôme de Busleyden, once provost of Aire, be sacred both to all who pursue the liberal arts and, above all, to candidates of theology. Busleyden, cheating even his heirs, bequeathed a large sum of money specifically to procure with a decent salary those who should profess the three languages at Louvain. His brother, Gilles de Busleyden, also deserves a large portion of this praise, for he so supports his brother's last will and testament, or, rather, is himself so steeped in liberal learning, that he prefers the money be devoted to supporting the studies of all rather than to enhancing his own coffers. Etienne Poncher, once bishop of Paris, now archbishop of Sens, a man worthy of the memory of all ages, diligently emulates this most splendid example, summoning from all sides with generous rewards those who would teach the languages.

[14] Aurelius Augustine does *not demand that you advance in* Hebrew and Greek literature *to prodigious fluency*, which, even in Latin, is the fortunate lot granted to only a few. *It is enough if you get as far as neatness and propriety of expression, that is, if you achieve some modest skill such as suffices for making judgments. For, to pass over all the other disciplines of humane learning, it is in no way possible to understand what is written if you are ignorant of the language in which it is written* – unless, perhaps, sitting idly by we prefer to wait with the apostles for this as some gift from heaven. *We must not, I think, listen to those persons who, though they waste away in sophistical trumpery* and illiterate literature *even to a decrepit old age, are accustomed to say, 'Jerome's translation is enough for me,'* – as those above all reply who do not care to know even Latin, so that for them, certainly, Jerome translated in vain.

[15] *But to disregard for the moment the fact that it matters very much whether you draw from the originating springs of Scripture or from any sort of pool whatever, what of the fact that certain things, because of idioms peculiar to the languages, cannot even be transferred to a foreign language without losing their original clarity, their native grace, their special nuance? What of the fact that some things are too small to be translated at all, as Jerome everywhere cries out and complains? What of the fact that many things restored by Jerome have perished due to the ravages of time – for example, his* New Testament *emended according to the Greek original*, or the marks of the obelus and the asterisk, or the prophets punctuated by phrase, clause, and full sentence? *What of the fact that either through the error or the indiscretion*

of the scribes the sacred books *were long ago corrupted and today at many points are being corrupted*? What of the fact that Jerome did not by himself restore everything, nor was he able to do so? What if he also wrongly emended or translated some things? Here, I beg you, desist from that tragical lamentation, 'O heaven! O earth!' Let the truth be told: however godly the man, however learned, he was a human being and able both to be led astray and to lead astray. Many things, I would imagine, escaped his notice, many things led him astray. *Finally, what of the fact that not even those* annotations *with which Jerome restored these texts are well understood if you are completely ignorant of the languages on whose evidence he depends?*

[16] *But if Jerome's translation sufficed once and for all, whatever was the point of assuring through pontifical decrees that the true reading of the Old Testament be sought in the Hebrew books, an accurate text of the New in the Greek sources* – the very thing Augustine teaches in more than one place? Lastly, *if the translation* we commonly use *was sufficient, how did it happen afterward that theologians of the first rank slipped as a result of so many manifest and shameful errors, which is so obvious that it can be neither denied nor concealed? Among these* are both Augustine, foremost among the ancients, and *Thomas Aquinas himself* (in my opinion *the most assiduous of all the moderns*) *– and let their curse be upon me if I lie or say this as an insult. Not to* speak at all *for the moment about the rest, who, in my* judgment *at least, are not to be compared with Thomas.*

[17] *If anyone has already grown too old for this, let him play the part of a prudent man, be content with his lot, and,* to whatever extent *possible, rely on the industry of others, provided he does not obstruct young people* of promise, *for whom* above all *this is written. And yet I, certainly, would not be the cause of despair even to the old, since I can name four men specifically, well known personally to me, and also distinguished by their books already published, who came to the study of Greek, none of them under the age of forty, and one forty-eight. Moreover, they themselves by their own work witness to the mastery they have achieved. If Cato's example means little to us, St Augustine, himself already a bishop, already* growing *old, returned to Greek, which as a boy he had indeed tasted – and loathed. Rudolph Agricola, the singular light and ornament of our Germany, neither was ashamed, great connoisseur of letters that he was, to learn Hebrew when he was already beyond his fortieth year, nor did he despair,* a man *as old as he was, for as a youth he had imbibed Greek. I myself* have already begun *my* fifty-third year, *and when I can, I come back to Hebrew, with which I made some acquaintance long ago. There is nothing,* in fact, *the human mind cannot achieve provided it has learned self-discipline, and provided it greatly desires something. For this task, as I said, some modest ability is enough, provided, of course, that it is free from temerity,*

which generally pronounces an opinion more boldly precisely as its judgment is less discerning. In this respect, youth is indeed more fortunate, but nevertheless *we must not despair of the elderly. The former offers in itself more hope, but to the latter, intensity of desire sometimes furnishes what the strength of youth does not provide for others. Moreover, in the letters* and prefaces *Jerome himself sufficiently refutes the opinion of Hilary and Augustine who think that nothing beyond the Septuagint is to be required for the books of the Old Testament and if he had not, Hilary's egregious mistake in the* word 'Hosanna' *quite adequately* did *so. St Ambrose, too, stumbled over the same stone.*

[18] But it is a human characteristic that each of us approves only so much as we can understand. Augustine checked the Old Testament against the Septuagint; much rather would he have checked it against the Hebrew verity if he had acquired the language. Elsewhere[4] also, when he was debating with Cresconius (if I remember correctly), and his opponent had introduced a text from Ecclesiasticus that made no sense, he bade him consult the Greek translation, as though the more reliably true text could be found there.

having some knowledge of the liberal disciplines

[19] *Further, if some rare felicity, 'some exceptional natural gift,' as we say, seems to give promise of a distinguished theologian, I am not averse to something Augustine welcomed* in the books *On Christian Doctrine, that such natural abilities be trained* suitably to one's age *and equipped through a* modest *and guarded acquaintance with the more liberal disciplines, namely, dialectic, rhetoric, arithmetic, music; above all, however, through a knowledge of the objects of nature, for example,* stars, animals, trees, jewels, *and, in addition, places – especially* those that *divine literature mentions. For it is the case that when territories are recognized* from cosmography, *we follow the narrative in our thought* as it passes before us, *and we are, as it were,* completely *carried away with it,* having a sense of pleasure, *so that we seem not to read about but to look upon the events narrated; at the same time what you have thus read sticks much more firmly.* In truth the prophets often stud their books with the names of places, like lights of a sort, and if anyone tries to investigate the allegory, he will not do so either safely or auspiciously if he has no knowledge of the setting of the places. *Now if we will learn from historical literature not only the setting, but also the origin, customs, institutions, culture, and character of the peoples whose history is being narrated or to whom the apostles write, it is remarkable how much more light and,*

---

4 Elsewhere ... there.] Added in 1522

if I may use the expression, life will come to the reading. The reading has to be quite boring and lifeless, whenever not only such things but also the terms for almost everything are unknown. The result is that, either shamelessly guessing or consulting absolutely wretched dictionaries, they make a quadruped out of a tree, a fish out of a jewel, a river out of a musician, a shrub out of a town, a bird out of a star, pants out of plants. *It seems* to them *profoundly learned if only they add 'It is the name of a jewel,' or, 'It is a species of tree,' or, 'It is a kind of animal,'* or whatever you prefer. *But often the understanding of the mystery hangs upon the very nature of the thing.*

[20] This principle Augustine reveals very clearly in On Christian Doctrine book 2, the sixteenth chapter, through some examples he brings in to demonstrate it. He also[5] tells, in the work he wrote Against Faustus the Manichaean, how he had asked that the fruit of the mandrake be brought to him so that he might deduce from either the form, taste, or smell something that would contribute to the explanation of the allegory of the mystic narrative about Rachel selling to her sister, Leah, at the price of that fruit the opportunity to lie with the husband they held in common. Moreover,[6] with how many words does St Ambrose, in his exposition of the thirteenth chapter of Luke, explain in what respects the fig tree differs from the other trees; he does so that it might become more evident how well this tree, as a type, fits the synagogue.

[21] On the other hand, certain people who have relied on dialectic alone reckon that they are sufficiently informed to discuss anything at all. They[7] attribute so much to this discipline that they suppose the Christian faith is finished and done for if it is not secured by the support of dialectic, though meanwhile they disdain grammar and rhetoric as utterly superfluous. And Augustine does indeed approve of anyone who grasps the principles of logical deduction, provided there is no trace of the disease peculiar to this skill – obstinate disputation and a passion for wrangling. But I ask you, what will you divide or define or infer if you do not know the essence and nature of the things you are discussing? How will it help you to have constructed a syllogism in the form of *celarent* or *baroco* when you dispute about a crocodile, if you do not know what kind of tree or animal a crocodile is? These things are not, in fact, learned so much from Aristotle's eight books of *Physics* (which alone are now taught in the schools) as from his extremely erudite commentaries on animals, from his books on *Meteorology*, from[8]

---

5 He also ... held in common.] Added in *1522*
6 Moreover ... synagogue.] Added in *1523*
7 They ... utterly superfluous.] Added in *1520*
8 from ... *Remembering*] Added in *1522*

his books *On the World, On the Soul, On Sense and Sensation, On Memory and Remembering*, from the *Problems*, from the books of Theophrastus *On Plants, On Winds, On Precious Stones*, from Pliny, from Macrobius and Athenaeus, from Dioscorides, from the *Natural Questions* of Seneca and other writers of this sort.

[22] In fact, even the poets contribute much to this part of learning, in whom descriptions of this sort frequently occur: for example, in Lucan, what an enormous account of drugs. But Oppian also professedly published on the nature of fish and wild animals, Nicander on harmful beasts. There are certain arts, classed by Augustine among the superstitious and reprehensible, from whose practices certain narratives in Scripture are drawn. It will help, therefore, to know the superstitious practices of even these arts, to the learning of which the reading of the poets who repeatedly portray the follies of magic is especially conducive. The books of Seneca on the superstitious worship of the gods would also be helpful if only they were extant: Augustine affirms in his work *The City of God*[9] that he had read them. And there are – or rather were – certain people who through their own laborious effort have endeavoured to ease the burden for Christians by explaining the terms and the nature of only those things that are mentioned in the divine books. Among these was Eusebius, bishop of Caesarea. And there are extant even today certain works of this kind, partly under the name of Jerome, but they are, as it is clear, mingled and mutilated. And yet many of us do not even read these; but if we meet some word from an unknown or foreign language, we appeal to Eberhard the Grecist as our Delphic oracle, or to that little book *On Hebrew Names* that reflects such mingled sources. To some, one book is sufficient for everything – the *Catholicon* or Isidore, whose work is more erudite than the *Catholicon*.

recognizing the power of figurative and poetic language, the virtues of the ancient theologians, the deficiencies of their modern counterparts

[23] *I also think that it will be useful for the young man destined for theology to be carefully practised in the figures and tropes of the grammarians and rhetoricians*, which are learned with little effort; also *to acquire preliminary experience in the allegorical explanation of stories*, especially

---

9 in his work *The City of God*] Added in *1522*

those that look towards good conduct. You might, for example, apply
the story of Tantalus to the rich man brooding over and gaping at his
wealth, and yet not enjoying it, or the story of Phaethon to the dangerous temerity of one who assumes a magistracy though he is unsuited
to bearing office. There should also be *practice in fables, and in comparisons*, on which I have published something; further, *and with respect to
rhetoric, those parts especially that treat 'essential questions,' propositions,
proofs, amplifications,* all of which Fabius treats very thoroughly, *and
that discuss the twin emotions, one of which, the gentler, is called
ethos, the other, more severe, is called pathos* – about these no one
wrote more carefully than Aristotle. *For a practical knowledge of these
things* especially *determines judgment, something that is of particular
importance in every kind of study. And since the theological profession rests
rather on emotions than on clever arguments, which even in pagan philosophers the pagans themselves ridicule, and Paul denounces in a Christian –
and in more than one place –* it will be well to be vigorously *practised
in this field throughout youth, so that later you might be able to engage
more skilfully in discussing theological allegories and commonplaces.* In
allegory Origen was most felicitous, in commonplaces Chrysostom
most abundant. *Augustine, in the first book On Order, saw this, if I am
not mistaken, when he bids his Licentius to return to his liberal studies from
which he was then preparing to depart, because studies of this sort make the
intellect more vigorous and lively in approaching as well other subjects* and
the serious disciplines. At the same time, Augustine counts a knowledge of poetry among the liberal arts. But it will be better, I think,
because of those disposed to dispute, to add the words of Augustine
himself. He says, 'You must return to those verses. For education in
the liberal arts – at least if it is modest and limited – makes its lovers
keener, more persistent, more prepared to embrace the truth, so that
they seek it more passionately, follow it more faithfully, and, finally,
cling to it more dearly.' Thus Augustine.

[24] *Otherwise, if anyone is imbued only with those silly, troublesome and
jejune little rules* – those, say, *of dialectic, or, more truly, as it is now* generally *taught, of sophistry (which itself, for all that, they make into one thing
after another every day with their new* and fabricated *problems) – one turns
out, indeed, to be unconquered in debate, but in treating divine literature,* in
preaching the sacred word, *God immortal! how flat we see they are, how
frigid, indeed, how lifeless!* The chief function of these was to set hearts
afire! *If anyone seeks* an example *of this*, let him read the homily of Origen
on Abraham, who had been ordered to sacrifice his son. In this story a
type and pattern is set before our eyes showing that the strength of faith
is more powerful than all human affections.

[25] It may be worth the trouble to consider carefully the details and with what and with how many devices the father's mind is assailed again and again. 'Take your son,' he says. Is there a parent whom the very term 'son' would not cause to waver when he heard it? But to make this battering ram the more effective he adds, 'only-begotten'; and not content with this he continued, 'whom you love.' This could have seemed enough to assault the breast of any man. There is added the name of the son, 'Isaac,' something extraordinarily pleasant to paternal feeling. Herein also the memory of the divine promise is aroused afresh, the promise where he had heard, 'In Isaac will your seed be named,' and, 'In Isaac will the promise be yours.' This[10] was a race that felt, beyond any other, parental love towards children. This most excellent man desired posterity; no hope of this remained if Isaac was cut off, for through him alone would posterity come. And yet God does not simply order him to be slain, but commands that he be sacrificed, so that feelings of parental devotion continually torture the old man's mind in the midst of the preparations. Many and heavy are the weights of the temptation. Over and above all these, he is ordered to ascend a lofty mountain at which he arrived only on the third day, so that for a long time the mind of the father was vexed with changing thoughts, human affection drawing him one way, the divine command urging him another. As they were going along, the boy, laden with the wood with which he was supposed to be burned, addressing his father who was carrying the fire and the sword, says, 'My father,' and the father replies, 'What is it, son?' At this point what a giant battering ram of paternal love do we suppose struck the heart of the old man? Indeed, who would not be moved to pity by the simple sincerity of the boy's submission to the father when he says, 'Here is the fire and the wood, but where is the sacrificial victim?'

[26] Consider now, I beg you, the strength and firmness with which the faith of Abraham, tested in so many ways, followed orders to the end. He does not talk back to God, he does not complain about the reliability of the promise, he does not lament his childlessness among his friends and relatives – for by such actions grief is somehow generally alleviated. Sighting in the distance the designated place, he bids his attendants stay where they are so that no one should thwart him as he fulfilled his orders. He loads the wood on his son, he himself places the pile on the altar, he himself binds his son and places him on the wood, to be sacrificed and consumed. He draws back his arm, brandishes his

---

10 This ... children.] Added in *1520*

sword, ready to cut the throat of his only son, in whom lay all hope of the posterity he earnestly loved – had it not been that suddenly the voice of an angel restrained the old man's right hand.

[27] Origen's discourse on this passage is fuller and more finely wrought, whether with greater pleasure to the reader, or greater profit, I hardly know, though he is, for the moment, engaged only with the historical sense. He does for the divine books exactly what Donatus does for the comedies of Terence in laying bare the intent of the poet. Would anyone see such things who had never applied himself to the more refined literature? who had scarcely tasted the precepts of grammar (and at that, from authors ungrammatical), then, soon hurried off to thorny arguments and dry and troublesome questions, spent the rest of his life in these? I could show with innumerable examples how insipid, not to say ridiculous, are the trifles and absurdities uttered by certain people whenever some saint is to be celebrated with a eulogy, or when a hymn or some other written text is to be used that calls for brilliance and emotion. To theologians of this kind we owe certain hymns and songs commonly called 'sequences' that no educated person reads without either laughter or nausea.

[28] For the present, however, it is not my concern to ridicule anyone's ignorance, but to invite young persons to the best system of study. Only, I shall say this in general: *if anyone seeks some ready proof of this, let him place those ancient theologians, Origen, Basil,* Chrysostom, *Jerome beside these more recent ones* and *let him compare them. He will see there a sort of golden river flowing, here some shallow streams, neither very pure nor much like their source.* There,[11] the oracles of eternal truth thunder forth, here, you hear the trifling fabrications of men, which, the more closely you investigate, the more they vanish like dreams. There you will make for the harbour of evangelical truth by a direct course, here you will be struggling among the tortuous intricacies of human questions, or dashing against the Scylla of pontifical power or upon the Syrtes of scholastic dogmas or upon the Symplegades of divine and human laws – unless you prefer to speak of the Charybdis. There an edifice resting upon the solid foundation of the Scriptures rises aloft, here a frame no less vacuous than vast is raised up to an enormous height, built upon the cunning but unreliable arguments of men, or even upon fawning flattery. *There,* as *in the most fruitful gardens, you will be* both delighted

---

11 There ... flattery.] The first three comparisons here ('There,' etc) were added in 1520, but the second ('There ... Charybdis') appeared only in the separate Froben edition of March that year.

and *filled to satiety, while here you will be torn and racked among* sterile thorns. *There all is full of grandeur, here nothing is noble, while many things are mean and hardly worthy of the dignity of theology* – to refrain, meanwhile, from a comparison of moral character.

[29] *But if one must delay a little longer in profane literature, I should prefer that at all events one do so in literature that is more closely related to the mystic books. I am aware with what arrogance some despise poetry as a subject worse than childish, with what arrogance they despise rhetoric and all good literature, as it is called – and is. And yet this* literature, however loathsome to them, *has given us those distinguished theologians, whom we are now more inclined to neglect than* either *to understand* or to imitate. If anyone asks for proof of this, let him consider how many who have tried to emulate this poetic or grammatical faculty (as they say) – whatever it is – have not succeeded. I refrain from names to avoid offence, though[12] every day they betray themselves by the books they publish. If they condemn the more refined literature why are they so anxious to aspire to refinement of speech? If they approve it why do they discourage from it those who would with more success embrace it? The writings of the prophets everywhere abound in poetic figures and tropes. *Christ clothed almost all his teachings in comparisons; this belongs especially to poets.* Augustine did not think it a childish exercise to note *the figures of the rhetoricians in* the writings of *the prophets and the Epistles of Paul*, also the pauses in the discourse and the full periods. He did this, moreover, in the books he entitled, not 'On Grammar' or 'On Dialectic,' but *On Christian Doctrine*, and what is that if not theological? As a bishop he was not ashamed in the same work to seek from the grammarians a difference of pronunciation and syntax. I shall not mention here that men worthy of immortality treated the mysteries of Christ in poetic verses – Gregory of Nazianzus, Damasus, Prudentius, Paulinus, Juvencus. The apostle *Paul himself* more than once made *use* of *the witness of poets. Where, in these* writings, pray tell, *is there anything that*, however clever and learned, *reflects Aristotle? that reflects* the ungodly *Averroës? Where is any mention of first and second intentions*, of the figures of syllogisms, *of 'formalities,' or 'quiddities' or 'haeceities' – with which everything* in their discussions *is stuffed?*

[30] Do those early Christian writers discourse with little wit because they do not dissect everything into corollaries and conclusions? Or because they do not say what they are about to say before they say it, and again point out that they have said what they sometimes did not

---

12 though ... embrace it?] Added in *1520*

say? Or because they do not cut to pieces every discourse, sliced up almost word for word. This part is divided into three, the first of these into four, and of these four, every one into three further: here the first, there the second. It is precisely these things – the very dullest – that seem to us erudite. Accustomed to these from boyhood, we comprehend only what has been dismembered piecemeal in this fashion. *In other professions it is* regarded as (and is) *a most excellent thing for each person to reflect his own principal authorities.* Virgil imitated Homer, Theocritus, and Hesiod, Horace imitated Pindar and Anacreon, *Avicenna Galen*, Galen Hippocrates, Cicero imitated Demosthenes, Xenophon Plato, *Aristotle*, who discussed everything, imitated *various men depending on the* various *subjects;* Theophrastus, Themistius, and Averroës imitated Aristotle. *Why have we alone dared to abandon in our entire method of discourse the principal representatives of our philosophy?* For what is so unlike, so discordant with the style of the prophets, of Christ and the apostles as that in which those who follow Thomas and Scotus now dispute about divine things. *Augustine thinks it was fortunate that he had encountered Plato above all* when he was still being led about by various errors, because *Plato's doctrines come so close to the teaching of Christ, and a transition from what is closely allied* and akin *is more easily made*.

[31] I should *not*, indeed, say these things *because I condemn the studies that we now* generally *see established in the public schools, provided they are treated* in a sensible and modest way, *and not alone*. But what sort of a thing is it to be afraid to profess oneself a theologian unless one has Aristotelian philosophy; to declare oneself even the standard-bearer in the rank of theologians, when one is without grammar, without rhetoric, without knowledge of all the ancient and more refined learning, and[13] to make confident assertions with great arrogance about the very things of which Paul did not dare to speak a word when he returned from the third heaven [2 Corinthians 12:1–4]? Accordingly, if they wish, *let the few whom just Jove has loved – to use the words of Virgil –* and who have the time to lose some part of their youth, *embrace those studies, too. I am educating the* theological recruit, *an ordinary one* and one in haste.

[32] *And yet, to speak my mind freely, it seems to me by no means safe for one marked out for theology to grow old in profane studies, especially those that are somewhat foreign to the enterprise. Those who coat their palate and tongue with wormwood taste the wormwood in whatever they then eat or drink, and to those that are out in the sun for a very long time, whatever they then see presents itself with that hue which they themselves* convey *when the blurring*

---

13 and ... heaven?] Added in *1520*

of the lens has impaired their vision. So to those who have spent a good part of 20
their lives in the Bartoluses and Balduses, in the Averroës, in the Holcots,
Bricots and Tartarets, *in sophistical quibbling,* in hotch-potch *summulae*
and collections – *to these divine literature does not have its true taste, but the
taste they bring to it. For though it may be nice in treating divine literature
to sprinkle it now and then with those exotic spices, so to speak, yet it seems* 25
*utterly absurd when you are treating a subject vastly different from all worldly
wisdom to prattle on about nothing except Pythagoras, Plato, Aristotle, Averroës, and authors further beyond the pale; to be struck with amazement at their
opinions as though these were oracles,* to protect[14] in earnest the dogmas
of our religion by the determinations and the demonstrations of these, 30
when, in the judgment of the most distinguished men, it is from such
authors that heresies have arisen, and with their weapons especially
that heretics assault us. 'Take away from the heretics,' says Tertullian,
'the wisdom of the pagans, so that they base their inquiries on the Scriptures, and they will not be able to stand.' But today nothing else receives 35
more attention from theologians. *Surely this is not to season the* celestial
philosophy of Christ, but to make it something quite other! Chrysippus is
censured because one could find entire tragedies in the commentaries
he wrote on logic. Someone might more justly censure us than him if
one should see that more than the whole Aristotle is found in the com- 40
mentaries of the theologians.

[33] *But if anyone cries out that apart from* a precise knowledge of *these
one is not a theologian, I, at all events, shall take comfort from the examples of
so many distinguished men – Chrysostom,* Cyprian, *Jerome,* Ambrose, *Augustine, Clement.* I should prefer to be with these, a midget rhetorician, than
to be a theologian along with some who imagine they are supermen. I 5
shall take comfort from the example, *finally, of Peter and Paul, who were
not only not versed in this knowledge but even condemn it sometimes.* At least
it is clear that they never used it.

[34] As Seneca says, 'Some things one ought to have learned; one
ought not to be learning them.' But what sort of sight is it for an eighty-year-old theologian to do nothing in the schools but either to teach or
practise the exercises in dialectic and philosophy appropriate to a forum
of debate? To chatter away endlessly here with no tongue to preach the 5
gospel of Christ, and right to the end of life to do nothing else than
dispute – not to say prattle. Those who prepare for battle are trained
above all in exercises that most assuredly lead to victory. Athletic trainers mould and shape the future athlete – selected while yet a boy – for

---

14 to protect ... theologians.] The rest of this paragraph was added in *1522.*

the contests that lie ahead, and direct everything to their goal. Now, the chief goal of theologians is to explain prudently divine literature, to give an account of the faith and not of frivolous questions, to discourse seriously and effectually on godliness, to elicit tears, to set our souls aflame for heavenly things. For this let our future theologian rehearse from the very beginning of his studies rather than grow old in alien literature.

keeping sight of the aims of the 'philosophy' of Christ

[35] *It would be more to the point*, in my opinion, *to hand down to our young tyro doctrines reduced* to a compendium and *to their chief particulars, and this above all from the Gospel* sources, *then from the apostolic Epistles, so that everywhere he might have clearly defined target points with which to set in line* his reading. *As examples of such teachings I note the following few*: that Christ, the heavenly teacher, *established in the world a new* sort of *people that depended entirely upon heaven, and distrusting all the supports of this world, was rich in a different sort of way, was wise, noble, powerful, happy in some different way*, and *that found its happiness by despising all* the *things the common crowd admires. These were a people who did not know envy or spite – no doubt because their eye was sound; who did not know impure desire inasmuch as they were of their own accord* castrated, practising in the flesh the life of angels; who did not know divorce, evidently either bearing or correcting every evil; who did not know the taking of oaths, as people who neither distrusted anyone nor deceived anyone; who did not know the love of money, as their treasure had been laid up in heaven; who were not titillated by vain-glory, as people who referred all things to the glory of Christ alone; who did not know ambition inasmuch as they were people *who, the greater anyone was, the more he submitted himself to all* on account of Christ; *who, not even when provoked, knew how to become angry or to curse*, much less to take revenge – in fact, *they strove to do well even to those who had harmed them*; whose manner of life was so innocent that it was approved even by the pagans; *who had been, as it were, born again, refashioned into the purity and the simplicity of babes; who, like the birds* and the lilies, *lived from day to day*; among whom there *was the greatest harmony, exactly like that among the members of the body* in *whom mutual charity made all things common*, so that when some good befell, assistance was given to those in need, while anything evil, if it occurred, was either removed or at least alleviated by the obligations of kindness. These were people who, as the heavenly Spirit was their

teacher, were so wise, *who so lived* according to the example of Christ, *that they were the salt and light of the world*, a city set on a hill and visible to all around; who, whatever they were able to do, this they were able to do in the interest of helping all; *for whom* this *life was of no consequence*, while *death was to be desired* because of their longing for immortality; *who feared neither tyranny nor death, nor* even *Satan* himself, *relying on the help of Christ alone; who* in every respect *conducted themselves in such a way that they were always girded, as it were, and ready for that final day.* [I note] that this is the target-point set out by Christ to which all the affairs of Christians must be directed – granted, meanwhile, that we must bear with and encourage the weak, until they make progress and, in gradual stages unobserved, grow into the measure of the fullness of Christ.

[**36**] These are the new teachings of our founder, teachings that no company of philosophers has handed down. This was the new wine that was to be poured only into new skins. These are the teachings through which we are born again from above – hence also Paul calls anyone who is in Christ a new creature [2 Corinthians 5:17]. The Peripatetics hold to the principles of Aristotle, the Platonists to the doctrines of Plato, the Epicureans hold to the tenets of Epicurus; much more does it befit us to hold to the teachings of so great a founder.

B1 The Unity in Variety of the Gospel

Accounting for the variety in the scriptural expression of Christ's teaching: difference of things taught

[**37**] But in these teachings there is some variety, because of the differences in persons and circumstances. Certain things our founder plainly forbids. The following belong to this category: among us there should not be divorce, jealousy, ambition, love of money, revenge, mistrust, disparagement. I shall soon point out a little more fully how much consideration and effort he has given to ensure that all such feelings are banished from the hearts of his disciples. Certain things he plainly prescribes for everyone. In this category are the precepts about mutual love, about forgiving the faults of our brothers, about each one taking up his cross – which, if you refuse to do, Christ does not acknowledge you as a disciple – about gentleness, when he says in the eleventh chapter of Matthew, 'Learn of me for I am gentle and lowly in heart, and

you will find rest for your souls' [11:29], about faith, which he demands everywhere, about kindness to all, and other precepts like these.

[38] Certain things he commends but does not require, enticing with a reward those who can fulfil them, without threatening punishment if they cannot. For in the nineteenth chapter of Matthew he calls eunuchs 'blessed' who have castrated and emasculated themselves on account of the kingdom of God; he does not call those unhappy who maintain a legitimate marriage in purity and chastity [19:10–12]. Perhaps to this class belongs Christ's word to the young man, 'If you wish to be perfect, go, sell all that you possess, and come, follow me' [Matthew 19:21]. Actually, the saying seems to me rather to pertain to all Christians, every one of whom ought to be so minded that if the glory of Christ requires anything of this sort he will gladly neglect everything – if, indeed, by the word 'perfect' Christ denotes a Christian. That young man was an upright Jew; it remained that he should become a disciple of Christ, and then follow the path of perfection. In human affairs, nothing is truly perfect, but each ought to have in his particular condition a zeal for perfection. Certain things Christ disapproves and rejects as unworthy of him, as in the twelfth chapter of Luke, when he had been invited to divide an inheritance, and said, 'Man, who appointed me as a judge or divider over you?' [12:14].

[39] In some cases Christ dissimulates, as it were, as though the matters do not pertain to him, or as though he is indifferent to them. A case in point is found in Matthew, the seventeenth chapter. He asks Peter, 'Who owes tribute to kings, sons or strangers?' [17:25] – as though he were unskilled and inexperienced in these things, since they were things that pertained to the base condition of this world. And, similarly, though he spoke as if the tax was not owed, still he asks that a two-drachma piece be paid, yet not for all, but only for himself and for Peter [17:24–7]. There is another case in point in the twenty-second chapter of Matthew when Christ, who had been questioned with treacherous intent, whether it was right to pay tribute to Caesar, asks that he be shown a coin, as though the coin were unknown to him [22:15–22]. When he had seen it he asks, 'Whose image and superscription is this?' as though this, too, he did not know. And his reply about rendering the tribute to Caesar is not without ambiguity: 'Give to Caesar the things that are Caesar's,' as though to say, 'If anything is owed to Caesar, pay it, but I am more concerned to admonish you to give to God the things that are God's.'

[40] In a very similar manner, he neither condemns nor openly absolves the woman taken in adultery in John the Evangelist, but admonishes her not to commit the sin again [8:3–11]. He was unwilling

to deprive necessary human laws of their own authority, and yet he who had come to save all was unwilling to be the author of condemnation, as far at least as this lay in him. In[15] doing so he gave at the same time an example to those who would follow in the place of Christ that they should be more eager to save sinners by their gentleness than to destroy them by their severity. Again, in Luke, when certain ones reported the novel and dreadful punishment inflicted upon the Galileans, whose blood Pilate had mingled with their own sacrifices, he neither approves nor disapproves the severity of the laws, but uses the story as an opportunity for warning: 'Do you think,' he says, 'that because they suffered such things these Galileans sinned beyond all the Galileans? No! I say to you, unless you regain your senses and repent, you all will perish likewise, just as those eighteen on whom the tower in Siloam fell and killed them' [13:1–5].

[41] For understanding the sense of Scripture some light will be shed from another source also, that is, if we consider not only *what is said*, but also *the words* used, *by whom and to whom they are spoken, the time, the occasion, what precedes and what follows*. For one type of discourse befits John the Baptist, another Christ. The untrained populace is taught one thing, the apostles are taught another. Again, one thing is taught to the apostles while they are still untrained, another when they have now become formed and educated. One sort of reply is given to those who interrogate with an insidious design, another to those who inquire with sincere intent. Finally, the very sequence of the narrative discloses, on thorough investigation, the thought that is otherwise obscure. Many times a comparison of passages unravels the knot of a problem, when what is said somewhat obscurely at one point is repeated at another point quite clearly.

difference of personae

[42] And since in almost all his discourse Christ speaks obliquely through figures and tropes, the candidate for theology will search out with a keen nose what role the speaker sustains – whether he speaks as head or members, shepherd or flock. For when Christ on the cross cries out to the Father, 'My God, my God, why have you forsaken me? Far from my salvation are the words of my transgressions' [Matthew 27:46], he speaks with the voice not of the head but of the members – this on the authority of Augustine. Likewise, when he is sad, when he is distressed,

---

15 In ... severity.] Added in *1520*

when he prays that the cup may be taken away, when[16] again, as though
correcting what he had said, he renounces his own will and submits to
the will of the Father, he seems to have taken upon himself the feeling of
the members. Again, when he says to the retinue that was threatening
him, 'If you seek me, let these go' [John 18:8], he plays the role of shepherd and bishop, the apostle of the flock. For if ever the storm-winds
of persecution rush in, it is the duty of the pastor to throw his own life
in front of the dangers for the safety of the flock. Moreover, when the
disciples flee in terror, when Peter denies the Lord, when he strikes
with the sword, then Peter assumes the persona of the flock still weak
and needing to be fostered towards a hope of better things. But again
when Christ, plaiting a whip, drives the crowd of money-changers out
of the temple, he plays the part of the chief pastor. Sometimes he speaks
expressing the feeling of others, as when he replies to the Canaanite
woman who was importuning him quite shamelessly: 'It is not good to
take the children's bread and throw it to dogs' [Matthew 15:21–8; Mark
7:24–30]. Here he speaks with the voice of the Jews, who regarded themselves alone as holy, and considered Canaanites, Samaritans, and the
other profane races as impure and as dogs, though in Christ there was
no distinction of race except in relation to the providential arrangement
of time. He knew that the attitude of this woman was to be preferred to
the confidence of the Jews, but he wanted to impress upon the minds of
his own race that those would share in the kingdom of heaven who had
broken into it by faith, regardless of origin.

[43] Again, when he asks his disciples, 'Who do you say that I am?'
[Matthew 16:15, Mark 8:29, Luke 9:20] he plays the role of the head.
Peter replies with the voice of, and in the place of, the whole Christian
people, 'You are the Christ, the Son of the living God,' for there is no
one in the body of Christ from whom this confession – 'You are the
Christ, the Son of the living God' – is not required. In like manner, the
words spoken to Peter, 'You are Peter, and upon this rock I will build
my church, and I will give to you the keys of the kingdom of heaven'
[Matthew 16:18–19], extend, according[17] to the interpretation of certain
people, to the entire body of Christian people. It is different when he
says to Peter, who had thrice declared his love, 'Feed my sheep' [John
21:15–17]. Here Christ represents himself as the chief shepherd, that is,
as the head, while Peter is a type of each and every bishop, to whom the
flock for which Christ died is not entrusted unless he loves Christ with

---

16 when ... Father] Added in *1520*
17 according ... certain people] Added in *1522*

an extraordinary love, and looks only to the glory of Christ. His words
were not, in truth, 'rule,' or, 'subdue the sheep,' but 'feed.' His words
were not, 'your sheep,' but, 'my sheep.' You are the shepherd of someone else's flock; you are not its master. See that in good faith you give to
the chief shepherd an account of the sheep entrusted to you. In the same
way, Paul does not, in my opinion, speak in his own voice in the Epistle
to the Romans, the seventh chapter, when, after a long lament about his
own flesh rebelling against the Spirit, he at last cries out, 'Wretched man
that I am, who will deliver me from the body of this death?' [7:24]; he
speaks rather with the voice of some other person, someone who was
still weak, still no match for his own desires.

[44] Now, although the method of taking personae into account is
especially important in the literature of the Old Testament, as in the
Prophets, the Psalms, the Song of Songs, nevertheless, it frequently has
a place in the New Testament also, especially in the Pauline Epistles.
Certain things, however, are put forward in such a way that they do
indeed pertain to all, but not without distinction. For example, when
Christ, speaking to the apostles, says, 'You are the salt of the earth; you
are the light of the world' [Matthew 5:13–14], this pertains to all who
profess the religion of Christ, but chiefly to bishops and magistrates.
Likewise, when he says, 'Be perfect, as also your Father in heaven is
perfect' [Matthew 5:48], he shows to all his people the end to which they
must strive; yet those who are in charge of the church of Christ must
especially manifest this.

difference of times: five periods of Christian time

[45] By taking into account the difference of times, like the difference
of persons, one dispels the obscurity in arcane literature. For not every
command, prohibition, or permission given to the Jews should be
accommodated to the life of Christians. Not that there is anything in
the books of the Old Testament that does not pertain to us, but because
many things that were handed down on a temporary basis as a type
and dim outline of things to come are destructive unless they are
allegorized – like circumcision, the sabbath, choice of foods, sacrifices,
hatred of an enemy, wars undertaken and waged in this spirit, a multitude of wives. These are things that in part are no longer permitted,
in part have utterly vanished like shadows in the gleaming light of the
gospel. However, with respect to the choice that one must consider –
whether to adapt these rules and customs in a straightforward manner

to our conduct, or to give them an allegorical interpretation – it is not my purpose to pursue the subject here, since Augustine has discussed this quite fully in the books *On Christian Doctrine*.

[46] Let the first time period, then, if you will, be that which preceded the life of Christ; the second, when the shadows of the former law were fading as the light of the gospel was near at hand and now approaching though it had not yet, in fact, arisen – as the sky gradually grows light when the sun, not yet risen, hastens to arise. Then it was still enough to be baptized with the baptism of John, to be invited to repent of one's former life. It was enough that the tax collectors be admonished to demand nothing beyond what had been set for them; it was enough that the soldiers be admonished to do violence to no one, to rob and pillage no one, but to be content with their wages [Luke 3:12–14]. Not that these things made them good men or truly Christians, but that they caused them to be less evil and prepared them for the preaching of Christ that was soon to follow. For John nowhere taught that one must not swear, must not divorce his wife, must take up his cross, must be kind to an enemy. These doctrines that made people Christians in the proper sense were being reserved for Christ. Perhaps to this period of time belongs also the first preaching of the apostles, when, with the example of John before them, they are bidden to call to repentance, to announce that the kingdom of heaven is near, to say nothing about Christ. Perhaps also the baptism with which they were at that time baptizing was of this sort, for the apostles were also then baptizing, as John bears witness, though Christ himself baptized no one – nor is it related at all in canonical literature that anyone had been baptized by Christ.

[47] Let the third period, if you like, be the time when Christ was now becoming widely manifest to the world through miracles and teaching, and the evangelical doctrine was being proclaimed – without, however, forbidding the observance of the Law. This time period includes also the beginnings of the nascent and still unformed church after the Holy Spirit had been given. Certain things, however, seem to belong specifically to this period: for example, all those parables about the cultivators of the vineyard who had killed the owner's son; about the wedding and the invitees who excused themselves; likewise Christ's predictions about the sufferings and the afflictions of preachers; and perhaps his admonitions to take up the cross, to shake off the dust from the feet, to greet no one on the way, to flee from city to city, to leave father and mother and wife; his precepts about the happiness of those who castrate themselves on account of the kingdom of heaven, about selling possessions and renouncing all affections, about frequently changing place; finally, his words about the signs that would follow those who believed

[Mark 16:17–18, John 14:12] – otherwise we would not be Christians today, for it is clear that these signs have not followed us. And yet, from the above, this much applies to us, that we are commanded to possess what we hold dear in such a spirit that we are ready to give it up for the glory of Christ whenever the need arises.

[48] To this same period of time belongs also the decision taken through Peter and James in the Acts of the Apostles that Gentiles who had come to Christ should abstain from eating anything that had been strangled, and from blood [Acts 15:20 and 29, 21:25], neither of which we regard as forbidden. This concession was made to the unconquerable obstinacy of the Jews, who would not have been able to associate with the Gentiles if these had had nothing at all of Judaism. Perhaps[18] we should view in the same manner the stumbling block before which the apostles with godly intent gave way at a time when the gospel was still of a tender age, when Judaism and paganism held sway. Today, would one not be a laughing stock who abstained from pork in the presence of Jews to avoid giving them offence? But the apostles continued to do so for some time. Accordingly, those questions that Augustine raises in a certain letter seem to me, at least, to have no point. One of them is this: is a Christian permitted to drink water from a spring or a well into which meat sacrificed to idols has fallen? Paul teaches that bishops should control their wives and children [1 Timothy 3:2–4, Titus 1:6–7]; today, the right to have wives is forbidden even to subdeacons. Paul wants a woman who is a believer to remain with her unbelieving husband [1 Corinthians 7:13–15], though Augustine and Ambrose[19] take a different view, and today the church judges otherwise. Paul does not want a Christian slave to leave his pagan master unless he has been given his freedom [1 Corinthians 7:20–4]; it is determined otherwise today. There are many other things of this kind that were instituted for use in those times but have later been consigned to oblivion or changed; for example, many sacramental ceremonies. Many rites were then not observed that we are now told to observe; for example, feast days and perhaps the private confession of sins – would that[20] at the present time we might use it as profitably as we use it indiscriminately!

[49] For the religion of Christ had by then been spread throughout the entire world and become established. The emperors were not

---

18 Perhaps … has fallen?] These several sentences were added in *1522*.
19 and Ambrose] Added in *1520*
20 would that … indiscriminately!] First in *1522*; previously, 'which at the present time we profitably use.'

persecuting it with their military arms, as they were accustomed to do, but were protecting it. They were not plundering but augmenting the resources of the church – for we have here, if you will, the fourth time period. New laws were introduced to match the transformation in the state of affairs. A few of these laws would seem to conflict with the tenets of Christ, unless we bring the Scriptures into harmony by observing the distinction of time periods.

[50] We can make a fifth time period now of the church falling away and degenerating from the pristine vigour of the Christian spirit. To this period, I think, belongs the Lord's saying in the Gospel that as iniquity abounds the love of many will grow cold; also, that there would be those who would say, 'Lo! here is the Christ; lo! there' [Matthew 24:12 and 23, Mark 13:21]. Paul,[21] writing to Timothy, seems to have designated this time: 'In the last days shall come on dangerous times, men shall be lovers of themselves, covetous, haughty, proud, blasphemers, disobedient to parents, ungrateful, wicked, without affection, without peace, slanderers, incontinent, unmerciful, without kindness, traitors, stubborn, puffed up, blind, and lovers of pleasures more than of God; having an appearance indeed of godliness, but denying the power thereof' [2 Timothy 3:1–5].

Securing the unity and purity of a scriptural understanding of Christ's teaching: the three circles of Christian society

[51] But to prevent such a great variety of times, persons, and things from overwhelming the reader, it might be of some value to distribute the whole people of Christ into three circles, all of which, however, have a single centre, Jesus Christ, towards whose absolutely unstained purity all must strive with all the power each person has. For we must never move the target from its place; rather all the actions of mortals must be directed towards the goal.

[52] Let those occupy the first circle, then, who, because they have, as it were, succeeded to the place of Christ, are closest to Christ, always cleaving to and following the Lamb [Revelation 14:4] wherever he goes. These are such persons as priests, abbots, bishops, cardinals, and popes. These must be as free as possible from the contamination of worldly

---

21 Paul ... power thereof.] Added in *1522*

things, such as the love of pleasures, the pursuit of money, ambition, the appetite for life. It is the responsibility of these to transfuse into the second circle the purity and light of Christ they have derived from nearby. The second circle contains the secular leaders. Though secular, their arms and their laws in some way serve Christ, whether by overthrowing the enemy in necessary and just wars and keeping the public peace, or by curbing criminals with lawful punishments. We may allot the third circle to the undiscriminated crowd as the most stolid and untutored part of this orb we are constructing, remembering that though it is the most stolid and untutored part, it nevertheless belongs to the body of Christ.

[53] Within the individual circles we may picture to ourselves a sort of differentiating order. For when priests offer sacrifices to God, when they feed the people with the food of the evangelical word, when they converse with God in pure prayers, and when they intercede for the welfare of the flock, or[22] when they meditate at home in private study to make the people better, they are no doubt dwelling in the purest part of their own circle. But when they comply with the inclinations of princes to prevent the latter from becoming provoked and arousing a worse commotion, when they unwillingly concede much to the frailty of the weak to prevent them from falling into things still worse, they are moving on the outside boundary of their circle, a boundary to which they proceed, however, only to draw others to themselves, not to become worse themselves. Of the elements of which this lowest world consists, each has its own place; but fire, which holds a place next to the lunar orb, though in its highest part it is most pure and transparent and most precisely like the nature of the sky, is, nevertheless, somewhat heavier and coarser where it actually borders the lower atmosphere. Likewise, the air is most like fire at the topmost edge of its circle, while in the lowest part, which borders water, it becomes thick. Perhaps the same can be said of water and earth. And meanwhile, fire, which is the chief active force, gradually carries off all things to itself, and as far as it can transforms them into its own nature. The earth, attenuated by the winds, it changes into water, water vapourized it changes into air, rarified air it transforms into itself. The borders serve to transform into the better, not into the worse. So also Christ would frequently accommodate himself to the frailties of the disciples; so Paul used to indulge the Corinthians in many things, though he distinguished sometimes what he set forth in the name of the Lord for the perfect and what in his own name he

---

22 or ... better] Added in *1522*

pardoned in the weak with the hope nevertheless that they would progress [1 Corinthians 3:2].

[54] Accordingly, when popes with their pardons and indulgences, as they call them, foster and encourage those who are slothful (or who are, perhaps, close to despair) until they progress to better things, they are not moving in the highest part of their circle. When they also pass laws about extorting praedial and personal tithes, about paying for the use of the pallium, about requiring the annates, as they name them, about defending with arms the patrimony of Peter, as they call it, about subduing the Turks in war, and about innumerable other things – though we grant that they are concerned with something that is necessary or at least useful to our common life, still no one would say that they are engaged in what is peculiar to the heavenly philosophy. And indeed perhaps popes, even if they particularly wished, could not regulate their laws – the laws they publish for the common life of human beings – in such a way that these would correspond in every respect to the precepts of Christ. Christ, as that purest source of all light and innocence, teaches things that taste of heaven. Popes are men and prescribe according to circumstances what seems helpful for people who are weak, and weak in so many different ways. Accordingly, it is impossible that sometimes among the prescriptions even of popes there should not be certain things that smack of human affections and in which you miss the innocence of Christ.

[55] Moreover, just as the lowest part of fire is lighter than the highest part of air, so it is proper that what is grossest in the pontifical regulations nevertheless comes closer to the straightforward candour of Christ than what is especially god-like in the laws of the Caesars or their magistrates. For since princes and magistrates are engaged in affairs that are connected with the lowest dregs and with the sordid business of the world, they must respond to their situation. Through their laws we do not happen at once to be good, but for the time being less evil. Accordingly, if these make regulations or decrees that depart somewhat from the precepts of Christ, take care ever and again not to mingle the most pure spring of Christian philosophy with the pools of these men, whatever sort such pools may be. Human laws ought to be sought from this archetype. The sparks of human laws are taken from the same light, but the gleam of eternal truth is reflected in one way in a smooth and polished mirror, in another way in an iron blade, in one way in a completely transparent spring, in another in a filthy pool.

[56] I have said these things so that we might not taint the celestial philosophy of Christ with either the laws or the doctrines of human beings. Let that target remain intact; let that one unparalleled spring be

unpolluted; let that truly sacred anchor of gospel teaching be preserved; in it one can take refuge amidst such dark mists of human affairs. May[23] that cynosure never become obscured for us, lest there be no sure constellation by which we might be put back once again on the right course when we have been enveloped in such great billows of error. May this pillar not be moved, in order that with its support we may withstand the force of this world, which always both sinks towards and carries one off to the worse. May that foundation remain solid and ready to give way before no blasts of opinion or storm winds of persecution – a secure foundation on which the good architect might place a structure of gold, silver, and precious stones – and when the hay and straw of the studied opinions of human beings have been consumed by fire, the foundation itself might remain for a better edifice. Men can make mistakes; Christ does not know how to err. Do not reject forthwith what human beings prescribe, but consider carefully who prescribes, to whom he prescribes, at what time, on what occasion, and, finally, with what intent the prescription is given; but[24] above all whether a prescription agrees with gospel teaching, whether it has the taste of the life of Christ and reflects his life. 'The spiritual person discerns and judges all things,' says Paul, 'he himself is to be judged by no one' [1 Corinthians 2:15]. But if the teachings of Christ are twisted to accommodate human laws, what hope, I ask you, is then left? Much less indeed if the divine philosophy is bent to accommodate human desires, and as the Greek proverb says, 'Let the Lesbian rule prevail.'

[sidenote on the critical use of ancient and modern theologians

[57] We must,[25] I think, take the same point of view about the writings of the ancient and the modern Doctors as about the laws established by human beings – the point of view just described. We ought not to be so

---

23 May ... Christ does not know how to err.] Added in *1520*. From this point, several major additions of *1520* break into the text of *1519* and are themselves later amplified by brief additions of *1522* and two major additions of *1523*. The *1520* additions extend from this point to the penultimate sentence of **71** ('... creeds grew'). See CWE 41 187 section 1.
24 but ... reflects his life] Added in *1520*
25 We must ... granted them] added in *1520*. At this point Erasmus inserted into the *1519* text a very long addition in *1520*, interrupted by two additions in *1522* (see nn 26 and 28) and a long addition in *1523* (see n 29). The *1519* text resumes at **67**; see n31.

devoted to any of these Doctors that we regard dissent at any point to be forbidden. Quite a few people today make a practice of doing this: here is one who has so devoted himself to the principles of Thomas or the doctrines of Scotus that he prefers to defend them even when they are false rather than swerve a single hair's-breadth, as they say, from the teachings of these Doctors, though the authors themselves do not want so much granted them – or,[26] to be more specific, though Augustine, a man so distinguished, wants his own books to be read in precisely the same way he himself was accustomed to read the books of others, however famous their authors were, that is (to use his own words), 'not with the necessity to believe but with the liberty to judge.' And yet[27] to those ancient writers, especially those whom, besides their outstanding erudition, both their venerable antiquity and their very holiness of life commend, it is right to grant this, that we interpret their writings in a kindly manner, and that wherever their lapses are too obvious to be concealed, we respectfully dissent from them, not pursuing human mistakes with clamorous reproaches, but attenuating and removing them as far as one can. We should feel the same way towards the teachings of the scholastics: let those teachings certainly have their weight on the exercise grounds of the disputations; let them be admitted as the definitions of human beings, as themes and subjects for debates, not as articles of faith, especially since in these matters the schools themselves do not agree with one another, nor do the same schools always approve the same definitions. And, indeed, it becomes more unbearable that every day new dogmas are set down, and upon these, as though sacred and inviolate, we build Babylonian towers rising all the way to heaven. We fight more fiercely to maintain these than we fight on behalf of the teachings of Christ.

some points of doctrinal controversy

[58] But certain tenets might seem to be of such a kind that the integrity of the Christian religion would remain nicely secure without them, some again of the sort that open a window for the destruction of true godliness. To understand more clearly what I mean, take an example of the first kind. A godly man practises reverently the confession of sins as

---

26 or ... judge.'] Added in *1522*, interrupting the *1520* insertion
27 And yet ... for the people.] Added in *1520*. The long *1520* insertion (see n25) continues here for four paragraphs to the end of **60**, where it is interrupted again by a *1522* addition (see n28), which is followed in turn by a lengthy insertion of 1523 (see n29).

the practice originated among our ancestors and gradually arrived at its present form, for he respectfully maintains the view that one ought not dissent on his own authority from what the public practice of Christians and the authority of leading men have approved. Not content with this obedience, certain people add their own tenet that this confession, since it is a part of the sacrament, had been instituted not by the apostles but by Christ himself. For, say they, the church does not have the right either to add any sacrament to the seven or to remove any from them – though they themselves attribute to one man the right or the full power to do away with purgatory if he wishes. To me, at least, this tenet does not seem entirely essential to piety. For of what importance is it to godliness whether a thing has been instituted by Christ himself or by the church inspired by the Spirit of Christ? Unless, perhaps, we fear we will lose the profit we gain from anything of this sort, using the holiest things for an unholy end! And yet I should not want these comments to be taken in any other way than as an example adduced for the purpose of illustration.

[59] Another example of the same kind seems to be the following. A good man believes that Christ was conceived from the Holy Spirit and born of a virgin. What need was there for so many definitions? Presently, the living body of a human being complete with all its limbs was fashioned from an absolutely pure little drop of the virgin's blood the size of a tiny wee spider; into this was placed at the same time a soul complete with all the gifts it now enjoys in heaven. To me, at least, it would seem to contribute to godliness if we either did not explore these things or at least explored them more reverently; but at the present time we affirm them in front of the unlearned populace as most definitively ascertained. Meanwhile, this too I would put forward only by way of illustration, for I prudently abstain both from multitudinous and from serious examples.

[60] Here is an example of the second kind: sometimes we attribute to princes more than we should, whether seeking something from them or following a custom we see commonly observed. For there are those who contract the whole body of the church into one man, the Roman pontiff, who alone, they say, cannot err whenever he makes a pronouncement on faith or morals. The whole world, they say, though it stands united in a different opinion, ought to trust the judgment of a single individual, the one pontiff; if it does not do so, it must be judged schismatic. And yet the very ones who attribute to the Roman pontiff more than even he himself acknowledges, attribute very little to him if anything stands in the way of either their greed or their ambition – then the inviolable scruples of religion are banished, then the enlightened

theologian inclines towards a universal council, then a summons to a synod is proposed. Does not teaching of this kind open a vast window to tyranny if such great power should come to an ungodly and destructive man? In addition, there are certain teachings of the scholastics – or rather of the monks – concerning vows, tithes, restitutions, absolutions, confessions, by which the souls of the simple, or at least of the superstitious, are grievously ensnared, bringing great harm to the people but exceptional advantage to those for whom, as for bad physicians, times are best when they are worst for the people.

[61] We[28] do not envy the majesty of the Roman pontiff. Would that he truly had what those attribute to him, and that he would not be able to slip in matters that pertain to godliness! Would that he might truly be able to deliver souls from the pains of purgatory! Nor do I deny that popular morality is prone to unrestrained licentiousness at every point and sometimes must be restrained by barriers like those mentioned – if only evangelical integrity permits you to coerce some, to ensnare the consciences of others, even if we admit that Platonic lie that the wise man deceives the people for the good of the one who is deceived.

[62] Now,[29] assuredly, an unbreachable wall arising from the jurisconsults, if I am not mistaken, has been taken over by the theologians, namely, the view that an indissoluble marriage arises from consent alone. To how many snares, how many anxieties, how many almost inexplicable difficulties does this tenet give rise? Nor do I see on what rational arguments or on what Scriptures it rests. But what harm would befall the Christian commonwealth if marriages were validated just as they were among the Jews, Greeks, and Romans? While, however, mutual consent would still be the principal part of marriage, it would not be 'stem and stern' as they say. I think that this too derives from the jurisconsults when it is said that if the cowl is assumed, a marriage that is indeed valid but not yet consummated is dissolved. 'This is done,' they say, 'in the interest of religion.' Is it religious to injure a bride? Is it not permitted to live a religious life within matrimony?

[63] Now the view that a marriage procured through fraud or deceit ought not to be dissolved unless a mistaken claim concerns the person or the person's status is one that does indeed have a certain human justification sufficiently probable. For I do not think it right for a marriage to be dissolved if a spouse who had been said to possess ten acres

---

28 We ... deceived.] Added in 1522
29 Now ... can have three wives.] This lengthy insertion appeared in 1523. The 1520 text resumes at the beginning of **66** (see n30).

is found to have only nine, or one who was said to be thirty years of age was thirty-six. But will it also seem right to compel a girl who is well born, virtuously reared, of holy character, of unspotted reputation to spend her life forever with a man who was deceitfully declared to come from a respectable family, though he is the son of some pimp – or worse? To spend her life with a man who was said to be rich when he has mortgaged even his life? with a man who was said to be upright and of blameless reputation when he is sunk deep in every kind of criminal act? with a man who was put forward as having a healthy body when he has leprosy or what is now called the French disease, which is just like leprosy? And yet we will more quickly give our approval to this than allow a scholastic tenet to lapse.

[64] No more pleasant are the consequences to which we are led ultimately by the precept that we must not commit any wrong, however trivial, to obtain a good result, however great. But if the pope, for reasons that in my opinion are not very important, dissolves a marriage between persons whom he, on his own authority, beyond the authority of Divine Scripture, has pronounced 'incompatible' (to use their expression), why does he not much rather render incompatible those who were deceived by a flagrant trick and have been caught in an unhappy marriage that is worse even than death to a girl of respectable station? Now this, too, was regarded as an article of faith many centuries back, that a solemn vow (as they call it) can by no means be broken, while one that is not solemn can. For it is irrelevant to this argument that the pope does not entrust a release of this sort to bishops or to parish priests, though he commonly entrusts a purchasable right to agents and to people of the most sordid and ignorant kind.

[65] Now, from the concept of spiritual kinship how many snares arise for us. Although the concept was introduced through a purely human law, nevertheless, theologians give an account of it as though it could not be otherwise. But the case was otherwise before the regulation arose, and perhaps it would be advantageous to repeal regulations of this sort. Away with those arguments from the similar, the like, the unlike in cases involving a special concession; away with them where there is no conflict with a right God has been pleased to grant. 'If kinship of the flesh is an impediment, much more kinship of the spirit' – why do we not rather argue thus: if kinship of the flesh makes me an heir, why not rather kinship of the spirit? 'No one can have two wives at the same time; therefore no one is able to have two parishes at the same time.' Why not argue thus: a bishop is able to resign or exchange his sacerdotal office, therefore a husband can do the same? The pope

grants that the same man can have three bishoprics; one can therefore concede that the same husband can have three wives.

[66] Every[30] day we hear complaints about these things from godly men who earnestly desire the good of the Christian flock. It is not for me or for people like me to tear down what has been accepted through common use. Still, it is right to desire that that Divine Spirit should blow upon the minds of popes and princes in order that they might wish to examine those things in such a way that more true godliness and less superstition attend to the people, and that less tyranny also is allowed to those whose good fortune is fed by the evils the public endures. And yet it is my desire to advance these things, too, only by way of example, for my intent at present is to teach, not to provoke.

B2a 'The Wonderful Circle and Harmony of the Entire Drama of Christ'

The unity of the Old and New Testaments

[67] In addition,[31] we will enjoy an important advantage if we diligently read through the books of both Testaments and consider closely that wonderful circle and harmony of the entire drama of Christ (if I may use the expression), a drama acted out for our sake by the one who was made man. If we do so we shall not only understand more correctly what we read, but we shall also read with a more certain confidence. For no lie is so skilfully fabricated that it is at all points consistent. Collect from the books of the Old Testament the types, and the oracles of the prophets: the types sketch out and represent in outline the Christ; the oracles point to his coming as though with the eyes of faith. Those[32] divine seers portrayed almost everything Christ did. There is nothing in his teaching that does not find a correspondence in some passage in the Old Testament, as Tertullian so nicely shows in the fourth book *Against Marcion*. Following the prophets comes the witness of the angels – of Gabriel announcing to the virgin a celestial marriage, of the angelic choir singing together at the nativity, 'Glory to God in the highest.' The

---

30 Every ... provoke.] Added in *1520*
31 In addition] The *1519* text resumes at this point; see n25.
32 Those ... *Marcion*.] Added in *1522*

witness of the shepherds soon is added, then of the Magi, of Simeon and Anna besides. Then comes the prelude in the preaching of John the Baptist, who now points out the presence of the one who the prophets predicted would come; and so that we might know what to expect from the one to come he adds, 'Behold the one that takes away the sins of the world' [John 1:29]. This one alone is the Lamb that knows no blemish; he is not only a lamb, but he also makes lambs. He does not promise his own a kingdom, pleasures, honours, or wealth, but he promises innocence if only people come to their senses and repent. Moreover, no true good will be absent if innocence is present.

[68] After this observe the entire sequence of his life, how he grew, making constant progress in the sight of both God and men [Luke 2:52]. Before God there is the commendation of a good conscience; among human beings there is the grace of an honourable reputation, which more happily attends true excellence when it has not been sought. He first gave proof of what he was when at the age of twelve he taught and, in turn, listened in the temple. Again, he became known to a few at a wedding, when he performed privately his first miracle – for he undertook the duty of preaching only when he had been baptized and commended by the sign of the dove and the voice of the Father, and, finally, only when he had been tested and tried by a forty-day fast and the temptation of Satan. Examine his nativity, his upbringing, his preaching, his death; you will find nothing but a model of poverty and humility, or rather, a model of all innocence. Just as his teaching in its entire orbit is self-consistent, so it is consistent with his life, consistent even with the judgment of nature itself. He enjoined innocence; he himself so lived that not even suborned witnesses found any convincing point of slander, though they sought it in various ways. He taught gentleness; he himself was led as a sheep to the slaughter. He taught poverty; we read that he himself never either possessed or sought anything. He gave no place to ambition and pride; he himself washed his disciples' feet; he taught that this was the way to true glory and immortality. He himself through the ignominy of the cross won the name that is above every name, and though he did not strive for any kingdom on the earth, he obtained dominion over heaven and earth alike [Philippians 2:8–11]. After his resurrection, he taught exactly what he had taught before. He had taught that the godly must not fear death, which[33] does not snuff out our life but gives us immortality, and for this reason he showed himself to his disciples, alive again. As they were looking on, he ascended

---

33 which ... immortality] Added in *1520*

into heaven that we might know to what point we must exert our efforts and refer all things. Last in order, that heavenly spirit descended; by its breath it made the disciples the men Christ wanted them to be.

[69] And[34] in all these things he was himself in a certain manner his own seer. For just as Christ did nothing that was not sketched out in outline through the types of the Law or was not predicted through the oracles of the prophets, so he did nothing worthy of memory that he had not earlier predicted to his disciples – about his death (the kind of death, the place of death, the effect of his death), about his burial, resurrection, return to heaven, the power of the Holy Spirit, the distress of the disciples, the defection of the Jews and the reception of the Gentiles, about spreading the gospel from its very small beginnings throughout the whole world, which took place wonderfully through the lowly and the uneducated, about the suffering of the disciples, the destruction of the city of Jerusalem, about the heresies that would shake the concord of the church. You see what great agreement there is at every point.

[70] You will perhaps find in the books of Plato or Seneca principles that are not inconsistent with the tenets of Christ. You will find in the life of Socrates things that in some way accord with the life of Christ. But in Christ alone will you find this circle and harmony of all things congruent with each other. In the prophets there are both many inspired sayings and many godly deeds; there are many in Moses and other men distinguished for the sanctity of their lives. In the case of no one else will you find such a completion of the cycle, a cycle that begins with the prophets, and comes full circle with the life and teaching of the apostles and martyrs. These expressed whatever Christ taught, fulfilled whatever he promised; they had drunk the same Spirit, they speak and teach the same things as Christ. Everything to this point is to be revered; the rest is to be read or even to be imitated with judgment and discrimination.

[sidenote on the authority of the sacred writings

[71] It[35] would perhaps not be unreasonable to establish some order of authority among sacred writings also, as Augustine did not scruple to do. First place is owed to those books about which the ancients never had any doubt. For me, at least, Isaiah has more weight than Judith or

---

34 And ... point.] Paragraph added in *1523*
35 It ... grew.] Except for the last sentence, this paragraph was added in *1520*, the last in the series of major additions in *1520* that began at **56**; see n23.

Esther, the Gospel of Matthew more than the Apocalypse attributed to
John, the Epistles of Paul to the Romans and the Corinthians more than
the Epistle to the Hebrews. Next place after these is held by certain
things that have been passed down to us by hand as it were, and have
reached even to us either from the apostles themselves or from those at
least who lived close to the times of the apostles. Among these I place
first of all the creed commonly known as the 'Apostles',' produced, if I
mistake not, at the Council of Nicaea. I believe it derives its name from
the fact that it manifests the weight, the moderation, and also the brevity of apostolic speech – and would that our eagerness to believe had
been satisfied with that one creed! When there began to be less faith
among Christians, both the number and the size of the creeds grew.
And yet even the apostles, while they resemble Christ, do not rise to his
majestic grandeur.

The harmony in variety of Christ's action and discourse: Christ a Proteus in his life and teaching

[72] Nor, in truth, does the diversity in Christ bring this harmony into
disorder. Rather, just as in song the sweetest harmony arises from different voices aptly ordered, so the diversity of Christ produces a fuller
harmony. He became all things to all people but without ever compromising himself. Sometimes he manifests the signs of his divinity – when
he commands the winds and the sea, when he forgives sins, when on
the mountain he presents to his disciples a new appearance, one more
excellent than that of a human being. At other times he plays the part
of a human being, concealing his divinity – when he is hungry, thirsty,
tired out from work, when in hunger he hurries to a fig tree, when he
mourns, when he is afflicted, and killed. Certain men, without their
asking, he calls to join him, some from their nets, Matthew from the
toll-house; certain people who wish to follow him he rejects. Of this you
have an example in Matthew, the eighth chapter, where a scribe says,
'Master, I will follow you wherever you go,' to whom Jesus replies,
'The foxes have holes and the birds of the sky have nests, but the son of
man does not have where to lay his head' [8:19–20]. Again in the same
passage he says to a man who seeks permission to leave, 'Follow me,
and let the dead bury their dead' [8:22]. He feared for the latter that he
should fall away; he knew that the former would be useless in work that
would be anything but dainty and delicate. Delighted by the enthusiasm of Zacchaeus, he invites himself on his own initiative to his house,
as you read in the nineteenth chapter of Luke [19:1–10]. Everywhere he

censures Herod as an ungodly Jew and, for that reason, worse than the
pagans. He calls him a fox in the thirteenth chapter of Luke: 'Go and
tell that fox' [13:32]. When he was led to Herod he did not deign even
to address him.

[73] Sometimes he performed a miracle quite voluntarily, as though
seizing an opportunity – the miracles, for example, of the fig tree that
withered at his curse, of the crowd that was filled with a few loaves of
bread, of Lazarus. At other times he acted seemingly with reluctance
and under compulsion. There is an example of this in the Gospel of
John, when at the wedding he replies to his mother, who was inconspicuously pointing out to him the lack of wine: 'Woman, what have you
to do with me? My hour is not yet come' [2:4]. Again, in Matthew, the
seventeenth chapter, when he was asked to heal the epileptic whom his
disciples were not able to help, deeply moved he exclaims: 'O faithless
and perverse generation, how long shall I be with you? How long shall
I suffer you? Bring him hither to me' [17:17]. He listens to the Canaanite
woman with reluctance – and only after she became importunate – and
he does not comply immediately [Matthew 15:22–8, Mark 7:24–30]. To
the leper, on the contrary, he shows a ready compliance, saying, 'I will,
be clean!' [Matthew 8:3]. Again, he flatly refuses to give the Pharisees
a sign when they ask for one. He says, 'An evil and adulterous generation seeks after a sign, and a sign shall not be given it but the sign of the
prophet Jonah' [Matthew 12:39]. In the same way in the sixteenth chapter he replies to the Pharisees and Sadducees who were pressing him
to give some sign from heaven, 'You know how to discern the face of
the sky; but can you not discern the signs of the times?' [Matthew 16:3]

[74] In some places he demands silence after performing a miracle, as
in Matthew, the ninth chapter, he gives to the blind men whom he had
healed a menacing order, 'See that no one knows it' [9:30], well aware
that they would spread the news abroad all the more. In precisely the
same way in the same Gospel, the twelfth chapter, he instructed the
many he had healed not to make him widely known [12:16]. However,
in the fifth chapter of Mark he does not accept the healed demoniac as
a companion; yet neither does he ask him to be silent, but to proclaim
among his own people – not Jesus Christ, but what had happened to
him through the kindness of God [5:18–19]. He demands a confession
from his disciples, saying, 'But who do you say that I am?' [Matthew
16:15]. He enjoins silence upon the demon, who openly confessed that he
was the Christ [Mark 1:23–6, Luke 4:33–5]. Again, elsewhere he claims
gratitude from those who conceal the kindness they have received; for
example, the woman who had ceased to haemorrhage after touching
his cloak. He said, 'Who touched me?' and persisted until the woman

acknowledged the kindness in the presence of everyone [Mark 5:25–34, Luke 8:43–8]. Similarly, he accuses of ingratitude the nine lepers who, though Jews, nevertheless did not return to give the glory to God [Luke 17:12–19].

[75] There is also another kind of difference in the miracles he performs. He heals some people without any trouble, as when he raises a girl with a word, 'Little girl, I say to you, "Arise"' [Mark 5:41]. He smears mud softened with spittle on the eyes of the blind man, and, content not even with this, he instructs him to wash in the pool of Siloam – and only then was the blind man aware of the kindness he had received in having his health restored [John 9:1–12]. Those ten lepers were not healed immediately but ordered to go to the priests; they were cleansed from leprosy as they went [Luke 17:12–19]. Further, when he is about to raise Lazarus, he even sheds tears, groans in the spirit, asks to be shown the sepulchre, orders the stone removed, and thus calls forth the dead man with a piercing cry [John 11:32–44]. Sometimes he is angry and addresses the disease in a menacing tone. It will be appropriate to philosophize where there are differences of this kind, and to investigate with a pious curiosity the mystery of the divine plan.

[76] He changes likewise in his responses. To those who ask questions to trick him he replies warily and obliquely – to the Pharisees, for example, who ask about divorcing one's wife, about paying tribute to Caesar, about the great commandment. When a coin is shown to him, he takes the opportunity to point out what they were not doing, since this was above all else what mattered. He retorts that their liberty in divorce had not been conceded on the basis of what was right, but granted to their unconquerable ill-will. Likewise with respect to the commandment, he shows that they were not doing what they knew should above all else be done. He attributes knowledge of the Law to the Pharisees, though he refuses to acknowledge their piety; he condemns the Sadducees for their folly because of their dull-witted inquiry, for they were men who did not understand what they read. Sometimes he gives no answer but to a question retorts with a question, like driving out a nail with a nail. For example, when asked by what authority he did what he was doing, he asks, in turn, whether they thought the baptism of John was from heaven or of human origin. Elsewhere he does indeed reply but follows up a question with a question – as in Matthew, the twenty second chapter, he asks the Pharisees, 'Whose son is Christ?' and when they had replied, 'David's,' he says, 'How does David, speaking in the Spirit, call him his Lord when he is his son?' [22:41–5]. In Mark, the twenty-sixth chapter, he says nothing in response to the witnesses; just so in the twenty-seventh chapter he is completely silent before Herod.

In the presence of Pilate he responds with a very few words, but not to everything; he says nothing to Caiaphas. Though bound, beaten, mocked, he makes no response; he does respond when struck with a blow. On the cross he said not a word in the face of the reproaches of the Jews, but he cannot restrain himself at the lamentation of the women who followed him.

[77] Sometimes he avoids the crowd, as though he found it wearisome; again, at other times, moved by compassion, he seeks the crowds of his own accord, and allows them to press in closely upon him. At one time he draws into the deepest solitude to pray; at another time he voluntarily takes himself to a very crowded assembly in the temple; at another, he stealthily slips from the hands of those who were lying in wait for him; for example, when he had been led to a mountain so that they might hurl him down from it; and again he secretly vanishes when the crowd was going to stone him. He entrusts to the disciples certain things they should preach; certain things he confides that are to remain unspoken for a time – the vision, for example, on Mount Tabor and the secret conversation with Moses concerning his death. He speaks in one way to his disciples, in another way to the common crowd. Finally, he shows himself to his disciples after the resurrection now in one form, now in another. Thus, though nothing is more straightforward than our Christ, yet with some hidden intent he represents a kind of Proteus by the variety of his life and teaching. This will perhaps be a cause of wonder to our new theological recruit, but to a person who is practised and attentive, it will not be difficult to track down the circumstances of the individual cases.

the problem of apparent contradictions in Scripture

[78] But we stumble less over such passages than we do over those that at first glance seem even contradictory. Cases of this are the following: in the Gospel of John Christ denies that John the Baptist is the light [John 1:8], though later he declares of the same John, 'He was a burning, shining light' [5:35]; and when he says to the still unformed apostles, 'You are the light of the world' [Matthew 5:14], likewise when he says, 'My teaching is not mine' [John 7:16], if anyone pays attention only to the surface meaning of the words, there seem to be inconsistencies. Again, in John, the sixth chapter, when he says, 'He who eats my flesh and drinks my blood has everlasting life' [6:54], but a little later, 'It is the Spirit that gives life, the flesh is of no avail' [6:63], does he not seem to be saying things that are contradictory? What you find in the next chapter is very similar. Although Jesus had said, 'You both know me and you

know from where I came' [7:28], he soon adds, as though disagreeing with himself, 'He who sent me is true, whom you do not know' [7:28]. Somewhere he says that he judges no one [John 8:15]; elsewhere he testifies saying, 'The Father has given all judgment to the Son' [John 5:22]. He forbids his disciples to be angry [Matthew 5:22], though we read that he himself had been moved by anger [Mark 3:5].

[79] Moreover, in certain narratives, the apparent variation lay open to the slander of the ungodly. For example, Matthew reports one blind man healed though Luke affirms that two were healed – likewise when sometimes one name seems to be substituted for another, when Stephen, in Acts the seventh chapter, seems to tell the story somewhat differently from the way it is found in Genesis – in the twelfth chapter, that is. Further,[36] in the number of years there is considerable inconsistency, and here and there the observant reader has trouble with the order of events in the Gospels. If difficulties of this sort sometimes arise, one should not be offended or doubt the trustworthiness of what is written, but should consider carefully all the details and then look for a way to resolve the problem. Our predecessors toiled with sweat in this very task; their assiduous efforts will help us if we do not find an answer that satisfies the mind.

proofs of Christ's double nature, human and divine

[80] Now, we must also attend carefully to the proofs by which Christ demonstrated his double nature of God and man. For who would hope for true salvation from one who was simply a man? On the other hand, who would believe that a being unconditionally God suffers anything? But he wanted us to return his love by loving him as a true man, who truly suffered for us, and not to doubt that he would fulfil what he had promised, since he was truly God. What of the fact that not even his example would be sufficiently effective if what was done in Christ was not done with true feelings, but was a sort of stage play, merely fictional, presented to the eyes? Of his human nature the signs are that he is conceived in the womb of a woman, of his divine nature that he is conceived from the Holy Spirit, of his human nature that he is born of a pregnant woman in the regular time, of his divine nature that his conception is without the agency of a man.

[81] That he was true man is shown by the fact that he repeatedly calls himself the son of Adam, by the fact that he grows up gradually

---

36 Further ... Gospels.] Added in *1523*

in accordance with the customary stages of life, by the fact that he eats, sleeps, hungers, thirsts, grows weary from a journey, by the fact that he is moved by human feelings. We read that he often pities the crowd, as in the twentieth chapter of Matthew [20:29–33]. In Mark, the third chapter, he is angry and grieves [Mark 3:5]; in the eighth chapter of the same Gospel he groans in the spirit [8:12]. Again, in the twelfth chapter of John, long before the passion, he is troubled in mind [12:27]; in the garden he suffers anguish of mind to the point of sweating bloody drops [Luke 22:43–4]. On the cross he thirsts, the usual result of that kind of punishment [John 19:28]. He weeps after looking upon the city of Jerusalem [Luke 19:41], and at the tomb of Lazarus he both weeps and is troubled in mind [John 11, 33, 35].

[82] On the other side, his divine nature was disclosed by so many miracles performed – and so easily and with such efficacious power – for he preferred that his divinity be shown by deeds rather than words. And yet even with words he bears witness that he is the Son of God sent from heaven, and that he had been in heaven and was in heaven when he was dwelling on the earth and repeatedly insisting again and again that God was his Father. Even the Jews understood this when they said, 'Though you are a man, you make yourself God' [John 10:33]. Last of all, when he rises from the dead, when he is carried to heaven, when he sends the Paraclete, who suddenly makes new men of the apostles. But just as this can be noted briefly, so it would extend the discussion too far to expand upon each point.

rejection of the Jews in favour of the Gentiles

[83] It also seems to belong to the careful investigation of the divine plan that we note in how many ways [God] wanted it to be manifest that the Jews, who long ago had been promised the Messiah and had awaited him, had through their own fault been rejected on account of their incredulity, while the Gentiles had been received into their place because of simple faith. Christ knew the hardness of his own race, a race that was farther from true righteousness for the very reason that it was puffed up with a false opinion of righteousness. He knew that this was a race utterly given to malicious accusation; accordingly, he did everything to prevent them from having occasion to expostulate with God that they were cheated of the promises beyond what they deserved. The prophets had predicted that the Gentiles would by faith break through to the grace of the gospel, while the Jews would by their own moral failing fall away from the promises. He wanted to be born among those to

whom he had been promised. He was heralded in song by the angels, proclaimed by the shepherds, revealed by the Magi, acknowledged by Simeon and Anna, pointed out by John the Baptist, commended by the utterance of the Father. He became well known through many miracles, he invited them with so many kindnesses, he taught such salutary doctrines, and yet no advantage was derived from these things. Blinded by envy, arrogance, and avarice, they killed the prophets, did not believe John, falsely and slanderously charged that the miracles were done with the help of Beelzebub, persecuted Christ himself. And yet all the while they took pride in the empty title of the Law and in a temple worthy of veneration throughout the world, saying, 'The temple of the Lord, the temple of the Lord, the temple of the Lord.'

[84] The Magi are the first of all to worship the boy; Herod, the Jew, persecutes him. When Christ at first had commissioned his disciples for the work of the gospel, he forbade them to go into the cities of the Samaritans [Matthew 10:5], and he did so with the specific design that the Jews should not find a captious reason to quibble on the grounds that they had been neglected by Christ. He calls a tax collector, who leaves all and follows him. The Pharisees, who had been invited in so many ways, set themselves to oppose. He offers them examples of faith from those whom they regarded as detestable and wicked. He presents to view the Canaanite woman, to whom at first he barely listened, then even thrust her back with an insult, but she conquered through her unconquerable faith, and forced Christ, as it were, to do a kindness – for is there anyone whom that cry of the woman would not successfully assault: 'Yes, Lord, for even the little dogs eat of the crumbs that fall from the table of their masters' [Matthew 15:27]? Do you hear, proud Jew, the Canaanite woman's modesty filled with trust? She, though rejected thus, nevertheless presses on and insists; you can be enticed by no kindness. Accordingly, she hears, 'O woman, great is your faith. Be it done for you as you desire' [Matthew 15:28]. What do the Jews hear? 'Your house shall be left to you, desolate' [Matthew 23:38]. And in Matthew, the twenty-first chapter, he openly casts in their teeth that the tax collectors and the harlots were, because of their ardent faith, going into the kingdom of God before such Jews [21:31].

[85] In Matthew, the eighth chapter, there is introduced the example of the centurion who trusted Christ so completely that he thought it of no importance for Christ to come to his house, since Christ could bestow health by his word and assent [8:5–13]. How do you feel about this, unhappy Jew? A centurion, outside the sacred circle of God's people and an army officer, a man who had not read the prophets, trusts Christ thus. And do you cry out against your Saviour, awaited now for

so many ages? Accordingly, he deserves to hear, 'Verily I say to you, I have not found so great faith in Israel' [8:10]. But to you what does he say? No doubt what we read in Luke, the eleventh chapter, 'The queen of the South will arise in judgment against the men of this generation and will condemn them, because she came to Jerusalem from the outermost parts of the earth to hear the wisdom of Solomon' [11:31]. He whose wisdom makes the wisdom of Solomon seem as nothing, willingly showed himself to you – and are you reluctant to hear him? The people of Ninevah, who accepted the preaching of Jonah [Jonah 3:1–10], will do the same; you spurn him with whom Jonah is not to be compared [Luke 11:32]. The example of Zacchaeus, who had climbed a tree in his eagerness to see Christ, is introduced. You hear, greedy Jew, an unholy man bearing witness about himself, 'Half of my goods I give to the poor' [Luke 19:8], so that you might understand that the kingdom of God is promised not to race, but to life and faith. Therefore in your presence Zacchaeus hears, 'Today salvation has come to this house, since this also is a child of Abraham' [Luke 19:9].

[86] A race that is naturally jealous – is it not incited to emulation by however many examples? is it not moved even by so many parables? In Luke, the eighteenth chapter, he introduces for you a tax collector: the man is a sinner, but he is humble, he implores mercy, and he is preferred to the just man who is proud [18:9–14]. In the seventeenth chapter he draws a portrait of yourself, when the nine Jewish lepers hide the kindness bestowed; only the Samaritan returns and gives thanks [17:11–19]. He signifies the same thing by the parable of the wounded man: the Jews pass him by; only a Samaritan takes him up to care for him [10:30–7]. We find the same point made in two parables in Matthew, the twenty-first chapter. The first parable is about two sons, one of whom promised his father he would carry out his orders but did not, the other, though he refused at first, soon came to his senses and did what he said he would not do [21:28–32]. The second parable is about the wicked tenants, who after first maltreating the slaves, finally killed the very son and heir [21:33–43]. So the evangelist adds: 'And when the chief priests and Pharisees had heard his parables, they knew that he spoke of them' [21:45]. Although they knew they were guilty, so far were they from any thought of repentance that there follows: 'And seeking to lay hands on him they feared the multitudes' [21:46].

[87] Moving in the same direction also is the parable that immediately follows about those invited to the wedding [Matthew 22:1–10]. In some cases the Jews offer excuses, in some cases they offer insult and injury to the slaves who were inviting them to the banquet. Rightly,

therefore, are the Jews passed over and the wedding tables are filled with an indiscriminate crowd of Gentiles.

[88] For what would you do with those who, when invited to salvation, stubbornly vent their anger against the one who is kindly caring for their interests? The parable of the hired labourers employed to do work in the vineyard [Matthew 20:1–16] has in view the same end – for the Jews murmur against us who have come later and nevertheless have been made equal to them in the grace of the gospel. I think the parable of the prodigal son also focuses on this point. In this parable the son who had maintained the justice of the Law is angry at his brother who had long wandered afar in the mazes of error but then came to his senses and repented, and for this reason was received with joy by a merciful father back into the family [Luke 15:11–32]. The Jew recalls his own good deeds, while the pagan does not have the sins of his former life cast in his teeth. In my opinion, the theme is exactly the same in the parable of the coin that was lost and found [Luke 15:8–10], in the parable of the wandering sheep brought back to the flock [Luke 15:3–7, Matthew 18:12–14], in the parable of the fig tree that was still unfruitful after three years, and was to be cut down in the fourth year unless it ceased to be unfruitful once manure had been applied [Luke 13:6–9], in the parable of the children sitting in the market place, chanting in alternation among themselves: 'We played the pipes and you did not dance; we sang a dirge and you did not mourn' [Luke 7:32].

[89] In these ways, so various, our most excellent Saviour wanted the obstinacy of the Jews made evident, an obstinancy worthy of their destruction. At the same time he was also reordering the minds of the disciples still somewhat tainted with Judaism, so that they should not be averse to receiving pagans into the fellowship of the gospel. For Peter, after he had heard from Christ, 'Go into the entire world and teach all nations, baptizing them in the name of the Father and of the Son and of the Holy Spirit' [Matthew 28:19], after the heavenly Spirit had been received, does not dare to receive Cornelius unless warned in a vision [Acts 10:19–20, 28–9]. In like manner, in John, the tenth chapter, Jesus advises the disciples about the future, saying, 'I have other sheep also that I must bring, and there shall be one flock' [10:16]. Again, in Luke, 'The kingdom of heaven suffers violence, and everyone uses violence towards it' [Luke 16:16]. Pagans, who were outside, broke into it by force; the Jews, who were within, were shut out because of their distrust. Jerusalem was turned into Sodom, and where formerly it used to be said, 'not my people,' there they are called the children of God. These words, spoken in a past era, belong to those ancient times; even

so, they also can be applied to every period of time. Every age has its
own Pharisees; every age is at risk if it misuses the kindnesses of God.

the innocence of Christ made plain

[90] Next after this it seems good to note in how many ways Christ
wanted his own innocence to be made evident to all, so that no one should
find anything with which to disparage the authority of this teacher. He
wanted to be born of parents who, though of humble means, were nevertheless blameless and upright, not because in the eyes of God the
sins of the parents are imputed to the children, but because the custom
generally prevails that anything perpetrated by the parents is thrown
up against the children more cruelly than against the very perpetrators
of the wicked deeds. The[37] widespread popular saying is by no means
without grounds, 'From the ugly raven comes the bad egg.' Indeed, he
wanted to have even a guardian[38] who was upright, of whom you read
in Matthew, 'Whereupon Joseph, being a just man' [1:19]. Angels from
heaven give their witness about the boy. Magi acknowledge his divinity with their gifts. Shepherds tell abroad what they had seen. Simeon
embraces the infant awaited so many ages. Anna, a widow most pure,
adds a corroborating witness. God the Father time and again cries out
from heaven, 'This is my beloved son; hear him.' Many were the times
that John gave witness about him. Even the demons acknowledge and
confess that he is the Son of God, although he is loath to be proclaimed
by them. Many are the times that the crowd wonders at the divine power
in him. In John, the seventh chapter, even the officers who were sent to
arrest and take him give their witness, 'Never did a man speak like
this man' [7:46]. Martha confesses, 'You are the Christ, the Son of God
who was to come into this world' [John 11:27]. The Samaritan woman
confesses, 'You are a prophet' [John 4:19]. The apostles confess, 'You are
the Christ, the Son of the living God' [Matthew 16:16]. For Christ frees
from all sin anyone who acknowledges God.

[91] Pilate also witnesses, 'I am free from the blood of this just man;
see to it yourselves' [Matthew 27:24]; his wife witnesses, too, 'Have no
dealings with that just man' [27:19]. Caiaphas, inspired by the prophetic
spirit, adds his witness, 'It is expedient for you that one man should
die for the people and that the whole nation should not perish' [John
11:50]. Even the hostile judges acknowledge his innocence, rejecting the

---

37 The ... egg.'] Added in *1522*
38 guardian] *nutricium* in *1523*, previously *vitricum* 'stepfather'

testimony of many; the witnesses themselves also show that they had been suborned and were lying. They have no charge to bring against him except a statement about destroying the temple and building it again, and they bring forward this statement itself in a sense different from that intended, and cast up at him what they had not understood. Unhappy Judas also confesses, 'I have sinned in betraying innocent blood' [Matthew 27:4]. At the cross the centurion confesses, 'Truly this was the Son of God' [Mark 15:39]. The wicked Pharisees also confess, who had no charge to bring against the crucified except that he was going to destroy the temple of God and raise it in three days [Matthew 27:62–4]. So free was he from any misdeed that no story could even be invented against him with any credibility.

how Christ, by his action and discourse, won over the whole world

[92] After this the piously curious reader will note in what ways or with what design Christ brought over to his own tenets an entire world divided into so many religions. For he did not subjugate the kingdoms of the world by machines of war, not through the syllogisms of philosophers or the enthymemes of the rhetoricians, not through wealth, not[39] through honours, not through the enticements of pleasures. He did not want any human aids to be mixed with this business, which he wanted to be due entirely to heaven. In the first place, the agreement of so many prophecies helped to induce trust, prophecies with which John [the Baptist]'s testimony agreed – for Christ did not suddenly renew the world. It is extremely difficult to root out of the human mind what we have imbibed from childhood, what has with common agreement been handed down from our ancestors. Long ago John played the prelude in the baptism of repentance, the apostles played the prelude announcing not yet the Messiah, but only that the kingdom of heaven was at hand. Christ begins the work through men uneducated and of humble station so that the world should not on this score claim anything for itself [1 Corinthians 1:26–9]. He puts up with these same men, long untrusting and unformed, so that they should not seem to have believed rashly. Thomas distrusts with a most stubborn persistence, and only upon feeling the prints of the nails and of the spear says, 'My Lord and my God' [John 20:28]. Why, even when Christ is about to ascend to heaven, he

---

39 not ... pleasures.] Added in *1522*

rebukes them all for their hardness of heart and the difficulty they had in believing what they had seen [Mark 16:14].

[93] He sprang from the Jews, a most wicked and obstinately rebellious race. He began, not in Nazareth, lest his native city should disparage his authority, but in Capernaum, a city corrupted by wealth and luxury. Openly he censures nothing that had been received on the authority of the community – for there is scarcely anyone who accepts such censure with equanimity. Everywhere he affirms the testimony of the Law, though he gives it a different interpretation [Matthew 5:17–48]. He adapted himself to those he was eager to attract: he became a human being to save human beings; he associated on familiar terms with sinners to restore sinners to health; to entice the Jews he was circumcised, was purified, he observed the sabbath, was baptized, fasted. He prevailed through gentleness, he prevailed through kindness, he prevailed through truth itself, whose power is more effective than any magic charm. Even wild beasts are tamed by such things.

[94] He confirms with the testimony of Scripture almost everything he asserts. Indeed, even when provoked by abuse, he responds either with the Scripture or with reasoned arguments. For in Matthew, the twelfth chapter, when it was said as a terrible insult that he cast out demons with the help of Beelzebub, he replied, 'Every kingdom divided against itself will be laid waste' [12:25]. And when he was struck at his trial, he said, 'If I have spoken wrongly, give testimony of the wrong; if well, why do you strike me?' [John 18:23]. He provided additional confirmation through miracles, but these themselves were nothing other than kind deeds and[40] on this ground, especially, distinguished from the illusions of magicians. And he made an unquestionable trustworthiness attend every miracle he performed. He did almost everything before a crowd as witness. He sends the lepers to the priests not to be cleansed but that it might be better established that they had been truly cleansed. A man widely known to be blind is healed, his parents are summoned, he himself is called back, and all these actions have only one objective, to build up the trustworthiness of the miracle [John 9].

[95] Everywhere he shows that he endures all his sufferings of his own will and with foreknowledge, and that he suffers not on his own account but for us. His teaching won no little confidence from the fact that he never strove for any reward for all his kind deeds – neither glory, nor wealth, nor pleasure, nor sovereign power – so that no suspicion of a ministry corrupted could be duly attached to him. And, lest it should

---

40 and ... magicians.] Added in *1522*

seem that he was seeking some personal gain while alive, the gospel trumpet did not sound throughout the entire world before the heavenly spirit was sent [Matthew 10:5–6, Acts 1:4–8]. Moreover, no witness is more efficacious among mortals than the witness of blood. By his own death and that of his disciples he declared the trustworthiness of his teaching – for I have already said something about the harmony of his whole life. But about his type of teaching, which generally consists of comparisons drawn from things most familiar to the common folk, and for this reason not only effective but also suited to the capacity of even the uneducated crowd, I shall say something a little later.

[96] It was generally with such forces that Christ, and the apostles after him, assaulted the obstinacy of the Jewish race. In[41] these ways, he who was contemptible in appearance and uneducated overcame the arrogance of the proud philosophy of Greece. By these means he put down the savagery of so many barbarian nations, a savagery unconquered by arms. By these means he brought under the yoke of faith the tyrants and satraps of the whole world, and drew them over to his laws. So declares the prophecy of Isaiah, where Christ is portrayed as one who, for all his gentleness, takes the nations by storm: 'Behold my servant whom I have chosen, my beloved, in whom my soul is well pleased. I will put my spirit upon him and he shall show judgment to the Gentiles. He shall not contend nor cry out, neither shall anyone hear his voice in the streets. The bruised reed he shall not break, and smoking flax he shall not extinguish till he send forth judgment unto victory. And in his name the Gentiles shall hope' [Matthew 12:18–21]. In this passage you do not hear of tortured syllogisms, you do not hear of threats and fulminations, you do not hear of troops armed with the sword, you do not hear of carnage and conflagrations. You hear rather of judgment, you hear of clemency, you hear of gentleness towards the meek, in whom there was some hope of moral progress. You hear of victory – not a victory wrenched out by the force of machines, but one sought through judgment. You hear of a victory that is not fearful for the vanquished, that does not plunder and oppress those who have been subjugated. What then? You are hearing that he is the sort of person on whom the Gentiles, vanquished by kindnesses, have fixed their hope of salvation. And yet since these are the means through which the Christian commonwealth arose, grew, and became established, who does not see that these are also the means through which it must be protected,

---

41 In ... uneducated] Added in *1520*; in *1519* 'He overcame the arrogance' etc.

The conformity of the life and teachings of the apostles to Christ's example

[97] Now,[42] if you like, let us consider in a brief comparison how the life and teaching of the apostles correspond to the pattern of their teacher. With what great cunning Paul everywhere acts like some chameleon, if I may use the expression, and turns himself into all things to bring some gain to Christ from every side. Thus, on one occasion feeling exalted, he gives himself precedence over all the apostles, on another occasion humbling himself, he says he is unworthy of the name of apostle [1 Corinthians 15:8–11, 2 Corinthians 11:5–6, 21–3]. On one occasion, when he has returned from the third heaven, he boasts of what he heard there, things forbidden to be told [2 Corinthians 12:2–4]. On another occasion, lowering himself to the humble state of the weak, he professes to know nothing but Jesus and him crucified [1 Corinthians 2:2–3]. At one time, he has wisdom that he speaks among the perfect, whom he feeds with solid food, at another, he feeds the Corinthians with milk, as being feeble [1 Corinthians 2:6, 3:1–3]. Somewhere again, suppliant and unassuming, he flatters those who deserved to be scolded, and forgets his own rank while he has regard for their salvation [1 Corinthians 1:4–7, 2:1–5, 4:8–13, etc]. Elsewhere, on the other hand, how harshly menacing are his words: 'Do you seek a proof of Christ dwelling in me?' [2 Corinthians 13:3] He never claims for himself tyrannical power, he everywhere calls the task he performs a ministry – he is nothing but a minister and a steward. And in the third chapter of the first Epistle to Timothy he refers to the bishopric as a 'work': 'One who desires the office of a bishop desires a good work' [3:1]. Paul ascribes to Christ and to God whatever he has done that is worthy of praise. Indeed, he is not reluctant to be the servant of all, provided that the loss of apostolic honour results in Christ's gain [1 Corinthians 9:19]. In our day, certain bishops regard their people as purchased slaves, or, rather, as cattle; Paul everywhere calls his people either sons or brothers. He represents himself as Philemon's partner, while he calls Onesimus a brother, though he was Philemon's slave, and a fugitive at that [Philemon 16–17].

---

42 Now ... flourishing so widely.] The passage running from here until almost the end of **103** was added in *1520*; see n44. For its significance, see CWE 41 187 section 2.

[98] Now this affability is particularly effective in making one's way into human hearts. Thus those whose business it is to tame wild beasts first adapt themselves in every way to the nature and disposition of the beasts. So wine slips soothingly into a person's body, and spreading at once through all the veins, it unleashes its force and places the whole person under its power. Accordingly, Paul entices with praise those he wishes to amend. When writing to the Romans, who were by nature headstrong, immediately, at the very beginning of the letter, he extols their faith [1:8], then expatiates on the vices of their former life under a persona that seemed not to be theirs: 'Because when they knew not God, etc,' and then, 'God gave them up to the desires of their heart' [1:21–4]. At length, when they had been softened and soothed, he dares to raise the recollection of their former life: 'What fruit therefore did you have in those things of which you are now ashamed?' [6:21].

[99] By the same design, when he is eager to recall the Athenians from their ingrained superstition, he did not immediately begin with, 'You are out of your minds, Athenians; you worship wicked demons as God.' Rather, he tells them how, as a recent visitor eager to learn, he was walking about intending to survey the rituals and the kind of religion they followed. He calls their wicked idols *sebasmata*, an ambiguous word that is appropriate to the representation of God as well as the deities. Moreover, since he knew the superstition handed down from remote generations of ancestors could not suddenly be eradicated, and that even the state laws forbade anyone to bring in foreign religions, he took part of an inscription and with remarkable dexterity turned it to an occasion to preach the gospel. 'I am not bringing in a new religion,' he says. 'Your altars attest that you worship a certain God that is unknown. Worship henceforth as a God you know the one you have worshipped as unknown.' And thereupon he confirms his words not with the testimony of the prophets, whose authority would have had little weight among the Athenians, but with that of Aratus, the Greek poet, 'For we too are his offspring.' Then he blames upon the times the fact that the Athenians had until that point been guilty of both impiety and immorality. Finally, he does not immediately call Christ God, but a man, through whom God had determined to restore the world. He affirms that no ordinary proof of this was the fact that he had called this man back to life after he was dead.

[100] With the Galatians, who had fallen away, he is in labour a second time, until Christ should be formed in them [Galatians 4:19], and he counsels the Romans not to reject the weak in faith, but to receive such and nourish them until they grow up [Romans 14:1]. Soon, in the fifteenth chapter, he inculcates the same lesson: 'Now we that are stronger

ought to bear the infirmities of the weak and not to please ourselves' [15:1]. And shortly after, 'Wherefore receive one another, as Christ also has received you to the honour of God' [15:7]. Tolerate those who now are what you once were; tolerate them with the same gentleness with which Christ tolerated and cherished you. Again, in the tenth chapter of the first Epistle to the Corinthians, he bids them be like himself, who with pliancy accommodated himself to all in all ways, 'not seeking,' he says, 'that which is profitable to myself, but to many, that they may be saved' [10:33]. Then, too, with what feeling, with what clemency, he calls back to a better mind the Galatians who had left so deserving an apostle for pseudo-apostles! You would not say that this was an apostle angry at those who had deserved punishment, but a dear mother feeling sick in sympathy with the sickness of her child. He invites them in the sixth chapter to follow the example of this gentleness: 'Brethren, even if a man be overtaken in any fault, you who are spiritual instruct such a one in the spirit of meekness, considering yourself, lest you also be tempted' [6:1].

[101] But notice, reader, what a large admixture of gentleness is found even in the very severity of Paul. For in the third chapter of the Second Epistle to the Thessalonians, he asks that the person who stubbornly refused to obey wholesome admonitions be noted and even shunned [3:14–15]. But to what end? That he should perish? By no means, but that he should become ashamed. It is enough for Paul if such a person comes to his senses and repents, if he acknowledges himself, if the sinner is ashamed of himself. What punishment is milder than this? And yet Paul mitigates even this: 'Yet do not regard him as an enemy, but admonish him as a brother' [3:15]. Moreover, in the fifth chapter of the First Epistle to Timothy he forbids a bishop to reprove somewhat disagreeably an older man taken in a fault, but Paul entreats him to admonish an older man as a father, errant younger men as brothers, old women as mothers, girls as sisters [5:1–2].

[102] But some will say, 'There might be a danger that from this gentleness many people will learn the wrong lessons about many things.' Rather this gentleness has made this world new, as no severity would ever have been able to do. If in ruling a realm clemency is very often more effective than severity, and if many kings have discovered this from experience – among them Jeroboam,[43] the son of Solomon – how much more becoming is clemency among those who are called fathers instead of lords, and to whom the sword has been given not to destroy but to heal [Romans 13:4]? Further, in the third chapter of Titus, he asks

---

43 Jeroboam] Added in *1522*

that even pagans be enticed by this stratagem: 'To speak evil of no one,' he says, 'not to be litigious, but gentle, showing all mildness towards all people' [3:2]. Here, once again, he assumes the persona of those who have turned from an immoral life to the religion of Christ: 'For,' says he, 'we ourselves also were sometime unwise and incredulous, erring, slaves to diverse desires and pleasures, living in malice and envy, hateful, having hatred for one another' [Titus 3:3]. Paul had never been a person like this, but he represented himself as having been such so that he would give them no offence.

[103] Peter, too, in the fifth chapter of his First Epistle admonishes – or rather entreats – other bishops as partners and associates to prove themselves to be shepherds of the flock entrusted to them, not lords, and to look after the work of Christ, not their own interests [5:2–3]. In the second chapter of Acts, in the speech where he, as first, began first to fulfil the apostolic task, he rejects the insult that the disciples were (as it was being said) quite deranged because filled with new wine [2:12–40]. Here again, with what gentleness does he do so, citing the witness of the prophet! Then he shows by logical argumentation that the oracle of the prophet fits not David but Christ. Even so, to avoid any offence here, he softens his speech, as though enticing them: 'Brethren,' he says, 'let me boldly speak to you' [2:29]. Soon, when they had become troubled in mind, he enjoins upon them nothing else than that they should come to their senses and repent, and be made new through baptism. Then, as though imputing their evil deeds to the age, he says, 'Save yourselves from this crooked generation' [2:40]. Then, in the next chapter, see how he extenuates the terrible crime of the Jews, who had killed Christ: 'And now, brethren, I know that you acted in ignorance, as did also your rulers' [3:17]. And he calls them the sons of the prophets, to whom especially Christ was promised [3:25]. Would you like to hear how much this civility accomplished? The number of believers had already grown to five thousand [4:4]! We, for our part, deaf to this teaching, blind to these examples, do nothing else than threaten and terrify; we do not teach, we compel, we do not lead, we drag – our point of reference in all these matters being our own glory and our own purse. We more readily cause a loss for Christ, however great, than we would allow the diminution of our own emoluments even by the merest fraction. Do you wish to know the result? You see how the borders of the religion of Christ have been contracted, a religion once flourishing so widely.[44] But I have frequently discussed these matters elsewhere; now let us pursue what we began.

---

44 The long addition of 1520 (see n42) ends here.

How Christ prepares those who are to preach the gospel: disciplining the affections

[**104**] We must also notice in what ways and how carefully he prepares those who are about to go out to preach the gospel. Our observation will enable those who today undertake the ministry of preaching Christ to understand the preparation they ought to acquire. The kingdom of heaven is being summoned; it is fitting that from this heavenly kingdom the earthly passions which hold sway in those who love the world be far removed. It is worth while to consider with what great zeal he banished all such passions from the hearts of his disciples. He took away luxury and the love of sensual pleasures with the parable of the rich reveller and the beggar Lazarus [Luke 16:19–31]. These come before our eyes, the one dragged down from temporary delights to everlasting torments in the realms of Tartarus, the other carried from the evils of this life to eternal rest. He takes away the pursuit of riches with the parable of the rich man who was enlarging his barns and promising himself a soft and pleasant life for many years, but on that very night death loomed up behind the wretched fellow, ready to take away once and for all what he had heaped up with the sweat of so many years [Luke 12:16–21]. Again, he removes the pursuit of wealth when he prohibits us from being concerned about tomorrow; when he asks that treasures, subject to neither moths nor thieves, be laid up eternal in the heavens; when he enjoins us to live from day to day, like lilies and little sparrows, relying on the goodness and the providential care of the heavenly Father; when in the tenth chapter of Mark, through the opportunity offered by the young man who had departed in sorrow as soon as he was told to abandon his wealth (for he was very rich), Jesus turned to his disciples and said that it was easier for a camel to go through the eye of a needle than for a rich man to enter the kingdom of heaven [10:17–25]. To convince his disciples of this from experience also, he sharply reminds them, when they are concerned about bread, of that miracle which they had seen a little before: with a few loaves and fishes several thousands had been filled, and so abundantly satisfied that many baskets full of left-overs were taken up from the feast. In addition, there is the time when he sends the disciples on their first preaching mission, carrying no provisions; on their return they confessed that they had lacked nothing.

[**105**] In many ways he roots out the affection one has for parents and kin (for affection also is frequently accustomed to call us aside from our zeal for godliness). He asks that they depend wholly on the heavenly Father, and call no one on earth 'father' [Matthew 23:9]; likewise,

he says that he does not acknowledge as a disciple one who will not renounce father and mother, sisters and brothers, and, lastly, even also his wife, when the work of the kingdom of God requires it [Matthew 10:37, Luke 14:26–33]. Though he had a mother of unexcelled piety, he himself is never fondly gentle with her. When she appeals to him in the matter of the wine, he says, 'O woman, what have you to do with me?' [John 2:4]. When he is scolded in the temple, he says, 'How is it that you sought me? Did you not know that I must be about my Father's business?' [Luke 2:49]. Again, in Matthew, the twelfth chapter, while [Jesus was] teaching the crowd, someone interrupted him on behalf of his mother and brothers, who wanted to meet with him. What an absence of fond affection in his response! 'Who is my mother, and who are my brothers?' [12:48]. Again, on the cross, he calls her 'woman,' not 'mother,' placing John in his own position [John 19:26–7].

[**106**] Now in regard to the love of honour and the disease of ambition, which is usually innate in noble and lofty natures, in how many ways does he root this out of the hearts of the disciples, knowing full well that this would be the chief bane of ecclesiastical princes! He allowed his disciples to feel this emotion so that he could more effectively eradicate it. It was from ambition that the sons of Zebedee request (through their mother, whom they had secretly directed to this end) that they sit next to Christ in the kingdom of heaven [Matthew 20:20–3]. It was from ambition that the disciples disputed among themselves who would be first in the kingdom of heaven. Accordingly, they hear from the Lord: 'The princes of the Gentiles lord it over them, and those who have power exercise it over their own. It shall not be so among you; rather, whoever will be greater among you, let him be your minister, and he that will be first among you shall be your servant' [Matthew 20:25–7]. And not content with this, he offers himself as an example: 'Even as the Son of man did not come to be ministered unto, but that he himself might minister to others, and give his life for many' [Matthew 20:28]. How little[45] is this speech concordant with a disposition towards ambition! He sets before them a lowly and insignificant child and says that no one will enter the kingdom of heaven who does not humble himself to the level of a little child.

---

45 How little] In *1519* and in *Froben* March *1520* 'Popes, how little,' thus making a direct address to the popes. 'Popes' was omitted in the February 1520 edition and in the later editions of 1522 and 1523.

[107] Again, in the twenty-third chapter of Matthew he openly attacked the pride and ambition of the scribes and Pharisees: making a display of themselves with their phylacteries broadened and their fringes extended, they strove to get the first seats at dinners and the first rows in the synagogues, and were delighted to be greeted in the market place with 'Rabbi' as a mark of honour [Matthew 23:5–7]. 'But you,' he says, 'Be not called Rabbi, for one is your master, and all you are brothers. And call none your father upon earth, for one is your father, who is in heaven. Nor be called masters, for one is your master, Christ. He that is the greater of you shall be your servant. Moreover, whoever will extol himself shall be humbled, and he that humbles himself shall be exalted' [23:8–12]. He makes the same point in the fourteenth chapter of Luke with the parable of the guests. Among these, the one who had chosen the last place is told to go up higher [Luke 14:7–11]. His invitation to the lowly to accept his soft and gentle yoke has the same import: 'Learn from me,' he says, 'For I am gentle and lowly in heart, and you will find rest for your souls' [Matthew 11:29]. Pride is a quality conducive to unrest, it strives for the position of honour, it is vengeful, and in never yielding to anyone it is never free from fighting. And yet no teaching is more effective than Christ's own life. For what puny little man would not be ashamed haughtily to extol himself, when he who is truly the highest girds himself with a towel and washes the feet of his disciples [John 13:3–12]? He is taken, he is beaten, he suffers insults and is lifted up on a cross as though he were a shameful criminal. Finally, by casting himself down to the farthest point he merited being raised to a position of highest honour [Philippians 2:5–11].

[108] Furthermore, many, many people are puffed up with the nobility of their race. This disease, though it is indeed common to all, nevertheless infected more especially the Jews, who were boasting incessantly of their father Abraham. [John the Baptist] says, 'Do not begin to say, "We are children of Abraham," for I say unto you that God is able from these stones to raise up children to Abraham.' And elsewhere [Jesus] calls all those 'children of Abraham' who resembled Abraham by their deeds, while he says that those who were boasting that they were children of Abraham were children of the devil – the parent they emulated by their wicked deeds [John 8:39–44]. Every kind of nobility among Christians must be judged by virtuous action, not by family trees. The person who is a slave to vices is the only one whose status is a matter of disgrace. Christ gives a centurion – a foreigner – precedence to Israelites [Matthew 8:5–13, Luke 7:2–10]. He prefers a Samaritan leper to Jews [Luke 17:11–19]. Again he prefers the Samaritan who cared for the wounded traveller to the priest and the Levite [Luke 10:29–37], who

used to despise the Samaritans as the vilest of people, while they themselves behaved as demigods.

[109] He banishes utterly the evil of rage, inviting us with so many parables to be clement and ready to forgive. So it is, in Matthew, the eighteenth chapter, with the parable of the slave who would not pardon a fellow slave, though he himself had experienced the mercy of their common master [18:23–5]. In that same chapter Jesus bids us correct the erring brother in private and without witnesses [18:15–17], and if a brother comes to his senses and repents seventy times seven times, he bids us forgive him as many times [18:21–2]. So also is it in the ninth chapter of Luke: as the Samaritans do not receive Christ, James and John say, 'Lord, do you want us to bid fire to come down from heaven to consume them?' [9:54]; but Christ at once summons them back from this fierce impulse to a disposition towards clemency, and sharply rebuking them, says, 'You do not know of what spirit you are. The Son of man came not to destroy souls but to save' [9:55–6].

[110] There is also another affection that lies in wait even for good men in the very midst of their good deeds, if they are not careful: trust in ourselves. Christ does not tolerate this disposition in his disciples. One who thinks he is godly is not godly enough. Christ scorns the Pharisee who was standing close by, proclaiming his merits; he acknowledges the publican who was standing far off, displeased with himself [Luke 18:9–14]. Likewise in Luke, the seventeenth chapter, he draws a picture for the sake of comparison, then explains that no thanks is owed to servants even if they have in every respect fulfilled their duty. He says, 'So you also, when you have done all that is commanded you, say, "We are unprofitable servants; we have done what we ought to do"' [Luke 17:10]. He makes the same point in the next [sic] chapter with the parable of the talents entrusted by a proprietor: the principal belongs to someone else, however small it is; whatever is acquired through our effort is acquired for the Lord, not for us [Luke 19:11–27]. Stewardship has been entrusted to us; woe betide us if we are remiss, but there is no reason to boast on our own account if we manage affairs dutifully. What we read in Matthew, the nineteenth chapter, has the same end in view. When a certain man asks him what good he had to do to have eternal life, he says, 'Why do you ask me concerning the good? One is good, God' [19:17]. Christ perceived the sickness of a man who was arrogating to himself the praise for his goodness, when all of our righteous acts are nothing else in the eyes of God than the rags of a woman that are soaked in her menstrual flow. Besides, in the same Gospel, the twenty-fifth chapter, he acknowledges only those who are themselves unaware of their own good deeds: 'Lord, when did we see you hungry

and fed you, thirsty and gave you drink? And when did we see you a stranger and took you in? Or naked and clothed you? Or when did we see you sick or in prison and came to you?' [25:37–9]. It is a most certain proof of true piety if, when you have with all your strength made every effort, you think yourself devoid of piety. The unjust are surprised if they have neglected some duty – so far are they from thinking themselves ungodly [25:41–4]. In Matthew, the seventh chapter, he acknowledges not even those who recall that they have even cast out demons through his name, that they have predicted the future, and have done many wonderful things [7:21–4]. He says, 'Truly I say to you, I do not know you.'

[111] The parable he puts before us in Luke, the twelfth chapter, invites the same conclusion, if I am not mistaken. Here, he warns us that no one, confident in his own justice, should appeal to a judge and risk the full rigour of the law, but ought rather to settle the quarrel with his adversary [12:57–8]. He makes the same point in the fifteenth chapter of John when he says, 'You have not chosen me, but I have chosen you, and appointed you that you should go and bring forth fruit' [15:16]. And a bit before in the same chapter he calls himself the vine, the disciples the branches [15:5]. If we bring forth any good fruit, everything must be credited to the stock; without the stock we are nothing but fuel for the fire [15:6]. Then in the next chapter the disciples are a little pleased with themselves when they say, 'Now we know that you know all things and do not need anyone to question you. By this we believe that you have proceeded from God' [John 16:30]. But how quickly does he thrust them back, and does not allow them to remain in that disposition: 'Now,' he says, 'you believe; behold the hour will come, and indeed has come, when you will desert me and scatter in all directions' [John 16:31–2]. Nor did he suffer Peter when with human self-confidence he was making magnificent promises in regard to himself: 'Even though all should be offended, I, at least, will not waver.' Jesus replied, 'Truly, I say to you that this night, before the cock crows twice, you will deny me thrice' [Mark 14:30]. Elsewhere, when the disciples were relating somewhat boastfully how successful they had been in their first attempt at preaching (for even the demons had been subject to them), he says, 'Truly I say to you, I saw Lucifer falling as lightning from heaven. Do not boast about the fact that the spirits are subject to you; boast rather that your names are written in heaven' [Luke 10:18, 20]. And it was not Peter alone who declared that he would be steadfast; his word was everyone's word. Nor was he alone in losing his self-confidence; the others also fled in terror [Matthew 26:35, 56, Mark 14:31, 50].

[112] This,[46] too, is generally ingrained in human nature, that everyone has a high opinion of himself, but a rather low opinion of others, a vice present in beginners and those who are only a little advanced, more than in the well-practised and the fully trained. Hence those who within a year have received the title and the profession of the seven liberal arts are proverbially reckoned among the 'wild beasts.' It was aptly and wisely said by someone that those who had gone off to Athens became, first, wise men, then philosophers (that is, those who are eager for wisdom), finally, ignorant and uneducated folk, because it was found that only when they had advanced as far as possible did they realize that they knew nothing.

[113] Accordingly, Paul, who had drunk deeply enough of the Spirit of Christ, everywhere with remarkable solicitude deters us from this disease that makes us not only untaught but unteachable. Everywhere he calls any virtue we have 'the gift of God' and 'grace,' and attributes it to Christ and to the Spirit of Christ. Thus, in the second chapter to the Ephesians he says, 'By grace are you saved through faith, and that not of yourselves, for it is the gift of God, not of works, that no one may boast' [2:8–9]. Again, in the tenth chapter of the Second Epistle to the Corinthians he says, 'He who boasts, let him boast in the Lord' [10:17]. What is meant by this expression, 'to boast in the Lord'? Surely that every virtuous act of ours be ascribed to the freely given kindness of Christ. But he speaks even more clearly in the third chapter of the same Epistle: 'And such confidence we have through Christ towards God. Not that we are sufficient to think anything of ourselves, as of ourselves, but our sufficiency is from God' [3:4–5].

[114] Moreover, in the ninth chapter of the Epistle to the Romans he shows that salvation comes to us only through the righteousness that is from faith. Furthermore, what he calls the 'righteousness from faith' is this: when we attribute absolutely nothing to our own deeds but acknowledge that whatever success we have as we try for the best with all our might is the result of his gift freely given. Elsewhere, he calls this the righteousness of God, to which he opposes the righteousness of human beings. He says, 'Wishing to establish their own righteousness, they have not submitted themselves to the righteousness of God' [Romans 10:3]. For he writes thus in the third chapter: '[...] even the justice of God by faith of Jesus Christ, unto all and upon all them that believe in him, for there is no distinction, for all have sinned and do

---

46 This ... upon the divine help.] This paragraph and the four immediately following it were added in *1520*. For discussion, see CWE 41 187 section 3.

need the glory of God. Being justified freely by his grace through the redemption that is in Christ Jesus, whom God hath proposed to be a propitiation, through faith in his blood, to the showing of his justice for the remission of former sins, through the forbearance of God, for the showing of his justice in this time, that he himself may be just and the justifier of him who is of the faith of Jesus Christ' [3:22–6]. What he writes in the fifth chapter agrees with this: 'For if by one man's offence, death reigned through one, much more they who receive abundance of grace and of the gift of righteousness shall reign in life' [5:17]. You see how everywhere he calls our righteousness 'grace' and 'gift.' But what has he added? – 'through one Jesus Christ' [5:17]. And yet in this whole Epistle does Paul aim at anything else than to take away the self-confidence of Jews and Gentiles alike, and to invite them to the help offered by Christ, placing no trust whatever in themselves? Our righteous deeds are nothing but a rag polluted with menstrual flow; our wisdom is folly [1 Corinthians 3:19]; our purity impure. But Christ is all these things to us: justice and peace and wisdom [1 Corinthians 1:30, Ephesians 2:14]. This he is as a result of the generosity of the Father, who first both freely loved us and freely bestowed upon us even this, that we should love him in return [1 John 4:7–12, 19, John 3:16].

[115] It is in line with this that Paul everywhere calls himself a slave of Jesus Christ. Whatever the slave does in the course of his duty is attributed to his master on whose order he acts. If he is remiss, he deserves punishment; if he completes the tasks assigned, no reward is owed him under contract, since he belongs wholly to his master. The same point is made when Paul designates the task he performs at one time a stewardship, at another a ministry. Trustworthy though your management may be, still, what you manage belongs to another; diligent though your administration may be, you administer the Lord's affairs. Indeed, writing to the Romans, he designates as 'grace' the very fact that he had been called to the apostolic ministry: 'By whom,' he says, 'we have received grace and apostleship' [1:5]; dealing with the Corinthians he calls it 'mercy': 'Concerning virgins,' he says, 'I have no commandment of the Lord, but I give counsel as having obtained mercy of the Lord to be faithful' [1 Corinthians 7:25].

[116] Therefore, Paul is eager entirely to root out of our souls this disposition, a disposition particularly harmful and destructive. Accordingly, in writing to the Romans he recalls the parable of the master, about the vine and the branches, with a comparison – the image of the olive tree and the wild olive grafted into it [Romans 11:17–24, recalling John 15:1–6]. It was of no benefit to the Jews to be the original branches; they were cut off because of their unbelief. It will be of no value whatever

to us to have been grafted into the olive tree and made partakers of its root if we practise the things for which we deserve to be cut off. He says, 'The branches were broken off that I might be grafted in. True; because of unbelief they were broken off. But you stand by faith; be not arrogant, but fear' [Romans 11:19–20]. And soon, 'I would not have you ignorant, brothers, of the mystery, lest you should be wise in your own conceits' [Romans 11:25]. What is this 'be wise in your own conceits'? Quite simply, 'trusting in yourselves.' Nor is there, in truth, a danger that if we should lay aside our confidence in our own strength, we might be more slack in our effort to reach the summit of virtue. Rather, since we are convinced that everything is possible with the assistance of God, and that no one lacks God's help except the one who refuses it, so much the more keenly will we enter upon this race-course, awaiting from him the beginning of the course, its progress, and a successful conclusion. No one trusts God more truly than one who entirely distrusts his own resources. No one has more strength than one who relies entirely upon the divine help.

[117] In addition to this, there is a strange power in the human sense of shame which often those cannot disregard who can disregard wealth and pleasures. Accordingly, Christ pronounces people blessed when others reproach them, bringing disgrace upon them with false slanders [Matthew 5:11]. He adds an example from his own experience: 'If,' says he, 'they have called the master of the house Beelzebub, how much more those of his household? The disciple is not above his master' [Matthew 10:25, 24]. And in Acts the apostles think it is to their honour that they were publicly beaten with whips, for God had thought them worthy to suffer dishonour for the name of Christ [Acts 5:40–1]. Elsewhere he promises a reciprocation of behaviour: 'Whoever will be ashamed of me before men, of him shall I also be ashamed before my Father, and the one who confesses me before men, I shall in turn acknowledge before the Father.' Paul does not boast about other things, only about the cross of our Lord Jesus Christ, though the world considers the cross to be the greatest disgrace [Galatians 6:14]. Paul also knows how to carry on the gospel through good report and bad, in such a way that if any glory came of it, he transferred the glory to Christ; if any ignominy, he considered it an honour to be slandered because of Christ.

[118] A final disposition would remain so deeply implanted in us by nature that it could seem unassailable, if all things were not possible with God [Matthew 19:26]. For who, through human resources, would make light of the fear of facing trial on a capital charge, disdain the cruelty of tyrants, the most savage punishments, lastly, death, too, and one that appears ignominious in human eyes? In respect to this also, Christ

bids his disciples to be without concern, enjoining them not to think of a speech by which they might defend themselves before tribunals; he would suggest what needed to be said, he would supply the eloquence which adversaries could not resist. Those are not to be feared who have power to kill the body, but are not able to kill the soul – and since this is safe, nothing of the whole person perishes, since he promised that not even a hair of our head would perish.

[119] What then is there that can either frighten or destroy those who are free from these dispositions? On the other hand, one who is subject to them cannot carry on the work of the gospel without flinching. A bishop sees what is good for the flock and wants to have regard for its welfare, but the affections immediately cry out, 'If you proceed in this direction revenues will immediately decrease, you will offend the prince, you will not get a cardinal's hat, you will be thought crazy.' No one, of course, should be deliberately angered, but if Christ's estate cannot otherwise be maintained, one must bear with a stout heart loss of possessions, dishonour to reputation, danger to life. The apostles nowhere provoke magistrates or princes, they do not cast in the teeth of the populace the disgraces of its former life. They only invite to Christ, to newness of life, to salvation, and they accommodate themselves to all, as far as permitted, to entice more people to Christ.

[120] But if we are so engulfed in the surge of human affairs that we cannot push on to where Christ and the soul's desire invite, we must nevertheless struggle in that direction with all our strength. Fortune has heaped wealth upon you. It may not be expedient to renounce it; hold it scornfully, and, to use the words of Paul, possess it as though you do not have it. Then you will feel less distress if some portion is docked, less fear if some loss looms overhead. You happen to have distinguished parents, to have found an outstanding woman as your wife: have them as though you do not have them, and possessing them will divert you less from piety. You have come into favour with a prince; do not on this score swell with pride, but rather turn this to use, as far as you can, in the interest of Christ. You are involved in the affairs of the court; free yourself to the best of your ability – meanwhile, however, culling from this evil any opportunity for benefit that presents itself.

[121] Meanwhile, always let Martha murmur against Mary, envious of her freedom from the daily cares [Luke 10:38–42]. Above all, let innocence be at hand; even bad men are ashamed to assail innocence. Let love be present, open and eager to do good to all. Let there be a gentle disposition, which either mitigates or endures the harshness of the ungodly. Let a guileless prudence be present, and a prudent candour, which avoids injury without inflicting injury on anyone. Let there be

present a most confident faith that does not doubt at all the promises of Christ. If those who follow in the place of apostles exhibited hearts and minds like this, then truly the church of Christ would deserve to be called the kingdom of heaven. At present, many are so far removed from this portrait that there are some who laugh at these things as worn out and useless, some who teach the direct opposite.

Finding a pattern for human life in the Gospels and Epistles, or how to 'philosophize' from Scripture

[122] Since, however, the goal of all of Christ's teaching is that we ourselves should live our lives in a godly and holy manner, it will be fitting to track down in the divine books the example and pattern for all the actions of our lives, searching chiefly, however, in the Gospels, from which our duties are especially derived. We must observe, therefore, how Christ himself conducted himself in different ways towards different people: towards his parents as a boy and as a grown-up (as a boy he obeys, when he teaches he gives them little esteem), towards his disciples, towards the proud Pharisees, towards those who question him insidiously, towards the ingenuous populace, towards the afflicted, among his own, among outsiders, among magistrates. We must observe also the ways in which everywhere he prepared and fortified his disciples by showing them how they ought to conduct themselves towards relatives and friends – he does not want these even to be greeted at the expense of preaching the gospel [Luke 10:4] – towards those who are well deserving and receive the grace of the gospel, towards those who reject it, towards persecutors, Jews, Gentiles, towards the weak or erring brother, or towards a brother who is beyond correction, towards ungodly judges, towards the flock entrusted to them, and the other things that we usually meet in the daily experience of life. I shall, if you like, mention some of these passages on account of the less well trained, so that they can more easily note the rest for themselves.

[123] There are two things especially that Christ constantly inculcates – faith and love. Faith ensures that we cease to trust ourselves and we place all our trust in God; love urges us to do good to all. First, in Matthew, the ninth chapter, he imputes to the paralytic the faith even of others: 'And Jesus seeing their faith' [9:2]. Shortly after, he does not help the blind men, who implore his mercy and help, until he has made a stipulation about faith: 'Do you believe,' he says, 'that I can do this for you?' [Matthew 9:28]. And when they replied that they believed, then at last he touched their eyes, saying, 'According to your faith be it done

to you' [Matthew 9:29]. Again, in the same chapter, he says to a woman
who has gained her health by touching his garment: 'Courage! daughter, your faith has made you whole' [9:22]. In the same Gospel, the fourteenth chapter, as the disciples were terrified and cried out for fear, he says, 'Take heart; it is I, fear not' [14:27], and almost immediately Peter, sustained by faith, following the example of his teacher, walks upon the waters. But when he loses confidence he sinks and hears, 'O man of little faith, why did you doubt?' [14:31]. And in the next chapter Jesus cries out (as though he had been compelled by the trust of the Canaanite woman to offer this kindness to a person to whom he did not wish to offer it): 'O woman, great is your faith! Be it done to you as you wish' [15:28].

[**124**] In Luke, the seventeenth chapter, he wants the leper to credit his health to faith: 'Rise,' he says, 'go your way, for your faith has made you whole' [17:19]. Again, in John, the fourth chapter, the faith of the ruler obtained salvation for his dying son. The Scripture says, 'The man believed the word that Jesus had spoken to him and went away' [4:50]. And already then, while he is returning home, his servants meet him and report his son's recovery. Once more in Matthew, in the sixteenth chapter, he scolds the disciples, who were concerned about bread, for their lack of faith [16:8–11]. In the same Gospel, the seventeenth chapter, the disciples wonder what prevented them from being able to heal the epileptic. He says to them, 'Because of your unbelief you were not able' [17:20]. And at once, showing them how great the power of faith is, he says, 'If you have faith as a grain of mustard seed, you will say to this mountain, move from here, and it will move, and nothing will be impossible to you' [17:20]. In the same Gospel, the twenty-first chapter, the disciples are astonished that the fig tree had withered as a result of Jesus' curse. He says to them, 'Truly, I say to you, if you have faith and do not doubt, you will not only do what has been done to the fig tree, but even if you say to this mountain: "Be taken up and cast yourself into the sea," it will be done. And whatever you ask in your prayers you will receive' [21:21–2]. Likewise in Mark, the tenth chapter, the blind man who was healed hears, 'Your faith has made you whole' [10:52]. In Luke, the eighth chapter, he says to the disciples who had come into danger because of the force of the storm, 'Where is your faith?' [8:25]. And soon in the same chapter the Lord Jesus says to the ruler of the synagogue, who was greatly troubled by the news of his daughter's death, 'Do not fear, only believe, and she shall be well' [8:50]. So great a thing is faith that any vice that corrupts the character of Christians usually arises from weakness in or want of faith.

[125] But on the matter of love, how does it help to specify? For what else does Christ teach, what else does he inculcate by his whole life except the most consummate love? This was the one thing he had come to teach us. For in Luke, the twelfth chapter, he says, 'I am come to cast fire on the earth, and what do I want except that it be kindled?' [12:49]. There[47] had to be some powerful reason why the Son of God came down to earth. He did not come down to take possession of the kingdom of the world, or to hand down to us a philosophy. He came, great envoy that he was, to set ablaze a huge conflagration of love, and for this reason he speaks of fire. Natural love is great, but it is ice in comparison with the love of Christ. Now, in John, that whole scene in the presence of his disciples – what he says, what he does as the time of his death is approaching – what else does it signify, what else does it manifest except a fiery love intensely burning? Who is so unfeeling that he reads those words without tears? This is that love stronger than death, which inflames the lover to the point where he despises death and effects what human aids cannot accomplish [Song of Solomon 8:6–7]. Love alone is the token by which he wanted his disciples to be distinguished from others when he said: 'By this all will know that you are my disciples, if you have love for one another' [John 13:35]. 'God,' says John, 'is love'; whoever falls away from love, falls away from God [1 John 4:16]. Accordingly, look what Matthew mentions in the twenty-fifth chapter when he explains and sets out in vivid array the deeds deserving of heaven. What are these? Wearing sordid clothes? fasting? choice of foods? mumbling a number of psalms? learning? miracles? None of these. What then? He says, 'You fed the hungry, you gave the thirsty drink, you received the stranger, you clothed the naked, you visited the sick, you sustained the prisoner with words of consolation' [25:35–6]. These are, precisely, the duties of love.

[126] Go through the whole New Testament: nowhere will you find any precept relating to ceremonies. Where is there a single word about food or clothes? Where is there any mention of abstaining from food or the like? Love alone he calls his commandment [John 15:12]. Discord arises from ceremonies, peace comes from love. In Matthew the Pharisees murmur against Christ because his disciples, constrained by hunger, were plucking the heads of grain – David, who did not scruple to eat the most holy bread, provides their precedent. Jesus says, 'But if you had known "I will have mercy and not sacrifice" [Hosea 6:6], you would never have condemned the innocent. For the son of man is Lord

---

47 There ... love of Christ.] Added in *1520*

even of the sabbath. The sabbath[48] was established for the sake of man, man was not created for the sake of the sabbath.' Now these were God's commandments, yet he does not want them to be observed whenever the ministry of love must be fulfilled. What, therefore, will obscure and insignificant men say when they demand that a person risk his whole life because of a prohibition against eating meats or because of petty regulations more inane than these?

[**127**] David,[49] in peril through hunger, dares to eat the sacred loaves though he himself was a secular man, nor does the priest feel any scruple in handing over the bread, though the law handed down by God had forbidden this [1 Samuel 21:1–6]. And do you permit, or rather, compel, an innocent brother to perish [Romans 14:15] because it is the good pleasure of men who are perhaps stupid or superstitious (at any rate invested with no public authority) to prohibit the eating of meat? Indeed, in these matters to what lengths does the tyranny of certain men go – tyranny more truly than superstition? At one time they allow meat broth, but forbid meat itself; certain ones, a little more indulgent, grant the intestines also. Occasionally they concede milk products, but keep us from eggs. Sometimes they permit nothing but bread and beer, and fruit from trees instead of meats. To be sure, I do not condemn anyone who undertakes such things through earnest piety. I do find it astonishing that a Christian wants to put a Christian's life in peril on account of the observance of things like this, that brotherly love is torn apart because of them.

[**128**] In John, the ninth chapter, a great commotion is raised because Christ had restored the sight of a blind man on the sabbath day [9:1–17]. In the same Gospel, the fifth chapter, they murmur at the cured paralytic, who had, at the bidding of Christ, taken up his pallet on the sabbath [5:1–12]. But in Matthew, the ninth chapter, they mutter to themselves because he forgave sins [9:1–7]. Elsewhere, because he had on the sabbath healed a bent and shrivelled woman, those murmur who did not scruple to rescue on the sabbath an ox or an ass that had fallen into the well [Luke 13:10–17]. Christ cries out that man was not created on account of the sabbath, but the sabbath was devised on account of man [Mark 2:27], and do you wish your laws to prevail so far that a Christian person must sooner perish than swerve from them a finger's breadth?

[**129**] Again, in Matthew, the fifteenth chapter, they murmur because the disciples took their food with unwashed hands [15:1–9]. But here

---

48 The sabbath ... sabbath.'] Added in *1522*
49 David ... because of them.] Paragraph added in *1522*

not only does the devout Lord excuse his disciples, but even turns the charge back against the critics: those were neglecting the commandment of God because of corban, which the avarice of the priests had devised. He calls it a commandment of God because it concerns a piety rooted in nature: to help parents is a matter of love. From this they were diverting people – with one concern, that something should accrue to the treasury. Christ cries out, 'Not that which goes into the mouth pollutes a man' [Matthew 15:11]. And do you require a Christian to eat fish at an enormous cost to his health? Rather, in comparison with you, you do not even regard as a Christian one who gives thanks to God when, under the constraint of his bodily disposition, he eats any kind of food on any day. The kindness that he calls 'alms' pleases Christ so much that in Luke, the sixteenth chapter, he praises the unjust steward, who, though cheating his master, came to the aid of debtors [16:1–9]. Is it not this same message that the apostles in their Epistles commend to us? And do we, almost deaf to all these things, burden with more than the Jewish regulations those who have been freed through the blood of Christ? Do we calumniate the innocent because of these regulations?

[130] But it is not part of this enterprise to pursue these things. As for what remains, I shall touch upon matters piecemeal as they arise, once[50] I have pointed out how the teaching and character of the apostles conform to this pattern, and above all, that of Paul, for no one resembled the preceptor Christ more than he. Would that those who have succeeded to the apostolic office and boast that they are called the vicars of Christ could deservedly apply to themselves the words with which Paul exhorts the Corinthians to true piety when he says, 'I ask you, be ye followers of me, as I also am of Christ' [1 Corinthians 4:16]. He repeats this in as many words in the eleventh chapter of the same Epistle [11:1]. It is therefore important to observe how there is not a page in Paul that does not abound in the frequent mention of faith and love, which he commends sometimes separately, sometimes jointly to his people. He brings the two together in the sixteenth chapter of the First Epistle to the Corinthians, concluding a lengthy exhortation with this 'epilogue' as it were: he says, 'Watch, stand fast in the faith, act manfully and be strong. Let everything you do be done in love' [16:13–14]. Again, in the

---

50 once ... with great disturbances.] This lengthy addition of *1520*, into which were inserted in 1522 only a few very short additions, concludes at **151/152**, whereupon the *1519* text broken off here after 'touch upon matters piecemeal as they arise' resumes with '[Meanwhile, this, too,] must be observed ...' (see n55). For discussion, see CWE 41 188 section 4.

first chapter of the Second Epistle to Timothy, he says, 'Hold the form of sound words which you have heard from me, in faith and in love in Christ Jesus' [1:13]. You see how he has joined faith and love, the two twin standard-bearers of all piety. And with these two terms he especially praises the Thessalonians in his Second Epistle to them: 'Because,' says he, 'your faith grows exceedingly and love abounds' [1:3]. He connects them in the First Epistle also – 'and reported to us your faith and love' [3:6].

[**131**] Likewise, in the Epistle to the Romans, the fifteenth chapter: 'Now the God of hope fill you with all joy and peace in believing, that you may abound in hope' [15:13]. Has he not joined together three heroines – faith, hope, and love [1 Corinthians 13:13]? For[51] what else is peace but mutual love? Now there is nothing in the Romans he praises sooner than their faith, and he thinks their most glorious renown was due to their faith; he says: 'Your faith is spoken of in the whole world' [1:8]. Indeed, on the strength of Habakkuk's testimony, he so fully credits to faith the essence of righteousness that he will not have the fact that Abraham pleased God, great man that he was, imputed to anything else than faith [Romans 1:17, Habbakuk 2:4]. And he confirms this view by the witness of Genesis: 'Abraham believed God and it was imputed to him for righteousness' [Romans 4:3, Genesis 15:6]. In the ninth chapter also, he ascribes to faith the fact that the Gentiles, though formerly idolaters, were admitted to true godliness; that the Jews, on the other hand, were rejected, a people who had persuaded themselves that they alone were close to God – the responsibility for this, he judges, lies precisely in the fact that the Jews did not trust the evangelical promises [Romans 9:30–2]. Lives stained with so many disgraceful and criminal deeds beyond the worship of idols did not stand in the way of the Gentiles; the solicitous observance of laws and the worship of the eternal deity did not help the Jews. Why? 'Because,' says he, 'not by faith, but as though from works' [9:32]. Moreover, he concludes that whole disputation, in which faith plays the leading role, with the final sentence, 'For all that is not of faith is sin' [14:23]. So great is the power of faith that virtue, destitute of faith, turns into vice.

[**132**] In addition, in the Second Epistle to the Corinthians, he shows that faith is the vehicle by which the whole course of life is borne to the eternal. He says, 'We walk by faith and not by sight' [5:7]. The only goal Paul had set before himself in performing his apostolic service was to bring all races under the yoke of faith. He calls this faith 'obedience' (or,

---

51 For ... love?] Added in *1522*

in the Greek, as he himself wrote, *hypakoe*), pointing out as he goes along that Christian faith is firm and solid only if inquisitive and subtle lines of reasoning have been thrust aside, and it trusts with simplicity and without critical investigation the promises of Christ. 'Through whom,' he says, 'we have received grace and apostleship for obedience to the faith in all nations' [Romans 1:5]. Moreover, writing to the Ephesians, he wants salvation to be credited to faith alone: 'By grace, he says, 'you are saved through faith, and that not of yourselves' [2:8]. Further, in the Epistle addressed to the Hebrews, with what elevated style, with what richness of language does he adorn the encomium of faith, justly attributing to the merit of faith almost all the mighty deeds of the ancient heroes [11].

[133] What now is the point of bringing forward some passages concerning love, when all of Paul everywhere breathes, resounds, thunders with nothing but the most ardent love? His words are pure fire, and yet you might think when you read him that you feel something still more ardent that the stammering of human speech is not able to express. Paul's tongue is fiery, but it suggests rather than exhibits the burning in his breast. Further, since love cements everything together, there is no place for discord wherever love holds sway: love makes all things common to all, so far as it lies within its power to do so. Therefore, with this, like a most auspicious omen, Paul begins all his Epistles invoking upon his people grace and peace in place of some outstanding good. It is with these same words that Peter, head of the apostolic senate, offers greetings: 'Grace to you and peace' [1 Peter 1:2, 2 Peter 1:2].

[134] Quite often the concluding statements correspond to the introductions. For Paul, as though he is about to finish the Epistle to the Romans, says, 'The God of peace be with you all. Amen' [15:33]. When he bids them greet one another with a holy kiss, what else does he commend than fraternal concord – for I interpret the Christian kiss to be of the heart, not of the mouth. It is a common practice to greet by touching cheeks; to wish well for everyone, with hearts united, is a kiss truly worthy of a Christian person. What? Does he not conclude the second Epistle to the Corinthians in the same way? 'Be of one mind,' he says, 'have peace' [13:11]. But what is 'be of one mind' except 'agree together'? Repeating the idea to implant it more deeply in our minds, he says, *eireneuete* 'have peace.' Not satisfied with even these expressions, he adds a reward that is by no means common or trivial: 'And the God of peace will be with you' [13:11]. Long ago, he was called God of powers, the 'God of armies.' For us he is called 'God of peace.' Such is the God Isaiah had seen when he calls him 'Prince of Peace' [Isaiah 9:6]. Further, Paul adds, as though concord were never sufficiently commended, 'The

grace of our Lord Jesus Christ and the love of God and the fellowship of the Holy Spirit be with you all, Amen' [2 Corinthians 13:14]. This might be attributed to chance, except that he concludes the First Epistle to the Corinthians in the same way: 'My love be with you all in Christ Jesus, Amen' [16:24]. It is some rare love he requests for the Corinthians, when for them it is his own love that he requests.

[135] Do you wish to hear how Paul loved Christ? 'I desire,' he says, 'to be released and to be with Christ' [Philippians 1:23]. What is sweeter or dearer than life? But he desires to be united with Christ at the cost of his life! Does he not seem to you to be beside himself from some sacred impulse of love when, in writing to the Romans, the eighth chapter, he bursts forth into these words, 'Who will separate us from the love of Christ?' [8:35]? He says that this love can be destroyed neither by death nor angelic forces [8:38–9]. Again, he sufficiently shows what affection he had for the godly when he desires to become anathema from Christ for the sake of the Jews who were stubbornly crying out against Christ [9:3].

[136] Does the Epistle to the Galatians have a different conclusion? When he wants to promise some great and wonderful reward to those who have not departed from the rule of evangelical doctrine, he prays for nothing else than peace: 'Whoever,' he says, 'shall follow this rule, peace be upon them' [6:16]. He prays similarly for the Colossians. He says, 'And the peace of God which surpasses all understanding keep your hearts and minds in Christ Jesus' [Philippians 4:7], and soon, 'These do, and the God of peace shall be with you' [Philippians 4:9].

[137] What, moreover, would we find if we extracted from the middle of Paul's Epistles passages that commend to us peace and concord? In the second chapter of the Epistle to the Ephesians he calls Christ himself peace. He says, 'He is our peace who has made both one' [2:14]. Elsewhere also he calls Christ the *mesites* 'mediator,' because as one who reconciles he comes midway between God and man. Likewise John, in his Epistle, calls God himself love – love is so united to God that whoever possesses one of these feels the presence of the other, whoever lacks one of these feels the absence of the other [1 John 4:16]. Again, in Ephesians, the fifth chapter, Paul makes love so proper to God that he thinks genuine and true sons of God are recognized by this native quality. 'Be imitators of God,' he says, 'as very dear children, and walk in love as Christ also has loved us' [5:1–2]. But see how much he attributes to love in the first chapter of the first Epistle to Timothy. He calls love the perfect completion of the entire Law: 'Now the end of the commandment is love from a pure heart, and from a good conscience, and from unfeigned faith' [1 Timothy 1:5]. Clearly, he is in harmony with the word of his teacher, who states that the essence of the Law lies in love of God and neighbour [Matthew 22:35–40].

[138] Again, in the fifth chapter of the Epistle to the Romans, he ascribes to love the solid strength of the Christian heart that is so far from yielding to the storms of evils that it even boasts in the afflictions it bears for Christ. 'Because,' he says, 'the love of God is poured forth in our hearts by the Holy Spirit who is given to us' [5:5]. Moreover, in the eighth chapter to the same he attributes to love so much that by its help everything is turned into good. He says, 'To those who love God everything works together for good' [8:28]. Where love grows cold, no laws, however many, suffice; where love is fervent, there is no need of law. Love and do what you will, for genuine love does not sin; it is its own law and everywhere prescribes what is best to do. Accordingly, with what a thundering voice does he declare the praises of love in the thirteenth and also in the fourteenth chapter of the first Epistle to the Corinthians! He calls this a most excellent way that makes people truly great in the work of Christ [7:20–3]. He prefers this to the other gifts: love is exceedingly beneficial, it is everywhere useful, it alone does not fail, it alone does not sin, without it the other virtues are defective and useless. Again, in the seventh chapter of the First Epistle to the Corinthians he so promotes concord that he does not want even mixed marriages broken up [7:12–16], and at another point not even a baptized slave parted from an ungodly master [7:20–3], thus judging that the essence of our calling is concord, not discord: 'God has called you,' he says, 'in peace' [7:15].

[139] In how many ways, therefore, does Paul inculcate this virtue! With what deep concern he deters from the things that break up concord and give rise to discord! However, no crop is so productive that these weeds are not intermingled there. God himself was the occasion of discord to the Jews; in refusing to share him with others, they ceased to have him by themselves. Paul frets at this in the third chapter of the Epistle to the Romans: 'Is God the God of the Jews only, or is he not also the God of the Gentiles?' [3:29]. But we must be on our guard that we do not experience what the Jews experienced then. There are so many differences among those who profess religion, and individually they each claim emulously for themselves the high merit of religion, just as though God acknowledges them alone and disregards the people. 'Our religion,' says Ambrose, 'is peace.' Where you see discord ruling, understand that religion is either absent or at least in trouble. It is for them to see what agreement there is among them. And[52] yet not even the common folk are now ignorant of this.

---

52 And ... of this.] Added in *1522*

[**140**] Again, contention must be avoided not only in life but also in sacred studies. Now, arrogance is the source of all discord, as long as each person attributes the utmost to himself, the least to the other, while no one gives in to the other. It is for this that the apostle so often scolds the Corinthians. He says, 'I beseech you, brethren, by the name of our Lord Jesus Christ, that you all speak the same thing and that there be no divisions among you, but that you be perfect in the same mind and in the same judgment' [1 Corinthians 1:10], and the rest that follows. And soon in the third chapter: 'For whereas there is envying and contention are you not carnal, and walk according to man?' [3:3]. Again, in the eleventh chapter, he reproves them because they were not celebrating even the Lord's supper in harmony, a supper that was the symbol of utmost harmony. He says, 'I hear that when you come together in church there are divisions among you, and in part I believe it' [11:18]. In the next chapter he chides them because they had found the occasion for dissension even in the very gifts of the sacred Spirit. Accordingly he at once calls them back to concord, using as an example the body and its members, and he appropriates everything as arguments for peace: that one God is common to all, that one Christ died equally for all, the one Spirit imparts his gifts to each as it wills, the one baptism through which we are all grafted into the body of Christ, the one bread that we all eat, the one cup in which we all equally share. For he speaks thus in the tenth chapter: 'For we being many are one bread, one body, who all partake of one bread and one cup' [10:17]. Likewise in the twelfth chapter: 'But all these things one and the same Spirit works, dividing to everyone according as it will. For as the body is one and has many members, and all the members of the body, though they are many, yet are one body, so also is Christ. For in the one Spirit were we all baptized into one body, whether Jews or Gentiles, whether bond or free, and we all have been called in one Spirit' [12:11–13].

[**141**] Moreover, writing to the Galatians, he so emphatically wants these nurseries of discord to be destroyed by baptism that he calls anyone initiated into Christ a new creation [6:15]. Further, in the sixteenth chapter of the Epistle to the Romans he asks that the originators of divisions also be avoided: 'Now I beseech you, brethren, to mark those who make dissensions and offences, contrary to the doctrine which you have learned, and to avoid them' [16:17]; and pointing out at once the source of this evil, he adds, 'For they that are such serve not Christ our Lord, but their own belly' [16:18].

[**142**] We have seen even in our day extraordinary turmoil among Christians. I have found that it has been stirred up precisely by those whose quest for gain the purer teaching of Christ seemed to obstruct.

You might have said that they would sooner overturn everything than refrain from innards once tasted. So tenaciously do they hold the wealth that is collected from absolutions shamelessly proclaimed, from arrangements, from dispensations, from empty promises many offer for sale under the pontifical name, from the application of merits, from consciences wrongly ensnared, from a false view of religion, from the delusion of helpless little women and the poor, ignorant populace. Ambition led many to raise this commotion: they grant so much to their own glory that they would rather Christ's doctrine be abolished than that they themselves appear to have been ignorant of anything. Many were infected by a two-fold disease: greed and ambition. I[53] do not, for the present, discuss how far the authority of the church or of the Roman pontiff prevails in matters of this sort. I only point out the sources of discord, sources that quite clearly arise from nowhere but our own desires.

[143] Paul, therefore, perceiving how great a plague discord is, inculcates and reiterates nothing sooner, more frequently, more passionately, than concord, peace, mutual love – not only with those who share our religion (which love [Paul] calls *philadelphia* 'brotherly love'), but also with those who were strangers to our mysteries. For thus he admonishes the Thessalonians in the fifth chapter of the First Epistle: 'See that none render evil for evil to anyone, but always follow that which is good towards each other and towards all' [5:15]. One has something more than concord with all when one is eager to do good to all.

[144] Again, in the twelfth chapter to the Romans: 'If it is possible, as much as it lies in you, have peace with all men. Do not avenge yourselves, dearly beloved, but give place to wrath' [12:18–19]. In passing, he intimates that concord cannot exist among people of a fierce and headstrong nature, where injury is immediately returned for injury, where no one ever gives up his own right in any respect, no one wishes to overcome a bad deed with a good deed [12:16–21]. For if this window is once opened to our hasty tempers, that we may justly avenge an intolerable injury, everyone who has been angered will think his case just, everyone will be deluded by his own mind. Accordingly, to keep us further from this pitfall, Christ and his imitator, Paul, exhort us to repay injury with a kindness. He says, 'Bless those that persecute you; bless and curse not' [Romans 12:14]; and soon, 'If your enemy is hungry, give him to eat, and if he is thirsty, give him drink; for doing this you will heap coals of fire upon his head. Do not be overcome by evil, but overcome evil with good' [12:20–1]. And where, meanwhile, are those who,

---

53 I ... desires.] Added in *1522*

though they wish to be regarded as the overseers of the Christian religion, stab a good man – and one who has benefited them – with tongues whose points have been daubed with deadly poison? They do it with persistent determination, with deliberate design, with devoted commitment, under the pretext of piety, which is the most wicked grounds for doing harm.

[145] In his own person Paul exhibited what he taught. For in the fourth chapter of the First Epistle to the Corinthians he says, 'We are reviled and we bless, we are persecuted and we suffer it, we are blasphemed and we entreat' [4:12–13] – clearly imitating him who on the cross itself prayed to the Father on behalf of those responsible for the cross [Luke 13:34]. How great, in fact, is Paul's displeasure when he reproves the Corinthians, because they were taking each other to court over financial matters, and did not accept injury and loss of property rather than loss of peace and concord [1 Corinthians 6:1–11]! But since, according to the comic poet, 'compliance wins friends, truth earns hatred,' Paul becomes all things to all people, taking on the character of a sort of polypus, if I may say so. He rejoices with those who rejoice, weeps with those who weep, he is pained along with those who have suffered offence, he is weak with the weak [Romans 12:15, 2 Corinthians 11:29]. For there is also a compliance appropriate to piety that everywhere accommodates itself to either the weakness or the opinion of another.

[146] I judge it superfluous to adduce testimonies from the Epistle of John, since he speaks of nothing but love and concord. Let us hear Peter, prince of our profession according to Christ [Matthew 16:13–19]. In the fourth chapter of the First Epistle, when he urges the principal obligations of piety – sobriety, vigilance, and prayers – he puts love before all of these. 'Be sober and watchful in prayers,' he says, 'but above all have mutual love among yourselves, and that constantly,' or as the Greek word seems to mean, 'with fervour' [4:7–8]. To commend this to us even more he says, 'Love will cover a multitude of sins' [4:8]. Meanwhile, how beautifully does Peter correspond to his teacher, from whom he specifically had heard, 'Follow me' [John 21:19]. His teacher says, 'Forgive and you will be forgiven' [Luke 6:37], and 'Many sins are forgiven her, because she loved much' [Luke 7:47], and 'Forgive us as we also forgive' [Matthew 6:12]. Why today are those who are weighed down by the burden of their sins summoned to pardons, arrangements for restitution, and similar remedies rather than to that which was set forth by Christ, by the chief apostles? Why do we prefer the doubtful to the certain? If anyone will compare the beginnings of the nascent church with these remedies, one will find only the auspicious signs of love. All alike with one heart and mind sit together in the same place;

they are equipped with tongues of fire [Acts 2:1–5]. The multitude of believers had one heart and one soul [4:32]. The resources of all are brought together for the common use [2:44–5, 4:34–5]. There is no mention anywhere of ceremonies.

[147] Now just as a resolute mind and true godliness are the companions of faith and love, so, when the latter languish or are absent, superstition thrives. And just as unalloyed godliness rests upon purity of mind, so superstition commends itself by ceremonies. Paul frequently designates the former by the word 'spirit,' the latter by the word 'flesh.' This, I think, is what he has in mind when he writes to the Galatians: 'Are you so foolish that when you began with the spirit, you are ending with the flesh?' [3:3]. Having begun from evangelical faith and love, are you sliding back into Judaism? In the twelfth chapter to the Romans he urges the same thing, albeit in a different way, that having abandoned Jewish rites, they should turn to the pursuit of a piety that lies within the mind: 'I beseech you, therefore, brethren, by the mercy of God, that you present your bodies a living sacrifice, holy, pleasing to God, your rational service' [12:1]. That he himself had done so he affirms when he writes in the first chapter to the Romans in this way: 'Whom I serve in my spirit in the gospel of his Son' [1:9]. While he still lived in the manner of a Jew, he worshipped God, but with appointed fasts, with new moons, sabbaths, washings, choice of foods. Now, having embraced another kind of worship, he worships the Father neither in the mountain nor in Jerusalem, for the Father delights in those worshippers who worship in spirit. Again, in the seventh chapter: 'That we should serve in newness of spirit, and not in the oldness of the letter' [7:6]. What he elsewhere calls the 'flesh' he here calls the 'letter.' He makes the same point in the fourth chapter of the First Epistle to Timothy, saying, 'Bodily exercise is profitable to some extent, but godliness is efficacious for all things' [4:8]. Why does he say 'to some extent'? Because it is advantageous to one, but not to another; it is fitting at one point but not at another; it is extolled today but will soon come into disfavour. The godliness that is of the mind is common to all and has a place everywhere.

[148] In addition, who does not know that nothing is more deadly than a counterfeit holiness? But there is no mask through which this more deceives than that of ceremonies. The common people especially are guided by what they see. Do you wish to hear with what great destruction the pretence of piety assails piety? Let us hear Paul as he speaks so prophetically in the third chapter of the Second Epistle to Timothy. 'But know this, that in the last days dangerous times shall come, and men will be lovers of themselves, covetous, haughty, proud, blasphemers, disobedient to parents, ungrateful, wicked, without affection, without

peace, slanderers, profligate, unmerciful, without kindness, traitors, stubborn, puffed up, lovers of pleasures more than of God, having an appearance indeed of godliness, but denying the power thereof' [3:1–5]. What does Paul add? 'Imitate these'? Certainly not, but, 'Avoid these; for of this sort are those who creep into houses and lead captive silly women laden with sins, who are led on by various desires' [3:5–6]. I ask you, reader, do you not think that Paul is pointing his finger directly at certain members from their orders who, though they are involved in the very heart and soul of worldly affairs, call themselves monks and make indigence a pretext as they strive for the luxury, the glory, and the tyranny of kings? And would that they were so few that the odium felt for such monks did not weigh down heavily upon the good ones! As it is, there are so many that the good ones are overwhelmed by the multitude of the evil ones and by their despotic power.

[149] Hear what Paul thinks about the feast days of the Jews, about the distinction of foods (for the sake of these things the Jews, though readily inclined to other crimes, would refuse not even death): 'One who regards the day, regards it unto the Lord, and one who does not eat, does not eat unto the Lord. Let everyone be fully persuaded in his own understanding' [Romans 14:6, 5]. Then soon, in the same chapter, 'The kingdom of God is not meat and drink, but righteousness and peace and joy in the Holy Spirit' [14:17]. What he writes to the Corinthians in the tenth chapter of the First Epistle accords with these statements: 'Whatever is sold in the marketplace eat, asking no question for conscience sake. The earth is the Lord's and the fullness thereof' [10:25–6]. Again, in the sixth chapter, 'Meat for the belly and the belly for the meats, but God will destroy both it and them' [6:13]. Moreover, with what strong feeling does he, in the second chapter to the Colossians, scorn the teachings of those who prescribe thus: '"Do not handle, do not taste, do not touch." All these things perish as they are used, and belong to human precepts and doctrines. In name, indeed, they have the appearance of wisdom, through scrupulous observance and abasement of mind and injury to the body, not through any assistance they offer in satisfying the needs of the body' [2:21–3].

[150] Paul, indeed, everywhere concerned for concord, advises that the strength of the perfect should bear the weakness of others [Romans 15:1] – but for a time, and on the principle that the weak progress and cease to be weak, and with respect to those things that have been too deeply implanted as a result of the former life to be able to be suddenly uprooted. Paul is indignant towards one who eats food that wounds the soul of a brother, a brother for whom Christ died [Romans 14:15]. But he is also indignant towards one who assesses the conscience of another

on the basis of such matters. 'Why,' he says, 'is my liberty judged by the conscience of another?' [1 Corinthians 10:29]. Occasionally there are times when a knowledgeable love adapts itself to another's weakness, but it does so in the manner of a teacher who comes down to the level of his pupil, in the manner of a physician who accommodates himself to the feelings of the sick. On the other hand, what sort of thing is it when we ourselves create the stumbling-blocks? When we find grounds for pride in them? When we think we are better simply because we are the weaker? Because we gratuitously attack those from whom we ought to have learned and voluntarily precede those whom we should have followed?

[151] 'What then?' someone will say, 'do you condemn ceremonies?' Far from it! I praise the rituals with which the church choir both long ago and today goes through its mysteries. These rituals bring something before us and add majesty to the divine worship, though even in these there should be due measure. But what I do not approve is this, that almost the whole life of Christians is, through human regulations, weighed down with ceremonies, that too much is attributed to these, too little to godliness; that simple souls, relying on ceremonies, neglect the pursuit of true religion; because of these the tranquillity of the Christian body is torn to pieces with great disturbances. For[54] about fifteen years now we have seen great turmoil in public affairs, schisms, wars, pillaging. If anyone asks for the sources, he will find that this entire evil takes its origin from ceremonies.

[152] Meanwhile, this, too,[55] must be observed, that Christ almost everywhere has compassion on the guileless crowd. It is against only the Pharisees, the scribes, and the rich that he thunders his fearful 'Woe unto you,' clearly suggesting that the piety of the people, whether it flourishes or flags, lies in the hands of bishops, theologians, and princes. From these every evil arises. He has compassion on the people, who, while the Pharisees are cultivating their own interests, wander destitute, like a flock of sheep abandoned by its shepherd, and scattered. It is thought that Christ fasted in the Jewish manner; the evidence for this view is that it is not he but his disciples who are blamed on this account, as you read in Matthew the ninth chapter [9:14–15]. This signifies that

---

54 For ... from ceremonies.] The remainder of this paragraph was added in *1523*. With the previous sentence the *1520* insertion beginning at **130** (see n50) is concluded, and the *1519* text is resumed in the next paragraph (see n55).
55 Meanwhile, this, too] Added in *1522*; previously, 'it' implied in the verb. The text of 1519, interrupted in 1520, continues here.

those who fill the role of pastor or of prince must avoid any occasion for false accusation. We read of Christ venting his rage only twice: against the chief men, in the twenty-third chapter of Matthew [23:1–36], and against the merchants in the temple, in the twenty-first chapter of the same Gospel [21:12–13]. In such actions Christ attested that the universal plague of the church would arise from these sources. He reveals that none is more receptive of evangelical teaching than the simple, the gentle, the humble; everywhere he embraces little ones, and proclaims that the kingdom of heaven belongs to them.

[153] By his own example, Christ shows that no one's counsel is to be accepted if it diverts one from piety. For he calls Peter 'Satan' – the Peter who just a little before had been warmly praised [Matthew 16:17–19] – and he orders this counsellor, who wished to lead the way, to follow by imitating his death, as you read in the sixteenth chapter of Matthew [16:24]. Christ indicates that certain things are to be done even beyond obligation so that public order should not be upset, for in the seventeenth chapter he bids the drachma to be paid, though he had affirmed that the sons of the kingdom are free [17:24–7]. In the twenty-first chapter of the same evangelist he teaches that nothing is more incurable than impiety masquerading in the form of piety. He says, 'Truly I say to you that the tax-collectors and the harlots go into the kingdom of God before you' [21:31]. The Pharisees, swollen with pride in the false appearance of holiness, everywhere cry out against the teaching of Christ. The tax-collectors and the harlots, acknowledging their disease, hasten to the physician. And in the very same passage he sets forth the parable of the two sons of whom the one is praised who fulfilled in fact what he had in words refused to do [Matthew 21:28–32]. With this parable Christ shows that true godliness lies in deeds, not in words, in internal disposition, not external appearance, in obedience, not ceremonies.

[154] In the twenty-third chapter of the same Gospel Christ advises that bishops and those who discharge the duties of legitimate office must be obeyed even if they are not entirely worthy, provided their instructions are right and good: 'The scribes and Pharisees have sat upon the seat of Moses etc' [Matthew 23:2]. Sometimes we must heed one who teaches the gospel even though he does not live in the gospel way. But in the same passage he censures the scribes and Pharisees because they weighed the people down with human regulations – which[56] were so far from contributing anything to true piety that sometimes on occasion they diverted one from it – and he implies that such authority figures

---

56 which ... from it] Added in *1522*

are to be disregarded in cases of this kind [23:3–4]. For elsewhere, too, he defends the apostles against the Pharisees, who were blaming them because they took their food with unwashed hands [Matthew 15:1–20].

[**155**] He shows that one must not rashly or suddenly rush into the ministry of preaching the gospel, for he himself had first received approval from so many witnesses: the witness of John, of the dove, of the Father. He withdrew after his baptism, fasted, was tempted, overcame, and then only when he had been on all sides tested and prepared did he teach; nor did he immediately set out the sum and substance of his teaching, but began from the preaching of John, calling people to come to their senses and repent of their former life. For no one desires the help of a physician unless he is dissatisfied with the state of his health.

[**156**] But with regard to the fact that Christ of his own accord calls certain people, like James, Andrew, Peter, and Matthew, while he rejects certain others who wanted to follow him – by this he wanted us to be warned that not just anyone should be received into the fellowship of our religion, but only those who draw near with an honest and guileless intent. A person's intent was, of course, crystal clear to him certainly to whom all things lay open; we, on the other hand, must search for it by conjectural inference.

[**157**] While Christ preached to all, he never enticed anyone to join him through flattery or human promises, nor did he compel anyone by force, though he was omnipotent. It was with kindnesses that he drew people; it was by the example of his life that he drew them, as did the apostles. Accordingly, one must consider whether those have the right sentiment who are eager to make the Turks Christians by the engines of war only. Rather let the voice of the theologians sound mightily among them, like the voice of the apostles; let a radiant integrity of life shine forth. Thus they become truly Christian.

[**158**] In Matthew, the eighth chapter, the Gerasenes, having looked upon the miracles of Jesus, ask him to depart from their borders, because he was useless for the things they desired [8:28–34]. So in our day there are many who prefer that evangelical teaching remain silent, as it opposes the pattern of their own lives.

[**159**] While still an infant, Christ flees to Egypt [Matthew 2:13–15], though as a man he offers himself of his own accord to the band of soldiers [John 18:3–11], indicating that there is a time to flee and to steal away, when it seems the imminent peril will not further the glory of Christ.

[**160**] With a most gentle mind he put up with his own apostles, for so long unformed and unbelieving, until they should gradually progress.

Thus priests ought to bear with the greatest mildness the feeble populace, until it advances bit by bit to better things.

[161] He also presented himself as affable and companionable, and open to all, avoiding the dinner parties not even of tax-collectors and sinners, but everywhere doing the work of the gospel. Likewise, it is appropriate for the bishops or their vicars to accommodate themselves to all, doing so in such a way, however, that they themselves do not come out the richer but make their people better. The prince has summoned you to the palace to be confessor or preacher. Do not occupy this position in order to carry off a bishopric, but so that the sins of the court may be fewer, and[57] you may relieve the oppressed when the opportunity arises.

[162] He attests in the thirteenth chapter of Matthew that close connections thwart those who have charge of the gospel: among his own people he performs fewer miracles because of unbelief. They say, 'Is not this the carpenter's son? Is not his mother called Mary, and his brothers James and Joseph and Simon and Judas? And his sisters, are they not all with us? Whence, therefore, does he have all these things?' [13:55–6]. Elsewhere his relatives are ready to lock him away, saying, 'He is beside himself' – as we read in the third chapter of Mark [3:21]. Accordingly, one who wishes to use his powers to help the many will have greater success abroad than at home.

[163] He everywhere defends the disciples, who had no answer to give on their own behalf, against the accusations of the Pharisees, as in Matthew, the twelfth chapter, when they pluck the ears of grain on the sabbath [12:1–8]; again, in the fifteenth chapter, when they take food with unwashed hands [15:1–9]; once more, elsewhere, when they do not fast as the disciples of John did [9:14–15].

[164] He teaches in various places that you must not strive to be praised by just anyone, but only by the good, and by those who praise only honourable things. For in the first chapter of Mark, when a demon cries out in the temple, Jesus replies to it: 'Be silent, and come out of him' [1:25]. In the same Gospel, the third chapter, when the spirits cry out, 'You are the Son of God,' he forbids them, with threats added, to reveal himself [3:11–12].

[165] He admonished Judas; he did not cast him out, nor did he even withdraw from the customary kiss, nor did he betray the man by whom he was to be betrayed – so highly did he value friendship and the intimacy of household companionship. In this he shows that a friendship

---

57 and ... arises.] Added in *1523*

once formed must not be rashly abandoned. Thus Martin also once endured his Brice.

[166] Peter comes to his senses and repents after his denial, when Christ fastens his eyes upon him [Luke 22:54–62]; Judas, moved by penitence for his deed, went off and hanged himself with a noose [Matthew 27:3–5]. This reveals two kinds of repentance: one that bears fruit and one that does not. Happy, then, is the sinner upon whom Christ looks when he has lapsed; unhappy is the one who turns away from Christ so that he cannot be seen. It is of some value to follow the Saviour even at a distance.

[167] By his own life the Lord shows us what we must do if at some time the ultimate storm of troubles rushes upon us, or the necessity of death, which awaits everyone. As death approaches he withdraws, watches, prays earnestly, prostrate on the ground, and as though his own defences had deserted him, he depends wholly on the aid of the Father. The martyr who measures his own strength will be no match for his ordeal!

[168] Christ rarely performed miracles that had no value beyond the astonishment they caused – the sort they now generally devise for saints. He healed, he fed, he freed from perils, all of which are acts of kindness. Accordingly, one who wishes to appear great in the church should reveal his greatness by deeds of this sort, deeds that help, not those that attest one's own power – with harm to the people.

[169] He shows in the parable of the sower that one must never be remiss in sacred teaching, even though not everyone profits from it. We must always sow;[58] it is enough if some seeds spring up. Although Christ with his disciples accepted certain things from friends who were offering them of their own accord, yet we do not read that he demanded or took anything except for the immediate needs of life [Mark 15:40–1]. Thus, those who preside over the Christian flock should teach without charge. People will be at hand to supply of their own accord what is needed, provided teachers act properly and seek nothing more than nature requires.

[170] The apostles show that we should take nothing from those who spurn salutary admonition, so that we do not appear to countenance their sins. For the apostles, following the instruction of the Lord, even shake off the dust from their feet against those who do not receive the gospel. Those who administer the sacraments of the church or who preach the doctrine of Christ must not be immediately forbidden to do

---

58 We must always sow] Added in *1520*

so even if their life does not adequately correspond. The Lord implies this in the ninth chapter of Mark, when he does not allow one who had performed miracles in the name of Christ to be forbidden, though he did not follow him [9:38–40].

[171] Jesus teaches that a good pastor sometimes withdraws and retires for complete peace and quiet so that he will have more freedom for prayer and for holy reading, and, restored by these things, will return to his episcopal duties with more vigour. Jesus shows this in the sixth chapter of Mark, taking his disciples to a lonely place to rest for a little while [6:31]. He shows in many places the sort of retreat appropriate to bishops, as he himself withdrew not for pleasures or for hunting expeditions but for prayer, for more intimate discussions with his disciples. Such were long ago the retreats of leading men, which, because of their solitude, they called monasteries.

[172] Christ cursed only the fig tree, which deceived him, as it were, with its leaves when he was hungry [Matthew 21:18–22, Mark 11:12–14, 20–4]. By this he signified that no type of person is more hateful to him than those who, under a cloak of godliness, are ungodly, and professing religion with their name and dress, live irreligious lives.

[173] He himself prayed frequently and so shows us that we must, with repeated prayers, earnestly entreat God for anything that pertains to our salvation. By frequently giving thanks to his Father he teaches us that whatever good comes to us we should credit to God. He also inculcated insistent prayer by some parables: for example the parable of the man who through his importunity compels his neighbour to arise at night [Luke 11:5–8]; similarly the parable of the widow who wearied the inexorable judge with her continual appeals [Luke 18:2–5]. In more than one place he also enjoins his disciples, 'Ask and you will receive' [John 16:24, Matthew 7:7–8, Luke 11:9–10].

[174] His own life teaches that the natural talent of an outstanding pastor flickers also in a boy and is betrayed by little sparks of a sort, for as a boy of twelve in the temple he offered a token and a taste of his wisdom. Likewise, at the wedding, before the baptism, he already practised, as it were, and by a miracle offered a prelude to his evangelical ministry, and anticipated his future preaching.

[175] One who wishes to undertake the work of gospel preaching must be cleansed from all the affections of the flesh and must set his mind on heavenly things only. At his baptism Christ was filled with the Spirit: by the impulse of the Spirit he was carried off into the desert; by the impulse of the Spirit he was carried away into Galilee, a victor after the temptation in the desert. This you read in Luke, the fourth chapter [4:1–14]. Then he entered the synagogue at Nazareth, and when a scroll

of Isaiah had been opened he came upon a passage about the Spirit: 'The Spirit of the Lord is upon me, wherefore he has anointed me. He has sent me to preach good news to the poor' [4:18]. He bids Nicodemus to be born not of the flesh, but of the spirit, not of the earth, but of heaven [John 3:3–8]. He breathes his Holy Spirit upon his apostles, who, after the resurrection, had been commanded to go and preach [John 20:21–3, Matthew 28:18–20]. Again, he sends a fiery spirit after the ascension [Acts 1:8].

[176] Certain ones want to be regarded as holy by virtue of the fact that they hide themselves from the gaze of the common crowd. But according to the example of Christ, one who is truly Christian does not shrink from the companionship of the weak if there is some hope that they will return to their senses and repent. At a banquet, he is touched by a woman who is a sinner, he converses apart and alone with an unknown Samaritan woman, who was living with her sixth lover; he dines with tax-collectors. For why would a loving and trustworthy physician shrink from the sick if there is hope for their health?

[177] In Luke, the fourteenth chapter, he teaches that one should perform a good deed without charge and without hope of interest accrued, and[59] expect no reward for kindnesses done except at the resurrection of the just. He teaches this in a parable he related, pointing out that it is not relatives, or neighbours, or the rich who are to be invited, but the poor, the disabled, the blind, and the lame [14:7–14].

[178] Although the common crowd of those who think themselves pious place the sum total of piety in pretty prayers and petty superstitious ceremonies, Christ shows in Luke, the fifteenth chapter, that the chief duty of piety, and the one most pleasing to God, is this: that one leads a sinner to come to his senses and repent. He inculcates this one idea in three parables: those of the lost sheep rescued although it was the last of one hundred [15:3–7], the lost coin found although it was the last of ten [15:8–10], and the prodigal son who came to his senses and repented [15:11–32]. And therein that supreme pastor, who was the only one of all completely free from all defects of the vices, teaches that a sinner who sincerely returns to his senses and repents must be received with joy, whereas we everywhere revile such, and receive them with an indelible brand-mark – just as though we were free from all wrong-doing!

[179] He everywhere refers his deeds and words to the Father as their author [John 5:19–47, 17:1–19]. He has thereby given us an example that

---

59 and ... the just.] Added only in *Schoeffer* 1519

we puny humans should make no claims for ourselves nor rely upon our own wisdom.

[**180**] Whatever ordinary life offered he generally turned into an opportunity for teaching godliness. A coin with the likeness of Caesar is shown to him; he turns the incident in this direction: that from the image of mind we recall what we owe to God. He urges upon the crowds the food that does not perish when they were flocking to him in quite large numbers because of the feast he had provided [John 6:22–33]. Again, in the same John when they demand some sign that could be compared to the manna long ago fallen from heaven, he invites them to the feast of his body, a feast far more sacred than any manna [6:30–51]. As the occasion was opportune, he invites to repentance those who told him of the extraordinary punishment of certain criminals [Luke 13:1–5]. He turns the children who were brought to him into an example of gentleness and modesty. He mentions his death and resurrection to those who were showing him the temple. A woman cried out that blest was the womb that had borne such a babe, blest the breasts that had offered milk to such a child. He redirects this utterance to show that they rather are blest who receive the divine word, and hence put forth the fruit that will never perish. But this method is too obvious to require illustration by citing examples.

[**181**] The fact that in John, the twelfth chapter, the Pharisees resolutely plan to kill Lazarus also is a type: the wicked hate not only Christ himself but also those through whom the name of Christ is made glorious [12:10–11].

[**182**] In the same Gospel one must note the circle in which Christ generally places himself, everywhere commending both the fellowship and the covenant-bond of Christians. In the twelfth and thirteenth chapters especially he shows that he is one with the Father, so completely that one who knows the Son knows the Father also, one who spurns the Son spurns the Father also [John 12:26, 44–5, 13:20]; nor is the Holy Spirit severed from this mutual participation. For so you read in the Epistle: 'There are three who give testimony in heaven, the Father, the Word, and the Spirit. And these three are one' [1 John 5:7]. Into the same partnership he draws his disciples, whom he calls his vine-branches, entreating them to be one with him just as he himself was one with the Father [John 15:4–5]. He imparts to them the Spirit that he shares with the Father, the Spirit that reconciles all things [John 20:21–3, 14:26, 2 Corinthians 5:18–19].

[**183**] He does not entrust to Peter the feeding of his sheep without Peter's triple confession of his love for Christ [John 21:15–17], implying that a bishop should have no other aim than the welfare of the flock and

the glory of Christ. And at once he shows to what end the true and faithful pastor should prepare himself, adding, 'Truly, I say to you, when you were young you girded yourself and walked where you would; but when you are old, you will extend your hands and another will carry you where you do not wish' [John 21:18]. For[60] one cannot be a true pastor whom financial gain, the pursuit of glory, the fear of princes, or even of death diverts from duty.

[184] It is in this way that it will be appropriate to philosophize over individual passages in the mystic volumes, especially in the Gospels – for I have introduced the above only as examples to show the way to others who will perhaps find better examples than these.

B2b The Figurative Character of the Language of 'Sacred Literature'

[185] But considerable difficulty lies in the very character of the speech in which sacred literature has been handed down to us. For Scripture generally speaks indirectly and under the cover of tropes and allegories, and of comparisons or parallels, sometimes to the point of obscurity in a riddle. Perhaps Christ thought it fitting to reproduce the speech of the prophets to which Jewish ears had grown accustomed, or he wanted to stimulate our sluggishness with this difficulty, so that fruit sought with effort might later be more pleasing, or through this design he wanted his mysteries to be covered and concealed from the profane and the ungodly without at the same time cutting off hope of understanding from godly investigators. Or perhaps he particularly liked the mode of expression that is most effectively persuasive, and, likewise, accessible to learned and unlearned alike, and familiar and completely natural, especially if similitudes are drawn from things best known to the common crowd; we read that Socratic comparisons were generally of this kind.

specialized tropes: parables or comparisons, allegories, riddles, and proverbs

[186] A parable is effectual, however, not only for teaching and persuading, but also for stirring the emotions, for alluring with its charm, for bringing clarity, for implanting one central idea deep within the mind,

---

60 For ... duty.] Added in *1520*. The 1519 text resumes at **184**.

beyond the possibility of escape. The mind is quite extraordinarily moved by the parable that is introduced concerning the prodigal son, who came to his senses and repented [Luke 15:11–32]. In this parable the story is told of a young man who demands from his father the portion of wealth that was coming to him; then with self-confidence he boldly ventures into a country far off. Soon, forgetful of his most indulgent father, he squanders with harlots and spendthrifts the resources given to him by the kindness of a parent. Finally, compelled by his utter want of everything, he acknowledges at last his madness, and a desire for the life he had left behind comes over him. The son returns, acknowledges his error; the father meets him, opens his arms to embrace his son. New clothes are brought out, a ring is offered, the fatted calf is killed, the whole house rings out with joy. In regaining the youth the old man rejoices as though the son had come to life again from the grave. There is no reproach for the rashness of the young man in demanding, nor for his luxury and wickedness in spending. The father's devotion no longer remembers these things. For paternal devotion it is enough that the son has come to his senses and repented, that the son has been restored to him. These images, I say, strike the mind more sharply than if, without a parable, one should say that God willingly receives a sinner provided the sinner sincerely repents of his former life, and God does not hold the sin against one who profoundly hates his transgressions. Just[61] as this idea steals into the minds of hearers more effectively through the allurement of a similitude, so it is etched more deeply when it is restated through the image of the wandering sheep that is brought back home on the shoulders of the shepherd after a long search [Luke 15:3–7] – likewise, through the parable of the coin that is finally found after it had been so eagerly sought [15:8–10].

[187] Again, there is the mystic parable from Genesis: Abraham everywhere digs wells, the Philistines fill up the pits by throwing earth in them, Isaac digs the same wells again and adds several more besides that have veins of living water [26:15–22]. When you introduce this parable, will you not be heard with greater pleasure than if you should simply say that one must seek in the divine books instruction for good living – that those who are devoted to earthly goods have no taste for these? Likewise, one who makes a bare statement of the virtues a bishop should possess will receive a less receptive hearing than if he applies as an allegory Aaron's entire vestments [Exodus 28:3–43], most carefully described by Moses.

---

61 Just ... sought.] Added in *1522*

The Figurative Character of the Language of 'Sacred Literature'   199

[188] In the same way,[62] suppose you explain that a person's desire entices to sin when the opportunity arises, that unless reason, which obeys the divine will rather than human affection, rules the person, a brief pleasure is purchased with death, that often, moreover, affection steals in under the cloak of necessity or some other honourable reason and deceives. This statement will delight or affect the hearer less than if you introduce the story of Genesis: God commands, the serpent sets the trap, Eve entices her husband to share her sin, soon punishment becomes the companion of the pleasure tasted [2-3].

[189] In addition, if someone should explain that one must with one's whole heart abandon vices and withdraw from association with the wicked, and must always progress towards the better things, until one has attained the reward promised to those who have persevered to the end, he will more forcibly move his hearers if he applies the allegory of the Hebrews who fled from Egypt under Moses' leadership, set themselves free from a harsh and base servitude, and after crossing the sea made their way through various stages, like points of progress in practising the virtues, to a land flowing with milk and honey. Again, one who teaches that true piety is a difficult thing and does not fall to the listless, but is scarcely acquired even with much industry and much struggle, will add much charm if he will adapt to allegory the battles and the uprisings that the Hebrews had against the Jebusites, the Philistines, and the other barbarian enemies.

[190] In addition, if you state in a straightforward way that nothing is more peaceful, nothing more pleasant than a good conscience that evil desires no longer molest, the auditor will be sleepier than if you add the wrapping of allegory: Isaac was born to Abraham and Sarah only when Abraham's body was dead, and it had ceased to be with Sarah after the manner of women [Genesis 18:11, Romans 4:19].

[191] However, it will not be the task of one who is writing a compendium to recount all these stories from the books of the Old Testament. It is enough to have shown by some examples that[63] there are things that appear in a more pleasing way through crystal or amber than if they are looked upon alone and bare. And somehow sacred things have more majesty if they are brought before the eyes under a cover than if they

---

62 In the same way ... shown by some examples] The addition, extending just beyond this and the next two paragraphs, appeared first in *1520*; see n63 and CWE 41 188 section 5, where three major areas of additions are identified, all made in *1520*, appearing from here to the end of the *Ratio*.
63 ... that there are ...] So in *1520*. In *1519* 'There are ...' See n62.

are seen absolutely bare. Thus[64] truth that has tormented us first under cover of a riddle is more pleasing once grasped – we who are the animal that walks first on four feet, then two, finally three. Now if someone should say that any good that dwells in us comes to us from Christ, its author, he will be understood, it is true; but if he will apply to this same thought the similitudes of the vine stock and the vine branches [John 15:1–10], of head and members [Ephesians 4:15–16, 1 Corinthians 12:12–27], of root and branches [Romans 11:16–24], the idea is at once placed before the eyes as though portrayed in a picture.

[192] Moreover,[65] just as Christ imitated the speech of the prophets, so Paul and the other apostles reflect the speech of Christ, projecting a theme visually, through parables, and, by frequent repetition, fastening it upon the mind. Thus Paul repeatedly calls us temples dedicated to God, and temples of the Holy Spirit, which it is forbidden to desecrate [1 Corinthians 3:16–7, 6:19, 2 Corinthians 6:16]. Thus also he concludes the whole discussion about the rejection of Israel and the adoption of the Gentiles with the parable of the olive tree and the wild olive, the root and the branches [Romans 9:1–11:24]. He calls 'leaven' the doctrine which, once handed down, influences many, indicating the large number by the term 'dough'; he calls those who are sound 'unleavened,' the corrupt, 'leavened' [1 Corinthians 5:6–9]. He says that those who are of a strong and resolute mind 'stand,' those who vacillate or sin 'fall' [Romans 14:4, 1 Corinthians 10:12], those who are dead 'have fallen asleep' [1 Corinthians 15:18, 1 Thessalonians 4:13], or those who neglect their salvation 'sleep' [1 Thessalonians 5:6], those who come to their senses and repent 'are awakened' [Romans 13:11], those who engage in the work of salvation eagerly and attentively 'keep watch' [1 Corinthians 16:13]. He calls a life sunk in error and vice 'night,' an honourable and blameless life 'day.' Occasionally, he calls the Last Judgment a 'day'; he calls 'day' a full and unerring judgment, which sometimes the word 'fire' also designates' – 'the fire will make manifest each person's work, of what sort it is.' He calls the gifts of the Holy Spirit 'treasures,' our bodies, or rather, ourselves, 'earthen vessels' [2 Corinthians 4:7]. He calls the human race a 'lump,' God a 'potter.' He says that the godly are vessels destined for honourable uses; the ungodly, he says, are vessels prepared for dishonour [Romans 9:21–3, 2 Timothy 2:20–1]. He calls the

---

64 Thus ... three.] Added in *1522*
65 Moreover ... course begun] This paragraph, the next, and the opening words of **194** added in *1520*; see n66.

frail body of a human being sometimes a 'dwelling,' sometimes a 'garment,' sometimes a 'tabernacle' [2 Corinthians 5:1–4].

[193] Through the similitude of the pedagogue and the young heir he shows that the Mosaic law was handed down for a limited time [Galatians 3:23–9]. He calls a kindness invested a 'sowing,' and the returns gained from a kind deed done he calls a 'harvest' [2 Corinthians 9:6]. He commends concord at one point under the figure of the body and its members [1 Corinthians 12:12], at another, under that of a building well constructed through a tightly fitting arrangement of stones in equilibrium right to the gable that provides their common peak [Ephesians 2:14–22]. Whatever in anything is coarser he calls 'flesh,' 'body,' or 'letter'; whatever is finer and is more like the force of the intellect he terms 'spirit' or 'mind.' He says that the teaching adapted to the capacity of the weak is 'milk,' the more complete teaching is 'solid food' [1 Corinthians 3:2]. In more than merely one place he shows through the parallel of marriage and its dissolution that the Mosaic law has been rendered of no effect since evangelical doctrine has succeeded to it. In the fifteenth chapter of the First Epistle to the Corinthians he treats the whole matter of the resurrection not by Aristotelian or Platonic enthymemes, but by comparisons, likening a body buried in the ground to a seed, citing wheat that has sprouted or a tree that has sprung up as an image of the glorified body [1 Corinthians 15:35–44]. Now it would be superfluous to recount the times he introduces a similitude from athletes and soldiers, from stadiums, boxers, war. In the ninth chapter of the same Epistle, with how many comparisons does he insistently repeat the same idea, that thanks is owed for a kindness provided: 'Who serves as a soldier at any time at his own charge? Who plants a vineyard and does not eat of the fruit thereof? Who feeds a flock and does not take the flock's milk?' [1 Corinthians 9:7]. Likewise, 'You will not muzzle the mouth of an ox that treads out the grain' [9:9]. Again: 'If we have sown spiritual things for you, is it a great matter if we reap your carnal things?' [9:11]. And again, 'Do you not know that those who work in the holy place have their food from the holy place, and those who attend at the altar partake of the sacrifices?' [9:13].

[194] But perhaps we are pursuing this at greater length than an account of method warrants. Accordingly, to finish the course begun: Christ[66] sometimes deceives his disciples temporarily through riddles of an allegorical nature so that what he wanted them to understand would stick more deeply later on. For example, in the sixteenth chapter

---

66 *1519* text resumes here; see n65.

of Matthew, when Christ warns the disciples to beware of the leaven of the Pharisees, it is the loaves they had forgotten that come to their minds, though he was speaking about avoiding the hypocrisy of the Pharisees [16:5–12]. Again, in Luke he bids them sell their tunics and buy a sword; they reply that two swords are at hand, and he says, 'It is enough.' When the opportunity arose, the words added incentive to Peter to set about the matter with a sword, though Christ was trying to pluck out of their hearts from its very deepest roots this desire to protect themselves by force against their persecutors [Luke 22:36–8, 49–51]. Likewise, when in John he speaks to those who were admiring the great edifice of the temple, and says, 'Destroy this temple and within a space of three days I will raise it up' [2:19], not even the apostles perceived that he was speaking about his body that was to be killed and that would live again within a period of three days. In addition, when in the same Gospel he says, 'A little while and you will not see me, and again a little while, and you will see me' [16:16], he signified as though with a riddle that he would shortly die, but would soon show himself to them from the resurrection right to the day of the ascension.

[195] Thus,[67] by whatever design, it pleased the eternal wisdom both to insinuate itself into the minds of the godly and, if I may use the expression, to deceive the minds of the profane through images sketched in outline only. For how many centuries do the Hebrews await their Messiah, the one so often promised? But what were the common crowd expecting? Some extraordinary ruler who would far extend the confines of their dominion, who would restore the Jews to liberty, who would bless their race with riches, who would lay waste with fire and sword the nations that were strangers to the law of Moses. But how vain and deluded was their expectation! Christ came, an example of lowliness and poverty; he came teaching that absolute power of a worldly sort was to be despised; he came exhorting us to take up the cross, and he himself led the way. Accordingly, when he came they turned away from him with a hatred that matched the zeal with which they had awaited his coming, deluded as they were by the fanciful images of their dull minds. But[68] in Matthew, with how many parables does he sketch out for us the kingdom of heaven: the sower whose seed fell

---

67 Thus ... many examples.] This paragraph and the next two with the first sentence of **198** were added in *1520* with the exceptions noted at nn68–70. For the continuation of the text in *1519*, see n71.
68 But ... pearl.] This sentence appeared already in *1519*, following the last sentence of the previous paragraph.

on different kinds of soil, then the sower of good seed, the grain of mustard, the little bit of leaven hidden in a large quantity of flour, the treasure buried in a field, the exceptional pearl [Matthew 13:3–45].

[196] One could put in the same class the practice of Paul, a man who always imitates Christ: he refers everything from its normal meaning to its inner meaning, which is always the sense that is truest, and also the most salutary and of the most extensive application. According to the general opinion, a Jew is one who has a little bit of foreskin cut off. According to Paul's interpretation, a Jew is a person who has a mind cleansed from earthly desires, while the uncircumcised is one who is led by base affections [Romans 2:28–9]. In the popular view the children of Abraham are those whose stock derives from Abraham. According to Christ and Paul the children of Abraham are those who in their moral life reflect the godliness and the trust of Abraham [John 8:39, Galatians 3:6–7]. Likewise, one who belongs to the race of Israel is called an Israelite; to Christ he is not an Israelite unless he is related to God through innocence of life [John 1:47]. When someone has kept the rules prescribed by the laws, this is commonly called 'righteousness.' With God it is not righteousness unless sincerity and purity of mind make the observance of the Law praiseworthy in the eyes of the one who looks deep within the innermost recesses of the heart.

[197] One who killed a sacrificial animal, or, as is done today, one who has consecrated the Eucharist, is said to have offered a sacrifice. But it is the one who suppresses and slays anger, lust, ambition, and other similar beastly desires that truly sacrifices to God. A building dedicated with the words of priests and with oil is said to be a temple dedicated to God; the mind[69] that bears the image of God and admits no likeness of turpitude is a truly sacred temple within [1 Corinthians 3:16–17, 2 Corinthians 6:16]. To burn incense before some profane statue is commonly defined as idolatry; true idolatry is to defy Christ because of foul lust, base gain, desire for revenge, tyrannical power. Those who have deserted to the side of the Turks are said to be apostates; true apostates are those whose life is in conflict with Christ and is enslaved to the world, and[70] is inconsistent with their baptismal profession. When someone spews out impious words against God, this is generally said to be blasphemy; but Paul, following the thought of the prophet, calls it blasphemy whenever the name of God is dishonoured because of the

---

69 the mind ... within.] First in *1522*; in *1520*: 'the mind that inwardly bears the image of God ... a truly sacred temple.'
70 and ... profession.] Added in *1522*

ungodly lives of those who profess the worship of God [Romans 2:23–4]. For why should we scruple to say that God is defamed by the evil practices of Christians, when in the Gospel [Matthew 5:16] the Father is said to be glorified by the good works of disciples? By the same reasoning it could be said that in the popular judgment those are called monks who profess themselves to be such by a specified kind of dress and food and established ceremonies, though in God's eyes he only is a monk whose mind is plainly dead to worldly desires.

[198] But I think I have sufficiently indicated with a few examples this method, too, since each person can with a little thought supply for himself many examples.[71] Closely allied and akin to these are proverbs; to this class belongs the following: 'We piped to you and you did not dance, we wailed and you did not weep' [Luke 7:32]. This means that the Pharisees were not aroused to repentance by the austerity of John or by the civility of Christ.

idioms of everyday speech, in Hebrew

[199] There are, however, tropes that belong not to the domain of grammarians or rhetoricians, but to the idiomatic character of speech; if an idiom is misunderstood the reader will frequently either be deceived or delayed. The Greek language has, in fact, many idiomatic expressions in common with Latin, some peculiar to itself. But Hebrew has many forms of expression different from both. We use the same idiom as the Greeks when we say that one who 'deserves well of another' 'does a kindness.' But we do not share in common with them the fact that their expression *eupathein*, that is, 'to be fortunate' [*bene pati*], is used idiomatically to mean 'to receive a kindness' [*beneficio affici*]. We share with them a common idiom for 'I am grateful' [*habeo gratiam*], *echo charin* [literally, 'I have thanks']; we do not share with them an idiom that expresses the same idea, *oida charin*, literally, 'I know thanks,' nor[72] do we share with them the idiom *memnesomai charin*, literally, 'I will remember thanks,' which expresses the same idea as the Latin idiom *referam gratiam* ['I will return a favour']. For 'one who has unknowingly welcomed angels as his guests' the correct expression in Greek is *elathen xenisas aggelous*, but in Latin we do not say, 'it escaped his notice receiving angels.'

[200] Now, although the apostles wrote in Greek, they retain in no small measure the idiom of Hebrew speech. Moreover, the Seventy who

---

71 The text of *1519* resumes here; see n67.
72 nor ... receiving angels.'] Added in *1520*

gave us the Old Testament in Greek retain a great many of the idioms of Hebrew speech. These were generally changed by Jerome, who did away with the old translation that Augustine cites in his work *On Modes of Expression* (if anyone would like to sample that translation). As a result of the Hebrew idioms in the Septuagint, one who has little proficiency in Hebrew, even if very skilled in Greek, sometimes does not follow the thought of the speaker. Let me produce one or two examples of this kind for the sake of illustration: 'who swears in heaven,' for the expression 'he swears by heaven'; and 'he believes in him' for the expression 'he trusts in him'; 'he confesses in him' for 'he confesses,' or, 'he acknowledges him'; 'in this they will know,' 'he struck in the sword' – 'by this they will know,' 'he struck with the sword'; 'I will be to him unto a father, he will be to me unto a son' – 'I will be his father, he will be my son'; 'two and two' for 'two by two,' 'more stronger than we' – 'stronger than we'; 'if a woman will be to a foreign husband' for the expression 'if she marries a foreign husband'; 'man man' for 'whoever'; 'of a man of a man' for 'of any man at all'; 'what things he did [to] their force' for 'what he did to their armies' – Augustine thought this was a Hebrew idiom, though I think it is Greek. Hebrew idiom adds a superfluous pronoun: 'Blessed is the people whose God is the Lord of it' [Psalm 144:15]. Also, 'he showed' for 'he made' [or, 'he did']; 'good good' for 'exceedingly good'; 'Mary of Cleopas' for 'Mary, wife of Cleopas'; 'James of Alphaeus' – 'James son of Alphaeus' is an ellipsis familiar in Hebrew. Likewise, 'all flesh' for 'all people,' 'many souls' for 'many persons,' 'word' for 'deed' – 'what is this word you have done to us?' – 'honour' for 'assistance,' 'mercy' for 'kindness.' Moreover, the translator is confronted with the same situation in rendering Greek idioms as in translating Hebrew idioms. But in the annotations that I have written on the New Testament I have in scattered fashion pointed out cases of this kind. And Aurelius Augustine did likewise in some books with the title *On Modes of Expression*. And yet Augustine could have occupied himself more profitably with this subject if in his annotations he had drawn from the Hebrew sources rather than the Greek. There exist also the annotations of the Greek writer Titanius, in this very genre a modern author as it appears.

other everyday tropes: heterosis, synecdoche, hyperbaton, hyperbole, etc

[201] Now a problem is frequently solved through other kinds of tropes also. For example, Matthew [27:44] and Mark [15:32] reported that the robbers who were crucified with Christ reviled him, though Luke tells

us that only one did so [23:39]. Augustine unravels the knot by saying that this is a case of *heterosis*, a change of number, where 'robbers' is used for 'a robber.' Again, he explains by synecdoche the statement that Christ was in the tomb for a period of three days, as also the passage written in Mark that he would rise again after three days, although he rose at daybreak on the third day. How many times, moreover, do Chrysostom and Jerome and Augustine scatter the obscurity of meaning by unravelling the intricacies of a hyperbaton. These[73] authors, I suppose, had not been read by a certain distinguished Scotist, who recently in a public assembly – and with the sharpest wit, as he thought – scoffed at people like me, who have laboured to show the order of words. He said, 'I learned to construe quite some time ago from Alexander, the grammarian.'

[202] Indeed, we frequently encounter hyperbole also, as in this passage: 'They mount up to heaven, they go down to the depths' [Psalm 107:26], where the Psalmist wanted us to picture the violent surging of storm-driven waves. A statement that goes beyond demonstrable reality is not necessarily a lie, but a trope is applied to make discourse more pungent and passionate. And no one should think it absurd to point out hyperboles in the divine books, for Origen does so, as does Chrysostom, and so do Augustine and Jerome.

[203] The following are examples: 'It is easier for a camel pass through the eye of a needle than for a rich man to enter into the kingdom of heaven' [Matthew 19:24] – whereas Christ wanted only this to be understood, that it is extremely difficult for a rich man to obey gospel teaching. Likewise, in Luke, when in the parable he asks that the disabled, blind, and lame be invited to a feast [Luke 14:12–14], all that is meant is that the unfortunate and the downcast should be supported by kindness freely given; again, when he forbids the apostles to greet anyone on the way [Luke 10:4] – whereas he wanted it understood that they must not act in such a manner that they delay the work of the gospel by losing any time due to human affections. When he forbids them to take wallet or staff for the journey, he meant that they ought to be free from those supports that most people provide for themselves when they are about to go on a journey. For there is no doubt that the apostles had wallets and staves, since Paul left both a cloak and a library at Troas [2 Timothy 4:13]. When he bids his disciples to live in the manner of lilies, he wanted them to realize that they ought to cast off the anxious concern to lay away provisions for the future [Matthew 6:28–33, Luke 12:26–31].

---

73 These ... grammarian.'] Added in *1520*

When he bids them to offer the left cheek to one who strikes on the right, what else does he mean except that an injury inflicted should not be returned [Matthew 5:39]? We must hold the same view, I think, about the tunic that was to be left with one who took away the cloak, and about walking of their own accord the second mile with the person who had compelled them to walk the first [5:40–1]. When he says that a person who does not hate father and mother is not his disciple [Luke 14:26, Matthew 10:37], he said more than he wanted inferred, for[74] he did not mean that parents should be hated, but that all affections should take second place to the concern for godliness and salvation. When he bids us to anoint our faces with oil so that we do not appear to fast, he means only that we should not strive to be ostentatious in doing good deeds [Matthew 6:17–18] – for I suppose that the apostles usually did not anoint their faces when they fasted.

[204] Origen points out that there is a hyperbole in the text we read in Genesis: 'He washes his robe in wine and his cloak in the blood of grapes' [49:11]. For who washes his clothes in wine? But from these words he wanted us to understand only the extraordinary and abundant fertility of the land. He also thinks that Paul's statement that the faith of the Romans is spoken of in the whole world is hyperbole, since their faith was unknown to many regions. St Augustine, in the letter to Publicola (which is numbered among the others as the 154th), thinks there is hyperbole in those words of Christ by which he forbids us to swear at all, either by the heaven or by the earth or by anything else: he said more than he meant in order to deter us more forcibly from perjury. I shall add Augustine's words, in case anyone should ask for them: '[…] if, at least, this is still a concern for us that in the New Testament it is said that we should not swear at all. This, indeed, seems to me to have been said not because to swear to the truth is a sin, but because perjury is a monstrous sin, from which he who admonished us not to swear at all wanted us to keep far away.' So far Augustine. Just as, when we use threats in forbidding children to swim, we say, 'If you so much as look at the pool, I'll kill you.' If we accept this interpretation, other passages also will be explained in a very similar way: 'Do not divorce your wife'; 'Do not resist evil'; 'Do not be angry' [Matthew 5:32, 39, 22]. For[75] when Christ took completely away from his people the right of divorce, he is expressing with vehemence his intent that they should not divorce without just cause. When he says that they should not avenge themselves

---

74 for … salvation.] Added in *1520*
75 For … unjustified anger.] Added in *1520*

even when injured, he means that they should not even think of inflicting injury. When he expresses his desire that they should not become angry whatever the provocation, he means that there is no place for homicide, reproaches, or unjustified anger.

[205] Now, Cyril and Chrysostom frankly admit that John's statement at the end of his Gospel – that the whole world could not contain the books that would have to be written about Christ [21:25] – is hyperbole. The[76] latter of these in his thirty-fifth homily on Matthew thinks a hyperbole underlies these words of Christ: 'What I tell you in the dark, speak in the light; and what you hear in the ear, preach upon the housetops' [10:27]. For Christ did not say anything in clandestine encounters or in hushed voice, nor did the apostles ever preach upon the housetops. But Christ characterizes what had been said to a few in Palestine as said in 'darkness' and in 'whispers,' in comparison with the light and the trumpet-sound of the gospel, which, through the apostles, soon shone forth and rang out among all the nations of the world – among people of the most exalted rank and among the humblest. I think it is also hyperbole when he forbids us to call anyone on earth 'father' [Matthew 23:9]; and again when he says that neither an iota nor even one little dot of the Law must be left unfulfilled [5:18], meaning that not one of the divine promises is to pass away; they can stand even if dots have sometimes been removed. But in the annotations with which I have clarified the New Testament I have pointed out some examples of this type, too.

[206] There are expressions that are akin to these; whether they correspond to tropes, I do not know, but at least they must be brought in line with common sense rather than forced to the quick, as they say. For example, when Christ forbids all swearing [Matthew 5:34], he means that one must not swear as the ordinary person swore for any reason whatever. When he forbids us to be concerned for the morrow [6:34], he means 'after the manner of the ordinary person' who, as though distrusting God, was tormented with anxious concern for the future. When he forbids us to resist evil [5:39], he means that evil must not be repelled with evil, as is usually done by the ordinary person; in any case it is permitted to reprove sinners, it is also permitted to restrain them. When he forbids his disciples to be called 'Rabbi' [23:8], he means not in the manner of the Pharisees, who were swollen with pride on account of this title. When he forbids verbosity in prayers [6:7], he means that one must not pray after the example of those who supposed that God

---

76 The ... the humblest.] Added in *1522*

was moved by a multitude of words rather than by disposition of mind; in any case we read that even Christ prayed at length [Luke 6:12]. In the same way he bids us not to be angry [Matthew 5:22], meaning the ordinary anger that leads to violence. In the same way he condemns a person who has said to his brother, 'You idiot' [5:22]; he has in mind the person who has done so by way of insult in the usual way. In any case, we read that Christ himself was moved by anger [Mark 3:5], and elsewhere he calls his disciples fools [Luke 24:25], and Paul calls the Galatians 'fools' [Galatians 3:1, 3] – but to reprove, not to assail. Godliness,[77] too, has its own anger; love also has its own reproof.

[207] The following are almost of the same sort. When in Matthew Christ says, 'I will have mercy and not sacrifice' [9:13, 12:7], he certainly wanted sacrifice, which he himself had appointed, but showing mercy comes before offering sacrifice. Again, when he says, 'My teaching is not mine' [John 7:16], he says that the teaching is not his, which as a man he attributed to the Father. Again, when he says that the Spirit was not yet because Jesus had not yet been glorified [7:39], he does not mean quite simply that the Spirit was not, but that that evangelical Spirit had not yet made its appearance among the apostles.

idioms of everyday speech, in Latin

[208] Indeed, Latin speech itself also has certain idioms of its own, which sometimes deceive those who are little attentive or less learned. An example of this type is in Mark, the fifth chapter, when those who came to Christ from the house of the ruler of the synagogue are said to come from the ruler of the synagogue [5:35]. We have this passage now long ago corrupted by those who did not recognize the special idiom of Latin whereby we Latin speakers say, 'we shall go "to me"' for 'to my house.'

other everyday tropes: irony, ambiguity, emphasis

[209] But you might perhaps be inclined to doubt whether one is permitted to find irony in the literature of the apostles and of the Gospels – though there can be no doubt that it is found in the Old Testament. Certainly in the eighteenth chapter of the third book of Kings, Elijah, mocking the prophets of Baal, says: 'Cry out with a louder voice, for he

---

77 Godliness ... reproof.] Added in *1520*

is a god, and perhaps he is talking, or he is at an inn, or is on a journey, or surely he is asleep, and must be awakened [1 Kings 18:27]. In the opinion of Theophylact, the Bulgarian bishop, irony can be perceived in these words of Christ, 'Sleep now and take your rest' [Matthew 26:45, Mark 14:41]. Again, in Paul, the sixth chapter of the First Epistle to the Corinthians, 'Those who are the more despised, set them to judge' [6:4] – this can be seen to have been said with irony, especially since there follows, 'I speak to your shame' [6:5]. Perhaps also those words of Christ are not very far from irony, 'It is not good to take the children's bread, and cast it to the dogs' [Matthew 15:26]; nor these, 'I came not to call the righteous but sinners' [Matthew 9:13]; for he did not truly believe that they were righteous, but he reproaches them because they thought they were righteous.

[210] There are many other figures of speech and figures of thought that contribute either the weight or the pleasure of discourse to the artistic arrangement. Although[78] the sense of mystic Scripture stands firm without them, through these figures the Scriptures steal into our minds more effectually and more pleasurably, and are discussed and expounded more felicitously. St Augustine, in his work entitled *On Christian Doctrine*, was not reluctant to point out at great length these figures in the sacred books. Donatus and Diomedes expounded all these figures with care, but Quintilian did so with even greater care in the ninth book of the *Rhetorical Institutes*. But just so that no one disdains this part of literary study as philological and trivial, Augustine in his work *On Christian Doctrine* directs that it be carefully learned as being useful for understanding the canonical books.

[211] Now, ambiguity is indeed a fault in discourse, but one that often cannot be avoided, though Fabius [Quintilian] advises that it must be avoided as much as possible. Augustine wants ambiguity to be so entirely avoided that he considers that a manifest solecism should sooner be adopted than an ambiguous expression used, and he prefers that we say *ossum* ['bone'] rather than *os* ['bone' or 'mouth'] if we refer to some one of those objects that are in the plural called *ossa*, not *ora*. In this, indeed, I entirely disagree with him, except[79] when one speaks in the presence of the simple folk – which is how Augustine felt, in whose time ordinary people then used to understand and to speak whatever kind of Latin they could. In any case, when did Augustine in any of his

---

78 Although ... felicitously.] Added in *1520*
79 except ... avoid ambiguity?] Added in *1520*

books ever say *ossum* to avoid ambiguity? In[80] the same way he never said *floriet* for *florebit* ['will flourish']. For a long time this was permitted – among those who were allowed to pronounce *flos* ['flower'] and *ros* ['dew'] as neuter nouns, as we say *os*. But now such things would be said with no more excuse than if someone speaking among educated people were saying *tempo* for *tempus* ['time']. But this difficulty [ambiguity] occurs more frequently in Greek than in Latin. Accordingly, I have in many places noted it and, where I could, I have eliminated it. Generally, however, it is removed either, on the one hand, by the arrangement of words (I mean a change in the order of words if the difficulty arises from word placement), or, on the other, by clarifying the ambiguous expression through paraphrase. This is precisely the path Augustine pursues, offering some examples.

[212] Doubtless, the special use of a word sometimes makes the discourse ambiguous, but this is peculiar not so much to the language as to the writer, inasmuch as among authors each has language that is peculiar to himself. One who has read nothing but Cicero will frequently have difficulty in the language of Quintilian. So Paul at one time calls kindred or blood relationship 'flesh,' at another time he designates the whole person as flesh; sometimes the grosser part of a person or of another thing of any sort at all is said to be flesh; occasionally, he designates as flesh the affection of a person that entices one to the vices. Similarly, he often calls 'body' that which consists of limbs; sometimes 'body' has for him the same force as 'flesh.' Somewhere they call that highest and heavenly one the Spirit; elsewhere they designate a mental impulse as 'spirit.' Again, the gifts of the Holy Spirit are said to be the gift of 'the Spirit'; sometimes the movement of this air around us is called wind [*spiritus*], as here: 'The wind [*spiritus*] blows where it will' [John 3:8]. Almost identical to this is Paul's statement: 'My spirit prays, but my understanding is without fruit' [1 Corinthians 14:14].

[213] Of the same kind are these expressions, too: when they say *fides* for *fiducia* [trust], since in Latin *fides* is used of the one who promises, as in the expression *dare fidem* [to give a pledge], or of one who does or does not fulfil a promise, as in the expression *solvere fidem* [to fulfil a promise]. *Praestare fidem* [to keep faith] does not designate the action of the one who trusts or believes, except when we say, 'I have confidence in you' [*habeo tibi fidem*], 'he deprives another of his credit' [*abrogate illi fidem*]. A further example: when in Paul one who helps is said to build, one who harms is said to destroy [Romans 14:19–20]; again, when he

---

80 In ... for *tempus*.] Added in *1523*

calls a kindness voluntarily conferred a 'blessing' [2 Corinthians 9:5]. But I have said more about these at various points in the *Annotations*, and have touched briefly on the subject in the Arguments I have written for the apostolic Epistles.

[214] The[81] special significance attached to words will also have to be noted. For this, a knowledge of the different languages is especially useful. It is a case in point when Paul calls himself a slave of Jesus Christ rather than a worshipper [Romans 1:1, 14:4–9], for a slave is entirely in the power of another, depends upon the will of his master, and whatever he intends to do, it is for his lord, not for himself. There is a similar case in the Epistle to the Corinthians, where he calls the apostles *hyperetai*, that is, ministers of Christ, and *oikonomoi*, that is, stewards of the mysteries of God [1 Corinthians 4:1]. A minister is an administrator and steward of someone else's property, not his own, and dispenses at his lord's will, not his own, what and how much each needs, according to circumstances. Thus bishops do not seek their own interests, they do not teach their own doctrines, but what belongs to Christ. They do not propound the same things to everyone, but attune their discourse to the receptivity of each. This[82] *emphasis* is most properly observed in the original language in which the author wrote – though St Hilary often even in the Psalms brings out the *emphasis* from the Greek translation.

[215] Sometimes there is also *emphasis* in the little word that seemed to have no importance in common speech. For example, we read in the twenty-sixth chapter of Leviticus, 'Keep my sabbaths and reverence my sanctuary' [26:2]: it is not without design that he has added the possessive ['my'], for this world, too, has its sabbaths, it has its sanctuary, too. A person who scrupulously abstains from manual work, without, meanwhile, refraining from oaths, harlots, intoxication, keeps his own sabbath, not the sabbath of the Lord. The person who hears the divine liturgy every day, who is signed with the cross, sprinkled with water, still all this while wishes his neighbour ill, all this while cheats, plunders, practises usury – this person is reverencing not the sanctuary of the Lord but his own sanctuary. For God speaks thus in Isaiah: 'Your new moons and your solemnities my soul hates' [1:14]. How is it that he speaks of 'their' new moons – the ones he himself had appointed? But it was they who had made these their own by keeping them improperly and not for the purpose for which he had appointed them. As when we

---

81 The ... receptivity of each.] This paragraph was added in 1522 except for the final sentence, added in 1523.
82 This ... Greek translation.] Added in 1523.

fast either because of frugality or vainglory, or fast committing meanwhile quite serious sins through other more shocking vices, this is our fast, not God's. Origen's observation is also relevant here: Jesus says to Peter, *hypage opiso mou* ['Get behind me'; Matthew 16:23], for Christ wants him to be an imitator of his death. To Satan he says only, *hypage opiso* ['Get behind'; Matthew 4:10], no doubt sending him away and not inviting to imitation one whose lamentable perversity he knew. Since these instances occur everywhere, there is no reason to pursue them; it is enough to have pointed to them.

specialized tropes again: allegories, parables, and the historical sense; the different levels of sense in Scripture

[216] But to return to allegories. Special care must be devoted to these, since almost all Divine Scripture, through which the eternal wisdom speaks with us in a stammering tongue, as it were, rests upon allegories. Unless these come to our attention, especially in the books of the Old Testament, the reader will lose a large part of the fruit. If[83] a passage were taken in a straightforward way, the sense of the words would sometimes be manifestly untrue, occasionally even ridiculous and absurd. And by a salutary plan[84] the divine wisdom has taken precaution lest, if no obstacle appeared in the historical text, we should suppose there was not any more meaning there. Accordingly the divine wisdom breaks up the course of the biblical reading with certain rough bogs, chasms, and similar obstacles, mixing in things either that cannot have happened or could not happen, or that, if they happened, would be absurd. In this way, the mind, barred by such obstacles from understanding the passage in the ordinary manner, might wander through more hidden byways and at length arrive at the place where the riches of a more recondite understanding are spread out. This pattern occurs not only in narratives, but in prophecies and precepts.

[217] And yet we must not remove all the historical sense in the divine books just because, for the reasons mentioned, certain passages are found through which the divine providence wished to compel, as

---

83 If ... absurd.] Added in *1522*. Beginning with this addition, a large part of this section (**216–33**) appeared first in additions made in *1522* and *1523*.
84 And by a salutary plan ... according to the literal sense] Apart from a snippet retained from *1519* (see n87) and a portion of **220** already inserted in 1522 (see n85) the whole passage from here to almost the end of **223** (see n88) was added in *1523*.

it were, our mental powers to explore the spiritual meaning. Generally both senses stand together. For I believe that God's precept, 'You shall not muzzle an ox when it treads out the grain' [Deuteronomy 25:4], had long ago been observed among the Hebrews also according to the historical sense. And yet Paul writes, 'Does God take care for oxen? Or does he not speak especially for our sake? For this was written for our sake, because one who ploughs should plough in hope, and one who threshes in the hope of receiving' [1 Corinthians 9:9–10].

[218] But if anyone should look for an example of an incongruous narrative, many are encountered straight off in Genesis itself. For how is it consistent that the first day of the created world, the second, and the third, for which both evening and morning are mentioned, were without sun, moon, stars – the first day, moreover, even without sky [Genesis 1:1–13]? Next, how incongruous to understand according to the historical sense that God, like some farmer, planted trees in Paradise, in Eden towards the East, and there he planted a certain tree of life, that is, a real tree that could be seen and touched; to understand that this tree had such power that whoever had eaten of its fruit with his physical teeth would receive life, that he planted also another tree from which, if anyone ate, such a person would understand the distinction between good and evil [2:8–9 and 15–17, 3:22–3]! The narratives that follow are almost as feeble: where it is said that God walks in Paradise in the cool afternoon air; that Adam hides under a tree [3:8]; that Cain withdrew from the face of the Lord [4:16]; finally, where it is written that God completed some portion of his work on each day and at last on the seventh day rested from his work, as though he was worn out [2:1–2].

[219] Inasmuch as the exterior form of this sort of story offends the reader at first blush, it advises him that under this covering there lies hidden some more recondite sense, so that he should ask what an allegorical day is, what is the division of days, what is the rest from work, what the planting, the tree of life, the tree giving knowledge of good and evil, what is the 'afternoon,' what is 'God walking in the cool air,' Adam lying hidden, what is the face of the Lord, what is 'departing from him'? But whoever will examine the books of the Old Testament, which abounds in tropes of this kind, will find many examples like these.

[220] The same thing is somewhat more rare in the New Testament, but, nevertheless, we may even here, perhaps, find narrative that is absurd according to the historical sense. For example, we read that the Lord was led away into a high mountain, from where he looked upon all the kingdoms of the world and their glory [Matthew 4:8]. How would anyone be able to show to corporeal eyes from a single

mountain – no matter how high – the kingdom of the Persians, Scythians, Indians, Spaniards, Gauls, Britons, and to show in what ways each particular nation does homage to its king? But as I have quite frequently said, this also occurs in the Prophets. Here[85] is a case in point – for[86] I want to be satisfied with a single example: Isaiah in the seventh chapter writes about Christ: 'Behold, a virgin shall conceive, and bear a son, and shall call his name Emmanuel' [7:14]. It is clear that the name given to Christ was not Emmanuel but Jesus. From this circumstance, indeed, certain Jews and heretics used to make their case that the Jesus whom we worship was not he whom God had promised through Isaiah. In fact, the prophet did not have in mind simply the appellation given but its meaning, for God began truly to be with us when Jesus was born, restoring the world through his Son. But what follows is even more absurd: 'For before he knows how to say father and mother, he will take the forces of Damascus and the spoils of Samaria' [Isaiah 8:4] – so reads Tertullian; certainly Jerome, too, applies the passage to Christ. How is it appropriate for a child to be called a warrior? Will a child with his squalling summon to arms an army, and give the signal for war not with a trumpet but with his rattle? Will he attack the enemy not from a horse and chariot but from the neck of his nurse or nanny, and press down on Damascus and Samaria instead of the breasts? As a result of this incongruity of expression, heretics denied that this prophecy belonged to Christ. But if you apply allegory, it will fit nicely the Gospel story, which relates that the three Magi had come of their own accord to Bethlehem to acknowledge the new king by offering gifts. This was a king who was bringing the whole universe under his control, not by troops or arms, but by celestial power and the sword of the evangelical word.

[221] Now in the case of the commandments in both Testaments we must not, it is true, doubt that certain ones must be observed according to the historical sense, for example: honour your father and your mother, worship one God, do not steal, do not swear falsely, do not kill [Exodus 20:12, 3, 15, 16, 13]. It is just as true that certain commandments seem incongruous if you look for nothing beyond the outer shell of the words. The Law prescribes that a boy be circumcised on the eighth day, and it was right that parents be punished who did not take care to have their little infants circumcised. But then Scripture says that a boy not circumcised is to be utterly cut off from his people [Genesis 17:12–14].

---

85 Here ... evangelical word.] This remaining portion of the paragraph was added in 1522 except for the short insertion in the first sentence; see next note.
86 for ... single example] Added in 1523

But of what was the boy himself guilty if he had not been circumcised? It is even more incongruous that although the Law enjoins observance of the sabbath on pain of death [Exodus 31:14], it nevertheless uses these words: 'But each of you will be in your houses; no one will be moved from his own place on the day of the sabbath' [Exodus 16:29]. For how is it possible for one to sit at home all day and not move from his seat? Not unlike these is the prohibition against bearing any burden on the sabbath [Jeremiah 17:21–2]. This kind of absurdity forced even the Jews themselves to look for some trope in these words, for they had no scruple about pulling an ox or an ass out of a pit into which it had fallen [Luke 14:5].

[222] One may find some prescripts of this kind in the literature of the Gospels, too. Here is an example: 'Do not greet anyone on the way' [Luke 10:4]. Are the apostles forbidden to offer a salutation to a person who meets them on their journey? Likewise, the prohibition against having two tunics each or shoes on the feet [Matthew 10:10]: how can this precept be kept, especially in regions frozen stiff with cold and frost? Again, the prescript that one who has been struck on the right cheek offer the striker the left also [Matthew 5:39] – especially when it is common practice for one who strikes with the right hand to strike the left cheek? These, too, I think, belong to the same genre: 'Let your loins be girded and your lamps be burning in your hands' [Luke 12:35], and, 'Give to everyone who asks of you' [Luke 6:30], for if you insist on a literal interpretation, it will not be right to deny a girl a night. In some instances,[87] the sense of the words is even destructive unless you apply the remedy of allegory, for example, 'Blessed are those who have made themselves eunuchs for the kingdom of God' [Matthew 19:12].

[223] Similar to this are the precepts about cutting out the right eye, about cutting off the right hand or foot [Matthew 5:29–30], about praying always [Luke 18:1] – which, in trying to observe according to the literal meaning of the words, certain people have won for themselves a place among the heretics. And yet the precept put forth by Christ in Luke is repeated by Paul [Romans 12:12, 1 Thessalonians 5:17]. For in the apostolic Epistles, too, certain things are found that bar us from the ordinary sense, and compel us to turn up, with the help of tropology, a sense worthy of the Holy Spirit. What pertinence has Paul's precept that

---

87 In some instances ... kingdom of God.'] This example was included already in *1519*, where it followed immediately upon the introductory remarks for the section beginning at **216**, in the place at which the insertions in *1522* (and *1523*) would subsequently be made; see n84.

if anyone is called when circumcised he should not put on a foreskin
[1 Corinthians 7:18]? What harm would there be if a circumcised Jew,
to avoid an indecent appearance, should put on a foreskin, provided
this could be suitably done? It would even be impious to want to keep,
according to the literal sense,[88] this prescript of Paul, 'For doing this,
you will heap coals of fire upon his head' [Romans 12:20]. It is Augustine's opinion that this text, too, is of the same kind: 'Unless anyone has
eaten my flesh or drunk my blood etc' [John 6:53–4]. Here, therefore,
as I have said, a knowledge of material things is useful; also to have
had practice beforehand during youth in poetical allegories, or even
in drawing comparisons from any kind of thing, and discussing them.
About comparisons I have long ago published a little book.

[224] There are those who turn the story of the New Testament also
to allegory. I very strongly approve, since it is sometimes necessary, and
very often pleasant and neat, provided one treats the matter skilfully.
It seems to me that Ambrose is, in this respect, sometimes extravagant,
if I may say so without offence to him; for example, when he says that
Peter, warming himself at the fire, did not feel cold in body, since the
season then could not be cold, but the coldness was that of the mind.
Ambrose neatly turns this into allegory when he says the following:
'But it was winter when Jesus was not acknowledged, when there was
no one who saw the light, when the consuming fire was denied' – and
the rest along the same line. But nothing prevents the facts of the narrative also from being trustworthy. Moreover, Ambrose adds: 'If we consider the time, it could not have been winter,' and a little later, 'The cold
was, therefore, of the mind, not of the body.' Indeed, we may grant that
during those months the daytime temperature in this region is warm
enough, yet even in places that grow very hot, the night can be cold.

[225] Very much like this are the comments that Ambrose adds concerning Peter's denial. They reflect subtle wit more than they provide
a true defence of Peter, for Christ had permitted Peter to fall so that by
returning to his senses and repenting through the compassion of Christ,
he might strengthen his brothers. And yet, that Peter could have sinned –
Ambrose wants this to seem so strange that not even the Gospel writers could understand his sin, as though it was a sufficient proof that
they did not understand a story about which their narratives varied,
although this occurs in several places. Then Ambrose twists the words
in Matthew and Mark when Peter replies to the girl who was betraying

---

88 The main *1519* text resumes here, after the series of insertions beginning in 216; see nn83–4.

him, 'I do not know what you mean' [Matthew 26:70, Mark 14:68], to give the sense that Peter had not denied the Lord, but had put himself at a distance from the woman's betrayal. But if even if anyone should press the point that Peter had indeed denied that he belonged to those who had been with Jesus the Galilean (or the Nazarene, as it is written in Mark), still Ambrose bends the words to the interpretation that Peter denied he had known as a Galilean or Nazarene one whom he knew as the Son of God. Again, Ambrose twists in the same direction the statement in Matthew, 'I do not know the man' [26:72], as if he who wished to be regarded as a disciple of God was not a disciple of the man. To confirm his interpretation, he cites from Paul: 'Paul, an apostle not from man nor through man, but through Jesus Christ and God the Father' [Galatians 1:1]. I am aware that some explain this otherwise, but it seems to me that Paul did not refer to Christ's human nature (which he did not take away from Christ), but by the word 'man' he wanted something quite weak and lowly to be understood, as when he says, 'Do I speak this after the manner of men? [1 Corinthians 9:8].

[226] Jerome[89] seems to criticize the comment in the short notes he wrote on Matthew: 'I know,' he says, 'that certain persons with pious feelings towards the apostle Peter have interpreted this passage to say that Peter did not deny God, but man, and the sense is, "I do not know the man, since I know him as God." The prudent reader perceives how frivolous this is. They defend the apostle in such a way that they make God guilty of a lie. For if Peter did not deny, then the Lord lied, who had said, "Truly, I say to you that on this night, before the cock crows, you will deny me thrice" [Matthew 26:34]. See what he says: you will deny me, not the man.' So far Jerome.

[227] It may well be that such things would be said cleverly and with applause in a school of declamatory rhetoric, but in sacred things one must not trifle; nor is it becoming to be clever, nor does it help to twist anything, lest we deprive of credit what is true while defending the false. The language of truth is simple according to the aphorism of the tragedian, but nothing is either simpler or truer than Christ. Perhaps we have the same thing when Augustine, in a certain homily about the woman caught in adultery, adapts to allegory the five husbands and the sixth man not her husband – rather forced, in my view. Now people philosophize everywhere over numbers – the numbers thirty, sixty, one hundred – adapting Hebrew matter to Greek and Latin numbers. Likewise, about the five thousand men who ate until full, the loaves, the two

---

89 Jerome ... so far Jerome.] Added in *1522*

The Figurative Character of the Language of 'Sacred Literature' 219

fishes, the talents (ten, five, and one), the three measures of flour, the[90] two sparrows, which they interpret as body and soul. Not that I would say that a mystery does not somewhere lie hidden in numbers, but that in certain cases alien and distorted interpretations seem to be proposed more[91] to display intellectual ability than to produce godliness, for with these they obscure the sacred teaching, just as Plato obscured philosophy with his numbers. And[92] yet now and then we want these petty comments to serve as the base on which we build a structure of serious dogmas. It is simplest, and also, I think, closest to the truth to take the ten, the five, and the one to mean the very much, the moderate, and the very little.

[228] Moreover,[93] I must in general advise the reader that in this matter Origen frequently errs, as do Ambrose, Hilary, and any others who gladly imitate Origen. For in their zeal to impose allegory upon the text, they banish the grammatical sense, quite unnecessarily. Therefore, whoever wishes to treat sacred literature seriously will observe moderation in interpretation of this sort. Moreover, it would be safest in tracing out allegories to follow the sources many of which the Lord himself opened up for us; Paul also some. But if anyone permits himself sometimes to indulge in allegories, he will be granted more forbearance when he does so in exhortation, in consolation, in rebuke than in asserting the truth. Ambrose seems sometimes to have attributed this to the joy of the Lord's day, for he writes thus: 'And since we have turned from typology to the moral interpretation, it is a delight on the Lord's day among so many pleasures of the believers to relax the mind, to add some clever pleasantries: Zacchaeus in the sycamore tree – doubtless the new fruit of the new time, so that in him this passage also was fulfilled, "The fig tree has put forth its green figs"' [Song of Solomon 2:13]. He admits that other things he has discussed in the same vein are somewhat forced, but they were given to delight the ears of believers, for it is better to relax the mind with pleasantries of this sort. Even though they do some violence to the Scriptures, still they put one in mind of something salutary.

[229] There are times when it is sufficient to have touched upon the chief point of the parable, even in those parables where allegory cannot be avoided. An example is the householder who remains on the watch for the thief in the night, which suggests nothing other than the

---

90 the two ... soul] Added in *1523*
91 more ... his numbers.] Added in *1523*
92 And ... dogmas.] Added in *1520*
93 Moreover ... salutary.] This paragraph was added in *1523*.

sudden and unexpected coming of that day [Matthew 24:43, 1 Thessalonians 5:2]. For[94] the sudden coming of Christ is not in every way like the thief who steals in unexpectedly. And if the householder had known the hour, he would have stayed awake. In our case, we must always remain on the watch, for the very reason that we do not know that time. Likewise, in the parable of the administrator who, in cheating his master, alleviated his debtors [Luke 16:1–13]: the analogy does not in every respect correspond – as though we also ought to attend to our own interests by fraud; rather, what in the parable is fraud against the master is in an allegorical sense faithfulness. That steward is said to be unjust because through falsified codicils he harmed the master and helped the debtors, and yet one who generously dispenses God's substance is said to be faithful. Now the steward was prudent: soon to be removed from his office, he took thought quickly and made friends for himself; by their kindness in turn he himself would be helped in the future. If such prudence is praised, how much more will God approve a similar prudence in us, should we, because we know that life is very short, hasten to bestow a kindness upon a neighbour from the gifts God has given us – especially since he whose gifts we dispense cannot be defrauded. Again, in the parable of the widow who shamelessly importunes the judge [Luke 18:1–8], the character of God does not correspond to the character of the ungodly judge, who neither feared God nor had regard for human beings. Again, in the parable of the nocturnal solicitor [Luke 11:5–8], the character of the man who lends bread to his friend is not consistent with God, for the man gave not because the solicitor was his friend but because the solicitor had worn him out with his tireless importunity; otherwise he would have refused. Accordingly, those who are eager to accommodate scrupulously all the parts of a parable to allegory frequently end up with more or less flat and trivial comments.

[230] There are those who disdain all allegories as arbitrary and dream-like. I strongly disagree with such people, since I see that, apart from allegory, many interpretations are either absurd or pernicious or futile, frivolous, and flat, and since it is clear that Christ used allegory and Paul interpreted some passages of the Old Testament allegorically. But just as I disagree with those, so I am not able to approve the inept allegorization by certain people who themselves invent the story they explain by allegory: a weary traveller sat upon the back of a huge dragon, having thought it was a tree trunk. Aroused, the dragon devoured the wretched fellow. The traveller is man, the dragon is the

---

94 For ... comments.] The remainder of the paragraph was added in *1523*.

world, which destroys those who rest upon it! And[95] others, sillier than these, have been published in regular books by certain people and are read by some with astonishing avidity. It is enough to accommodate to allegory the narratives found in sacred literature, should the subject so demand, provided we ourselves invent nothing in addition. I have heard a certain theologian of Paris who drew out the parable of the prodigal son to forty days, so that[96] it equalled the forty days of Lent, inventing details of the son's journey both as he went away and as he returned: now he was in an inn eating meat-pies prepared from tongues, now he was passing by a watermill, now[97] he was playing with dice, now he was lounging in some low tavern, now he was doing this, now that – and the theologian would twist the words of the prophets and evangelists to accommodate the trifles of this sort that he had composed. And meanwhile, he seemed to be a god to the unskilled multitude and to the rather thick-headed men of importance.

[231] The[98] zeal of such interpreters brings scarcely more profit than the zeal of those who, with plenty of leisure on their hands, have attempted to make theological matter fit figures and various outlines of letters (among whom, it seems, was Rabanus), or of those who attempt the same thing through fabricated pictures quite a bit more insipid than is the portrait of Cebes. This method has reached such a degree of inquisitive refinement that there have actually been people who have forced mystical meanings upon the game of pawns, or chess, as it is commonly called. Jerome has good reason to laugh at those who twist the tales of poets to apply to Christ – unless something is aptly turned in the direction of morals, when, for example, the tale of Proteus is directed against the fickle, the tale of Phaethon against the rash, of Tantalus against the avaricious and stingy, the tale of Midas against the stupid rich, of Danae against justice corrupted by money, the tales of Ixion and the Danaids against those who labour in vain. For there is no doubt that the ancients invented many narratives for this purpose.

[232] No mode of teaching, however, is more familiar or more effective than teaching by means of the comparison of similar things. Christ, who wanted his teaching to be in the highest degree accessible to the people, took his parables from the most common things. For who has

---

95 And ... avidity.] Added in *1522*
96 so that ... Lent] Added in *1520*
97 now ... tavern] Added in *1520*
98 The ... commonly called.] The first two sentences of this paragraph were added in *1523*.

not seen seed being cast on the ground? Who has not looked upon fisherman casting their nets? Who does not know that branches dry up when cut off? And these common things he makes marvellously fresh and new, adapting them to his philosophy. It belongs to the few to discuss the exceedingly acute[99] subtleties of the sons of Scotus; anyone at all is ready to philosophize in these comparisons. You see the sun arising; you rejoice. What pleasure will you feel if that sun of righteousness should arise before the eyes of your heart? Disease of the body is troublesome; how much more troublesome the disease of the soul. You shrink away from the contagion of a physical plague; much more must the contagion of pestilential morals be avoided. You think a garden blooming with all sorts of flowers, flourishing with all sorts of trees, an elegant thing; what a spectacle is the soul flourishing with innocence and abounding in every kind of virtue! You see a serpent; you have an example of Christian prudence. You see a dove; you have an image of Christian guilelessness. You see the deer; you have a symbol suggesting the eager pursuit of divine literature. You see a lamb; you have a type of the gentleness that harms no one. Winter bears down; you are admonished to bear up in adverse circumstances through the expectation of better fortune. Summer caresses; you are admonished to prepare for hardship to come. Old age is burdensome; you aspire to immortality. Youth is pleasant; you are admonished to prepare for the old age to come the supports of learning and the virtues. Thus, whatever this visible world offers to the corporeal eyes, of this you will find the archetype in the realm of the soul.

[233] Now, the sources from which allegories are to be sought are explained by Dionysius, in the work entitled *On the Divine Names*, in part by Augustine in *On Christian Doctrine* book 3, where the rules of Tyconius have been set forth and explained. Tyconius, in spite of the fact that he was, in the first place, incapable of good expression and, in the second, a Donatist, Augustine holds in rather more respect than we hold certain orthodox writers. I myself shall perhaps contribute something, if I find the leisure to complete a book I began long ago on theological allegories. Meanwhile, I shall add this one comment. *It is not enough to observe how in diverse things the eternal truth shines out in different ways – according to the historical sense*, which is straightforward, according to *the tropological sense*, which is concerned with morals and our life together, according to *the allegorical sense*, which investigates the hidden things of the head and the whole mystical body, according

---

99 exceedingly acute] Added in *1520*

to *the anagogical sense,* which touches upon the celestial hierarchy (for I see that certain people make such a division). One must also *consider in each of these individually what levels there are, what differences, what method of treatment is there. In how many ways does Origen treat Abraham's temptation from God,* and, *although he is engaged with history, still what topics does he find*! This is *not to mention,* meanwhile, *that* a *type receives a different shape, as it were, according to the variety of things, the diversity of times, to which it is accommodated. For example, the husks the swine feed upon,* with which in desperation the prodigal son is eager to fill his starving belly [Luke 15:3–32], *can be made to fit riches, pleasures, honours, worldly erudition, and yet you are still engaged in tropology. Further, that whole parable can be applied to the Jewish people and the Gentiles* of that time. The Gentiles come to their senses, repent, and are welcomed, the Jews murmur; and their common father soothes both. And now from the variation in persons and times to which the parable is being accommodated, a virtually new face is put upon the discourse, about which I have said something above. Furthermore, if anyone, perhaps, should look for a model to imitate, Origen is a most felicitous craftsman in handling allegories, while Ambrose is assiduous more than felicitous, except[100] that both are extravagant and generally more unfavourable to the historical sense than is proper.

A2 Elements of a Method for the Study of Scripture *(concluded)*

Means to the goal of personal transformation through study of Scripture, *continued*: knowing the 'testimonies' of Scripture at first hand, respecting their contexts

[234] Moreover, the theological candidate *must* especially *be advised of* this *also, that he learn to cite appropriately the testimonies of* sacred *Scripture, not from little summas* or review-lists or cheap and *trifling homiletical texts, or* other *excerpt-collections* of this sort *that have been poured back and forth* and mingled together *already an infinite number of times, one deriving from another, but from the sources themselves. He should not imitate certain people who are not ashamed to twist* forcibly *the oracles of the divine*

---

100 except ... proper.] Added in *1523*

wisdom to a sense foreign to them, sometimes even to the opposite sense. To save him from this, his first concern should be to learn thoroughly from those ancient interpreters the central thought of all the books of the Old and the New Testament. I have heard certain men, quite extraordinarily practised in the wrestling-schools of the Sorbonne, who in a packed assembly would philosophize at length – though the theme they had in the usual manner set out had not been understood, not even to the letter, as they say – and, to the great embarrassment of learned men, they would rant on, 'running beyond the olive trees,' as the Greek proverb has it. *There are some who bring their* own *doctrinal formulations with them,* and, imbued with popular opinions, *compel* arcane *Scripture* to serve *these, though one's own judgments should rather be sought from Scripture.* Hilary points this out with a fine turn in the first book *On the Trinity.* For him, the best reader of the divine books is one who looks for the understanding of the words from the words, rather than imposes it on them, and who has carried away more than he brought; nor does he compel the words to appear to signify the understanding he had assumed before the reading. *There are some who drag Scripture to the support of public moods and mores,* and since it suits to adopt this rule when they are considering *the course that should be followed, it is with the patronage of Scripture that they defend popular behaviour.*

[235] *Furthermore it is, indeed, a less obvious but for that very reason more harmful kind of distortion when we misuse the words of divine Scripture to interpret the church* – which is the body of Christ – *as the priests, the world* (a word that signifies evil affections) *as Christian laity,* just as though these do not belong to the church; *meanwhile applying* specifically *to monks what is said about* all *Christians.* Thus[101] we place in the world those whom Christ chose out of the world, and judge that those have been, as it were, removed from the world, who are out of the world as much as kidneys are outside the body of a living being. *What is said about divine worship we divert to ceremonies alone; what is said about the duty of the priest we refer to the prayers alone, however said.* Meanwhile,[102] with this whole explication violence is done to sacred literature, and the structure of an empty building is placed upon rotten foundations.

[236] Accordingly, whoever wishes to use the Scriptures rightly *should not think it enough to have picked out four or five little words* without *considering rather the context from which the words arise.* Frequently the sense of this or that passage depends upon what has preceded. He should weigh

---

101 Thus ... living being.] Added in *1520*
102 Meanwhile ... foundations.] Added in *1520*

carefully by whom the words are said, *to whom, the time, the occasion, the words*, the intent, *what has preceded, what follows. For it is from gathering and weighing these things that one grasps the meaning of what is said.*

[237] In these matters, this rule, too, must be observed, that the sense we elicit from obscure words should conform to that circle of Christian teaching, should conform to the life of Christ, finally, should conform to natural justice. Thus[103] Paul, urging the Corinthians that women should pray with their heads veiled, men, on the other hand, with heads uncovered, appeals to nature itself as evidence [1 Corinthians 11:4–15].

[238] I[104] must here indicate the error of those who take from the sacred books (in which various things are set forth in accordance with the difference in times, circumstances, and persons) only those bits that tend to justify their own inclinations, although no one understands a human law who has not examined carefully each of its principal parts, one by one. Hear the divine word, but hear all of it. You are a bishop; you are pleased that Christ said to Peter, 'I will give to you the keys of the kingdom of heaven' [Matthew 16:19]. But mark the words spoken to him when he dissuades Christ from facing the cross: 'Get behind me, Satan, because you savour not the things that are of God, but that are of men' [Mark 8:33]. Remember what was said to the same Peter: 'Follow me' [John 21:19, 22]. You are the pope; it is gratifying to be called the vicar of Christ, but meanwhile let the example of Christ, the death of Christ, come to mind. The one who succeeds to the office and title of Christ ought to succeed to his disposition and will. You are a priest; you are flattered by the words spoken to the apostles, 'Those whose sins you forgive, are forgiven' [John 20:23]. But notice what has preceded: 'Receive the Holy Spirit' [John 20:22]; mark what was said to these same apostles, 'Go and teach all nations' [Matthew 28:19]. You are pleased that Paul says presbyters are worthy of a double honour, but add what he adds, 'who rule well' [1 Timothy 5:17]. You put to your advantage the injunction in the books of the Old Testament that tithes be given to the Levites; but add to this the command that tithes be given to those excluded from a share in the land when it was divided, that tithes be given to those who would always attend on sacred things and be free for this alone, that tithes be given to those whose portion was the Lord God. How far from all this are those who now require from the populace more than the tithe. We plume ourselves because Peter said priests are a royal race [1 Peter 2:9]; but it does not occur to many that these

---

103 Thus ... evidence.] Added in *1523*
104 I ... healing.] This paragraph was added in *1520*.

same people must exhibit that of which Christ spoke: 'You are the salt of the earth; you are the light of the world' [Matthew 5:13, 14]. You are flattered because you imagine that Christ's words to Peter, 'Feed my sheep' [John 21:17], were also addressed to you; but remember, meanwhile, that he who said this demanded thrice the promise of love, even an extraordinary love, towards himself – for[105] he says, 'Do you love me more than these?' [John 21:15]. You preside over other bishops, but you are commanded to be superior to them also in love, you are commanded by the example of the supreme pastor to guard the safety of all at the cost of your own life [John 10:11–15]. You rejoice that your place on earth is next to Christ, but remember that it is your duty also to be next to him in sanctity of life. If we use sacred literature in this way, then, and only then, will it bring us health and healing.

[239] Certain people shamelessly turn the divine Scripture aside to a sense utterly foreign to it, like the man who twisted the words in Habakkuk, 'The tent-curtains of the land of Midian will tremble' [3:7]. These words were spoken about the tents of the enemy, but he twisted them to refer to Bartholemew, who had been flayed, as the story goes (though the story lacks credibility). Or like the man who, with utmost folly, diverted the statement found in the book of Judith, 'Circling round the valley, they came to the gate' [Judith 13:10 = 13:12 in the Vulgate], to the argumentation in the four books of Peter Lombard, who wrote the theological 'sentences.' And[106] what is even more subtle is this: he wants to see in these same words an allusion to the Lombard's name and surname! I would not be reporting these things if these same persons had not published their ditties, and if people were lacking who read such stuff eagerly and in earnest.

[240] There are those who play with the words of divine Scripture, and, as happens in the centos of the poets, use them, as though in sport, in a sense foreign to them. St Bernard sometimes does so – with more grace than gravity, at least in my judgment – for this distinguished man had drunk so deeply from sacred literature that Scripture appeared everywhere. Today, if some people want to seem amusing, they pervert the mystic words, turning them into scurrilous jokes, which is not only ignorant but also impious, and deserves to be punished. Jerome throws in the face of Origen the charge that he sometimes does violence to the Scriptures, though I think Origen's purpose is to lead us far away from the frequently sterile letter. Rather, nearly everyone of the ancients

---

105 for ... more than these?'] Added in *1522*
106 And ... in earnest.] Added in *1520*

sometimes twists the Scriptures whenever they contend with an adversary, even Jerome himself, as he virtually confesses at one point. In these endeavours, therefore, one must observe very carefully whether any violence is being done to the sacred words – unless someone thinks it is right to do so whenever an enemy has to be taken, or the souls of the weak have to be deterred from vices.

[241] I think the right way is to treat the sacred words appropriately and without violation. If you take care at first to do this as well as you can, later you will do so with ease besides. Although I should like this principle to be maintained everywhere, it is, nevertheless, especially appropriate to maintain it when we are dealing with an opponent of our religion, or when falsehood is being refuted and the truth affirmed, or when the sense of mystic Scripture is being expounded. Otherwise, the effect is that we not only fail to carry the point we are establishing, but we become a laughing stock to our own adversary. And yet in my opinion there is no other respect in which the ancients were more at fault.

[242] This is the case, I think, with Ambrose in the sixth chapter of the second book *On the Holy Spirit*. Against the Arians, he infers from the passage in Paul's Epistle to the Philippians, the third chapter, 'who in spirit serve God' [3:3 Vulgate], that the Holy Spirit is plainly called God; for he connects these two words, *pneumata* [spirit] and *theos* [God], though a different sense is expressed by the Greek words. The Greek means rather that we worship God not with ceremonies and corporeal victims, but with our spirit – especially since the definite article is not added to 'spirit,' which,[107] it would seem, ought to have been added at this point if he had been thinking of that Divine Spirit. Again,[108] there is another example in Ambrose when he expounds the passage in the Second Epistle of Paul to Timothy, the second chapter, 'But in a great house there are not only vessels etc' [2:20]. With great irritation he rejects and hisses off the stage the interpretation of Novatian, who interpreted the great house of the rich man as the world, which consists of the good people and the bad. To prove his point Ambrose cites the gospel passage, 'You are not of the world, but I have chosen you out of the world' [John 15:19]. But this divine declaration does nothing for the case against Novatian, for Novatian was thinking of this visible world, which embraces every kind of thing, while Christ, on the other hand, figuratively designates by the 'world' the desires to which is subject the common crowd of human beings who seek temporal and fleeting

---

107 which ... Divine Spirit.] Added in *1522*
108 Again ... Novatian.] The remainder of the paragraph was added in *1520*.

things instead of eternal. And there was no reason why, through hatred of Novatian, Ambrose should have been vexed at a good interpretation, which even St Chrysostom follows, though he had no connection with the heresy of Novatian.

[243] Another case: from the words of the Canaanite woman, 'Have mercy on me, O Lord, Son of David' [Matthew 15:22], Bede concludes and strongly affirms that with perfect faith the woman had believed that Christ was both God and man (which not even the apostles themselves, I think, had, at that time, believed). Bede[109] bases his interpretation especially on the fact that the text goes on to say that 'she fell and worshipped Jesus' – but does everyone who addresses another with the name of lord acknowledge him as God? Is it unusual to seek help of this kind from holy men also? Does not[110] Mephibosheth in the second book of Kings fall forward upon his face and do obeisance to King David? [2 Samuel 9:6]. Is it not written of Cornelius in the Acts of the Apostles that, falling at Peter's feet, he worshipped him [10:25] – and this is not to recount many other passages. It seems to me quite brash to assert rigorously anything on the basis of an argument whose refutation would occur at once even to a poorly educated man. And so that no one may falsely charge me with reporting Bede's comments in a deliberately inaccurate way, I shall add the words of Bede himself: 'For she has great fullness of faith who, entreating the kindness of the Saviour, says, "Have mercy upon me, O Lord, Son of David." For since the one she calls Son of David she also calls Lord, it is crystal clear that she believed this one was true man and true God.' Soon there follows: 'But in this, that after many tears she at length falls upon the ground and worships him, saying, "Lord, help me!" she shows that she is not in the slightest degree doubtful about the divine majesty of the one whose power, she had learned, was to be worshipped as the power of God.' Such are the words of Bede.

[244] Again, there is a case in Augustine on the words of the Baptist found in John, the first chapter: 'And I did not know him, but[111] he who sent me to baptize with water said to me, "He upon whom you will see the Spirit descending and remaining upon him, this is the one that baptizes with the Holy Spirit"' [1:33]. Augustine thinks these words a powerfully effective weapon for putting to rout all the hosts of the Donatists, interpreting that this alone had hitherto lain concealed from John,

---

109 Bede ... worshipped Jesus'] Added in *1522*
110 Does not ... words of Bede.] The remainder of this paragraph was added in *1522*.
111 but ... Holy Spirit."'] Added in *1520*

that Christ had reserved the authority of baptism for himself – for John knew all the rest:[112] he[113] knew that Jesus was the Son of God, he knew that he was God and man, he knew that he was the Christ, he knew that he had come to redeem and save the human race; he knew that he was the one who had come to baptize with water and the Holy Spirit. What, then, did the Father teach him by the sign of the dove? Doubtless this, that Christ would keep his baptism for himself, and would give it over not even to any of his disciples. Now, Augustine speaks at length in this vein, and with plausibility sufficient indeed for those who were persuaded that the Donatists were mad – as indeed they were. For even the very form of the discourse shows that he had accommodated that discussion to the minds and ears of those present and to the circumstances of that time.

[245] But if the matter were to be taken seriously, if, taking up arms, one would have to meet with an adversary in hand-to-hand combat, I do not see what force these weapons would have, though by relying on them among his own people Augustine scored a sort of triumph for himself. I do not wish for the present to probe too deeply why baptism has been permitted to all, when the administration of the other sacraments has been entrusted to so few, especially when each of the following statements was made by the same person to the same people: 'Go, baptize all nations' [Matthew 28:19] and 'Whose sins you forgive, they are forgiven them' [John 20:23]. Moreover, I do not intend to consider whether, just as the right to absolve is taken away, so the right to baptize can be taken away; then, whether the church cuts anyone off with the intent that afterwards he does not perform any ecclesiastical duty; further, whether Donatists believed that those who have once truly received baptism and fallen back into ungodly living have to be baptized again, or whether those who have been baptized with water in heresy and by heretics have truly received baptism. Nor do I wish to inquire whether what Augustine has propounded regarding the sacraments and the mark imprinted rests on sufficiently effective arguments. For I do not disagree at all with him on the issue, and I regard the Donatists not only as heretics, but also as schismatics and raging mad brigands. And he easily persuades me – with whatever

---

112 At this point the text in *1519* contained a sentence that was removed in *1520* when a long addition was inserted; see next note.
113 he ... win a victory.] The remainder of this and the next two paragraphs to the end of **246** were added in *1520*.

arguments – because the authority of the church and hatred of schism persuades even without proof.

[246] Meanwhile, we consider only whether this Gospel passage is sufficiently effectual to refute the error of the Donatists. For in the first place, what Augustine asserts and drives home so many times – that John was ignorant only of the fact that Christ was keeping baptism especially for himself – will have no effect upon the adversary. For the statement, 'This is he who baptizes' [John 1:33], does not adequately prove Augustine's claim, since the Gospel adds, 'with spirit and with fire,' distinguishing not the author of baptism but the kind of baptism. With respect to John's baptizing, he was baptizing on the authority of God [Matthew 21:23–7, Mark 11:27–33, Luke 20:1–8]. Besides, if from the words 'This is the one who baptizes' one contends that no one but Christ baptizes, how does Paul say that he baptized the household of Stephanas [1 Corinthians 1:16]? How does Christ give to the apostles the mandate, 'Go and baptize' [Matthew 28:19], if he alone baptizes? Nor does it immediately follow that, if Christ is the author of all the sacraments, these are for this reason conferred through anyone at all. The Donatists assumed that heretics were outside the fellowship of the church, outside of which there was no baptism. To establish this point, Cyprian uses many testimonies from the Scriptures and likewise a great many arguments, and with him many bishops whose votes are recorded in the Acts of the Synod of Carthage. For me at least, what the church has defined is in every way approved. I have brought these things forward only to show by way of example a passage that has been twisted to win a victory.

keeping a theological commonplace book, construing obscure passages of Scripture in the light of clearer ones

[247] *What I am now about to say will perhaps offer an advantage of the highest importance to anyone who applies the principle with skill. It is this: either prepare for yourself or take over from someone else a number of theological headings under which you put everything you have read, placing them into something like little pigeon-holes so that you might the more readily produce or store away what you wish, when you please – I note by way of example the subject of faith, of fasting, of enduring evils, helping the weak,* enduring ungodly magistrates, avoiding offence to the simple, the study of sacred literature, *godly devotion* to parents or children, Christian charity, honouring the leading people, envy, disparagement, chastity, *and*

other things of this kind (for countless *categories can be imagined*). *Arrange these in order according to opposites or similarities, as I once pointed out in my Copia also. Whatever is noteworthy anywhere in all the books of the Old Testament, in the Gospels,* in Acts, *in the apostolic Epistles, that either agrees or disagrees should be listed under the appropriate category. In fact, if anyone likes, he can bring to these topics what he deems will be of use from the ancient commentators; likewise, lastly, from the books of the pagans. I rather think I notice from Jerome's own writings that he used this method. If something has to be discussed, materials will be ready at hand; if something is to be clarified, a comparison of passages will be easy.*

[248] *For in the opinion of not only Origen but of Augustine also, the best method of interpreting divine literature is this: to make an obscure passage clear through a comparison of other passages, to explain mystic Scripture from mystic Scripture,* the sacred from the sacred. From[114] this, indeed, not only will one reap the advantage that the meaning, not otherwise understood, will be perceived, but authority will be added. For although the authority of divine Scripture everywhere even with a single word is sufficient for us, still sometimes cases arise where there can be ambiguity about the interpretation, especially when even the ancients quite often disagree. Accordingly, if many passages agree, they will stimulate confidence; if they disagree or are even in conflict, they will arouse us to a more thorough investigation. A case[115] in point: the Lord says, 'No flesh shall see me and live' [Exodus 33:20], and yet Luke says on the authority of Isaiah [40:5, 52:10], 'All flesh shall see the salvation of God' [Luke 3:6]. Again, Paul says, 'Flesh and blood shall not possess the kingdom of God' [1 Corinthians 15:50], and yet Job's words are: 'And in my flesh I shall see my God' [19:26]. Likewise, in the Gospel Christ forbids us to be angry [Matthew 5:22], and yet in the Psalms we read, 'Be angry and sin not' [4:4]; hence it follows that either Christ did not have in mind just any anger at all, or the words of the psalmist must be understood not as teaching us to be angry but that if anger wells up, it should not reach the point of becoming injurious. Likewise, here is a case: Christ at one point allows his disciples to take staff and wallet for their journey; elsewhere again he forbids them even these.

[249] This contradiction lies sometimes only in the words, sometimes in deeds, sometimes in a mixture of both. I have just given an example

---

114 From ... arcane discourse.] The remainder of this paragraph and the next two paragraphs to the end of **250** were added in *1520*, with the exception of a short insertion in *1522*; see next note.
115 A case ... Likewise] The first three of the following instances were added in *1522*.

of contradiction in words. Concerning deeds, this can be an example: though Peter patiently endured whipping and imprisonment by the Jews [Acts 5:17–21, 40], he did not extend the same mildness to Ananias and his wife Sapphira, but announced to them, when he had sharply rebuked them, their immediate end [Acts 5:1–11]. Again, with mildness and gentleness he calls an unbelieving people back to their senses to repent [Acts 2:37–40, 3:17–26]; Ananias and Sapphira he does not likewise urge to return to their senses and repent, but punishes them on the spot. And yet he does not punish Simon, who was about to buy the gift of the Holy Spirit, although he had already been baptized, but admonishes him to come to his senses and repent, holding out to him some hope of pardon if he changed [Acts 8:9–24].

[250] The following can serve to exemplify the mixed genre: Christ in the Gospel forbids all oaths [Matthew 5:34], and yet Paul swears so many times in his Epistles [Romans 1:9 and 9:1, 2 Corinthians 1:23, 1 Timothy 2:7]. Christ bids us turn the left cheek to one who strikes us on the right [Matthew 5:39]; he himself, when struck at his trial, even expostulated with the striker [John 18:23]. So far is Paul from offering the other cheek that, in return for a blow, he hurls at the high priest, his judge, a rebuke that was not much more gentle than a blow [Acts 23:2–3]. Likewise, when we read, 'You will destroy all who speak a lie' [Psalm 5:6], yet we read that certain excellent persons employed the lie, like Abraham and Judith [Genesis 20:2–13, Judith 10:11–13, 11:1–19]. In these cases, therefore, the deeds of the saints, contradicting as it seems the teaching of the sacred books, remind us that there lies in the words a different sense from the one the discourse projects at first glance. Moreover, this comparison of passages will bring the further benefit that we shall recognize with more certainty the idioms and tropes of arcane discourse.

having Scripture, especially the New Testament, constantly in hand and mind, committing it to memory, assimilating it inwardly

[251] *And now, furnished with these things, let* our theological tiro[116] *engage in constant meditation on divine literature, let him 'take care to turn by night, by day' its pages. Let him have the Scriptures always in hand, always in pocket; from Scripture let something always sound in his ears, or meet his eyes*

---

116 our theological tiro] First in 1522; previously 'him'

or hover within his mind. What has been fixed deep within through constant use will become a part of one's nature. In my opinion *it will not be ill-advised to learn the divine books word for word* even though they are not understood. For this opinion Augustine is my authority; by the words, 'even though not understood,' I take him to mean, 'even if you do not yet catch the mystic sense.' For to do what we see being done among some monks, and to learn the Psalms exactly as parrots learn the words of human beings, has more tedium than benefit. Not only do things we understand stick in the memory more readily and more tenaciously, but also with greater usefulness.

[252] I should like this memorization to be done first with *the books of the New Testament, which contribute so much more effectively to our profession that today they* can almost[117] *suffice even by themselves,* now that, clearly, the teaching of Christ has been spread abroad and implanted in the minds of all. For long ago it was necessary to appeal to the authority of the Old Testament to lead the Jews to the faith. Now we have little to do with the Jews, and for other people the books of the Hebrews do not have the same authority, though I would not deny that the greatest benefit is received from those books if anyone, by applying allegory, accommodates them either to the Christ sketched out in them, or to morals – and if one does not do so to excess, but now and then. There are some passages to which it is silly to apply allegory verbatim, because many details are put in not to add some special meaning, but to maintain the course and sequence of the narrative; so[118] Augustine teaches, and along with him John Chrysostom in the sixty-fifth homily on Matthew, where he expounds the parable of the men hired for the vineyard [Matthew 20:1–16]. With us, therefore, the first place of honour should be given to the New Testament, through which we are Christians and where Christ is much more distinctly portrayed for us than in the Old; the next place to the Old, and in *the Old to those books that have a particularly close correspondence to the New,* like the books of *Isaiah. And yet if, by arranging passages as I have said, you frequently compare* the *Pauli*ne Epistles *with the Gospels, and compare Isaiah and the rest of the Old Testament passages with both, these will of their own accord stick in the memory and become fixed there.*

[253] *If this labour deters some people, I ask that each reflect on this: how is it appropriate that the future theologian commit to memory the petty rules of sophistic, commit to memory commentaries on Aristotle (such as they are)* – or even a paraphrase – *commit to memory the so-called 'conclusions'*

---

117 almost] Added in *1522*
118 so ... vineyard.] Added in *1522*

and arguments of Scotus, *but is reluctant to bestow the same effort upon the divine books, from whose springs all theology flows – such, at least, as truly is theology?* But how much more satisfying it is to swallow this labour (not to say 'tedium') *once and for all than to have recourse to dictionaries, summaries, and indexes – with labour ever recurring* in endless round *– whenever you have to cite or discuss something!* They do as certain people like myself do, *who, having no dishes at home, whenever they need goblet or plate beg their neighbour for one to use.* But our wise man rightly advises to drink water from your own well [Proverbs 5–15]. So far should you be from any necessity to beg from someone else that you will rather draw from your own spring to give to others. Therefore, passing by those jumbled formularies and the sullied pools of summaries, *make your own breast a library of Christ.* As the prudent head of a household, *bring forth from it as from a storehouse things new or old* [Matthew 13:52], *as the occasion demands. Things penetrate the minds of the hearers in a much more lively way when they come forth from your own heart as though with the vigour of life than when they are filched from the mishmash of others.*

reading Scripture in the light of the exegesis of the ancient theologians, becoming like them

[254] But meanwhile *someone asks, 'Well, surely* for your part *you don't think Divine Scripture so easy* and accessible *that it can be understood apart from commentaries?'* Why not to some extent, that is,[119] to the degree sufficient not for theatrical display, but for sound teaching, *if its teachings have been learned first, and that comparison of passages, as I have described, has been applied. In any case, what else have they done who* were the *first to publish commentaries on Divine Scripture? Chief among these is Origen,* who so began to weave this lovely web that no one after him dared to put a hand to it. Then[120] Tertullian, older than Origen, and a man so prodigiously learned in Divine Scripture that Cyprian with good reason used to call him his master. *What prevents others from arriving at the same goal as these if they proceed by the same path?*

[255] I do not say these things because I want to give authority to anyone to pass over the commentaries of the ancients, and to claim or even hunt for himself a knowledge of Divine Scripture. *Rather let the labour of the ancients save us from part of the work, let us find assistance in their commentaries, provided, first, that we choose the best of them, for example,*

---

119 that is ... sound teaching] Added in *1522*
120 Then ... master.] Added in *1522*

Origen, who is so far ahead that no one else can be compared to him; after him, Basil, Nazianzus, Athanasius, Cyril, Chrysostom, Jerome, Ambrose, Hilary, Augustine; second, that we read even these with judgment and discrimination, though I want them to be read with respect. *They were men: certain things they did not know, at points their minds wandered, sometimes they were nodding, they conceded some things to the heretics in order to overcome them in any way at all (for at that time all things were seething with the contentions of the heretics)*; certain[121] *things they imparted for the ears of those to whom they were then speaking.*

[256] *Moreover, to virtually every one of these are falsely ascribed many titles that are in circulation; and, indeed (what is more shameful) in their books many passages have been added by others, as, in the case of Jerome, at least, I have publicly demonstrated,* and[122] *then in Cyprian, and I shall perhaps demonstrate the same thing in Augustine. It would not be that much trouble to do the same with the rest, that is, with Origen, Ambrose, and Chrysostom. But here, too, if the reader does not have eyes for cases like this, there is a danger that he will take the whim of an imposter or fool as an oracle of Jerome or Ambrose.* Thus, today certain men 'praise those whose thoughts rise higher than the sun.' So says Jerome in a certain discourse, so Augustine in one of his homilies, 'To the Hermit Brethren' – as though such men were pronouncing an oracle from a tripod.

[257] A choice, should, therefore, be made not only of authors, but also of works. And among authors there is not only this distinction, that the Greeks surpass the Latin writers, the ancients the recent, but also that even in individual characteristics one is better than another. For[123] example, no one is more instructive than Origen, no one treats commonplaces more felicitously than John Chrysostom, in the exposition of sacred literature Jerome has deserved no ordinary praise, Thomas [Aquinas] is very clear, Scotus quite subtle and studied. Among works you must take care not to take for the genuine and the true something that is bastard and supposititious.

[258] Accordingly, *since* there is not the leisure *to go through* everything – for there is such a great number of books, and time is so fleeting – it remains that first of all *we read the best. What does one gain by investing good time badly in these neoterics, who are more truly compilers than interpreters? In the first place, how many things there are in these that you must*

---

121 certain ... then speaking.] Added in *1523*
122 and then in Cyprian] Added in *1520*
123 For ... studied.] These two sentences were added in *1523*.

afterward unlearn with greater effort! Secondly, if there is anything good in them, you will find that it has been drawn from the ancients, but generally *maimed and mutilated, because the moderns have been compelled on account of their ignorance of languages and essential subjects to omit many things (and these possibly the best) since they did not understand them. What of the fact that a good many of them do not even gather their materials from the ancients, but filch them from collections that have themselves quite often have been* mingled *and* mixed together, *as though they had been drawn from the very last of a series of pools, so that they taste almost nothing like their source? Further, to prevent the appearance of having contributed nothing of their own, these people add a sprinkling of their own fantasies, or mix in something from some cheap author born but a day ago – as 'when a cook mixes many sauces together,' as Plautus says. Finally, granted that they teach the same things* as the early writers, *how frigid all things are with them, how mean they seem because of the most ineloquent stammering* of their speech! *But Jerome so seasons and enriches all things with sweet delights that when he wanders from the truth* or *digresses from the subject, he still teaches more that is good than they do when they deliver the subject correctly – not to mention further that we ourselves do become altogether like the authors with whom we are constantly engaged. For the properties of foods are not transferred into the condition of our body in the same way as reading affects the mind and character* of the reader. *If we are occupied with dry, frigid, artificial, thorny, and quarrelsome writers, we will inevitably become like them. But if we are occupied with those who truly* taste *of Christ, who glow, who are alive* and active, *who both teach and manifest true godliness, we shall resemble these, at least to some degree.*

Polemical coda: the difference between this practice of theology and the current kind

[259] *But, you will say, if there is nothing further, I shall be inadequately prepared for the scholastic palaestra. Well, we are training not a pugilist but a theologian, and a theologian who prefers to express with his life rather than in syllogisms what he professes. There is no reason why you should be so greatly displeased with yourself if among those* you are regarded as *not much of a theologian, since among them not even Jerome himself would have any response to make, possibly not even our very Paul. At fault is not theology itself, which was not created thus, but its treatment by certain individuals who have dragged down that entire discipline to the subtleties of dialectics and to Aristotelian philosophy, so that there is much more philosophy than*

theology there. And yet it is possible for some rhetorician or mathematician or musician to discuss the same thing in such a way that no one will now understand it except one who has first learned the whole essence of these disciplines. But why is it necessary for the theologian to make definitive responses to all the petty questions of everyone? Of these there is neither number, nor measure, nor end, while a thousand spring forth afresh, like the hydra's head for every one lopped off.

[260] *There are some things it is not really pious to investigate; there are some things of which we can be ignorant without any cost to our salvation; in the case of some things greater erudition is revealed by being doubtful and, with the Academics, by withholding judgment, than by making a pronouncement.* For what is the profit if I torture myself about whether God is able to create a person without sin; whether God is one when one [of the persons] has been distinguished from him; whether it is possible to establish relation without foundation and termination; whether the soul of Christ could have been duped or could have deceived; whether this proposition, 'God is a beetle,' is as possible as this one, 'God is a man'; whether[124] the power of generation in the Father is something absolute in him or a quality of the Father; whether the Persons are established in their personhood through relations of origin; whether all the ages of eternity make one age; whether grace and charity are different; whether grace is in the essence of the soul or in its potential; whether the body was formed and quickened before the Word was enfleshed; whether the soul of Christ was given the highest grace that can be bestowed upon a creature; whether the soul of Christ knows all things in the Word that the Word itself knows; whether the soul of Christ grieved at the moment of its conception; whether the fire of hell is of the same kind as ours?

[261] Some[125] things it is enough to have investigated to a limited degree; to pry too far is forbidden. St John Chrysostom[126] in the tenth homily on John's Gospel thinks it sufficient for us to have learned that in the person of Christ the divine nature had been joined together with the human body and soul in some ineffable bonding, such that the

---

124 whether ... same kind as ours.] The remainder of the paragraph was added in *1522*. At this point Erasmus introduced into the *1519* text large insertions in *1520, 1522*, and (one) in *1523*. The *1519* text picked up again at **272**; see n138 below and, for further precision on the splicing and recycling of material in successive editions, CWE 41 699 nn1089 and 1116.
125 Some ... predecessors.] This paragraph was added in *1520*, the first in a long addition, later broken by insertions in *1522* and *1523*, running to **272**.
126 John Chrysostom] First in *1522*; in *1520*, 'Ambrose'

same *hypostasis* embraced natures distinct from one another – but he does not think we should further examine how this was done. He says, 'Do not, then, seek the "how" of this; it happened as Christ himself knows.' But among us how many questions have arisen, how many opinions, how many factions of those who dispute whether Christ assumed human nature in general or in its individual particularity, or whether he is in some third way called God and man! And though there was little agreement on this subject among the ancients, a certain man has recently also arisen, and shown a new way, rejecting the opinions of his predecessors.

[262] In[127] his fourth homily on Matthew, Chrysostom also shows that the evangelist did not dare rashly to define anything about the nativity of Christ according to the flesh. Matthew demonstrates only that the Holy Spirit was the artificer of that marvellous conception, and in this way the evangelist succinctly freed himself from all questions. Chrysostom says, 'What the omnipotent spirit of God has done is not incredible.' What that spirit has accomplished by its own hidden plan is to us inscrutable [Romans 11:33]. For us it is enough to believe, to retain, to revere, what has been written. In the same passage Chrysostom very much wonders at the rashness, or rather, the madness (as he calls it), of those who delve into that eternal nativity by which he is begotten outside of time and which no human words are able to express nor is any human mind able to conceive. But if this opinion from a most holy man were one we accepted, clearly we would regard a good part of scholastic theology as superfluous, and those who strive for a knowledge of sacred doctrine would be relieved of the largest part of their labours.

[263] If[128] these were activities undertaken for amusement in conversations and at dinner parties, one could put up with them. As it is, these things are both taught and learned in the schools; in these labyrinthine puzzles[129] the life of the young and even of the old is wasted, as though these were matters especially worthy of a theologian. These are preferred to the writings of Jerome, Ambrose, Cyprian, and Hilary, and,[130] indeed, to the divine books. If people give some proof of themselves in these trifles, they become bachelors without having read a

---

127 In ... part of their labours.] This paragraph was added in *1522*.
128 If ... in every respect.] This paragraph and the first sentence of the next were added in *1520* except for a short addition in *1522*; see n130.
129 labyrinthine puzzles] First in *1523*; previously, 'trifles'
130 and ... Pauline Epistles.] Added in *1522*

Gospel or the Pauline Epistles. And yet, the more recent theologians seem to have exerted themselves especially to this end that they might appear to have added something to the ancients. To me, it seems not only superfluous but also dangerous so anxiously to investigate with human argumentation things that belong to matters of faith. For one seems to have some doubts who draws together with such solicitude and such investigative diligence the arguments with which one may either attack or defend what has been handed down to us – handed down not so that we might dispute, but that we might believe. And it often happens that when one is tracking everything down with more inquisitive diligence than piety, certain considerations arise that shake and uproot the solid core of faith. I myself know some people who used to admit that they were led so far by the subtleties with which Scotus treats the subject of the Eucharist that they absolutely were wavering and were scarcely able to free themselves from their perplexity.

[264] I should not ask anyone to trust me if it were not that St Chrysostom agrees with me in every respect. For[131] in the first homily on Matthew, it is on this count that he warns us against the books of the philosophers. They do, indeed, discuss virtue, but in a confusing and tiresome way, as when Stoics, Epicureans, Academics, and Peripatetics contend among themselves with intricate disputes about what is the honourable and in what lies the good. Further, though virtue is something to be practised, these spend their whole life investigating what it is. Certain things, therefore, are harmful simply because they are taught in a way that is verbose and obscurely involved, though Christ wanted his teaching to be completely straightforward, and easy and accessible even to farmers. He sets forth his teaching in words few and clear: 'You shall love the Lord your God with your whole heart and your neighbour as yourself' [Luke 10:27]. Surely someone who prattles on with so many subtleties about the nature of God, and raises so many complicated questions on the subject of charity – what it is, how it is received, where and to what extent it is appropriate to manifest it – is harmful by the very fact that he delays the person who is hastening to the thing itself? And love itself you would more quickly find among simple, uneducated people than among those who endlessly debate.

---

131 For ... but also] The remainder of this paragraph, the next paragraph, and part of the first sentence of **266** were added in *1522*. The 1520 text continues at n133.

[265] Some time ago, I happened to be debating with a certain theologian, in other respects a learned and irreproachable man, but one who had been far too long occupied with the subtleties of Scotus. Our subject was the sacraments, and there was not much on which we agreed. Turning to one who was seated beside him, he said, 'If this fellow[132] should bend his efforts towards teaching Greek to someone, he would not be able to accomplish this in a few days. And how can he himself possibly understand at once what a sacrament is?' A fine thing it is, indeed, if for ten long years we must debate what a sacrament is when the benefit of the sacraments is essential for everyone's salvation!

[266] Chrysostom also censures disputation among Christians that is philosophical and clever more truly than godly, not only in many other places, but also when[133] he expounds the passage in Paul in which the latter warns Timothy against fables and interminable genealogies [1 Timothy 1:4]. It will be better, I think, to set down Chrysostom's words: 'Do you see,' he says, 'how Paul condemns inquiries of this sort, and tries to cut them off? For where there is faith, there is no need for searching. Where the restless investigation of anything is unnecessary, what need is there for inquiry? Searching does away with faith, for one who searches has not yet found; one who searches is able to believe only with difficulty. For this reason Paul urges us not to be occupied with inquiries like this. For if we are seeking we are no longer believing, for faith puts at rest our mind and our thinking.' Then, at those who throw in our faces the shifty excuse that Christ himself has bidden us to seek in order that we might find, to knock in order that the door might be opened [Matthew 7:7, Luke 11:9], to search the Scriptures wherein we find life [John 5:39], Chrysostom hurls this retort, that the seekers are those who are engaged with great ardour of soul in the sacred books rather than in the petty questions of human beings; who ask God with pure prayers, that he impart his Spirit, which searches in us even the deep things of God[134] [1 Corinthians 2:10]; by saying that we have been ordered to search, not because we should be always seeking, but for this reason, that we should cease to seek when we have been assured by the authority of the Scriptures. So far Chrysostom.

---

132 this fellow] First in *1523*; in *1522*, 'Erasmus'
133 but also when ... superstitious multitude?] Added in *1520*. The addition includes the remainder of this and the subsequent three paragraphs to the end of **269**. For a significant revision in *1522/1523*, see n135.
134 of God] Omitted in *1522*

[267] To this it should be added that it has not been said, 'Search Aristotelian philosophy to see whether the resurrection of the dead can be taught with its help,' but, 'Search the Scriptures.' And Paul, in the passage from Timothy, showing how far the scrutiny of arcane Scripture should be taken and to what goal the learning of theology should be directed, says, 'The end of the commandment is charity from a pure heart and a good conscience, and from faith unfeigned' [1 Timothy 1:5]. We must therefore philosophize in sacred literature just so far as our diligence leads to these things Paul has mentioned. In truth, those who have not set before themselves this goal, but aim to bring forward a number of paradoxes and novelties in order to be an object of admiration to the populace (which always admires vanities!), these become 'mateologians' instead of theologians. Paul portrays these in the following words: 'From which things some, going astray, are turned aside to vain babbling, desiring to be teachers of the Law, understanding neither the things they say nor whereof they affirm' [1 Timothy 1:6–7].

[268] Even such things could be borne if this stage play were being acted out within the walls of academic institutions. But now this exhibitionism has invaded the sacred discourses themselves (why should I not say 'sacred' when sermons were once a part of the sacrifice?). How often have I been ashamed of it! How often have I lamented the lot of the people! I see the plain and artless multitude, open mouthed and eager to hang upon every word of the speaker, to await food for its soul, desiring to learn so that it might return home better, and there some theologast (whose reverent bearing and appearance almost make him an object of adoration) is tossing about some intricate and insipid question from Scotus or Ockham, showing how far he has progressed in the Sorbonne, and looking for the favour of the people by this display. Meanwhile, a large part of the assembly goes home, clearly, as the Greek proverb has it, 'gaping like a wolf.' Others repeat to one another how much this young man has read, how talented he is: what would he not be able either to construct or to demolish? No one is delighted except the few who are infected with the same disease – these have something to wrangle over during their supper.

[269] This is the teaching that James calls 'sensual' and 'devilish.' It is different from that which Paul, writing to Timothy, designates as 'sound teaching,' to be handed down in sincere rather than sophistical discourse, effectual at one and the same time both for urging on the laggards and for comforting the downcast, and for confuting adversaries. Then, soon, he portrays the mateologians in these words, 'For there

are many also not subject, who talk nonsense and deceive minds, on whom silence must be imposed. They overturn entire houses, teaching what they ought not for the sake of base gain' [Titus 1:10–11]. If only we had such preachers as the former type – for then these admonitions of mine might seem to have been to no purpose. But whenever we hear those of the latter kind commending papal indulgences in such a way that the whole speech smells of nothing but filthy profit, betrays nothing but an agent contracted for a fee; whenever, in undisguised adulation, they attribute more power to the Roman pontiff than he himself either acknowledges or demands; whenever they boast of their own benefactions to which the people owes its welfare; whenever[135] they each extol with extravagant praises their own saint, all the while vaunting boastfully their own order; whenever they try to persuade that the evil spirit has no power over those who are buried in the habit of this or that saint, that the home that has the cloak of such a saint will be blessed, that the person who wears the garb sacred to the saint will recover from disease, that one who looks daily upon a picture or a statue of Christopher will not perish miserably: whenever one who has been consecrated for the preaching of the gospel babbles from the pulpit these inanities and others more shameful than these, who would not lament? who would not have compassion on the undiscerning and superstitious multitude?

[270] With[136] what weariness for good people are the companions of Dominic or Francis often heard while both groups bear aloft their own saints with much too boastful praises! I myself heard a certain man who would not hesitate, I know well, to swear that no more distinguished theologian had ever come out of Friesland than himself; who used to proclaim the praises of Catherine of Siena: that while still a girl she knew from memory all the rules of the holy Fathers – of Benedict, Francis, Bridget, and the like; that Jesus himself, taking the girl as his bride, placed the ring on her finger with his own hands; that so intimate was the companionship between Jesus and the girl that they frequently walked together in the bedroom from one end to the other, talking with one another about various things, 'just like a girl and a youth,' said he, 'who are desperately in love with one another' – and

---

135 whenever ... from disease] Thus the revised text of *1523*, after removal of references to Franciscans and Dominicans inserted in *1520*. This revised text should have been in place in *1522* but had then been partly scrambled in type; for details, see CWE 41 707 n1125.
136 With ... are intelligent.] This paragraph was added in *1523*.

he added a vulgar expression that signifies extra-marital love. That we might stand even more in awe, he added, 'So intimate was their companionship that they frequently said their "hours" together in alternating responses: he would chant first, "Lord, open thou my lips," and she would then respond, "And my mouth shall show forth thy praise" [Psalm 51:15].' When he was preaching these and many other things of the same sort, he saw, I suppose, someone laughing, and he swelled up with anger in his whole being. He said, 'Someone might say that these are idle tales, but the same person will also be able to call the story of Lazarus' resurrection and the other stories reported in the Gospels "idle tales."' What could one have heard more impious than this utterance? Last of all, as though the talk here had not been sufficiently absurd, he promised that he would tell some similar tales about his Catherine every day throughout the entire octave. I report this not to besmirch anyone, for I designate no one, but to advise theologians not to speak with absurdity like this in front of the people, some of whom are intelligent.

[271] But[137] to return to contentious questions. See how anxiously Paul warns his own Timothy against them. He says, 'Do not contend with words, for it leads to nothing except to the subversion of the hearers' [2 Timothy 2:14]. Then, soon, when he had bidden him divide rightly the word of truth, he added, 'But avoid the language of empty novelties' [2:15–16]. Again, to Titus when he had reminded him of many things that contribute to godly ways, he urges him – pressingly – to reject foolish questions and genealogies and contentions that come from the Law [Titus 3:9]. Writing to Timothy, he calls these controversies *logomachiai* ['word-battles'], for which he says certain men have a morbid craving, though from these nothing comes but envy, strife, wrangling, evil suspicions, conflicts among persons corrupted in mind, destitute of truth, who prefer their own gain to godliness [1 Timothy 6:4–5].

[272] No one should, however, take these remarks of mine to imply that I utterly condemn those who have left us nothing but questions, or that I reject scholastic disputes. From these truth is quite often elicited just as fire flashes forth from striking flint-stones together. But I am asking for moderation in these, and discrimination. Moderation will guard us from searching into everything, discrimination from searching just

---

137 But ... In any case] This paragraph and the first few sentences of the next were added in *1520*.

anything at all. In any case there are[138] many things even in the books of the neoterics worth learning, but they should be treated in a manner suitable to one's age, tasted moderately, handled soberly and chastely. For studies of this kind were completely unknown among theologians long ago; then, after they had crept in (as usually happens in human affairs), they grew gradually to a vast extent, a point from which they have now begun in some universities to be regarded more cautiously and with more moderation, as in Cambridge in England, and Louvain in Brabant. These studies do not, on this account, flourish less, but they flourish more truly.

[273] But what sort of spectacle is it for an eighty-year-old theologian to have a taste for nothing but sophisms only and,[139] to the very end of his life, for nothing but clever prattling? I once saw a good many of this sort at Paris: if it had been necessary to produce a passage from Paul, they would think they had been quite transported to another world. Accordingly, *if anyone has been endowed with such great power of intellect that he is able to embrace both kinds of studies*, then, at least as far as I am concerned, *let him go! Let him go where his abilities beckon – and good luck go with him. But it is, nevertheless, from* the studies advocated here *that one should begin; in these*, I think, *the greater* and the *better part of life should be spent. But if one of the two kinds must be abandoned, I can only confess the absolute truth, that this is the side I should prefer to favour. It is better to be a little less the sophist than to have little understanding of the Gospels and the letters of* the apostles. *It is preferable to be ignorant of certain doctrines of Aristotle rather than not to know the precepts of Christ. Finally, I should prefer to be a godly theologian with* Chrysostom, *than to be undefeated with* Scotus.

[274] *This, at least, cannot be denied, that the teaching of Christ has been defended and illuminated by those ancient theologians, whom I should allow to be set aside only if it were clear that by the cunning ever so cunning and the subtleties ever so subtle in which these scholastics engage either a single pagan has been converted to faith in Christ or a single heretic has been refuted and changed. For if we are willing to admit the truth, the fact that fewer heresies today exist*, or at least are obvious, *we owe to the stake* more truly *than to syllogisms. Is there any kind of knot that can be tied with dialectical subtlety that the same subtlety may not untie if both sides are free to make whatever assumptions they wish?* What have you gained if you tie a knot that cannot be undone, to which, however, sometimes not even the one who ties

---

138 there are] The *1519* text resumes here; see n124.
139 and ... prattling?] Added in *1520*

it gives his consent? *But those simple writings, effective through their truth, not their subtlety, were able in the course of a few small years to make new the peoples of the whole world.*

[275] But let us dismiss the comparison of studies. In these, to each let his own study be honourable, and, to use the words of St Paul, let everyone be at rest with *his own mind* [Romans 14:5]. *Let anyone who likes scholastic debates follow,* by his own choice, *what is taught in the schools,* provided[140] he does not rate too highly the dogmas of the school, provided he does not continue in this too long. For I have seen many men, already grey, who tried to be reconciled to that ancient theology, but the attempt did not turn out very well because it was made too late.

[276] *But if anyone prefers to be trained for godliness rather than for disputation, he should occupy himself* at once *and above all with the sources, should occupy himself with those writers who have drunk most nearly from the sources.* If any uncertainty arises with regard to matters that pertain to godliness, a sound and prudent man will not lack a wholesome response from the divine oracles. Paul has trustworthy advice even when he does not have a command from the Lord [1 Corinthians 7:25]. *A holy prayer to God will compensate for what has been lost in syllogisms.* Ultimately, *you will be a theologian sufficiently unconquered if you succumb to no vice, yield to no desires, even if you leave a* contentious disputation *the loser. Whoever teaches Christ purely is an exceedingly great teacher.* If they consider it base not to know the definitions of Scotus, it is more base not to know the ordinances of Christ. If it is not very theological to fail to grasp the writings of Durandus, it is even less theological to fail to grasp the writings of Paul. A theologian gets his name from the divine oracles, not from human opinions.

[277] A good part of theology is inspiration, which comes only to a character that has been completely cleansed. And[141] yet there are no people who claim this power with greater arrogance than those whose lives are wholly enslaved to ambition, frequently also to lust and gluttony, lives corrupted on all sides by dissimulation, pretence, and hypocrisy. They boast that they are heralds of the evangelical doctrine, they make themselves the pillars of the Christian religion, on whose word the undiscerning multitude hangs. Christ doubtless perceived their deeds when he lamented the lot of the people who were wandering like sheep scattered and without a shepherd [Matthew 9:36]. For our

---

140 provided ... school] Added in *1520*
141 And ... duty.] The remainder of the work was added in *1520*, with an exception as noted below.

times also have their pharisees and their rabbis, our times have their hypocrites; they have their phylacteries with which they commend themselves to the simple-minded rabble – and[142] would that they did not deceive the leaders also. We must therefore pray to Christ either to change this pharisaical breed for the better, or to drive them away from his flock. And I have said this, not to hurt good men, but to remind the evil of their duty.

---

142 and ... also.] Added in *1523*

Explanatory Notes

[1]

1–2 **my revised version of the New Testament**] Erasmus speaks of the first (1516) edition of his New Testament as a revision and correction of the Vulgate or standard Latin translation of those books, which was traditionally attributed to Jerome; see **16**.

7–8 **the speed ... demanded brevity**] For the circumstances in which the first edition of the New Testament was completed, see above 41–2 and CWE 41 56–7.

9–10 **in such a way that this piece can, if one likes, be added as a preface**] The *Methodus* of 1516 was expanded to create the *Ratio* in 1518, when it was published separately from the New Testament. This new *Ratio*, a major hermeneutical essay in its own right and no longer merely prefatory in character, appeared as a preface to the New Testament in the edition of 1519 only. Approximately 90 per cent of the *Methodus* was incorporated into the *Ratio*. Passages taken over into the *Ratio* from the *Methodus* are printed in italic type in the present edition.

[3]

1 *Not the least part of a task is to know how to set about it*] See *Adagia* II i 1 CWE 33 15–17, where Erasmus describes three methods of 'setting about a task.'

18–19 **many-headed** *statues of Mercury*] In antiquity, busts of Mercury in a form with either two or four heads were placed at crossroads to mark out the roads and establish boundaries.

21–2 *'I shall do the work of a flintstone ... sharpen a sword.'*] Horace *Ars poetica* (*Art of Poetry*) 304–5

248 Explanatory Notes

[4]

2 *On Christian Doctrine*] So the title of the handbook by Augustine, *De doctrina christiana* (begun c 396, completed 427), is commonly translated, though it would be more accurately rendered 'On Christian Teaching' or even 'On Christian (Intellectual) Culture.' The work was highly influential in later centuries and Erasmus knew it from early in his career.

3–4 **a certain Dionysius**] Pseudo-Dionysius, long generally assumed to be the Areopagite converted by Paul (Acts 17:34), was a Neoplatonizing Christian of the late fifth to early sixth century, whose works (written in Greek) were popular in Latin translation in the sixteenth century. With the qualification 'I suppose,' Erasmus implicitly questions the traditional date and identification of this author.

9 *a fatter Minerva*] For the image see *Adagia* I i 37 CWE 31 85–6.

[5]

2 *like 1,2,3*] For the expression see *Adagia* III vii 58 CWE 35 250–1.

5–6 *neither* **Platonic** *nor* **Stoic** *nor* **Peripatetic**] 'Stoic' and 'Peripatetic' identify the philosophical schools that found their origin in, respectively, Zeno (320–280 BC) and Aristotle (380–300 BC). The Academy of Plato (429–347 BC) gave rise to the Academic school.

10 **Hippocrates**] An allusion to the Hippocratic oath. Hippocrates of Cos was probably a contemporary of Socrates (469–399 BC). His name is also attached to a body of ancient medical works.

11 *Julius Firmicus*] Julius Firmicus Maternus (c AD 300–after 360) wrote a book on astrology, the *Mathesis*, while still a pagan. After his conversion to Christianity, he wrote *On the Error of the Pagan Religions*.

[6]

1 **In Exodus**] For the allusions in this passage, see Exod 19:10–12, 19:24, 20:21–4:18, 3:1–4:17.

15–16 **Paul calls the exposition of arcane Scripture not philosophy but prophecy**] On prophecy as the exposition of Scripture, see eg Erasmus' paraphrases on 1 Cor 12:10 CWE 43 151–2, 1 Cor 13:2 CWE 43 157–8, and Acts 15:32 CWE 50 99.

Explanatory Notes 249

[7]

2 **the prophetic term 'taught by God'**] 'Taught by God': *theodidaktos*. The Greek word is found in 1 Thess 4:9, while the phrase 'taught of God' appears in John 6:45, quoting Isa 54:13.

3–4 **an eye of faith ... that sees nothing but the heavenly things**] For the 'sound' eye, see Matt 6:22 and Luke 11:34. The 'eyes of doves' is an expression found in the Vulgate of the Song of Solomon 1:15 (Vulgate 1:14) and 4:1. For the dove as an image of the heavenly Spirit, see Matt 3:16, Mark 1:10, Luke 3:22.

5–7 ***This incomparable pearl ... a soul thirsting for nothing else***] For the images, see Matt 13:46 (pearl), Pss 42:2, 63:1, 143:6 (thirsty soul). On desire as a precondition of learning, see Erasmus' paraphrase on Acts 8:31 CWE 50 61.

10–12 **The palace of this queen ... an extremely low portal**] Compare *Enchiridion* ('the doorway is low') CWE 66 34. The image of palace and queen suggests the common designation of theology as 'the queen of the sciences.'

16–17 **Pythagoras ... certain magical numbers**] See *Adagia* I i 2 on 'odd and even numbers,' listed under 'The Precepts of Pythagoras,' CWE 31 40–1.

[8]

1–3 ***Let ungodly curiosity be absent***] Erasmus, like Augustine, frequently warns against the dangers of *curiositas*. See eg the critique of the theologians in the *Moria/Folly* CWE 27 126–7.

8 *certain mysteries*] In his *Annotations* on the New Testament, Erasmus repeatedly notes that the Greek word *mysterion* 'mystery' has the sense of 'something hidden,' which he expresses most often by the Latin *arcanum* or *secretum*, and he stipulates that the *mysterion* is to be shared only with the 'initiates,' never with the 'profane.'

[9]

1–3 **Augustine wants us ... to read books of human learning with judgment and discrimination**] See eg Augustine *De doctrina christiana* 2.39.58. Erasmus sets up a contrast between 'human books' and the divine Scriptures, each of which requires from the reader a distinctive approach.

7–12 **as for example, when you read that God is angry ...**] References to Exod 4:14; Num 11:1 (God becomes angry); Gen 6:6 (God repents); Luke 22:36 (buying swords); Matt 5:39 (not resisting evil).

[10]

4–6 *Let this be your first and only goal ... that you be changed ... transformed into what you are learning*] Already in the *Enchiridion* (1503) CWE 66 34, Erasmus had described in very similar terms the proper approach to the study of Scripture.

7 **affections**] *affectus*, an important word in the Erasmian psychology; see above 57–62 and note on **23**/13–15

8–9 *not if you debate more keenly*] A reference to the 'disputations' that were a regular part of scholastic education

14 **interrupt the reading**] 'Reading': *lectio*, a term long in use to designate both the scientific investigation of Scripture, as in the schools, and the devotional reading of Scriptures, as in the monasteries.

[11]

8–15 **St James admonishes ...**] Erasmus paraphrases James 3:15–17, mingling the Latin idiom of the Vulgate with that of his own translation of those verses.

[12]

6–7 **in *On Christian Doctrine* book 2**] Augustine *De doctrina christiana* 2.11.16

14–15 *the pitiful stammering of a single 'half-language'*] Probably a reference to the language of the scholastic theologians whose speech Erasmus elsewhere described as stammering, eg in *Moria* CWE 27 130.

[13]

2 **Jérôme de Busleyden**] Jérôme de Busleyden (c 1470–1517), doctor of law, provost (ie mayor) of St Peter's at Aire, a small town not far from St Omer, and councillor to Charles, heir to the Spanish kingdoms and

future emperor. His will provided funds for the establishment of the *Collegium Trilingue* in Louvain, a project partly inspired by Erasmus, whom Busleyden knew well. After Jérôme's death, Gilles (1465–1536), his eldest brother, helped to carry out the plans for the *Collegium Trilingue* and continued to support it once it had been established.

10–11 **Etienne Poncher**] Etienne Poncher (1446–1525), lawyer, diplomat, and churchman. He became bishop of Paris in 1503, and archbishop of Sens in 1519. Others confirm Erasmus' appreciation of him here as a patron of learning.

[14]

7–9 **unless, perhaps, sitting idly by we prefer to wait with the apostles for this as some gift from heaven**] Erasmus' guarded sarcasm may reflect a concealed response to criticism of his 1516 annotation on Acts 10:38, where he had observed that the apostles spoke idiomatic vulgar Greek. A similar point had been made by Augustine *De doctrina christiana* prol 5.

[15]

1–5 *But to disregard for the moment the fact that it matters very much whether you draw from the originating springs of Scripture or from any sort of pool whatever* ...] For this general critique of translations, see Augustine *De doctrina christiana* 2.13.19. The contrasting images of spring and pool, which are very common in Erasmus' New Testament scholarship, had been deployed by Jerome in his arguments for retranslating the Old Testament directly from the Hebrew.

6–7 *as Jerome everywhere cries out and complains*] See eg the preface to Jerome's translation and expansion of the *Chronicle* of Eusebius of Caesarea.

9–11 **the marks of the obelus and the asterisk, or the prophets punctuated by phrase, clause, and full sentence**] The use of the obelus and asterisk to mark passages that ought to be added to or omitted from a received text was borrowed from the practice of classical grammarians, and had been extended to biblical texts by Origen, who was Jerome's guide in such matters. The segmenting of the texts of certain biblical books by units of sense (*per cola et commata*), also promoted by Jerome, was taken over from the classical rhetoricians.

12 **the sacred books**] The Latin word used by Erasmus for 'books' at this point in the *Ratio* is *codices*, which designates the text in its material form (ie 'manuscripts').

15–16 **that tragical lamentation, 'O heaven! O earth!'**] Terence *Adelphi* 790

[16]

1 *Jerome's translation*] For most of Erasmus' contemporary readers, this would mean the Vulgate Bible. But Erasmus insisted that the Vulgate Bibles in circulation could not, strictly speaking, be Jerome's translation, since in his commentaries Jerome himself is found correcting translations that became enshrined in the Vulgate Bible, while Vulgate Bibles of the sixteenth century manifestly differed among themselves. Thus while the Vulgate Bibles of the sixteenth century included versions of Jerome's translation, 'Jerome's translation' and the Vulgate Bible are not synonymous. Hence also Erasmus could say, as here, that many things in the Gospels as emended by Jerome had perished.

2 *pontifical decrees*] Apparently a reference to the *Constitutions* of Pope Clement V, promulgated in 1314 after the Council of Vienne, which ordered that teachers of Hebrew, Arabic, and Chaldean (ie Aramaic) be appointed at five universities, to assist in the conversion of heathens. That legislation is cited elsewhere by Erasmus as if it mandated instruction in Greek: see Ep 149:49–59 CWE 2 26; and Ep 182:205–8 CWE 2 96, the preface to his edition of Valla's *Annotationes* (Paris 1505) on the Vulgate text of the New Testament.

2–3 *the true reading of the Old Testament ... an accurate text of the New*] 'Testament' here translates *instrumentum* in the text of the *Methodus* and *Ratio*. The title page of Erasmus' first edition (1516) designated the New Testament by the phrase *Novum instrumentum*, defended by him as a more precise rendering of the sense of the Greek *diatheke* as a contract or covenant made in writing, since in Roman legal practice *testamentum* could also refer to a purely verbal engagement. Though regularly used by earlier Latin writers such as Jerome and Augustine, the term was not well received, and subsequent editions bore the familiar title *Novum Testamentum*.

4 **the very thing Augustine teaches**] See Augustine *De doctrina christiana* 2.11.16 and *De civitate Dei* (*City of God*) 15.14.2, where, however, the Septuagint (ie the Greek translation of the Hebrew scriptures made before the Christian era) is also granted an independent authority.

8–10 **the ancients ... the *moderns***] Erasmus distinguishes between the 'moderns' (*neoterici*), meaning the scholastics of the Middle Ages, and the 'ancients' (*vetustiores*), meaning the Church Fathers or authorities of the early church. For his general attitude to Thomas Aquinas and other 'moderns,' see 63–79 above and note on **57**/2. Thomas Aquinas (c 1225–1274), an Italian Dominican, was a pupil of Albertus Magnus (c 1200–1280), from whom he acquired the interest in Aristotle that shaped his theology and culmininated in his *Summa theologiae*.

[17]

5 *four men*] The identity of these four is uncertain. One of them was probably Erasmus' friend John Colet, Dean of St Paul's Cathedral in London.

9 *Cato's example*] The tradition that the elder Cato took up the study of Greek in old age is attested by Cicero and Plutarch. Erasmus makes the same reference at *De pueris instituendis/On Education for Children* CWE 26 321.

9–10 *St Augustine ... returned to Greek*] Augustine recalls his dislike of Greek as a schoolboy in *Confessions* 1.13.20. It was only after 420, in the last decade of his life, when hard pressed by opponents, that he attempted a comparison of a few texts of Greek Christian theologians, in the original language, with their translations.

11 **Rudolph Agricola**] Rodolphus Agricola (1444–1485), born near Groningen in the Netherlands, graduated in arts from the Universities of Erfurt and Cologne. From 1469 until 1479 he spent much of his time in Italy, where he translated many works from Greek into Latin. After his return to northern Europe, he vigorously advocated humanistic studies, first at Groningen, then at Heidelberg, where he began the study of Hebrew in 1484. In *Adagia* I iv 39 CWE 31 348–50 Erasmus gives a short account of Agricola, presenting him as 'most worthy of the highest public honour,' and claiming that 'among the Greeks he was the best Greek of them all, and among the Latins the best Latin.'

15 **my fifty third year**] Erasmus celebrated his birthday on 28 October. The year of his birth is disputed, but a convincing case has been made for 1466.

16 *Hebrew, with which I made some acquaintance long ago*] Erasmus took up the study of Hebrew at the same time as Greek, shortly after his return to France from England in 1500, but soon abandoned it, 'put off by the strangeness of the language'; Ep 181:41–4 CWE 2 87.

24–8 *Jerome himself sufficiently refutes the opinion of Hilary and Augustine ... St Ambrose, too, stumbled over the same stone*] Commenting

254 Explanatory Notes

on Ps 119:28 in his *Tractatus in Psalmos*, Hilary of Poitiers warns that 'it is not prudent to digress from the translation of the Seventy.' Augustine frequently affirms the authority of the Septuagint and in a letter to Jerome (Ep 71.4) argues that it is preferable to translate from it rather than from the Hebrew. Hilary in his *Commentarius in Matthaeum* 21.3 (on Matt 21:9) claims that in Hebrew 'Hosanna' signifies the 'redemption of the house of David,' and Ambrose in his *Expositio evangelii secundum Lucam* 9.15 (on Luke 19:37–8) explains the expression as 'redeemer of the house of David.' Jerome Ep 20, recalling Hilary's interpretation, analyses the word to show that the intent is 'Save, Lord, I beseech you,' and so demonstrates the necessity of returning to the 'Hebrew sources.'

[18]

2–3 **Augustine checked the Old Testament against the Septuagint**] He did so, for example, in the *Locutiones in Heptateuchum* and the *Quaestiones in Heptateuchum*, both written in 419.

5 **when he was debating with Cresconius**] See Augustine *Contra Cresconium Donatistam* 2.27.33.

[19]

1 *'some exceptional natural gift'*] *alba indoles*, with *alba* 'white' used idiomatically to express excellence

2–3 *something Augustine welcomed* **in the books On Christian Doctrine**] Augustine *De doctrina christiana* 2.16.23–18.28, 27.41–31.49, and 39.58–40.61

5–6 *the more liberal disciplines, namely, dialectic, rhetoric, arithmetic, music*] Erasmus omits 'astrology' from the otherwise identical list in the *Methodus*, but adds 'stars' among the 'objects of nature' in the list that immediately follows here. For a similar catalogue of subjects needed by the teacher to expound secular literature, see *De ratione studii/On the Method of Study* CWE 24 673–4.

18 *culture*] *cultus*, but the word can also mean 'worship' (as frequently in Erasmus) and 'dress,' and the latter may be intended here; see eg the paraphrase on Acts 13:15 CWE 50 86, where dress appears as a cultural phenomenon that can throw light on the scriptural narrative. Augustine *De doctrina christiana* 2.25.39 lists distinctions in 'dress and bodily ornament' (*habitu et cultu corporis*) among the useful and

necessary human institutions (*instituta*) that Christians are bound to observe.

23–4 They make a quadruped out of a tree] In this sentence, 'they' has no immediate referent, but Erasmus clearly has in mind those who, although without a liberal education, nevertheless attempt to expound Scripture; he may be pointing to professors of scholastic theology, or perhaps more generally to the medieval exegetical tradition.

[20]

1–2 This principle Augustine reveals very clearly in *On Christian Doctrine* book 2] Augustine *De doctrina christiana* 2.16.23

3–4 in the work he wrote *Against Faustus the Manichaean*] Erasmus accentuates the dramatic setting. Augustine *Contra Faustum Manichaeum* 2.56 says merely that, when he happened to see the fruit, he was very pleased because of this very passage in Genesis (30:14–16) and so he investigated the nature of it, using the senses of sight, smell, and taste. Finding it flat to taste but pleasant to smell, he concluded that the mandrake's fruit was a biblical figure of those who acquire the odour of a good reputation for their work in the church.

9–10 St Ambrose, in his exposition of the thirteenth chapter of Luke] Ambrose *Expositio evangelii secundum Lucam* 7.168–72 (on Luke 13:6–9)

[21]

6 And Augustine does indeed approve] Augustine *De doctrina christiana* 2.31.48

11–12 a syllogism in the form of *celarent* or *baroco*] *Celarent* and *baroco* were the names given to two patterns or figures in which syllogisms were constructed; see Piltz *World of Medieval Learning* 99–102.

14–20 Aristotle's eight books of *Physics* ... the *Natural Questions* of Seneca] For the works, genuine and spurious, here attributed to Aristotle, see Rist *Mind of Aristotle* 3–36. The list is very similar to that prescribed for the Arts degree in medieval universities. Theophrastus (c 371–286 BC) was an associate and successor of Aristotle and a prolific author on a wide range of subjects. Dioscorides from Cilicia (first century AD) wrote a work in five books, *Materials of Medicine* (*Materia medica*), which lists approximately seven hundred plants and more than one thousand drugs. Seneca the Younger (4 BC–AD 65) wrote a work in seven books,

Natural Questions (*Naturales quaestiones*), in which he discusses such natural phenomena as 'light in the sky,' waters, earthquakes, etc; Erasmus published an edition of the work in 1515. The remaining authors cited are encyclopedic. Pliny the Elder (AD 23–79) wrote a *Natural History* (*Naturalis historia*) in thirty-seven books. Macrobius (fl early fifth century AD) wrote a commentary, including considerable astronomical lore, on the dream of Scipio (*Commentarii in somnium Scipionis*), a narrative found in the sixth book of Cicero's *De republica*. He also wrote the *Saturnalia*, ostensibly a dialogue on the Roman feast of that name, but filled with information on many subjects, such as history, geography, and the sciences. The *Sophists at Dinner* (*Deipnosophistae*) by Athenaeus, a Greek-speaking Egyptian (fl c AD 200), is a book on gastronomy that also discusses fruit, wine, musical instruments, furniture, etc. With this list of encyclopedic authors compare the list in *De ratione studii/On the Method of Study* CWE 24 672–5.

[22]

2–3 **in Lucan, what an enormous account of drugs**] The Roman poet Lucan (AD 39–65) gives an account of various kinds of poisonous snakes in *The Civil War* (*Bellum civile*) 9.700–838.

3–5 **Oppian ... on the nature of fish and wild animals, Nicander on harmful beasts**] Two works are attributed to Oppian (fl AD 200), a Greek-speaker from Cilicia: the *Cynegetica* (on animals and hunting) and the *Halieutica* (on fish and fishing). Only the *Halieutica* is regarded as genuine. Nicander of Colophon (probably mid-second century BC) wrote a work, the *Theriaca*, on snakes, spiders, insects, and drugs effective against their poisonous bites and stings, as well as a work, the *Alexipharmaca*, describing antidotes to various poisons.

5–6 **arts, classed by Augustine among the superstitious and reprehensible**] Augustine *De doctrina christiana* 2.18.28–29.46 mentions in particular magic, astrology, and clairvoyance. He condemns such knowledge, though his discussion proceeds from an effort to show that some pagan learning, even when associated with superstition, is a necessary aid to the reading of the Scriptures.

11–12 **Augustine affirms in his work *The City of God***] At *De civitate Dei* 6.10–11 Augustine speaks of a 'book against superstitions' by Seneca the Younger.

16–17 **And there are extant even today certain works of this kind**] Numerous *Onomastica*, books explaining biblical names, appeared in

Explanatory Notes 257

antiquity. Eusebius (c 260–c 340), author of the *Ecclesiastical History*, compiled one such, listing the names of places alphabetically for each book or group of books in the Bible with information about each place. Jerome translated this work into Latin under the title *On the Location and Names of Hebrew Places* (*De situ et nominibus locorum Hebraeorum*).

20–1 **Eberhard the Grecist ... or ... that little book *On Hebrew Names*]** Eberhard of Béthune (twelfth century) wrote a grammar in verse, *Graecismus*, in which he explained Latin words derived from Greek, and so was nicknamed *Graecista*. Jerome wrote a book *On Hebrew Names* (*De nominibus Hebraicis*), in which names found in both Testaments are listed alphabetically with meanings given.

23–4 **the *Catholicon* or Isidore]** Erasmus widely deplored the use in education of compilations and word-books, of which he frequently mentions two, the *Catholicon* and the *Mammotrectus*. Isidore of Seville (AD 560–636) wrote an encyclopedic work, the *Etymologiae* or *Origines*, which offered an explanation of many terms.

[23]

2–4 *the figures and tropes of the grammarians and rhetoricians ... the allegorical explanation of stories*] For 'figures and tropes,' see note on line 12. On allegory, see *De copia/Foundations of the Abundant Style* CWE 24 336, 611–13 and *Enchiridion* CWE 66 67–9. Erasmus at one time intended to produce a separate work on scriptural allegory; see Ep 211:28–36 CWE 2 141 and *De copia* CWE 24 635.

6–7 **the story of Tantalus ... the story of Phaethon]** The story of Tantalus, condemned to hunger and thirst in the midst of food and water that he cannot enjoy, is told by Homer *Odyssey* 11.582–92; Horace *Odes* 2.18.36–8 makes Tantalus the type of the rich man. Phaethon attempted to drive the chariot of the sun across the sky, only to crash to the earth: Ovid *Metamorphoses* 2.1–328.

9–10 *comparisons,* **on which I have published something]** Erasmus refers to his *Parabolae sive similia/Parallels* or 'Comparisons' (1514) CWE 23 135–277. See **223**/21.

12 **all of which Fabius treats very thoroughly]** 'Fabius' is Marcus Fabius Quintilianus, ie Quintilian (c 30–before 100 AD), author of the *Institutio oratoria* (*Training of the Orator*), a standard resource for humanist rhetoricians of Erasmus' time. Quintilian discusses tropes in *Institutio oratoria* 8.6.1–76 and figures in 9.1.1–9.3.102. For his distinction between the two, see 9.1.4–5: a trope is an expression in which the normal meaning

of a term has been replaced by an artful signification; a figure is a pattern of thought or speech different from the norm. 'Essential questions' (*status*) refers to the fundamental basis on which a case rests: whether the issue at stake is one that must rely on conjecture, definition, or a consideration of 'quality,' ie, in forensic cases a consideration of the character of the offence (*Institutio oratoria* 7). The proposition sets out succinctly at an early point precisely what the advocate will argue (*Institutio oratoria* 4.4.1–9). Proofs, defined as artificial (those based on conjecture) and inartificial (those based on direct evidence such as witnesses), comprised both confirmation and refutation (*Institutio oratoria* 5). Amplification, though a stylistic feature (*Institutio oratoria* 8.4.1–29), was often associated with the peroration (*Institutio oratoria* 6.1.1–55) as a part of the speech between the proof and the conclusion. Figures, tropes, comparisons, and allegories are discussed at length at **185–233**.

13–15 **the twin *emotions* ... about these no one wrote more carefully than Aristotle**] 'Emotions': *affectus*. In Quintilian *Institutio oratoria* 6.1.7–25, *affectus* is used in speaking of swaying judgment by appeal to emotions. The contrast that Erasmus goes on to make between *affectus* 'feeling,' 'emotion' and *probatio* 'rational argument,' 'proof' is found in rhetorical theory (eg *Institutio oratoria* 6.2.3–7), but the word acquires a broader connotation in Erasmus' various discussions of it; see above 57–62. Aristotle discusses *ethos* and *pathos* in his *Rhetoric* 2:1–17 and *Poetics* 6 and 14–15. See too the long discussion in Quintilian *Institutio oratoria* 6.2.1–36.

18–19 ***clever arguments, which even in pagan philosophers the pagans themselves ridicule, and Paul denounces in a Christian***] Among pagans, Aristophanes *Clouds* 877–1112 lampoons sophistical argumentation; Erasmus places Aristophanes 'first among the poets' in *De ratione studii* CWE 24 669. Paul scorns 'subtle argument' and 'the wisdom of this world' at 1 Cor 1:17–29 and 3:18–21. See also Erasmus' paraphrase on 1 Tim 1:4 CWE 44 7–8.

22–4 **In allegory Origen was most felicitous, in commonplaces Chrysostom most abundant**] In *Enchiridion* CWE 66 69 Erasmus describes Origen as 'by far the predominant figure' after the apostle Paul in 'opening up certain sources of allegory,' and elsewhere similarly characterizes Chrysostom by his fondness for commonplaces. On the use of commonplaces in theological argument, see further **247**.

30–1 **the words of Augustine himself**] Augustine *De ordine* 1.8.24. At this point in the dialogue, Licentius has just confessed that he is beginning to find philosophy 'more beautiful' than the poets' tales of lovers and is ready to abandon them altogether. For the same reference, expressing the same idea, see *Enchiridion* CWE 66 33.

[24]

8–9 **the homily of Origen on Abraham**] Origen *In Genesim homiliae* 8.2–6 (on Gen 22:1–14). Erasmus had given a much briefer analysis of the passage in the *Methodus* CWE 41 444. The expression 'this story ... is set before our eyes' points to the rhetorical force of vivid description (*enargeia*).

[25]

10–11 **the promise where he had heard, 'In Isaac will your seed be named,' and, 'In Isaac will the promise be yours'**] The first citation is of Gen 21:12. Erasmus evidently takes the second citation from Origen's homily (8.2), where the preacher appears to echo such passages as Heb 11:18 and Gal 3:16.

[26]

8 **He loads the wood on his son**] 'Loads': *onerat*. This may be a mistake for *exonerat*: 'he removes the wood from his son.'

[27]

3–4 **the historical sense**] the literal meaning of the narrative, the author's supposed intent

4–5 **what Donatus does for the comedies of Terence**] Donatus, a grammarian of the fourth century AD, wrote a commentary on the plays of Terence, noting figures of speech, the meanings of words and phrases, and clarifying syntax.

9 **dry and troublesome questions**] *quaestiones*, one of the prevailing methods of education in the medieval university

14–15 **certain hymns and songs commonly called 'sequences'**] musical settings of rhymed poetry, used in the liturgy for certain feasts of the church

[28]

4 *those ancient theologians, Origen, Basil,* **Chrysostom,** *Jerome*] For these and other ecclesiastical writers of the second through the eighth centuries AD, see the Conspectus of Church Fathers Cited in the *Ratio*, below 329–33.

12–14 **the Scylla of pontifical power ... the Syrtes of scholastic dogmas ... the Symplegades of divine and human laws ... the Charybdis]** Scylla and Charybdis are the proverbial twin hazards that threatened sailors travelling through the straits of Messina between Italy and Sicily (Homer *Odyssey* 12.73–110); the Syrtes are the treacherous sandbanks north of the coast of Libya; the Symplegades (ie the 'Clashing Rocks') are the fabled floating rocks at the mouth of the Black Sea, which crushed ships that endeavoured to pass between them, until they were stabilized after the Argonauts had successfully sailed through them. 'Divine and human laws' here is an allusion to canon and civil law embodied in the two codes *corpus iuris canonici* and *corpus iuris civilis*.

[29]

2–3 *the mystic books*] ie the Scriptures, here *arcani libri*. See note on 8/8.

4–5 *good literature, as it is called – and is*] *Bonae litterae* 'good literature' designates the Greek and Latin literature whose study was encouraged by Renaissance humanists for its supposed power to inculcate both a polished literary style and a sound moral and intellectual life. The range of such literature is suggested by Erasmus' choice of authors in *De ratione studii* CWE 24 666–91, where patristic authors mingle with classical authors. In describing secular literature as 'profane,' Erasmus apparently wishes to refer to the root meaning of the compound: the literature that lies *pro* 'in front of' (ie outside of) the *fanum* 'temple,' in this case literature, mainly classical, authored by non-Christian writers; the term does not imply an inherently negative judgment upon the literature.

16 **comparisons**] *Parabolae*. See Ep 312:28–9 CWE 3 44: 'For the Greek *parabole*, which Cicero Latinizes as *collatio*, a sort of comparison, is nothing more than a metaphor writ large.' See 96 above.

16–19 **Augustine ... figures of the rhetoricians ... pauses in the discourse and the full periods**] Augustine *De doctrina christiana* 4.7.11–20.58

22–3 **pronunciation and syntax**] Augustine *De doctrina christiana* 3.2.2–4

24–5 **Gregory of Nazianzus, Damasus, Prudentius, Paulinus, Juvencus**] See the Conspectus of Church Fathers Cited in the *Ratio*, below 329–33.

25–6 **Paul himself more than once made *use* of *the witness of poets***] See Acts 17:28, 1 Cor 15:33, Titus 1:12.

28 *Averroës*] Latinized version of the name of the Islamic philosopher Ibn Rushd (1126–1198). He wrote paraphrases and commentaries on the works of Aristotle.

29–30 *first and second intentions,* **of the figures of syllogisms,** *of 'formalities,' or 'quiddities' or 'haeceities'*] For the 'figures of syllogisms,' see note on **21**/11–12. Erasmus routinely spills these and similar terms when expressing his disdain for scholastic method; eg *Moria* CWE 27 126–7, *Paraclesis* CWE 41 416. 'First' and 'second intentions,' for example, are terms that refer to the consideration of a thing as it is in itself and as it is known or perceived. The rest of this specialized vocabulary is from the same tool-box. See further Piltz *World of Medieval Learning* 57, 241–2.

[30]

6–8 **This part is divided into three ... here the first, there the second**] The penchant of scholastic theologians for complex division is well illustrated by the *Summa theologica* of Thomas Aquinas, and in his commentary on the *Sentences* of Peter Lombard.

12–17 *Virgil imitated Homer* ... **Themistius and Averroës imitated Aristotle**] Virgil's debt to Homer is manifest in the *Aeneid*, and to Theocritus, a Greek pastoral poet (early third century BC), in the *Eclogues*; in the *Georgics* he offers advice to farmers as the Greek Hesiod (fl c 700 BC) does in his *Works and Days*. Horace in his *Odes* emulates his Greek predecessors in the lyric, including Anacreon (second half of the seventh century BC), and in his victory odes follows the tradition of Pindar (b c 518 BC). There is a complex relation between Ibn Sina (980–1037), an Islamic physician-philosopher whose name was Latinized as Avicenna, and Galen (129–c 210). Galen admired Hippocrates and derived many of his medical principles as well as his anatomical descriptions from the Hippocratic corpus (see note on **5**/10); this comparison was added in *1520*. The comparison between the Latin and Greek orators Cicero (106–43 BC) and Demosthenes (384–322 BC) emerged in antiquity. Xenophon (c 430–354 BC) wrote several works that recall those of his contemporary Plato (c 429–347 BC). Theophrastus (c 342–258 BC), a companion and pupil of Aristotle, continued the latter's method of discussion and observation. Themistius (c AD 317–388) expounded Aristotle, as did Averroës (Ibn Rushd), whose writings were influential in western medieval thought.

20 **Thomas and Scotus**] For Thomas (Aquinas) see note on **16**/8–10 above. Duns Scotus (c 1266–1308), a Scottish Franciscan, lectured on the *Sententiae* of Peter Lombard at Cambridge, Oxford, and Paris and wrote a commentary on them; he also wrote on several of Aristotle's works, including the *Metaphysics*.

262 Explanatory Notes

21–4 *Augustine thinks ... more easily made*] Augustine *Confessions* 7.9

[31]

11 *the words of Virgil*] Virgil *Aeneid* 6.129–30

[32]

21–3 **Bartoluses and Balduses ... Holcots, Bricots, and Tartarets ... summulae and collections**] Bartolus of Sassoferrato (1314–after 1357) and his pupil Baldus degli Ubaldis (1319 or 1327–1400) were university men and commentators on Roman civil law. The Frenchman William Durand (1230–1296) was a specialist in canon law and the liturgy. The Englishman Robert Holcot (d 1349) commented on the *Sentences* of Peter Lombard, a core text of scholastic theology. Both Thomas Bricot (d 1516) and Pierre Tartaret (d 1522) were members of the faculty of theology at the University of Paris and experts on Aristotle and the *Summulae logicales* of Petrus Hispanus (1205–1277; Pope John XXI 1276–7). The *summulae* were compendia widely used in medieval education.

33–5 **'Take away from the heretics,' says Tertullian, 'the wisdom of the pagans ... and they will not be able to stand'**] Tertullian *De resurrectione mortuorum* 3.6

36–7 **the celestial *philosophy of Christ***] As he gets into his stride in the *Ratio*, Erasmus will develop a distinctive theory of how Christ himself, through the medium of the biblical text, models the activity of 'philosophizing' that he wants his followers to adopt. On the assumptions underpinning that theory, which shapes much of the rest of the treatise and accounts for some otherwise surprising turns in the argument, see the essay by Cummings above, 48–62.

37–9 **Chrysippus ... on logic**] Chrysippus of Soli (280–207 BC) succeeded Cleanthes as head of the Stoic school in 232 BC. The comment reported by Erasmus is made by Diogenes Laertius *Lives of the Eminent Philosophers* 7.7.180.

[33]

3–4 *Chrysostom,* **Cyprian, Jerome, Ambrose, Augustine, Clement**] See the Conspectus of Church Fathers Cited in the *Ratio*, below 329–33. In the *Methodus* CWE 41 440 the name of Clement comes immediately before those of Peter and Paul, suggesting that Clement of Rome (fl c 96), traditionally placed third in the succession of Roman bishops after Peter, is meant.

6–7 *Peter and Paul ... condemn it sometimes*] See eg 1 Cor 1:19–21, Col 2:8.

[34]

1–2 **As Seneca says, 'Some things ... learning them'**] Seneca *Epistulae morales* 88.2

[35]

4 *target points*] *scopi*, plural; but in the singular just below. *Scopus*, a transliteration of the Greek *skopos*, in the New Testament found only in Phil 3:14, where Erasmus translated *praefixum signum* 'the mark set out ahead' in place of the Vulgate's *destinatum* 'appointed end,' is a favourite word of Erasmus: see *Enchiridion* CWE 66 61 and 63 ('place Christ before you as the only goal,' 'Christ our only goal,' where 'goal' translates *scopus*) and CWE 43 384–5 n43 (paraphrase on Phil 3:14).

6 *a new sort of people*] See especially Matt 5–7 for many of the traits subsequently described; other details are suggested by other New Testament passages. The portrait Erasmus draws is, however, somewhat classicized.

10–38 *These were a people ...*] In the following extended passage, the subject, technically *populus* 'people,' slips in sense between the collective people and individual persons.

38 *... and ready for that final day*] From this point, down to **233**, the *Ratio* is independent of the earlier *Methodus*.

[36]

2–3 **This was the new wine that was to be poured only into new skins**] See Matt 9:17, Mark 2:22, Luke 5:37.

6–8 **the principles of Aristotle ... doctrines of Plato ... tenets of Epicurus ... teachings of so great a founder**] 'Principles,' 'doctrines,' 'tenets,' 'teachings': *placita, decreta, scita, dogmata*. According to Seneca *Epistulae morales* 95.10, the first three terms are more or less equivalent to the

Greek *dogmata*. These four terms are frequent throughout the *Ratio*, and context has, to a great extent, determined which of the four English equivalents given here will render the Latin in any particular case.

[37]

5–7 **I shall soon point out ... hearts of his disciples**] These vices have in general been mentioned in the course of the preceding description of Christian virtues. The promise 'soon to point out, etc' is fulfilled at **104–21**.

8–14 **In this category ... and other precepts like these**] For these precepts, see John 13:34–5 and Rom 13:8–10 (mutual love); Matt 18:15–35 and Luke 17:3–4 (forgiving one's brothers); Matt 16:24–7, Mark 8:34–8, Luke 9:23–6, also Matt 10:32, Luke 12:8 (taking up the cross, acknowledged by Christ); Matt 21:18–22, Mark 11:22–4 (faith); Matt 5:43–8, Luke 6:27–36 (kindness to all).

[38]

3–4 **For in the nineteenth chapter of Matthew he calls eunuchs 'blessed'**] The saying about eunuchs in Matt 19:10–12 is framed by the qualification that not all are able to receive it. Eunuchs are not, however, called 'blessed' in this passage. Here in the *Ratio* 'unhappy' translates *infelices*, 'blessed' renders *beati*.

11–12 **if, indeed, by the word 'perfect' Christ denotes a Christian**] In making the point that the word 'perfect' applies to all Christians, Erasmus excludes the possible inference that it is meant only of monks; see also the conclusion of the *Enchiridion* CWE 66 127.

[40]

3–4 **He was unwilling to deprive necessary human laws of their own authority**] Apparently a reference to the Old Testament law ordering adulterers to be stoned; see John 8:5, and for the law, Lev 20:10.

15 **you regain your senses and repent**] *Resipueritis. Resipiscere* 'regain one's senses' appears to be Erasmus' preferred Latin word to translate the Greek *metanoein*, routinely translated in English Bibles as 'repent.' For the sake of clarity, the word is given a double translation here and at other places in the *Ratio*.

[41]

2–4 **if we consider not only** *what is said,* **but also** *the words* **used,** *by whom and to whom they are spoken, the time, the occasion, what precedes and what follows*] The exegetical principle outlined here had been expressed in a different context in the *Methodus* CWE 41 446 and will be expressed again at **236**.

[42]

3 **what role the speaker sustains**] 'Role': *persona* (pl. *personae*), often in what follows rendered simply by 'persona.' In Erasmus' view, to recognize in biblical discourse the voice of the speaker is to have found an important clue to the sense of a passage. This exegetical principle had been developed by the Church Fathers in their interpretations of the Psalms, and is deployed by Erasmus in his own *Expositions of the Psalms*, begun in 1515 while the first edition of his New Testament was still in preparation; see eg CWE 63 9 (Ps 1), 81–2 (Ps 2), 154–68 (Ps 3). Erasmus turns here to the *persona* understood as a trope, since the language conveys 'obliquely' a concealed identity. He will offer later a more sustained and conventional discussion of figures and tropes at **185–233**.

7–8 **this on the authority of Augustine**] See Augustine *Enarrationes in Psalmos* 21.3 (on Ps 22:1), and also 37.6 (on Ps 38:3, with reference to Ps 22:1), where the exegete attempts to establish a theological foundation for his hermeneutical concept of the head (Christ) and the members (the church).

8–11 **when he is sad ... he renounces his own will and submits to the will of the Father**] See Matt 26:36–46, Mark 14:32–42, Luke 22:39–46. This biblical narrative provided the occasion for a vigorous debate between Erasmus and John Colet in 1499, represented in in *De taedio Iesu/The Distress of Jesus*, published in 1503 along with the *Enchiridion*: see CWE 70 2–67, and especially 20–1, where Erasmus traces to Augustine the view that in the garden Christ took upon himself the 'members' frailty.'

16–18 **when the disciples flee in terror, when Peter denies the Lord, when he strikes with the sword**] See Matt 26:56 and Mark 14:50 (disciples flee); Matt 26:69–75, Mark 14:66–72, and Luke 22:54–62 (Peter denies Christ); John 18:10 (Peter strikes with a sword).

20–1 **when Christ, plaiting a whip, drives the crowd of money-changers out of the temple**] The synoptic Gospels all narrate the event: Matt 21:12–13, Mark 11:15–17, Luke 19:45–6. John (2:15) notes that Jesus made a whip.

266 Explanatory Notes

28–9 **the providential arrangement of time**] *Temporis dispensatione*: an allusion to history divided from a Pauline and Augustinian theological perspective into three periods – before the Law, under the Law, under grace. Soon, however, in a more striking schematization, Erasmus will divide the periods of time into five, so that a third period intervenes between those of Law and grace, sharing characteristics of each, while the fourth and fifth periods demarcate the Christian era.

30–2 **he wanted to impress upon the minds of his own race ... regardless of origin**] This interpretation of the story of the Canaanite woman is elaborated in the paraphrase on Mark 7:24–30 CWE 49 93–4 (published 1524), which as here alludes clearly to Matt 11:12 (= Luke 16:16). The paraphrase on the corresponding passage in Matt 15:21–8 CWE 45 236–9 (published 1522) emphasizes the constancy and faith of the Gentile in contrast to the disbelief and malice of the Jews.

[44]

6–13 **For example, when Christ ... especially manifest this**] Erasmus' paraphrase on the Sermon on the Mount reflects the ambiguity of audience assumed here: in the paraphrase on Matt 5:13, the audience immediately in view comprises 'apostles, bishops, and teachers'; in the paraphrase on 6:2, Jesus addresses 'whoever is a follower of the gospel law' (CWE 45 93, 113).

[45]

15–16 **Augustine has discussed this quite fully in the books *On Christian Doctrine***] Augustine *De doctrina christiana* 3.10.14–25.35. The choice is between a tropological and an allegorical interpretation.

[46]

15–16 **These doctrines ... were being reserved for Christ**] See Matt 5:33–7 (swearing); Matt 5:31–2 (divorce); Matt 16:24, Mark 8:34, and Luke 9:23 (taking up the cross); Matt 5:43–8 and Luke 6:32–6 (kindness to enemies).

17–19 **the first preaching of the apostles ... say nothing about Christ**] See Matt 10:5–15, Mark 6:7–13, Luke 9:1–6. In these narratives the disciples are not forbidden to speak of Christ, but neither are they told to

Explanatory Notes 267

preach Christ. Erasmus seems to interpret Jesus' instruction assuming an implied reference to the two levels of truth appropriate to the two levels of learning, rudimentary insruction for beginners, the 'mysteries' for the 'perfect.'

21 **as John bears witness**] See John 4:1–2. In his paraphrase on John 4:2, Erasmus in the persona of the evangelist explains that Jesus did not baptize because he wished to show that preaching was more important than baptizing (CWE 46 53 with n2).

[47]

4–6 **This time period ... after the Holy Spirit had been given**] For this 'time of accommodation,' when the Law was still practised by Jewish Christians, see Erasmus' paraphrase on Acts 15:19–20 CWE 50 98, and his 'Argument' (ie synopsis) for Romans, CWE 42 8.

7–9 **all those parables ... who excused themselves**] See Matt 21:33–43, Mark 12:1–12, Luke 20:9–18 (vineyard); Matt 22:1–10 and Luke 14:15–24 (wedding).

9–15 **Christ's predictions ... frequently changing place**] The sequence of allusions in this passage suggests that while Erasmus may be citing from memory, he is drawing upon two extended passages in Matthew along with the synoptic parallels: (1) the mission of the apostles (Matt 10:5–23, 34–9) and (2) sayings that radicalize perspectives on family and possessions (Matt 19:16–30). For the synoptic parallels see Mark 6:7–13 and 13:9–13, Mark 10:17–31, Luke 10:1–12 and 21:12–19, and Luke 18:18–30.

[48]

12–13 **But the apostles continued to do so for some time**] Apparently a reference to Gal 2:1–14 (Peter and Barnabas withdraw from eating with Gentiles) and Acts 16:1–3 (Paul circumcises Timothy).

13–16 **those questions that Augustine raises in a certain letter ... meat sacrificed to idols has fallen?**] Augustine Ep 47.4

20–1 **Augustine and Ambrose take a different view, and today the church judges otherwise**] See Augustine *De fide et operibus* 16.28 and *De coniugiis adulterinis* 1.1, and Ambrosiaster *Commentarius in epistulam Pauli ad Corinthios* (on 7:13–15), a work formerly attributed to Ambrose, and hence now to 'Ambrosiaster' (ie pseudo-Ambrose). For the 'Pauline

Privilege' (ie the dissolution of marriage between a believer and a non-believer), see CWE 43 96 n34.

[51]

3 **three circles**] Erasmus published in outline the image of the three circles in August 1518 in the letter to Paul Volz that served as a preface to a new edition of the *Enchiridion*, CWE 66 14–17.

[52]

9–12 **Though secular, their arms and their laws ... lawful punishments**] Erasmus discusses these topics in his 1516 *Institutio principis christiani/Education of a Christian Prince* 6 ('Enacting or amending laws') and 11 ('On starting war') CWE 27 264–73, 282–8. For his writings on the just war, see the introduction to the colloquy 'Military Affairs' CWE 39 53–5.

13–14 **the undiscriminated crowd as the most stolid and untutored part of this orb**] The inferiority of commoners is sharply contrasted with the character of the good prince in the *Institutio principis christiani* CWE 27 212–14.

[53]

13–17 **Of the elements of which this lowest world consists ... lower atmosphere**] Erasmus borrows from Stoic physics: the elements – fire, air, water, and earth – are a continuum, converting into one another to form increasingly dense substances as they descend from the highest to the lowest regions, and, in the reverse direction, converting again into increasingly light substances.

[54]

1 **popes with their pardons and indulgences**] Erasmus consistently criticized the contemporary practice of granting indulgences, from the *Moria* (1511) CWE 27 114 onwards.

5–8 **praedial and personal tithes ... the pallium ... annates ... the patrimony of Peter ... subduing the Turks in war**] 'Praedial tithes,' tithes on the fruits of the earth; 'pallium,' a circular band worn by a metropolitan bishop imposed as a symbol of his jurisdiction; 'annates,' tax on the first year's income of an ecclesiastical benefice; 'patrimony of Peter,' the estates that belong to the church. In 1517 the Fifth Lateran Council voted to call a crusade against the Turks.

[56]

6 **cynosure**] *Cynosura*, the constellation of the Little Bear, by which, according to Cicero (*Academica* 2.20.66, *De natura deorum* 2.41.106), the Phoenicians steered their ships.

8–16 **this pillar ... that foundation ... better edifice**] For the image of the pillar, see 1 Tim 3:15; for that of the architect and building, 1 Cor 3:10–15; for the winds beating upon the foundation, Matt 7:24–7.

27 **the Lesbian rule**] *Adagia* I v 93 ('By the Lesbian rule') CWE 31 465 explains this proverbial expression by quoting from book 5 of Aristotle's *Ethics* on 'the leaden rule used in Lesbian architecture,' whereby 'the rule changes to fit the shape of the stone and does not remain a rule.'

[57]

1 **ancient and the modern Doctors**] ancient Christian teachers (the Church Fathers) and those of more recent times (scholastic theologians). See note on **16/8–10**. For an appeal, similar to the one made here, to allow a harmonious coexistence between the 'ancients' and the 'moderns,' see the dedicatory letter to Erasmus' *Paraphrase* on Ephesians, CWE 43 476–8 (1520 version) and 284–97 (1521 version).

8 **a single hair's-breadth, as they say**] See *Adagia* I v 6 CWE 31 390–1 for this and similar expressions.

13–14 **'not with the necessity to believe but with the liberty to judge'**] Augustine *Contra Faustum Manicheum* 11.5

29 **Babylonian towers rising all the way to heaven**] See Gen 11:1–9.

[59]

3–7 **Presently ... complete with all the gifts it now enjoys in heaven**] The thought is elliptical: as the number of definitions grew, the time soon came when they reached the absurdity mentioned here. The tone is satirical.

[60]

13–14 **a universal council ... a synod**] General Councils were convoked by the pope, whereas synods were assemblies of diocesan priests under the presidency of the bishop, but Erasmus may be using the terms here without precision. The Fifth Lateran Council, called by Pope Leo X, to whom Erasmus dedicated his edition of the New Testament, had concluded in 1517.

17–18 **vows, tithes, restitutions, absolutions, confessions**] The practice of making vows, like that of making confession, was a frequent target of Erasmus' criticism, as was the role of monks in taking advantage of these practices. In another *1520* addition to the *Ratio* at **142**, Erasmus will speak again of practices he deplores for the financial gain they bring; there the term 'absolution' (*remissio*) is evidently used for 'indulgence.'

[61]

8 **that Platonic lie**] In Plato *Republic* 3.389B–D, 5.459C–E, Socrates argues that the rulers of his imagined commonwealth may use deception to breed children possessing the excellence required by the state. For the 'noble lie,' see the *Republic* 3.414B–415D.

[62]

1 **an unbreachable wall**] *Murus aeneus*, literally 'a wall of bronze,' an expression explained by Erasmus in *Adagia* II x 25 CWE 34 137 as 'a precise and immutable decision,' citing Horace *Epistles* 1.1.60.

3–4 **the view that an indissoluble marriage arises from consent alone**] There is a clearer articulation of the problems outlined here in Erasmus' major work on the subject, *Institutio Christiani matrimonii/The Institution of Christian Matrimony* (1526) CWE 69.

8 **as ... among the Jews, Greeks, and Romans**] In *Institutio Christiani matrimonii* CWE 69 245–8, Erasmus cites evidence from Roman, Jewish, and Greek sources to show that marriages in these societies were subject to the authority of parents.

10 **'stem and stern'**] In *Adagia* I i 8 CWE 31 56–7, Erasmus explains the proverb as signifying 'the sum of the whole business, everything that is important and essential for it.'

11 **if the cowl is assumed**] if the husband takes monastic vows

13-14 **Is it not permitted to live a religious life within matrimony?**] Erasmus frequently affirmed that the truly religious life belongs as well outside the monastery as within it; see eg *Enchiridion* CWE 66 57–8.

[63]

15-16 **the French disease, which is just like leprosy**] Erasmus' horror at the 'French disease' (syphilis) is conveyed in the colloquy 'A Marriage in Name Only' CWE 40 842–59.

[64]

11-12 **a solemn vow ... one that is not solemn**] The distinction is explored in *Institutio Christiani matrimonii* CWE 69 258–63, 284–7.

15 **a purchasable right**] Perhaps a reference to the sale of indulgences

[65]

1 **the concept of spiritual kinship**] On this see *Institutio Christiani matrimonii* CWE 69 269–70.

[67]

2-4 **that wonderful circle and harmony of the entire drama of Christ ... a drama acted out for our sake**] What follows is an expansion and re-elaboration of the passage in the *Methodus* CWE 41 442–4 that noted the 'whole course and circle of Christ's life.' The idiom now is of acting out a play, *fabulam peragere*.

7 **For no lie is so skilfully fabricated that it is at all points consistent**] The liar's proverbial inconsistency is the theme of *Adagia* II iii 74 CWE 33 175.

9 **the types sketch out and represent in outline the Christ**] In Christian exegesis, 'types' (Greek, *typoi*) are events in the Old Testament that foreshadow the gospel dispensation. Thus eg the Israelites' crossing of the Red Sea in Exodus could be interpreted (as already by St Paul, 1 Cor 10:1–6) as a type or prefiguration of Christian baptism. Erasmus also uses 'type' in a more general sense to mean an event that prefigures or serves as a model for other events: see **181**.

13 **as Tertullian so nicely shows**] Tertullian *Adversus Marcionem* 4.6–43

14–18 **the witness of the angels ... then of the Magi, of Simeon and Anna besides**] The allusions, except for that to the Magi (Matt 2:1–15), follow Luke's narrative (1:26–38, 2:1–38). For the 'celestial marriage,' see the paraphrases on Matt 1:20 CWE 45 43–4 and on Luke 1:34–5 CWE 47 43–6.

18–19 **the prelude in the preaching of John the Baptist, who now points out ...**] John 1:24–36. For John's ministry as a prelude, see the paraphrase on John 1:28–9, 36 CWE 46 30, 33. 'Points out' renders *digito indicantis*, literally, points with a finger; see the paraphrase on Mark 1:14 CWE 49 14.

[68]

5–12 **He first gave proof of what he was ... the temptation of Satan**] Luke 2:41–7 (teaching in the temple); John 2:1–11 (wedding at Cana); Matt 3:13–4:11, Mark 1:9–13, Luke 3:21–2 and 4:1–13 (baptism and temptation). Erasmus appears here to place the wedding chronologically before the baptism and temptation, as he will do later; see note on **174**.

16–22 **he himself so lived ... washed his disciples' feet**] Matt 26:59–63, Mark 14:55–61 (witnesses suborned); Isa 53:2, Acts 8:32 (sheep to the slaughter); Matt 8:20 (possessed nothing); John 13:1–15 (footwashing)

26–32 **He had taught that the godly must not fear death ... that heavenly spirit descended ...**] Matt 10:26–33 (fear death); Acts 1:9–10 (Ascension); Acts 2:1–4 (Spirit descended); for the transformation of the disciples, see the paraphrases on Acts 2:1–14, 42–7 CWE 50 13–17, 25–6.

[69]

13 **You see what great agreement there is at every point**] References assumed in this paragraph apparently include Matt 20:17–19, John 12:32–3 ('the effect of his death'); John 14:1–17 and 16:19–21 ('distress of the disciples'); Matt 21:33–43, Mark 12:1–9, Luke 20:9–18 (parable of the keepers of the vineyard as allegory of 'the deception of the Jews and the reception of the Gentiles'); the miniature apocalypses of Matt 24, Mark 13, and Luke 21 understood as predictions of the gospel preached to the entire world, the suffering of the disciples, the destruction of Jerusalem, and the emergence of heresies. For the events of the spread of the gospel

and the sufferings of the disciples, the narrative of Acts is the main New Testament source.

[70]

1–3 **You will perhaps find in the books of Plato or Seneca ... accord with the life of Christ**] The principle implied here is expounded in the colloquy 'The Godly Feast' CWE 39 192–4.

[71]

1–3 **to establish some order of authority among sacred writings also as Augustine did not scruple to do**] In *De doctrina christiana* 2.8.13 Augustine reflects a traditional order of the biblical books: historical books, wisdom literature, Prophets, and New Testament. 'Also' appears to allude to a similar preferential order for secular authors implied in the allusion just above to Plato and Seneca, for which see *De ratione studii/On the Method of Study* CWE 24 666–76. As the following allusion to the Apostles' Creed indicates, the 'sacred writings' or 'sacred books' (*sacris voluminibus*) extend beyond the biblical canon.

3–4 **those books about which the ancients never had any doubt**] For the 'ancient witness' to the canon of Scripture, see notably Eusebius *Ecclesiastical History* 3.25, 6.25, and 7.25. Critics often challenged Erasmus on the doubts he expressed about some books of the New Testament.

11–12 **the creed commonly known as the 'Apostles',' produced, if I mistake not, at the Council of Nicaea**] In his late (1533) *Explanatio symboli/Explanation of the Creed* CWE 70 252–3, Erasmus distinguishes clearly the Apostles' Creed from the Nicene Creed, and says that the former was probably 'the first of all,' CWE 70 253. However, as Craig Thompson notes in regard to the colloquy 'An Examination Concerning the Faith,' Erasmus 'is disposed to date [the Apostles' Creed] from the first Council of Nicaea,' CWE 39 432 n16.

15–16 **When there began to be less faith among Christians both the number and the size of the creeds grew**] See also *Explanatio symboli* CWE 70 253: 'The impious inquisitiveness of philosophers and the perversity of heretics gave rise to a multitude ... of creeds,' a statement Erasmus had prefaced by noting, in addition to the Apostles' Creed, the Nicene, the Constantinopolitan, the Athanasian, and 'several others.'

[72]

4 **He became all things to all people**] The language is taken from 1 Cor 9:22, where it is used by Paul of himself. For Erasmus, as will appear from **97–102**, Paul was imitating Christ in this.

5–7 **when he commands ... presents to his disciples a new appearance**] Matt 8:23–7, Mark 4:35–41, Luke 8:22–5 (commands winds); Matt 9:2, Mark 2:5, Luke 5:20 (forgives sins); Matt 17:1–8, Mark 9:2–8, Luke 9:28–36 (is transfigured)

9–11 **when he is hungry ... killed**] John 4:6–7 (weariness, thirst); Matt 21:18–21, Mark 11:12–14 (hunger and the fig tree); John 11:35 (mourning)

12–13 **some from their nets, Matthew from the toll-house**] Matt 4:18–22, Mark 1:16–20, Luke 5:1–11 (fishers); Matt 9:9, Mark 2:14, Luke 5:27–8 (Matthew)

26–7 **When he was led to Herod he did not deign even to address him**] Luke 23:9. Herod here is Antipas, son of Herod the Great by Malthake, a Samaritan. Like his father, Antipas often disregarded traditional Jewish law and cultivated the goodwill of pagan Rome, on whose power his authority rested. Jesus appears to have censured Herod at only one other point in the Gospels, Mark 8:15.

[73]

2–4 **the miracles ... of the fig tree ... of the crowd ... of Lazarus**] Matt 21:18–21, Mark 11:12–14 (fig tree); Matt 14:15–21 and 15:32–9, Mark 6:30–44 and 8:1–9, Luke 9:12–17, John 6:4–13 (loaves); John 11 (Lazarus)

[75]

12 **Sometimes he is angry**] Jesus expresses anger in Mark 3:5, and 'rebukes' unclean spirits in Mark 1:25 and 9:25, while in John 2:13–17 his action in driving out the merchants from the temple is interpreted as 'consuming zeal.' Erasmus may have in mind as well such passages as Mark 1:43 and Matt 9:30.

13–15 **It will be appropriate to philosophize where there are differences of this kind, and to investigate with a pious curiosity the mystery of the divine plan**] An important qualification of Erasmus' occasional criticism of 'philosophizing' and his frequent attacks on *curiositas*: the imaginative exploration of Scripture leading to insights conducive to genuine piety – because they open up the significance of salvation history for Christian living – is 'philosophizing' emerging from 'pious curiosity.'

[76]

2–10 **to the Pharisees ... he shows that they were not doing what they knew should above all else be done**] Matt 19:3–9, Mark 10:1–12 (divorce); Matt 22:15–21, Mark 12:13–17, Luke 20:20–6 (tribute); Matt 22:34–40, Mark 12:28–34, Luke 10:25–8 (the great commandment). The assertion that the Pharisees leave undone the most important things may, in addition, echo Matt 23:23–4 and Luke 11:42.

10–13 **He attributes knowledge of the Law to the Pharisees ... condemns the Sadducees ...**] See eg Matt 23:1–13 (Pharisees); Matt 22:23–32, Mark 12:18–27 (Sadducees). In his paraphrase on Matt 23:1–13 CWE 45 312–16, Erasmus forcefully interprets the character of the Pharisees portrayed here.

14–15 **like driving out a nail with a nail**] See *Adagia* I ii 4 ('To drive out one nail by another') CWE 31 148–9.

15–17 **when asked by what authority ... from heaven or of human origin**] Matt 21:23–7, Mark 11:27–33, Luke 20:1–8

21–3 **In Mark, the twenty-sixth chapter ... silent before Herod**] 'Mark' is a mistake for 'Matthew'; see Matt 26:59–63. The encounter with Herod is narrated only in Luke 23:6–12.

24–9 **In the presence of Pilate ... the women who followed him**] Matt 27:11–14 (encounter with Pilate); Matt 26:57–64 and Mark 14:53–62 (encounter with Caiaphas): in both Gospels, Jesus, though silent at first, eventually responds briefly to the high priest. In John 18:19–24 he responds to him at some length. For the binding, beating, and mockery, see Matt 26:67, 27:1–2, 27–31 and Mark 14:65, 15:1–20; for the blow, John 18:19–23; for the reproaches of the Jews, Matt 27:39–43, Mark 15:29–32, Luke 23:35–7; for the lamentation of the women, Luke 23:27–8.

[77]

1–3 **Sometimes he avoids the crowd ... press in closely upon him**] Jesus may be thought to avoid the crowd in such passages as Matt 8:18, 14:13, Mark 3:9, 6:46–7, John 6:15. For his compassion for the crowds, see Matt

9:36, Mark 6:34; for the press of the crowd, see Mark 2:2, 5:24, 31 and Luke 8:19–21. Jesus welcomes the crowd in Luke 9:11.

3–9 **At one time he draws into the deepest solitude to pray ... secretly vanishes when the crowd was going to stone him**] Mark 1:35 (withdraws to pray); Luke 4:28–30 (escapes from those lying in wait); John 8:59 (escapes stoning). The reference to the crowded assembly in the temple may allude to passages where the narrative implies large numbers, eg Matt 21:12–24:1, Mark 11:11–13:1, Luke 19:45–21:38. See also John 7:10–44, where the 'crowds' are said to be present.

9–12 **He entrusts to the disciples certain things ... the secret conversation with Moses concerning his death**] Matt 10:5–7, Luke 9:1–2 (message to be preached); Matt 17:1–9, Mark 9:1–9 (message to remain unspoken). Luke alone records that the conversation with Moses and Elijah concerned the 'departure' of Jesus (9:31). In Matt 17:9 and Mark 9:9, Jesus forbids the disciples to report the vision; in Luke 9:36 the disciples 'did not report what they had seen.' The Gospels do not identify the mountain as Tabor.

12–13 **He speaks in one way to his disciples, in another way to the common crowd**] See eg Matt 13:10–17, Mark 4:10–12.

14–15 **he shows himself to his disciples after the resurrection now in one form, now in another**] The appearance of Jesus in different forms after the resurrection is described especially in the narratives of Luke 24 and of John 20 and 21; see also Acts 1:3.

16 **a kind of Proteus**] For the figure of Proteus in classical mythology, see *Adagia* II ii 74 CWE 33 113–14 and note on **231**/11–15 below. Erasmus made frequent use of it, eg as an image for theological allegory (*De copia* CWE 24 611), to describe the changing passions of the soul (*Enchiridion* CWE 66 49–50), or for the slippery evasiveness of heretics (*In psalmum 1* CWE 63 17).

[78]

1–2 **passages ... that at first glance seem even contradictory**] Discussion of the difficulties caused by apparent inconsistencies and contradictions in the biblical narrative had been an important feature of biblical exegesis from antiquity, and was one of the drivers for Erasmus' *Annotations*, on which see 80–92 above.

[79]

2–3 **Matthew reports ... Luke affirms ...**] A reference apparently to Matt 9:27–31, 20:29–34, and Luke 18:35–43, where, however, one blind man is found in Luke's narrative, two in Matthew's; see also Matt 12:22, where one man, both blind and deaf, was healed.

4–7 **when Stephen, in Acts ... in Genesis ...**] In Gen 12:1–6, God's call comes to Abram in Haran, and he moves to Canaan; in Acts 7:2–4, God's call comes to Abraham [*sic*] in Mesopotamia 'before he lived in Haran'; he then moves to Haran, and later to Canaan.

7–9 **in the number of years ... the order of events in the Gospels**] See eg the problems in determining the number of years in the *Paraphrase on Acts* 7:6 and 13:20 CWE 50 50 n11 and 86 n44. For difficulties in the order of events in the Gospels, see eg the story of the cleansing of the temple, placed at the beginning of Jesus' ministry in John 2:13–22, but at the end of the ministry in the synoptic Gospels, for which see Matt 21:12–13, Mark 11:15–19, Luke 19:45–6.

[81]

2 **calls himself the son of Adam**] By 'son of Adam' Erasmus refers to the title 'Son of Man' used frequently of Christ in the Gospels, eg in Matt 8:20, 9:6, Mark 2:10, 28, etc.

2–3 **he grows up gradually in accordance with the customary stages of life**] See Luke 2:40, 52 and *Ratio* 68.

5–6 **he often pities the crowd, as in the twentieth chapter of Matthew**] At Matt 20:34 it is the blind men that Jesus pities, not the crowd that follows him. For Jesus' pity towards the crowds, see eg Matt 14:14.

11–12 **he thirsts, the usual result of that kind of punishment**] For Erasmus' explanation of Christ's thirst on the cross, see the paraphrase on John 19:28 CWE 46 213 with n38.

[82]

4–5 **he bears witness that he is the Son of God sent from heaven**] Erasmus' paraphrase on John 1:1–2 and the preceding preface provide an exposition of the relation between Father and Son, CWE 46 15–19.

[83]

2–6 **the Jews ... had ... been rejected ... the Gentiles had been received into their place ...**] See Rom 9–11 and the paraphrase on these chapters, CWE 42 52–69.

6–8 **Christ knew the hardness of his own race ... a false opinion of righteousness**] See the paraphrase on Matt 10:5–6 CWE 45 166–7 with n10.

11–14 **The prophets had predicted ... fall away from the promises**] That 'the Gentiles would by faith break through' is a reference to a saying of Jesus recorded in both Matt 11:12 and Luke 16:16. It is interpreted here as in the paraphrases on these verses: see CWE 45 185–6 with n25 and CWE 48 96–7 with n18. The New Testament writers interpreted prophetic writings as predictions of the exclusion of Jews and the inclusion of Gentiles, an exegetical tradition extended by Christian theologians in later periods.

15–18 **He was heralded in song by the angels ... commended by the utterance of the Father**] The stories of the birth and infancy of Jesus are in Luke 2 and Matthew 2:1–15; John the Baptist points to Christ in John 1:29, 36; the 'commendation' of the Father, by the voice from heaven at Jesus' baptism, is recorded in Matt 3:17, Mark 1:11, and Luke 3:22.

21–3 **they killed the prophets ... persecuted Christ himself**] Matt 23:29–36, Luke 11:47–52 (killing the prophets); Matt 21:25–32, Mark 11:31, Luke 20:1–8 (disbelieving John); Matt 12:24, Mark 3:22, Luke 11:15 (Beelzebub)

25–6 **'The temple of the Lord ...**] See Jer 7:4, with the paraphrase on Acts 21:28 CWE 50 128.

[84]

1 **The Magi are the first of all to worship the boy**] Matt 2:1–18. Although the narrative of Luke 2:15–20 suggests that the shepherds found Jesus before the Magi, the shepherds are not said to have worshipped him.

6–7 **He calls a tax collector, who leaves all and follows him**] Matt 9:9, Mark 2:14, Luke 5:27–8; only Luke observes that Levi 'left all.'

10–14 **the Canaanite woman ... forced Christ, as it were, to do a kindness ... successfully assault**] Matt 15:21–8, Mark 7:24–30. The image of violence ('forced ... assault') alludes to the saying of Jesus in Matt 11:12 and Luke 16:16.

[85]

23–4 **'Today salvation has come to this house, since this also is a child of Abraham'**] Erasmus quotes his own translation (from *1519*), which makes 'this' in the concluding clause refer to 'house.' In his annotation on Luke 19:9, he explains that on this reading 'house' stands for the *paterfamilias*.

[89]

12–14 **Again, in Luke ...**] The citation mingles Luke 16:16 with Matt 11:12 as found in the Vulgate and Erasmus' New Testament.

16–17 **Jerusalem was turned into Sodom ... children of God**] Gen 19:24–9 (destruction of Sodom). The two final clauses in the sentence allude to Hos 1:8–10, 2:23, Rom 9:25–6, and 1 Pet 2:10. From Christian antiquity, Christians regarded the destruction of Jerusalem as a sign that the Jews were no longer 'God's people.'

[90]

6–9 **the custom generally prevails ... perpetrators of the wicked deeds**] For sins imputed to children, see Exod 34:7 and Num 14:18.

10 **'From the ugly raven comes the bad egg'**] A saying also quoted by Juvenal *Satires* 13.142

10–11 **he wanted to have ... a guardian ...**] In the *Paraphrases* Erasmus is generally careful to qualify the relation of Jesus to Joseph. See eg the paraphrase on Luke 3:23 CWE 47 119, where the narrator explains that Joseph was Jesus' father legally but that the relationship was concealed to facilitate the preaching of the gospel.

12–16 **Angels from heaven ... a corroborating witness**] For the birth stories, see Matthew 2 and Luke 2.

17 **'This is my beloved son; hear him'**] The quotation in the form given here follows closely the text of Luke 9:35 and Mark 9:7, combining the versions of Erasmus and the Vulgate.

17–21 **Many were the times that John gave witness ... the demons ... the crowd wonders at the divine power in him**] Matt 3:11–14, Mark 1:7–8, Luke 3:15–17, John 1:19–36 (John's witness); Mark 3:11–12 (witness of the demons and Jesus' reluctance); Matt 7:28–9 and 13:54–5, Mark 5:42 and 7:37 (astonishment of the crowd).

24 **... who was to come into this world'**] For this clause Erasmus follows his own translation.

[91]

6–8 **Even the hostile judges ... suborned and were lying**] Matt 26:59–65, Mark 14:55–9. The point is underlined in the paraphrases on these passages, CWE 45 358–9 and CWE 49 165–6.

8–11 **They have no charge to bring ... what they had not understood**] Matt 26:60–1, Mark 14:58. For the 'sense intended,' see John 2:19–21.

[92]

4–5 **the syllogisms of philosophers or the enthymemes of the rhetoricians**] Some ancient rhetoricians called the enthymeme a 'rhetorical syllogism' or an 'incomplete syllogism' and distinguished it from the regular syllogism by the fact that its parts were less clearly defined or less complete, but both Cicero and Quintilian say that properly speaking the enthymeme was an argument drawn from incompatibles or contraries; see Quintilian *Institutio oratoria* 5.14.1–2, Cicero *Topica* 13.55.

14 **the apostles played the prelude**] See Matt 10:5–15, Mark 6:7–13, Luke 9:1–6, 10:1–12 for the apostolic mission. On the 'limitation' of the message, a feature of the 'second time period,' see **46** with note there on lines 17–19. Among the images of theatre, frequent in the *Paraphrases*, that of 'prelude' commonly signifies early anticipations of the full gospel.

[93]

2–4 **He began, not in Nazareth ... but in Capernaum, a city corrupted by wealth and luxury**] Matt 4:12–17, Luke 4:16–37. The characterization of cities, especially maritime cities, as wealthy and corrupt is formulaic in Erasmus' writings.

9–11 **he associated ... was baptized, fasted**] Matt 9:10–13, Mark 2:15–17, Luke 5:29–32 (association with sinners); Luke 2:21–4 (circumcision and purification); Luke 4:16, 31, Mark 1:21 (sabbath); Matt 3:13–4:2, Mark 1:9–13, Luke 3:21–2 and 4:1–2 (baptism and fasting).

[94]

2–3 **he responds either with the Scripture or with reasoned arguments**] Classical rhetoric distinguished between 'artificial' arguments, based on reasonable deduction, and the primary evidence of testimony.

13 **He sends the lepers to the priests**] In Luke 17:12–14, a number of lepers are sent to the priests and are healed on the way; in Matt 8:1–4, Mark 1:40–4, Luke 5:12–14, a single leper is healed, then sent to the priest.

[95]

1–3 Everywhere he shows ... that he suffers not on his own account but for us] Matt 16:21–3, Mark 8:31–3, Luke 9:22 (Jesus predicts his sufferings); John 10:17–18 (Jesus suffers of his own will and for humanity).

13–16 But about his type of teaching ... I shall say something a little later] See **185–93** and **216–33**, where Erasmus comments on various forms of similitudes, including allegories.

[97]

3–5 With what great cunning Paul everywhere acts like some chameleon, if I may use the expression ... from every side] See 1 Cor 9:19–23 and Erasmus' annotation on Rom 1:12 CWE 56 37 ('to be comforted together'), where, as here, Erasmus notes Paul's characteristic *vafrities* 'cunning.' For Paul as 'polypus,' see **145**.

21–2 he everywhere calls the task he performs a ministry – he is nothing but a minister and a steward] For the apostles as 'only ministers and stewards,' see the paraphrases on Rom 15:19 CWE 42 85, on 1 Cor 4:1–2 CWE 43 60–1, and on Acts 20:24 CWE 50 123.

[99]

4–6 Rather, he tells them how ... the kind of religion they followed] Erasmus summarizes Paul's speech to the Athenians recorded in Acts 17:22–31. The paraphrase on these verses (CWE 50 108–11) abundantly illustrates the principle of accommodation asserted here.

6 *sebasmata*] See the annotation on Acts 17:23 (*et videns simulacra vestra*): 'Whereas a word denoting idols would have been offensive, *sebasmata* is a word that embraces everything we venerate – altars, shrines, statues, monuments ...'

11–12 he took part of an inscription and with remarkable dexterity turned it to an occasion to preach the gospel] In his annotation on Acts 17:28 (*ignoto deo*), Erasmus cites Jerome, who indicated that the full inscription there cited by Paul read, 'To the gods of Asia and Europe and Africa, to unknown and foreign gods,' that it was Paul's cunning (*vafrities*) to select only part of the inscription, and that even in the part excerpted Paul had changed the plural to the singular; see Jerome *Commentarius in epistolam ad Titum 1* (on Titus 1:12).

15–18 **not with the testimony of the prophets ... but with that of Aratus, the Greek poet, 'For we too are his offspring'**] Erasmus cites the Greek as in Acts 17:28. Aratus (315–240/239 BC) of Soli in Cilicia had been identified by patristic writers as the author of the poem from which this half-line was taken, and he is so identified in the paraphrase on Acts 17:28 CWE 50 110. The poem was famous in antiquity and well known in the Renaissance; see CWE 50 110 n48.

[102]

6 **Jeroboam, the son of Solomon**] Erasmus means Rehoboam, Solomon's son, from whom Jeroboam took the northern tribes of the kingdom that had earlier been united by David (1 Kings 12:1–20).

7–8 **those who are called fathers instead of lords**] For the king as a father-figure, ruling through clemency and extending mercy, see *Institutio principis christiani* CWE 27 228–30, 256. An allusion to the prince-bishops of the sixteenth century may be intended.

[103]

27–9 **You see how the borders of the religion of Christ have been contracted ...**] A reference to the Islamic conquests: Constantinople had fallen in 1453, and in 1516 and 1517 the Turkish king Selim I had conquered Syria and Egypt and begun to move against Europe. In August 1521 Belgrade fell to the Turks under Suleiman the Magnificent (cf Ep 1228:60–1). In a 1523 addition to the famous adage *Dulce bellum inexpertis* ('War is a treat for those who have not tried it'), Erasmus, discussing the Turkish menace, wrote 'What a small corner of the world is left to us!' (*Adagia* IV I 1 CWE 35 433).

29–30 **But I have frequently discussed these matters elsewhere**] Eg in the passage in the preface to the 1518 edition of the *Enchiridion*, beginning 'At this moment war is preparing against the Turks,' CWE 66 10–12.

[104]

17–22 **Again, he removes the pursuit of wealth ... the providential care of the heavenly Father**] See Matt 6:34 (concern for tomorrow); Luke 12:33 and Matt 6:19–20 (treasures); and, for the expression 'laid up eternal in the heavens,' 2 Cor 5:1, 1 Pet 1:4. Matt 6:25–33 and Luke 12:22–31 speak of lilies and, respectively, of birds and ravens; for sparrows see Matt 10:29–31 and Luke 12:6–7.

27–32 To convince his disciples ... left-overs were taken up from the feast] Matt 16:5–12, Mark 8:14–21 (concern about bread); Matt 14:15–21, Mark 6:34–44, Luke 9:12–17, also Matt 15:32–8, Mark 8:1–10 (miracle of the loaves and fishes).

32–4 In addition, there is the time when he sends the disciples ... they had lacked nothing] Matt 10:5–15, Mark 6:7–13, Luke 9:1–6, 10:1–20 (mission); Luke 22:35 ('confession' on return).

[106]

1–4 Now in regard to the love of honour and the disease of ambition ... the chief bane of ecclesiastical princes] According to the paraphrase on Matt 20:24 CWE 45 287, Jesus wanted to remove utterly ambition and envy from the 'hearts of all who would accede to the duties of the apostles'; see also the *Enchiridion* CWE 66 121–2 ('Against Ambition'), and, for 'the first case of ambition in the church,' the paraphrase on Acts 6:1 CWE 50 46.

19–21 He sets before them a lowly and insignificant child ... the level of a little child] Erasmus appears to follow the Matthean version of the story of the ambition of James and John (Matt 20:20–8), with its parallel in Mark 10:35–45, attaching to it, however, the story about the child as told in Matt 18:1–5 with its parallel in Mark 9:33–7 and Luke 9:46–8.

[108]

5 "We are children of Abraham"] For the expression, see Luke 3:8 (with its synoptic parallel, Matt 3:9) and John 8:33.

10–11 Every kind of nobility among Christians must be judged by virtuous action, not by family trees] Kinship defined in terms of spiritual and moral likeness is a commonplace to which Erasmus frequently appealed; see *Adagia* IV iii 36 CWE 36 25 ('He is his father's son') and the paraphrase on John 8:37–41 CWE 46 115–17.

[109]

13–14 'You do not know of what spirit you are. The Son of man came not to destroy souls but to save'] These verses from Luke, though included

[110]

2–3 trust in ourselves] *Fiducia nostri*, which may also be rendered by 'self-confidence.' In Erasmus' theological vocabulary, the word characteristically invites, as here, a contrast between reliance upon merits achieved by one's own works and reliance upon the freely given grace of God for salvation.

4–6 Christ scorns the Pharisee who was standing close by ... he acknowledges the publican who was standing far off] The spatial indicators here, 'standing close by ... far off,' are explained as relative measures of self-confidence in the paraphrase on Luke 18:11–13, CWE 48 118–19: 'The Pharisee, standing next to the mercy seat as if he deserved to speak with God at close quarters, prayed ... the tax collector, entirely dissatisfied with himself ... stood far away from the sacred objects ...'

23–4 the rags of a woman that are soaked in her menstrual flow] For the image see the Vulgate of Isa 64:6. See also **114/27** below and 102–3 above.

33–7 In Matthew, the seventh chapter ... 'Truly I say to you, I do not know you'] In the citation Erasmus conflates Matt 7:23 with Matt 25:12.

[111]

16 'Now,' he says, 'you believe ...'] Here and in Erasmus' translation a statement, but in most editions of the Bible (and in Erasmus' paraphrase, CWE 46 191) a question.

20–1 'Even though all should be offended, I, at least, will not waver'] A free rendering of Mark 14:29 and Matt 26:33.

[112]

4–6 Hence those who within a year have received the title and the profession of the seven liberal arts are proverbially reckoned among the 'wild beasts'] The statement may reflect a popular jibe at those who had recently received the degree of Master of Arts and had thus become entitled to teach in a University. The seven liberal arts – the trivium (grammar, logic, and rhetoric) and quadrivium (arithmetic, music, geometry, and astronomy) – provided the traditional basis for an arts degree.

6–11 It was aptly and wisely said by someone ... that only when they had advanced as far as possible did they realize that they knew nothing] A similar statement is attributed to Menedemus, a Greek philosopher (fl 300 BC) from Eretria in Euboea, in Erasmus' *Parabolae/Parallels* CWE 23 187:3–7; see also Socrates' story in Plato *Apology* 20C–22E.

[113]

3–4 Everywhere he calls any virtue we have 'the gift of God' and 'grace'] Erasmus attempts to offer a systematic analysis of the Pauline doctrine of grace in *De libero arbitrio/On Free Will* CWE 76 27–33.

[114]

3 what he calls the 'righteousness from faith'] For the expression 'righteousness from faith' (*iustitia ex fide*), see Rom 9:30 and 10:6; for the expression 'righteousness of faith' (*iustitia fidei*), Rom 4:13. While 'righteousness,' as used here to translate the Latin *iustitia*, is the common English rendering of the Greek *dikaiosyne* in such passages, it is clear from Erasmus' *Paraphrases* that for him the Latin term conveyed an inherent forensic metaphor that is lost in this English translation.

[115]

1–2 Paul everywhere calls himself a slave of Jesus Christ] Rom 1:1, Gal 1:10, and Phil 1:1; also 1 Cor 4:1 and Titus 1:1. *Servus* in Latin is both 'slave' and 'servant'; the context here invites the less ambiguous image of 'slave.' See also **214**.

6–7 Paul designates the task he performs at one time a stewardship, at another a ministry] In the Vulgate and in Erasmus' translation, Paul frequently designates his work as a *ministerium* 'ministry,' himself as a *minister* 'minister'; see eg Acts 20:24, 2 Cor 5:18, 1 Tim 1:12 (ministry); Rom 15:16, Eph 3:7, Col 1:23, 25 (minister). Less frequently do we find *dispensatio* 'stewardship,' and *dispensator* 'steward'; see 1 Cor 4:1, 2.

[116]

19–21 **so much the more keenly will we enter upon this race-course, awaiting from him the beginning of the course, its progress, and a successful conclusion]** An allusion to the three aspects of 'particular grace': 'the first stirring up, the second continuing, the third bringing to completion': *De libero arbitrio* CWE 76 32. 'Race-course': *stadium* as in 1 Cor 9:24 (Erasmus' translation and the Vulgate); see also Heb 12:1–2.

[117]

11–14 **'Whoever will be ashamed of me before men ... I shall in turn acknowledge before the Father']** Erasmus brings together sayings of Jesus from two contexts, Mark 8:38 (Luke 9:26) and Matt 10:32–3 (Luke 12:8–9).

16–19 **Paul also knows how to carry on the gospel ... an honour to be slandered because of Christ]** For Paul's ministry through good report and bad, see 2 Cor 6:3–4 and 8; for his reaction to slanders, 2 Cor 12:10, Phil 1:17–18. Paul's boasting is a recurrent theme in his Epistles: eg Rom 15:17, and especially 2 Cor 10:13–15, 11:10. For Paul's modesty, see Erasmus' annotation on Rom 15:19 CWE 56 407–8 ('of wonders in the strength of the Holy Spirit').

[118]

6–10 **Christ bids his disciples to be without concern ... he would supply the eloquence which adversaries could not resist]** Matt 10:19–20 and Mark 13:11, but the imagery here reflects especially Luke 12:11–12 and 21:14–15, where forms of the Greek verb *apologeomai* are found, commonly associated with the speech of or for a defendant in a public trial; hence here the word *apologia* 'speech.'

10–13 **Those are not to be feared who have power to kill the body ... not even a hair of our head would perish]** The first part of the sentence alludes to Matt 10:28, the last part to Luke 21:18.

[119]

12–14 **They only invite to Christ ... to entice more people to Christ]** See 1 Cor 9:20–2. Erasmus' characterization of apostolic action as neither

Explanatory Notes 287

provoking nor reproaching, but inviting, is set in relief in the paraphrases on Acts 2:37–40, 4:1–21, 5:26–9 CWE 50 22–3, 30–5, and 42–4.

[120]

3–10 **Fortune has heaped wealth upon you ... divert you less from piety**] These comments on wealth, parentage, and spouse apparently allude to 1 Cor 7:29–31, though the words on wealth specifically attributed to Paul are paraphrastic. See the similar admonition in the *Enchiridion* CWE 66 62–3.

[121]

6–7 **Let a guileless prudence be present ... without inflicting injury on anyone**] Perhaps an allusion to Matt 10:16; see the paraphrase on the verse, CWE 45 170–1.

[122]

5–6 **We must observe ... how Christ himself conducted himself**] For the scheme of thought underlying this section down to **184**, including the long passage from **130** to **151/152** inserted in *1520*, see note above on **32/36–7** and further reference there.

15–17 **towards those who are well deserving and receive the grace of the gospel, towards those who reject it**] Matt 10:11–14, Mark 6:10–11, Luke 9:4–5, 10:5–11

17–19 **towards persecutors, Jews, Gentiles ... towards ungodly judges, towards the flock entrusted to them**] See eg Matt 5:11–12, 44, 10:23 and Luke 21:12–13 (persecutors); Matt 10:5–6, 16–20, Mark 13:9–13, Luke 21:12–15, also Matt 15:22–8, Mark 7:25–30 (Jews and Gentiles); Matt 18:10–22 (the brother, weak or incorrigible); Matt 10:17–19, Mark 13:11, Luke 21:12–15 – though the expression may recall Luke 18:1–8 (the ungodly judges); John 21:15–17 (the flock entrusted).

[125]

10–14 **Now, in John, that whole scene in the presence of his disciples ... what else does it manifest except a fiery love intensely burning?**]

A reference apparently to John 13–17, pointing especially to the foot-washing scene and the Last Supper (chapter 13).

17–21 **Love alone is the token ...**] Echoing John 13:34–5, Erasmus frequently remarks that love is the special sign that marks Christians; see eg the paraphrase on those Johannine verses, CWE 46 166, the paraphrase on Acts 2:44, CWE 50 25, and the *Querela pacis/Complaint of Peace*, CWE 27 301.

[126]

5–12 **In Matthew ... the sake of the sabbath'**] For the story, see Matt 12:1–8, Mark 2:23–8, Luke 6:1–5. For the quotation, Erasmus follows closely the Vulgate of Matt 12:7–8, but the *1522* addition is a paraphrase of Mark 2:27.

14–17 **What, therefore, will obscure and insignificant men say when they demand that a person risk his whole life because of a prohibition against eating meats or because of petty regulations more inane than these?**] Erasmus often attacked the regulations for fasting imposed by the church, along with 'ceremonies' (ie special rules of conduct) in general, as he does in this and the following paragraph. In 1520 he received a papal dispensation from eating fish during Lent; see the colloquy 'A Fish Diet' CWE 40 677–721, first published in 1526.

[129]

14 **The kindness that he calls 'alms'**] 'Alms': *eleemosynam*, in the Vulgate (as in Erasmus' translation) among the words of Jesus in eg Matt 6:2–4, Luke 11:41 and 12:33.

[131]

23–4 **that whole disputation**] 'That whole disputation' may refer simply to chapter 14. However, in the context of the preceding citations from Romans, it appears that Erasmus intends rather almost the entire book of Romans (1–14), for which the last verse of chapter 14 provides the definitive climax.

Explanatory Notes 289

[132]

13–14 **in the Epistle addressed to the Hebrews**] Here, as in the *Paraphrase* on Hebrews (CWE 44 212 n3), Erasmus accepted the traditional attribution of Hebrews to Paul.

[133]

8–9 **love makes all things common to all**] See *Adagia* I i 1 ('Between friends all is common') CWE 31 29–30.

[134]

7–8 **a kiss truly worthy of a Christian person**] For the 'kiss of peace,' see Rom 16:16 (and Erasmus' paraphrase, CWE 42 88–9), 1 Cor 16:20, 2 Cor 13:12, 1 Thess 5:26.

14–15 **Long ago, he was called God of powers, the 'God of armies'**] In the annotation on Rom 9:28 CWE 56 272 ('bringing to completion the word'), Erasmus explains that in the Septuagint the Hebrew 'Sabaoth' is sometimes rendered by 'omnipotent,' sometimes by 'powers.' In the Vulgate, including the Vulgate of the Psalms according to the Hebrew, one generally finds the expression *Dominus exercituum* 'Lord of armies,' though in the Vulgate of the Psalms according to the Septuagint, the expression is *Dominus virtutum* 'Lord of powers.' English Bibles characteristically translate 'Lord of Hosts.'

[136]

5 **the Colossians**] A mistake for 'the Philippians'

[137]

4–6 **Elsewhere also he calls Christ the *mesites* 'mediator,' because as one who reconciles he comes midway between God and man**] Gal 3:19–20, 1 Tim 2:5. In his annotation (1519) on Gal 3:19 ('in the hand of an intercessor') CWE 58 60–1, Erasmus observes the difficulty of translating the Greek word *mesites* 'mediator.'

[138]

10 **Love and do what you will**] *Dilige et fac quod vis*. Erasmus quotes the famous dictum of Augustine *In Ioannis epistulam ad Parthos tractatus* (*Tractates on the First Epistle of John*) 7.8.

[139]

13 **'Our religion,' says Ambrose, 'is peace'**] This citation has not been traced.

[140]

12–13 **a supper that was the symbol of utmost harmony**] For Erasmus' interpretation of the supper, or the breaking of bread, as a symbol of harmony, a view expressed in various writings, see the paraphrase on 1 Corinthians 11:18–26 CWE 43 145–8 (1519).

[142]

1–2 **We have seen even in our day extraordinary turmoil among Christians ...**] Probably a reference to Luther's appearance on the ecclesiastical scene and the reaction to it.

5 **refrain from innards once tasted**] There was a saying that 'It is risky for a dog to taste once the innards.'

6–10 **... from absolutions ... arrangements ... dispensations ... empty promises ... application of merits ... the poor, ignorant populace**] In the spring of 1517 Johann Tetzel, a Dominican, had preached a papal indulgence that did much to stir Luther into action. For the sale of indulgences by the monks, see also the colloquy 'Military Affairs' CWE 39 58 and 62 n24. 'Arrangement' (*compositio*) referred to an arrangement for paying restitution for a theft. Belief in the church's 'treasury of merits' facilitated the sale of indulgences especially on behalf of the dead. See also the note on **60/17–18**.

[144]

17–18 **the overseers of the Christian religion**] 'Overseers': *antistites*. The word is found in early Christian texts referring to both priests and bishops. It is probable that Erasmus uses the word here to include, as well, monks and professors of theology, men specifically noted for their poisonous tongues in *Lingua* (1525) CWE 29 352–3.

[145]

10 **'compliance wins friends, truth earns hatred'**] Terence *Andria* 68
10–11 **Paul becomes all things to all people, taking on the character of a sort of polypus, if I may say so**] For the description of Paul as 'chameleon,' see **97**.

[147]

19–21 **he worships the Father neither in the mountain nor in Jerusalem, for the Father delights in those worshippers who worship in spirit**] See John 4:21 and 24, where Jesus replies to the Samaritan woman that in the future neither the Samaritan holy place (the mountain) nor the Jewish holy place (Jerusalem) would be the centre of worship, because worship would be spiritual.
22–3 **What he elsewhere calls the 'flesh' he here calls the 'letter'**] See the long disquisition on 'flesh and spirit' in the *Enchiridion* 'Fifth Rule' CWE 66 65–84, especially 70.

[151]

2–3 **I praise the rituals with which the church choir both long ago and today goes through its mysteries**] For Erasmus' appreciation of ritual in the liturgy 'both long ago and today,' see the dedicatory letter to Prince Ferdinand for the *Paraphrase on John* CWE 46 7–8.
10–12 **For about fifteen years now we have seen great turmoil in public affairs, schisms, wars, pillaging**] In 1523, when this addition to the text was inserted, the beginning of these events would have fallen around 1508, date of the formation of the League of Cambrai (France, Spain, the Holy Roman Empire, and the papacy against Venice), which was

followed in 1511 by the Holy League (Spain, the empire, Venice, joined by England against France). The intervening years saw the advent of Luther and the war between the emperor Charles and Francis I of France that broke out in 1521.

[152]

3–4 **his fearful 'Woe unto you'**] Matt 23:1–36, Luke 11:37–52 (woes against the Pharisees and scribes); Luke 6:24–5 (woes against the rich)

6–8 **He has compassion on the people ... scattered**] Matt 9:36, Mark 6:34, John 10:12

17–20 **He reveals that none is more receptive of evangelical teaching than the simple ... the kingdom of heaven belongs to them**] Eg Matt 5:3, 18:4, 19:13–15, Mark 10:13–16, Luke 18:15–17

[153]

7 **so that public order should not be upset**] On 'public order' see further the paraphrase on Rom 13:1 CWE 42 73–4 and the annotation on the same verse ('those, however, which are from God') CWE 56 347; also the *Institutio principis christiani* CWE 27 235.

14–16 **The tax-collectors and the harlots, acknowledging their disease, hasten to the physician**] Matt 9:9–12, Mark 2:13–17, Luke 5:27–31

[154]

4–5 **'The scribes and Pharisees have sat upon the seat of Moses etc'**] The 'etc' contains the focal point: 'So practise and observe whatever they tell you, but not what they do' (Matt 23:3).

[155]

3 **so many witnesses**] For witnesses at the baptism of Jesus, see Matt 3:11–17, Mark 1:7–11, Luke 3:15–17, 21–2, and John 1:29–34.

4–6 **He withdrew after his baptism, fasted, was tempted, overcame, and then only when he had been on all sides tested and prepared did he teach**] For the temptation and the beginning of Jesus' ministry, see Matt

4:1–17, Mark 1:12–15, Luke 4:1–22. Erasmus seized every opportunity in the *Paraphrases* to stress the need for proper preparation, for time-tested approval, before undertaking ministry.

[157]

5–7 those ... who are eager to make the Turks Christians by the engines of war only] See the vivid parallel: 'Destroy a Turk to make a Christian' *De bello Turcico/On the Turkish War* CWE 64 242, with the introductory essay 202–9. The Fifth Lateran Council (1512–17) was called with the intent of planning for a war against the Turks, and the Turkish advance into Europe in the 1520s added to the sense of danger felt by Erasmus and his contemporaries.

[159]

3–4 there is a time to flee and to steal away] An allusion to the ancient proverb, 'He that fights and runs away may live to fight another day': *Adagia* I x 40 CWE 32 252.

[161]

1–3 He also presented himself as affable and companionable, and open to all, avoiding the dinner parties not even of tax-collectors and sinners] See eg Matt 9:9–11, Mark 2:13–16, Luke 5:27–30 (Levi), Luke 19:2–10 (Zacchaeus).

[165]

2–3 nor did he betray the man by whom he was to be betrayed] In his paraphrases on John 13:25–6, Erasmus follows exegetical tradition in explaining that Jesus indicates his betrayer privately to John alone, not to the other disciples; CWE 46 164 with n29.

5–6 Thus Martin also once endured his Brice] Brice (Latin *Brixius*, d AD 444) was a badly behaved protégé of Martin of Tours, who often expressed contempt for his master; Sulpicius Severus *Dialogus* 3.15.

[166]

7–8 It is of some value to follow the Saviour even at a distance] An allusion to Peter, who, before his denial, had followed Christ at a distance: Matt 26:58, Mark 14:54, Luke 22:54.

[167]

3–6 As death approaches ... he depends wholly on the aid of the Father] Matt 26:36–46, Mark 14:32–42, Luke 22:39–46. As here, so elsewhere Erasmus interpreted Jesus' prayer in Gethsemane as an instructive example; see eg *De taedio Iesu* CWE 70 64.

[168]

2–3 the sort they now generally devise for saints] Although Erasmus severely criticized the contemporary practice of venerating the saints, he himself advocated a corrected and qualified veneration of them. Among his important statements on the saints and their relics, see the *Enchiridion* (1503) CWE 66 63–4, the *Modus orandi Deum/On Praying to God* (1524) CWE 70 186–201, and the colloquy 'A Pilgrimage for Religion's Sake' (1526) CWE 40 621–50.

[169]

1 the parable of the sower] Matt 13:3–9, 18–23, Mark 4:3–9, 14–20, Luke 8:4–8, 11–15

[170]

3–5 For the apostles, following the instruction of the Lord, even shake off the dust from their feet against those who do not receive the gospel] See the story of Paul and Barnabas at Pisidian Antioch (Acts 13:51), who follow their master's instruction to shake off the dust from their feet (Matt 10:14, Mark 6:11, Luke 9:5).

[171]

9–10 **Such were long ago the retreats of leading men, which, because of their solitude, they called monasteries**] 'Monastery' is an anglicization of the Latin *monasterium*, coined from the Greek *monasterion*, which is derived from the Greek verb *monazo* 'to be alone.'

[174]

4 **at the wedding, before the baptism**] Erasmus reverses the order of events in the Gospel narrative, as previously at **68**.

[175]

1–3 **One who wishes to undertake the work of gospel preaching must be cleansed from all the affections of the flesh and must set his mind on heavenly things only**] The same contrast is exploited in the *Enchiridion* CWE 66 46–54.

11–12 **not of the earth, but of heaven**] The Greek *anothen* 'again' or 'from above' leads to ambiguity in John 3:3, where the text can be read as either 'born again' or 'born from above.' The *1520* addition here reflects the latter.

[176]

5–9 **At a banquet ... hope for their health**] Luke 7:36–8 (woman at the banquet); John 4:7–26 (Samaritan woman); Matt 9:10, Mark 2:15, Luke 5:29 (tax collectors); Matt 9:12, Mark 2:17, Luke 5:31–2 (physician).

[180]

2–4 **A coin with the likeness of Caesar ... what we owe to God**] Matt 22:15–22, Mark 12:13–17, Luke 20:20–6

11–13 **He turns the children who were brought to him into an example of gentleness and modesty**] All three synoptic Gospels narrate two stories, virtually doublets, of Jesus with children. In each case the first of these, Matt 18:1–5, Mark 9:33–7, Luke 9:46–8, offers a lesson in modesty, while the second, Matt 19:13–15, Mark 10:13–16, Luke 18:15–17, reflects the gentleness of Jesus in contrast to the harshness of the disciples. The addition of *1522* may derive from Erasmus' work on the *Paraphrase on Matthew* (1522), where in the paraphrase on 18:1–5 the lesson of modesty is sharply drawn; CWE 45 259.

13–14 **He mentions his death and resurrection to those who were showing him the temple**] Erasmus conflates the narrative of John 2:18–22 with the synoptic narrative of Matt 24:1–2; see also Mark 13:1–2, Luke 21:5–6.

14–18 **A woman cried out ... the fruit that will never perish**] Luke 11:27–8, John 15:16, Matt 13:8

[181]

1–2 **The fact that in John, the twelfth chapter, the Pharisees resolutely plan to kill Lazarus also is a type**] For the sense of 'type' here, see the note on **67/9**.

[182]

7–9 **For so you read in the Epistle: 'There are three who give testimony in heaven, the Father, the Word, and the Spirit. And these three are one'**] Erasmus cites the text as widely found in the Vulgate tradition, but the words describing the 'testimony in heaven' of 'the Father, the Word [ie the second person of the Trinity], and the Spirit' (known to philologists as the 'Johannine comma,' where 'comma' means part of a sentence, as in Latin) are omitted by the best witnesses to the Greek text and were omitted from the text and translation of Erasmus' New Testament in 1516 and 1519. As a result of a vigorous debate, the missing words were added in the 1522 New Testament, with a large annotation. For the story of the events that led to the inclusion of the words in the last three editions of the New Testament, and for the significance of the words in debates on the divine Trinity, see CWE 41 200 with n781 and 309 with n1291.

[184]

1–2 **It is in this way that it will be appropriate to philosophize over individual passages in the mystic volumes**] For 'mystic,' used of Scripture, see **29**. Here the meaning of the expression 'to philosophize' (*philosophare*) has been amplified largely by the useful and practical application, in the preceding discussion, of Scripture to the life of the Christian individual and society. Erasmus will now proceed to discuss the literary modalities of Scripture.

[185]

2–5 For Scripture generally speaks indirectly and under the cover of tropes and allegories, and of comparisons or parallels, sometimes to the point of obscurity in a riddle] Erasmus describes the use for rhetorical purposes of comparisons and parallels in *De copia* CWE 24 616–26; for tropes, parallels, and allegories, see note on **23**/12. For brief definitions, including 'riddle' (*aenigma*), see *Ecclesiastes/The Evangelical Preacher*) (1535) 3 CWE 68 930–4. For the figurative mode of speech in Scripture, especially in relation to the role of persona, see **42**.

5–11 Perhaps Christ thought it fitting ... or he wanted to stimulate our sluggishness with this difficulty ... or through this design he wanted his mysteries to be covered and concealed from the profane and the ungodly ...] The second and third of these explanations for the obscurity in Scripture had been commonplaces of the Christian exegetical tradition since late antiquity; similar arguments were advanced in classical, medieval, and Renaissance defences of poetry.

15 Socratic comparisons] See eg in Plato's *Republic*, the fable of the race generated in the womb of earth (allegory of the metals), the allegories of the line and the cave, and the myth of Er, respectively 414B–416B, 509D–511E, 514A–517E, and 614B–621B.

[186]

1–2 not only for teaching and persuading, but also for stirring the emotions, for alluring with its charm] 'For alluring with its charm': *ad delectandum*. The phrases recall the classical formulation of the primary goals of good oratory: to instruct, to move, and to delight – *docere, movere, delectare*; Quintilian *Institutio oratoria* 3.5.2; 8.Pr 7.

26–7 the allurement of a similitude] 'Of a similitude': *similitudinis*. In Erasmus' New Testament vocabulary, *similitudo* appears to include various forms of 'likeness,' and according to context may be translated 'similitude,' 'parallel,' 'metaphor,' or 'simile.' In *De copia*, 'similitudes' are included as 'examples' along with 'parallels or comparisons, analogies, and anything else of the sort' (CWE 24 607), while 'simile' is abundantly exemplified (641–4).

[187]

1–4 there is the mystic parable from Genesis: Abraham everywhere digs wells ... veins of living water] Origen *In Genesim homiliae* interprets Isaac's wells as the 'living word of God (13.1.3), the mystical interpretation of Scripture (13.2.4), and 'heavenly as opposed to carnal perceptions' (13.3–4).

9–10 if he applies as an allegory Aaron's entire vestments] Origen *In Exodum homiliae* 9.4 offers an allegorical interpretation of the dress as priestly virtues.

[189]

8–9 made their way through various stages, like points of progress in practising the virtues, to a land flowing with milk and honey] 'A land flowing with milk and honey' is a frequent designation in the Hexateuch for Canaan; eg Exod 3:8, 17, Lev 20:24, Num 14:8, Deut 6:3, Josh 5:6. For the progress 'through various stages,' see Exod 17:1.

12–14 the battles and the uprisings that the Hebrews had against the Jebusites, the Philistines, and the other barbarian enemies] For the battles against the Jebusites and 'other barbarians,' see eg Josh 11:9–15, 2 Sam 5:6–9, and 1 Kings 9:20–1, where the Jebusites are mentioned; the story of the battles with the Philistines is told in the books of Judges to 2 Chronicles.

[191]

8–9 the animal that walks first on four feet, then two, finally three] An allusion to the famous riddle of the sphinx: what is it that walks on four legs, then on two, finally on three? In Greek legend the riddle, to which the answer is 'man,' was solved by Oedipus.

10–11 any good that dwells in us comes to us from Christ, its author] For the expression and thought, see Rom 7:18, 8:9–11 and James 1:17.

[192]

20–2 he calls the Last Judgment a 'day'; he calls 'day' a full and unerring judgment, which sometimes the word 'fire' also designates'] 'Night' and 'day' serve as metaphors of contrasting conduct in Rom 13:12–14, 1 Thess 5:5–8. 'Day' refers to the Last Judgment in Rom 2:5, 16, 2 Tim 1:12, 18 and 4:8. Erasmus cites the last part of 1 Cor 3:13; in the full verse, both 'day' and 'fire' appear as images of judgment.

[193]

9–11 Whatever in anything is coarser he calls 'flesh,' 'body,' or 'letter'; whatever is finer and is more like the force of the intellect he terms 'spirit' or 'mind'] Rom 6:6, 7:24, 8:13 (body); Rom 7:25 and 8:3–4, 1 Cor 3:3 (flesh); 2 Cor 3:6 (letter); Rom 8 and 2 Cor 3:6 (spirit); Rom 11:34 and 12:2, 1 Cor 2:16 (mind).

13–15 In more than merely one place he shows through the parallel of marriage and its dissolution that the Mosaic law has been rendered of no effect ...] Rom 7:1–4 seems to be the only passage in the Pauline corpus where the marriage-dissolution comparison illustrates the relationship of the old and new covenants. In 1 Cor 7, however, Paul discusses at length marriage, and Christian terms for its dissolution. See also Gal 4:21–31.

17 not by Aristotelian or Platonic enthymemes] On the enthymeme, see note on **92/4–5**.

20–2 Now it would be superfluous to recount the times he introduces a similitude from athletes and soldiers, from stadiums, boxers, war] See eg 1 Cor 9:24–6 (athlete, stadium, boxer); 1 Cor 9:7 (soldier); Eph 6:12–17 (war); and 2 Tim 2:4–5 (athlete, soldier).

[194]

12 Peter to set about the matter with a sword] For the identification of Peter as the swordsman, see John 18:10. The paraphrase on this passage reflects the disciples' incomprehension of the riddle: 'Jesus left [them] in this very dull-witted state for the time being' CWE 48 197. Luke 22:36–8 was cited in *Ratio* 9 as an example of a biblical problem.

15–16 when in John he speaks to those who were admiring the great edifice of the temple] That Jesus was addressing those who were admiring the temple is a detail taken from the synoptic Gospels, where the destruction of the temple is foretold: Matt 24:1–2, Mark 13:1–2, Luke 21:5–6.

[195]

11–13 he came teaching that absolute power of a worldly sort was to be despised; he came exhorting us to take up the cross, and he himself led the way] Matt 20:25–8, Mark 10:42–5 (despising power); Matt 10:38 and 16:24, Mark 8:34, Luke 9:23 (taking up the cross).

[196]

1–3 Paul ... refers everything from its normal meaning to its inner meaning] In the *Enchiridion* CWE 66 34, Paul is listed first among those 'who depart as much as possible from the literal sense.'

13–14 to Christ he is not an Israelite unless he is related to God through innocence of life] In the paraphrase on John 1:47, Nathaniel is defined as a true Israelite in comparison with false Israelites, CWE 46 36; in the paraphrase on Mark 7:24–30, the Canaanite (Syrophoenician) woman acquires a place among the sons of Israel, CWE 49 93–4.

14–18 When someone has kept the rules prescribed by the laws, this is commonly called 'righteousness' ... innermost recesses of the heart] See 1 Sam 16:7 and the allusion to it in the paraphrase on Acts 15:8 CWE 50 96–7; also Jer 11:20, 17:10, 20:12. The paraphrase on Rom 12:1–2 offers a broad exposition of this theme, CWE 42 69.

[197]

2–4 it is the one who suppresses and slays anger, lust, ambition, and other similar beastly desires that truly sacrifices to God] For this commonplace interpretation of 'sacrifice,' see the paraphrases on Rom 12:1–2 CWE 42 69 and the annotation on Rom 12:1 ('reasonable service') CWE 321–2; also *Enchiridion* CWE 66 71.

[199]

1–2 tropes that belong not to the domain of grammarians or rhetoricians] From antiquity, grammarians were teachers of literature at an elementary stage, while rhetoricians taught effective expression to students at a more advanced stage. For tropes as taught by Quintilian, see note on **23/12**.

8–10 **But we do not share in common with them the fact that their expression *eupathein*, that is, 'to be fortunate' [*bene pati*], is used idiomatically to mean 'to receive a kindness' [*beneficio affici*]**] In other words, whereas the word *eupathein* is used in Greek to mean both 'to be fortunate' and 'to receive a kindness,' Latin speakers wishing to express the latter idea would not use *bene pati*, literally 'suffer well' (the strict equivalent of the Greek), but *beneficio affici* (as here).

18 **'it escaped his notice receiving angels'**] *Latuit accipiens angelos*, a reference to Heb 13:2, where the Greek verb is plural. Erasmus' Latin expression here represents his own translation, which he defended in his annotation on the verse.

[200]

5–6 **Augustine ... his work *On Modes of Expression*]** Augustine *In Heptateuchum locutiones libri septem*. Each 'book' is comprised of short notes on 'modes of expression' or 'sayings' in one of the first seven books of the Old Testament, as found in a Latin version of the Bible then in use; see following note.

7 **the Septuagint**] According to a tradition embodied in our literary sources, first in the *Letter of Aristeas* (c 130 BC) and followed by numerous later authors, Jewish and Christian, Ptolemy II Philadelphus (308–246 BC) commissioned seventy-two Jewish elders to translate the Pentateuch into Greek. This translation (and by extension the translation of the Hebrew Scriptures in general) became known as the Septuagint from the number of translators (Latin *septuaginta* 'seventy'). In fact the Septuagint had a more complex origin than the tradition allowed. Translations based on the Greek versions provided Latin texts of the Bible (referred to in general as the *vetus latina* 'old Latin version'), which appear to have existed from at least the middle of the second century. It was the old Latin version of the Gospels that Jerome revised, ostensibly at the request of Pope Damasus; in the case of the Old Testament, however, after an initial and unsatisfactory attempt to provide a translation (perhaps based on the *vetus latina*) according to the Septuagint, Jerome made his own translations from the Hebrew. Although Augustine seems to have used Jerome's revision of the Gospels, for the Old Testament he preferred the old Latin version based on the Septuagint.

Differences between the Vulgate and the Latin cited in Augustine's *In Heptateuchum locutiones* are readily apparent.

21–2 **'Blessed is the people whose God is the Lord of it'**] Erasmus cites the Vulgate according to the Septuagint, not according to the Hebrew. Jerome had made Latin (Vulgate) versions of the Psalms from both languages. In the verse cited here, the Vulgate carries over into the Latin the Greek construction.

33–5 **Augustine could have occupied himself more profitably with this subject if in his annotations he had drawn from the Hebrew sources rather than the Greek**] Athough Augustine introduces the *In Heptateuchum locutiones* as a study of idioms Greek and Hebrew, it is evident that in this work his point of reference was normally the Greek text of Scripture. He himself was never more than minimally proficient in Greek.

35–6 **the annotations of the Greek writer Titanius**] There is no indication that Erasmus knew much about this author, whoever he may have been.

[201]

4–6 **Augustine unravels the knot by saying that this is a case of *heterosis* ... where 'robbers' is used for 'a robber'**] Augustine *De consensu evangelistarum* 3.16.53. For the trope of heterosis, see *De copia* 1.13 CWE 24 321–4. Erasmus refers to Augustine's solution again in *Ecclesiastes* 3 CWE 68 890.

6–9 **he explains by synecdoche ... at daybreak on the third day**] Augustine *De consensu evangelistarum* 3.24.66. See Matt 12:40 and Mark 8:31, but also Matt 16:21 'on the third day.' For synecdoche, see *De copia* 1.23 CWE 24 341, also *Ecclesiastes* 3 CWE 68 891–4.

12–16 **a certain distinguished Scotist ... Alexander, the grammarian'**] Alexander de Villa Dei wrote a Latin grammar in verse, the *Doctrinale*, c 1200. He is cited by Erasmus with other despised medieval sources in *Antibarbari/The Antibarbarians* CWE 23 36. Although the Scotist to whom Erasmus refers cannot be identified with certainty, it may be assumed that he is the Franciscan Henry Standish, on whom see CEBR III 279–80. For a construal of this episode that would be less disparaging of the unknown Franciscan, see the essay by Ocker above, 76.

[202]

6–8 **And no one should think it absurd to point out hyperboles in the divine books, for Origen does so, as does Chrysostom, and so**

Explanatory Notes 303

do Augustine and Jerome] For hyperbole, see *De copia* 1.28 and 1.46 CWE 24 344 and 385; also *Ecclesiastes* 3 CWE 68 824–34, where the same Fathers as are mentioned here are shown to have explained certain passages in Scripture by appealing to this rhetorical figure.

[203]

11–12 **When he forbids them to take wallet or staff for the journey**] At Matt 10:10 and Luke 9:3 both staff and wallet are forbidden; Luke 10:4 forbids only the wallet; Mark 6:8 permits a staff.

[204]

1–3 **Origen points out that there is a hyperbole …**] Origen *In Genesim homiliae* 17.8. Homily 17 is not in fact the work of Origen, but of his Latin translator Rufinus of Aquileia (c 345–411).

5–6 **He also thinks that Paul's statement … is hyperbole**] Origen *In epistolam ad Romanos* 1.9 (on Rom 1:8); see also Erasmus' annotation on Rom 1:8 ('in the entire world') CWE 56 33. This and the preceding passage from Genesis are both cited in *Ecclesiastes* 3 CWE 68 830, 833.

17 **So far Augustine**] Augustine *Ep* 47.2 (in the now-standard numbering of his letters), commenting on Matt 5:34–6

[205]

1–4 **Cyril and Chrysostom frankly admit that John's statement … is hyperbole**] Cyril of Alexandria *Expositio sive commentarius in Iohannis Evangelium* 12 (on 21:25); John Chrysostom *In Ioannem evangelistam homiliae* 88.2

4 **in his thirty-fifth homily on Matthew**] Chrysostom *In Mattheum evangelistam homiliae* 34 at 35.2 (on 10:27)

16 **must be left unfulfilled**] *omittendum qui non impleatur*. In spite of *iota* and *apiculum*, the neuter antecedents, the masculine *qui* evidently presupposes the Vulgate *apex* ('dot' or 'tittle'), masculine.

18–20 **in the annotations with which I have clarified the New Testament I have pointed out some examples of this type, too**] It was in a 1519 addition to his annotation on Matt 5:18 (*iota unum aut apex*) that Erasmus first noted the hyperbole: 'I think this statement also was spoken in hyperbole ... he affirms that nothing at all has been promised or brought forth in the law of Moses that is not fulfilled in the gospel' ASD VI-5 136:636, 644–5.

[206]

3 **forced to the quick, as they say**] *ad vivendum exigenda*, ie forced into a strictly literal interpretation. See *Adagia* II iv 13 CWE 33 196, where it is stated that the expression is used 'of the analysis of something with needless precision and pedantry.'

[209]

4 **the third book of Kings**] The Vulgate, following the Septuagint, named the books of Samuel the first two books of Kings. Hence 3 and 4 Kings in the Vulgate are equivalent to 1 and 2 Kings in most modern Bibles.

7–9 **In the opinion of Theophylact, the Bulgarian bishop, irony can be perceived in these words of Christ, 'Sleep now and take your rest'**] Erasmus follows the Vulgate in reading these words as a command, not a question. When he composed the *Ratio* he had only recently identified Theophylact accurately, having previously cited him as 'Vulgarius.' In the early summer of 1518 he had been able to prove that the commentaries on Scripture translated into Latin and circulating under the name of Athanasius were in fact the commentaries of Theophylact (d. after 1125). For Theophylact's comments, see PG 123 449D–452A.

[210]

6–8 **St Augustine, in his work entitled *On Christian Doctrine*, was not reluctant to point out at great length these figures in the sacred books**] Augustine *De doctrina christiana*, especially 3.29

8–10 **Donatus and Diomedes expounded all these figures with care, but Quintilian did so with even greater care in the ninth book of the *Rhetorical Institutes***] For Aelius Donatus, see note on **27**/4–5. Diomedes (late fourth/early fifth century), like Donatus, wrote an *ars grammatica*. Quintilian's 'Rhetorical Institutes' ie *Institutio oratoria* (9.1.10–18 on figures of speech and figures of thought)

Explanatory Notes 305

[211]

1–3 **ambiguity is indeed a fault in discourse ... Fabius [Quintilian] advises that it must be avoided as much as possible**] 'Ambiguity': *amphibologia*; in some classical sources *amphibolia*. See Quintilian *Institutio oratoria* 2.9 (the figure exemplified), 8.2.16 (as a vice).

3–7 **Augustine ... prefers that we say *ossum* ['bone'] rather than *os* ['bone' or 'mouth'] if we refer to some one of those objects that are in the plural called *ossa*, not *ora*]** Augustine *De doctrina christiana* 3.3.7. *Os*, nominative singular (genitive *ossis*, plural *ossa*), is the standard Latin word for 'bone,' though *ossum*, a 'less correct' form for the nominative singular, was also used. *Os* (genitive *oris*, plural *ora*) is the word for 'mouth.' Since one might understand *os* to mean either 'bone' or 'mouth,' Augustine argued for keeping the distinction between the two clear by using the 'less correct' form *ossum* for 'bone,' reserving *os* unambiguously for 'mouth,' though the form is nowhere else attested in his writings (including sermons) as transmitted to us. This example appears repeatedly in Erasmus' work.

12–17 **In the same way he never said *floriet* for *florebit* ... people were saying *tempo* for *tempus* ...**] *Floreo* is a second conjugation verb with its future properly *florebit*, not *floriet*, as though it were a fourth conjugation verb. Erasmus alludes to the *De doctrina christiana* 2.13.20, where Augustine notes that congregations sing Ps 132:18 (Vulg 131:18) using *floriet* not *florebit*. *Flos* and *ros* (long 'o') are both masculine and are different in pronunciation from the neuter *os* (short 'o'). Erasmus regards *tempo* as a careless deviation from *tempus, temporis* (compare Italian *tempo*).

19–20 **I have in many places noted it and, where I could, I have eliminated it**] The reference is to Erasmus' annotations and translation of the New Testament.

20–1 **the arrangement of words**] 'Arrangement of words': *compositione*; see Quintilian *Institutio oratoria* 9.4.1–9.

23–4 **This is precisely the path Augustine pursues, offering some examples**] Augustine *De doctrina christiana* 3.2.2–5.19

[213]

1–8 **Of the same kind are these expressions, too: when they say *fides* ... except when we say, 'I have confidence in you' [*habeo tibi fidem*], 'he deprives another of his credit' [*abrogate illi fidem*]**] This brief discussion anticipates methodologically the lengthy annotation added in 1527 on Rom 1:17 ('from faith unto faith') CWE 56 42–5.

12–13 the Arguments I have written for the apostolic Epistles] 'Arguments,' ie summaries, were composed for the Epistles by Erasmus in 1518 and published with the *Ratio verae theologiae* in November 1518, though they were also bound and sold separately; see CWE 41 112.

[214]

1 The special significance attached to words] 'Special significance': *emphasis*. Erasmus defines *emphasis* in the annotation on Rom 1:1 ('set apart for the gospel of God') CWE 56 7–8 with n3, and he frequently points out the *emphasis* of words in his *Annotations*. See also note on **115/1–2**.

16–17 St Hilary often even in the Psalms brings out the *emphasis* from the Greek translation] On the 'Greek translation,' see note on **200/7**. Hilary of Poitiers refers to the Greek to elucidate the text at eg *Tractatus in psalmum 2* 35 (on Ps 2:9) and *Tractatus in psalmum 51* 12 (on 51:4).

[215]

19–23 Origen's observation is also relevant here ... To Satan he says only, ***hypage opiso*** **['Get behind'; Matthew 4:10] ...**] Origen *Commentarius in Matthaeum* 12.22. Erasmus here misquotes Matt 4:10, which in his text of the New Testament (and in the preferred reading) expresses Jesus' command with a single word *hypage* 'go.'

[216]

1 But to return to allegories] See already **185–98**. The treatment of allegory that follows can be compared with the extensive discussion in *Ecclesiastes* 3 CWE 68 930–72. By 1508 Erasmus was planning a work on 'scriptural and theological allegories,' Ep 211:44–50 CWE 2 141. He refers again in the *De copia* to a 'short work I have in hand on scriptural allegories,' CWE 24 635:11–12. Three editions of the *De copia* (1512, 1514, 1517) had preceded the *Ratio* of 1518/1519, and Erasmus may have regarded the discussion here as the completion of or an alternative to a preliminary sketch previously made for a study of biblical allegories. See also 39 above.

9 **the historical text**] *historicus contextus*. The 'historical text' is a near equivalent to the 'literal text,' as 'historical sense' is to 'literal sense,' but carries a somewhat broader connotation, pointing more suggestively to the biblical text as a historical construction in a context of real historical events.

[220]

9–10 **But as I have quite frequently said, this also occurs in the Prophets**] See eg **185** and *Enchiridion* CWE 66 34, 68.

14–16 **From this circumstance, indeed, certain Jews and heretics used to make their case that the Jesus whom we worship was not he whom God had promised through Isaiah**] Erasmus might have gathered this information from the writings of Tertullian, to whom he presently refers.

21–2 **so reads Tertullian; certainly Jerome, too, applies the passage to Christ**] Tertullian *Adversus Marcionem* 3.13.1; Jerome *Commentarius in Isaiam prophetam* 3 (on 8:1–4). Erasmus adopts Tertullian's biblical text, in which the historical improbability (the infant will capture Damascus) is patent. The Vulgate text approximates that in modern translations (Damascus will be captured), where the scenario portrayed is historically quite possible.

23–7 **Will a child with his squalling summon to arms an army …? Will he attack the enemy not from a horse and chariot but from the neck of his nurse …?**] The phrasing here is taken from Tertullian *Adversus Marcionem* 3.13.2 with very little change.

33 **sword of the evangelical word**] An expression adapted from Eph 6:17

[222]

1–7 **One may find some prescripts of this kind in the literature of the Gospels, too. … how can this precept be kept, especially in regions frozen stiff with cold and frost?**] Compare the interpretation Erasmus gives in **203** of these precepts considered as tropes.

15–16 **'Blessed are those who have made themselves eunuchs for the kingdom of God'**] The beatitude expressed here ('blessed') is without explicit warrant from the New Testament text of either Erasmus or the

Vulgate, but Erasmus elsewhere also treats this passage from Matthew as if it took that form.

[223]

3–4 **according to the literal meaning of the words**] In this paragraph 'literal meaning' renders *sensum verborum* and 'literal sense' translates *grammaticum sensum*; see note on **219/9**.

15–17 **It is Augustine's opinion that this text, too, is of the same kind: 'Unless anyone has eaten my flesh or drunk my blood etc'**] Augustine *De doctrina christiana* 3.16.24

17–20 **Here, therefore, as I have said, a knowledge of material things is useful; also to have had practice beforehand during youth in poetical allegories, or even in drawing comparisons from any kind of thing, and discussing them**] See **19–24** above.

21 **About comparisons I have long ago published a little book**] An allusion to the *Parabolae sive similia/Parallels*, published first in 1514, CWE 23 130–277. See 96 above.

[224]

4–16 **It seems to me that Ambrose is, in this respect, sometimes extravagant ... yet even in places that grow very hot, the night can be cold**] Ambrose *Expositio evangelii secundum Lucam* 10.76 (on Luke 22:54–62). For the expression 'consuming fire,' see Heb 12:29. Erasmus himself, in his paraphrase on Luke 22:61–2, interprets tropologically the night, the cold, and the fire: CWE 48 204.

[225]

1–18 **Very much like this are the comments that Ambrose adds concerning Peter's denial ...**] Ambrose *Expositio evangelii secundum Lucam* 10.78–81. Ambrose's exposition of the Gospel story is set out in detail in *Ecclesiastes* 3 CWE 943–7.

3–5 **for Christ had permitted Peter to fall so that, by returning to his senses and repenting through the compassion of Christ, he might strengthen his brothers**] Luke 22:32 ('strengthening the brothers'), 22:61–2 (the compassionate glance of Christ and Peter's repentance).

See, too, the paraphrase on these verses: Peter, 'touched by his Lord's gaze ... struck with intense grief ... wept bitterly' CWE 48 204.

16–18 **Ambrose bends the words to the interpretation that Peter denied he had known as a Galilean or Nazarene one whom he knew as the Son of God**] Peter is said to have been with 'Jesus the Galilean' in Matt 27:69, with 'Jesus the Nazarene' in Mark 14:67. That Ambrose saw in narrative variation the proof of the evangelists' incomprehension is evidently an inference of Erasmus.

18–23 **Again, Ambrose twists in the same direction the statement in Matthew ... To confirm his interpretation, he cites from Paul ...**] For Ambrose's interpretation of Matt 26:72 and Gal 1:1, see *Expositio evangelii secudum Lucam* 10.82–4.

[226]

1–2 **Jerome seems to criticize the comment in the short notes he wrote on Matthew**] Jerome *Commentarius in evangelium Matthaei* 4 (on 26:72). 'Short notes': *commentariolis*; in the prologue to the commentary, Jerome describes his work as a 'brief exposition.'

[227]

2 **school of declamatory rhetoric**] *schola declamatoria*. In Roman schools, boys were often applauded for the extravagant treatment of declamatory themes: Quintilian *Institutio oratoria* 2.2.9–12. There may also be an allusion to Christian homiletical training, with an explicit critique of 'display' oratory in preaching.

5–6 **The language of truth is simple according to the aphorism of the tragedian**] Euripides *Phoenician Women* 469

7–9 **Augustine, in a certain homily about the woman caught in adultery ...**] Augustine *In Ioannis evangelium tractatus* 15.21 (on John 4:16–20). Augustine proposes that the five husbands are the five senses and the sixth man is 'understanding.' The expression 'woman caught in adultery' is taken from John 8:3.

10–11 **the numbers thirty, sixty, one hundred**] These numbers occur in the parable of the sower: Matt 13:3–23, Mark 4:3–20.

11–14 **Likewise, about the five thousand men who ate until full, the loaves, the two fishes, the talents (ten, five, and one), the three measures of flour, the two sparrows, which they interpret as body and** soul] Matt 14:15–21, Mark 6:34–44, Luke 9:12–17, John 6:4–13 (the five thousand, the loaves and fishes); Matt 25:14–30, Luke 19:12–27 (talents – Erasmus conflates details from the two accounts); Matt 13:33, Luke 13:20–1 (flour); Matt 10:29 (sparrows).

18–19 **just as Plato obscured philosophy with his numbers**] Erasmus may have in mind passages in Plato's *Timaeus* (eg the account of the creation of the soul 35A–36D). Those who 'obscure sacred teaching' may include the Christian Cabbalists, of whom Johann Reuchlin (d 1522) was one, and to whom Erasmus gave the full status of hero in the colloquy (1522) 'The Apotheosis of Johann Reuchlin' CWE 39 244–52.

19–21 **And yet now and then we want these petty comments to serve as the base on which we build a structure of serious dogmas**] This is in the same vein as the satirical portrait in *Moria* CWE 27 132–4 of preachers who establish Trinitarian and Christological doctrine on the basis of clever but manifestly erroneous interpretation of biblical details.

[228]

7–8 **the sources many of which the Lord himself opened up for us; Paul also some**] By 'sources' (*fontes*) Erasmus appears here to refer to the parables of Jesus, especially 'allegorizing' parables such as 'the wicked tenants' (Matt 21:33–46, Mark 12:1–12, Luke 20:9–19), and 'the sheep and the goats' (Matt 25:31–46). The Pauline Epistles provide examples of allegorization, eg the stories of Hagar and Sarah and their sons (Gal 4:21–31) and of the Israelites in the wilderness (1 Cor 10:1–6); and note also the allegorized metaphor of the 'potter and the clay' (Rom 9:20–4).

11–21 **Ambrose seems sometimes to have attributed this to the joy of the Lord's day ... still they put one in mind of something salutary**] Ambrose *Expositio evangelii secundum Lucam* 8.90 (on Luke 19:4)

[229]

11 **analogy**] 'Analogy': *collatio*. See Ep 312:28–9 CWE 3 44: 'For the Greek *parabole*, which Cicero Latinizes as *collatio*, a sort of comparison, is nothing more than a metaphor writ large.'

14–17 **That steward is said to be unjust ... is said to be faithful**] The intepretation offered in this 1523 addition is identical to that already given in Erasmus' paraphrase of the same passage CWE 48 88–94.

Explanatory Notes 311

[230]

1–2 **There are those who disdain all allegories as arbitrary and dream-like**] In the *Enchiridion* CWE 66 34–5 Erasmus contrasts the 'modern theologians' who 'stick to the letter' with the exegetes of antiquity: 'I have heard tell of some individuals who were so pleased with these petty human commentaries that they despised the interpretations of the ancient Fathers as if they were dreams ...'

12 **in regular books**] Erasmus apparently has in mind such books as the *Gesta Romanorum*, a widely circulating compilation of entertaining stories whose details were allegorized to provide a moral application; see the *Moria*, where he cites the *Gesta*, which, he says, some 'proceed to interpret,' adding in 1522, 'allegorically, tropologically, and anagogically,' CWE 27 134.

16 **a certain theologian of Paris**] The target of these remarks has not been identified.

[231]

4 **Rabanus**] Rabanus Maurus (c 780–856) was active as a teacher and abbot of the monastery at Fulda (818–42), and, later, archbishop of Mainz (847–56). His biblical scholarship was voluminous. His earliest work was the *De laudibus sancti crucis*, in which the outlines of figures such as the victorious Christ, the seraphim, etc, were superimposed upon a written text with acrostic verses. The figures were 'explained' in a *declaratio* following each.

6 **the portrait of Cebes**] Cebes, one of Socrates' disciples, and an interlocutor in the *Phaedo*, was a sophist thought (probably wrongly) to be the author of the *Pinax* 'The Portrait,' which gives an imaginary picture of human life. He is also mentioned in *De copia* CWE 24 582.

8 **the game of pawns**] *Ludus latrunculorum*, the name for the 'game of pawns' in antiquity; see Seneca *Epistulae morales* 106.11.

9–10 **Jerome has good reason to laugh at those who twist the tales of poets to apply to Christ**] Jerome Ep 53.7, characterizing as 'puerile' the efforts of some to apply the verses of Virgil to Christ; Erasmus comments on the passage in his edition of Jerome's epistolary works and other opuscula, CWE 61 223–4.

11–15 **the tale of Proteus ... of Phaethon ... of Tantalus ... of Midas ... of Danae ... of Ixion and the Danaids ...**] See *Enchiridion* CWE 66

67–8 and *De copia* CWE 24 610–14, where most of these stories appear allegorized, and where Erasmus notes stories invented by the poets intending a tropological or allegorical interpretation. **Proteus** is the old man of the sea who transformed himself into different shapes to escape those who tried to lay hold of him. **Phaethon** was the son of Apollo and Clymene, and was granted his rash request to drive the sun-god's steeds across the sky, but, being unable to control them, perished in the attempt. **Tantalus**, whose sin was variously identified in the tradition, was punished by being placed in a pool whose waters receded when in agonizing thirst he tried to drink, and over which were branches of luscious fruit which he could never reach. **Midas** was granted his wish that all he touched should turn to gold, so that he could neither eat nor drink. **Danaë**, fated to give birth to a son who would kill his grandfather, was locked away in a tower, but Zeus came to her in a shower of gold and impregnated her. **Ixion**, who repeatedly dishonoured the trust placed in him, was chained to a wheel that rolled perpetually through the air. The **Danaids**, the fifty daughters of Danaus, were forced to marry their cousins, the sons of Aegyptus, but on their wedding night all but one killed their husbands, and for this crime were condemned to carry water in jars perforated like sieves.

[232]

4–7 **For who has not seen seed being cast on the ground? Who has not looked upon fisherman casting their nets? Who does not know that branches dry up when cut off?**] Matt 13:3–23, Mark 4:3–20, Luke 8:5–15 (seed); Matt 13:47–50 (net); John 15:1–8 (branches).

9 **sons of Scotus**] *Scotidae*. Erasmus mockingly uses the aggrandizing patronymic. Duns Scotus (see note on **30/20** above) was called *doctor subtilis* 'the subtle teacher.'

11–12 **What pleasure will you feel if that sun of righteousness should arise before the eyes of your heart?**] For the expression 'sun of righteousness,' see Mal 4:2, for 'eyes of the heart' Eph 1:18 and the paraphrase on the verse CWE 43 310–11. Erasmus exemplifies with this and the following images what it means for a Christian to 'philosophize,' in his sense of the verb.

19–23 **You see a serpent ... a dove ... the deer ... a lamb ...**] Matt 10:16 (serpent and dove); Ps 42:1 (deer); Luke 10:3, Isa 53:7, and Acts 8:32 (lamb).

29–30 **Archetype**] *idea*; the language echoes Plato, who distinguished the visible world from the world of 'ideas' or archetypes.

Explanatory Notes 313

[233]

1-4 **Now, the sources from which allegories are to be sought are explained by Dionysius, in the work entitled** *On the Divine Names,* **in part by Augustine in** *On Christian Doctrine* **book 3, where the rules of Tyconius have been set forth and explained**] For Dionysius see note on **4/3-4**. In *De doctrina christiana* 3.30.42-37.55 Augustine describes Tyconius' rules for interpreting Scripture. These rules are introduced at a point where Augustine attempts to show how ambiguities in both literal and figurative expressions may be detected, and where he has cited 'tropes,' 'allegory,' 'enigma,' and 'parable' as examples of figurative expression (3.29.40). Tyconius (fl 370-90) was an older contemporary of Augustine and a biblical commentator (though a layman) in the separatist Donatist church of ancient North Africa, hence regarded by Augustine as a 'heretic' (3.31.44). He is best known for his 'Book of Rules,' which has survived intact and is also summarized in book 3 of *De doctrina christiana*.

8-9 **a book I began long ago on theological allegories**] For Erasmus' intention to write a book on Scriptural allegories, see note on **216/1**. At this point the *Ratio* begins to incorporate much of the latter part of the *Methodus*. There is an expanded statement in *Ecclesiastes* 3 CWE 68 932-4 of the brief definition given here of the four senses of Scripture (historical, tropological or moral, allegorical, and anagogical) recognized by Christian exegetes since the early Middle Ages.

18-20 *In how many ways does Origen treat Abraham's temptation from God,* **and,** *although he is engaged with history, still what topics does he find*!] Origen *In Genesim homiliae* 8 (on Gen 22:1-14)

25-6 *that whole parable can be applied to the Jewish people and the Gentiles* **of that time**] In Erasmus' paraphrase on this passage, the parable is 'applied to' Jews and Gentiles, and the husks are interpreted as the 'world's empty pleasures,' an exegesis there described as 'in accordance with the mode of the time,' CWE 48 74-9.

28-31 **And now from the variation in persons and times to which the parable is being accommodated, a virtually new face is put upon the discourse, about which I have said something above**] For the rejection of the Jews and the reception of the Gentiles as the theme of the parables, see **83-9** and, for variation in persons and times, **42-50**.

[234]

3 *little summas*] The 'little *summas*' were a genre widely popular in the Middle Ages and disdained by Erasmus; see **32**.

15-16 'running beyond the olive trees,' as the Greek proverb has it] In *Adagia* II ii 10 CWE 33 82-3 Erasmus says the proverb is applied to one who 'does or says irrelevant things that have no connection with the matter in hand.'

19-24 **Hilary points this out with a fine turn in the first book *On the Trinity* ...**] Hilary *De Trinitate* 1.18.

[235]

6-7 **we place in the world those whom Christ chose out of the world**] See John 15:19 and the letter to Paul Volz, prefatory to the 1518 edition of the *Enchiridion* CWE 62 22: 'Now men are called monks who spend all their time in the very heart of worldly business ...'

[236]

3 *context*] See 41.

[237]

1-4 **this rule, too, must be observed, that the sense we elicit from obscure words should conform to that circle of Christian teaching, should conform to the life of Christ, finally, should conform to natural justice**] See 68/14-16: 'Just as his teaching in its entire orb is self-consistent, so it is consistent with his life, consistent even with the judgment of nature itself.'

[238]

3 **times, circumstances, and persons**] See 37-45.

21-7 **You put to your advantage the injunction in the books of the Old Testament that tithes be given to the Levites; but add to this ... that tithes be given to those whose portion was the Lord God**] For the injunction that tithes be given to the Levites, see Num 18:21-4 and Deut 14:27-9; for the exclusion of the Levites from a portion of the land, see Num 26:52-62; for the Levites' sacred duties, Num 3:5-13, 8:14-19, 18:2-6, 21-4; for God as their portion, Num 3:12, 8:16; for the expression,

Num 18:20, where God says to Aaron, a Levite, 'I am your portion and your inheritance,' and Pss 73:26, 119:57.

28 **We plume ourselves**] *cristas erigimus*. For the expression, see *Adagia* I viii 69 CWE 32 163–4.

[239]

5 **Bartholemew, who had been flayed, as the story goes**] There are various legends of Bartholemew's missionary endeavours and martyrdom, including death by flaying (portrayed in Renaissance art eg by Michelangelo in 'The Last Judgment' in the Sistine Chapel) and beheading.

9–10 **Peter Lombard, who wrote the theological 'sentences'**] Peter Lombard (c 1100–1160) taught in the cathedral school in Paris, becoming bishop of Paris in 1154. He published extensive commentaries on the Psalms and the Pauline Epistles, but his four books of *Sententiae* (so named because they contained the *sententiae* 'opinions' of the Fathers) became a standard text for the systematic study of theology. In his annotation on Matt 1:19 (*nollet eam traducere*), Erasmus speaks of him as 'a good man and for his day a learned man, one not to be despised,' but also, in a less positive tone, as a rhapsodist who 'stitched together' his book from the opinions of others, regretting that this collection of opinions, designed to give answers, served only to open the door to an unending stream of questions.

[240]

2 **the centos of the poets**] Tertullian *De praescriptione haereticorum* 39.3–5 refers to the custom in antiquity whereby words and clauses were taken from an existing work and placed in a new arrangement to create an entirely new composition. A Christian author, Proba (c 360), made a *cento* by taking lines and half-lines from Virgil's poetry to create a poem that followed primarily the narratives of Genesis and Exodus; her work was widely used in schools in the Middle Ages.

3 **St Bernard**] Bernard (1090–1153) entered the Cistercian monastery of Citeaux in 1112, and in 1115 established a new house at Clairvaux, of which he became abbot. Active in ecclesiastical politics, he preached the Second Crusade (1147). His sermons on the Song of Songs, reflecting a mystical theology, became a classic of Christian spirituality.

8–11 Jerome throws in the face of Origen the charge that he sometimes does violence to the Scriptures, though I think Origen's purpose is to lead us far away from the frequently sterile letter] Jerome *Commentarius in Ieremiam prophetam* 5 (on 27.3–4 and 9). Though Jerome had originally found in Origen a congenial exegete, he became a severe critic after accusations of heresy were levelled against Origen in Palestine in AD 393. For Erasmus' appraisal of Jerome's relation to Origen, see his *Life of Jerome* and the preface to his edition of the *Opera omnia* II (1524) in CWE 61 33–4, 37, 100–1.

11–13 nearly everyone of the ancients sometimes twists the Scriptures ... even Jerome himself, as he virtually confesses at one point] Elsewhere Erasmus did not hesitate to point to Jerome's unscrupulous use of Scripture, particularly in his books against Jovinian and Helvidius, where Jerome himself acknowledges that his interpretations are not always consistent with one another; see eg Jerome *Adversus Iovinianum* 1.13 and *Adversus Helvidium* 20.

[242]

1–2 Ambrose in the sixth chapter of the second book *On the Holy Spirit*] Ambrose *De spiritu sancto* 2.5.45–7

6 a different sense is expressed by the Greek words] According to Erasmus, Ambrose argues that, since the Greek reads 'who serve [the] Spirit God,' the Spirit must be equated with God, thus refuting the Arians. In fact, the Greek witnesses to the biblical text vary, giving the sense of either 'worship God in the spirit' or 'worship in the Spirit of God.' They do not, however, allow for Ambrose's interpretation.

11–26 there is another example in Ambrose when he expounds the passage in the Second Epistle of Paul to Timothy ...] Ambrosiaster *Commentarius in epistolam Pauli ad Timotheum secundam* (on 2 Tim 2:20). Erasmus did not distinguish Ambrose, bishop of Milan, from Ambrosiaster the commentator; see 330–1.

14 Novatian] Novatian was a presbyter of the Roman church, who wrote letters on behalf of the Roman clergy after the martyrdom of the bishop of Rome, Fabian, in 250. After the election of the new bishop, Cornelius, whether through jealousy or in protest against Cornelius' lax policies towards those who had lapsed in the Decian persecution, Novatian had himself consecrated bishop and so became a rival to the new pope. Though excommunicated by a Roman synod, he was able to establish his own church throughout the Roman world. This exposition of 2 Tim

Explanatory Notes 317

2:20 does not appear in the authentic works of Novatian. It is evident, however, that a rigorist who was reluctant to extend the church's peace to the lapsed and sought a 'pure church' would prefer to understand the 'great house' with its two kind of vessels as the world rather than the church.

24–5 **a good interpretation, which even St Chrysostom follows**] John Chrysostom *In epistolam secundam ad Timotheum homiliae* 6 (on 2 Tim 2:20)

[243]

2–7 **Bede concludes and strongly affirms ... Bede bases his interpretation especially on the fact that the text goes on to say that 'she fell and worshipped Jesus'**] Bede *Homiliae genuinae* 1.19 (For the Second Sunday of Quadragesima). 'Fell down and worshipped Jesus' conflates the Vulgate of Mark 7:25 ('fell at his feet') and Matt 15:25 ('worshipped him').

9–11 **Does not Mephibosheth in the second book of Kings fall forward upon his face and do obeisance to King David?**] Erasmus cites the Vulgate, 'do obeisance.' On the designation of this book as the book of Kings, see note on **209/4**.

[244]

5–7 **Augustine thinks these words a powerfully effective weapon for putting to rout all the hosts of the Donatists**] Augustine's argument may be found in *De baptismo contra Donatistas* 5.13.15 (AD 400/401) and *In Ioannis evangelium tractatus* 5 (AD 406–7). Against the Donatists, who believed that the effective power of baptism resided in the minister, Augustine insisted that the effective power of baptism lay in Christ, the author of Christian baptism, and was unaffected by the moral status of the minister. He resolved the problem of how John the Baptist could say that he did not know who Jesus was by arguing that, while John knew that Jesus was the Christ, it was only when the dove descended that he learned that Christ was to be the author of the baptism administered by the church, whose power therefore lay in its author, not its ministers. On the Donatists, see the second note on **245/20–2**.

17–20 **For even the very form of the discourse shows that he had accommodated that discussion to the minds and ears of those present and**

to the circumstances of that time] Augustine's *De baptismo contra Donatistas* was written for Catholics at the request of 'brothers' who had demanded it (1.1.1), in a tone accommodated to sympathetic readers (1.2.3). The *Tractates* on John's Gospel (see previous note) were delivered in the presence of a public audience to which Augustine accordingly adjusted his style.

[245]

19 **the mark imprinted]** *character*. Erasmus reflects Augustine's image used to illustrate his view that the 'tattoo' received at baptism administered even by heretics is indelible and need not be repeated; *De baptismo contra Donatistas* 1.4.5, *In Ioannis evangelium tractatus* 6.15.

20–2 **I regard the Donatists not only as heretics, but also as schismatics and raging mad brigands]** The movement of the Donatists arose in North Africa after the persecution of Diocletian (303–5). They took their name from Donatus, successor to their first bishop Majorinus, elected in Carthage in protest against the elevation of Caecilian, whose consecration (some claimed) had been invalidated by the participation in the ceremony of a *traditor* – one who had handed over the Scriptures to pagan authorities during the persecution. Hence from its origin Donatist theology focused on the question whether sacraments had validity when administered by those outside the church of the Holy Spirit. By the end of the century, the Donatists had become the dominant church in North Africa, and Augustine undertook to engage them on the central question of the sacraments; above all, of baptism. As Erasmus suggests, Donatists agreed that lapsed Christians did not need to be rebaptized, unlike those who had received baptism from individuals regarded by them as heretics living outside the church of the Spirit. For some time, bands of brigands called *Circumcelliones*, who appeared to be on the Donatist side, terrorized parts of the North African countryside, but imperial legislation against the Donatists put the movement on the defensive, and by the early sixth century there is little evidence of their survival as a schismatic movement.

[246]

7–8 **the Gospel adds, 'with spirit and with fire']** Erasmus conflates the text of John 1:33, 'This is he who baptizes with the Holy Spirit,' with the synoptic texts of Matt 3:11 and Luke 3:16, 'He shall baptize you with the Holy Spirit and with fire.'

19–21 **Cyprian uses many testimonies … the Acts of the Synod of Carthage**] Cyprian, bishop of Carthage (d 258), anticipated the Donatists in taking a rigorist view on the question of the rebaptism of heretics and schismatics, claiming, against Stephen of Rome, that there could be no true baptism outside the 'Catholic' church, a position he argues in Epp 69–74. Church councils (or synods) held at Carthage in AD 255 and 256 had pronounced on these matters.

[247]

12–13 *as I once pointed out in my Copia*] See *De Copia* CWE 24 635–48, also *De ratione studii* CWE 24 672–3 and 33–4 above. 'Theological headings' here translates *locos theologicos*, a phrase in which *loci* is shorthand for *loci communes* or 'commonplaces.'

17–18 *I rather think I notice from Jerome's own writings that he used this method*] The same inference is made in Erasmus' *Life of Jerome* CWE 61 33.

[248]

1–4 *For in the opinion of not only Origen but of Augustine also, the best method of interpreting divine literature is … to explain mystic Scripture from mystic Scripture*] Augustine *De doctrina christiana* 2.9.14 and 3.26.37. Origen consistently observes this principle, which was widely acknowledged in early Christianity.

12–14 **'No flesh shall see me and live' … 'All flesh shall see the salvation of God'**] Erasmus' rendering of the passage from Exodus creates a contrast between 'no flesh' and 'all flesh.' For the Hebrew idiom that uses 'flesh' for 'people,' see **200/25–6**.

22–4 **Christ at one point allows his disciples to take staff and wallet for their journey; elsewhere again he forbids them even these**] Staff is forbidden in Matt 10:10 and Luke 9:3; it is permitted in Mark 6:8. Wallet is forbidden in Matt 10:10, Mark 6:8, Luke 9:3; it is permitted in Luke 22:36. In general, compare the earlier discussion on apparently contradictory statements in Scripture at **78–9**.

[250]

15–17 **this comparison of passages will bring the further benefit that we shall recognize with more certainty the idioms and tropes of arcane**

320 Explanatory Notes

discourse] See the extensive discussion of idioms, tropes, and the hidden sense of Scripture at **185–233**.

[251]

2–3 *let him 'take care to turn by night, by day' its pages*] See Horace *Ars poetica* 269, recalled to the same effect at the conclusion of the *Enchiridion* CWE 66 127 and n13. The idea is also biblical: Psalm 1:2. See 30–1 above.

3–4 **Let him have the Scriptures always in hand, always in pocket**] Likewise in the *Paraclesis*, CWE 41 421: 'Why do we not carry these books near our heart, have these books always in our hands?'

8–10 **For this opinion Augustine is my authority ...**] Augustine *De doctrina christiana* 2.9: 'Our first concern is to know those books even though they are not yet understood.'

[252]

8–10 **I would not deny that the greatest benefit is received from those books if anyone, by applying allegory, accommodates them either to the Christ sketched out in them, or to morals**] For allegorical and tropological (or moral) exegesis, see **233**.

14–17 **Augustine teaches, and along with him John Chrysostom ...**] Augustine *Enarrationes in Psalmos* 8.13; John Chrysostom *In Matthaeum evangelistam homiliae* 64 3 (on 20:1–16)

21 **like the books of *Isaiah*] 'Books': *libri*, probably an error for 'book'

21–2 **by arranging passages as I have said**] An allusion to the topical arrangement of biblical material: see **247**.

[253]

4–5 **the so-called 'conclusions' and arguments of Scotus**] The strong tradition of commentary and paraphrase of works by Aristotle, originating in antiquity, continued to Erasmus' time. Scotus' method was to proceed from arguments to conclusions, though the conclusions themselves might summarize the arguments. For his study of Aristotle's *Metaphysics*, Scotus provided an entire book of more than three hundred 'conclusions.' *Conclusio* was, in fact, a term commonly used in the sense of 'thesis.'

[254]

9–11 Tertullian ... a man so prodigiously learned in Divine Scripture that Cyprian with good reason used to call him his master] This statement of Cyprian is recorded in Jerome *De viris illustribus* 53. Tertullian did not write commentaries as such, but his work is thick with biblical quotations that receive exposition and commentary along the way.

[255]

18–20 *Origen ... Basil, Nazianzus, Athanasius, Cyril, Chrysostom, Jerome, Ambrose, Hilary, Augustine*] For these writers, see the Conspectus of Church Fathers Cited in the *Ratio*, below 329–33. Erasmus lists six Greek Church Fathers, followed by four of their Latin-writing counterparts. 'Nazianzus' is Gregory of Nazianzus. When Erasmus wrote the *Methodus*, much of the work of the Greek authors mentioned here was available only in Latin translation, while problems of authenticity and attribution – to which Erasmus presently refers – rendered the corpus of both Latin and Greek authors uncertain. Nevertheless, in his own *Annotations* and *Paraphrases* Erasmus drew on all the authors mentioned here.

[256]

3–7 *as, in the case of Jerome, at least, I have publicly demonstrated, and then in Cyprian, and I shall perhaps demonstrate the same thing in Augustine. It would not be that much trouble to do the same with the rest, that is, with Origen, Ambrose, and Chrysostom*] In his editions of the works of Jerome, beginning in 1516, Erasmus placed in a separate volume the works that he believed were falsely ascribed to that author. He published an edition of Cyprian in 1520. He had begun to prepare a new edition of Augustine in 1517, but it was not fully completed until 1529. His edition of Ambrose appeared in 1527, of Chrysostom in 1530, and of Origen in 1536.

9–13 Thus, today certain men 'praise those whose thoughts rise higher than the sun.' So says Jerome in a certain discourse, so Augustine in one of his homilies, 'To the Hermit Brethren' – as though such men were pronouncing an oracle from a tripod] These references remain uncertain. In his Jerome edition, Erasmus recognized as spurious the homily 'To the Hermit Brethren' CWE 61 87. The quotation 'praise those ... sun' is printed in Greek in the *Ratio* and may go back to a familiar joke in Aristophanes *Clouds* 225, cited by Jerome in his *Commentarius in epistolam ad Titum* 2:15. The oracles of Apollo at Delphi were uttered by a priestess sitting on the lid of a pot-shaped vessel placed on a tripod; see Virgil *Aeneid* 3.84–93.

[257]

7–8 **Thomas is very clear, Scotus quite subtle and studied**] The positive evaluation here of Duns Scotus is somewhat unusual for Erasmus; but see the essay by Ocker above, 63–79, esp 66, 68. In the *Methodus* CWE 41 431 he calls Thomas Aquinas the 'most assiduous of the moderns' (ie among scholastic theologians of recent centuries – also called 'neoterics' below – as distinct from the Church Fathers or 'ancients') and in his *Annotations* he makes frequent use of Aquinas' compilation of patristic exegesis of the Gospels, the *Catena aurea*.

[258]

9 *essential subjects*] *rerum*, presumably referring to the subjects Erasmus recommended along with languages as basic to understanding the Scriptures; see **19–22**.

18–19 **as 'when a cook mixes many sauces together,' as Plautus says**] Plautus *Mostellaria* 277, and for the context 273–7: For a woman the best smell is no smell at all. When perfume and sweat are mixed together, the smell is the same as when a cook mixes sauces together.

[259]

5–6 *if among those* **you are regarded as** *not much of a theologian*] 'Those' here are persons trained in scholastic theology.

16 *like the hydra's head*] The hydra had a dog-like body and numerous snaky heads (seven, according to Erasmus, *Adagia* I iii 27 CWE 31 258, but the number varies; see *Adagia* I x 9 CWE 32 238). When the heads were cut off, they were each replaced by two or three more. The hydra was slain by Hercules, who cauterized the wound when each head was cut off, thus preventing its sprouting again. The image appears

[260]

3–4 *by being doubtful and, with the Academics, by withholding judgment*] 'By witholding judgment' is expressed in the text here by the Greek *epechein*, a term in the techical vocabulary of the ancient Sceptics. The Academics, though deriving from Plato's Academy, came to assume a posture of scepticism; for their practice of 'withholding judgment,' see Cicero *Academica* 1.12.45–6. In *Moria* CWE 27 118 Erasmus appears to reflect his own predilection for Academic scepticism.

5–21 **For what is the profit if I torture myself about whether God is able to create a person without sin ... whether the fire of hell is of the same kind as ours**] In 1519 Erasmus added to the brief annotation of 1516 on 1 Tim 1:6 (*in vaniloquium*) a long list of 'foolish' questions of the kind debated in scholastic theology; virtually all the questions posed here both in the *1519* text and in the *1522* addition (see n124 on the text) can be found in that annotation, some of them repeated almost verbatim. For a mocking description of the 'vain questions' of the theologians, see *Moria* CWE 27 126–30, a description that, with only a few exceptions, belongs to the edition of 1511.

8 **to establish relation without foundation and termination**] This language is found in the commentary of Duns Scotus on the *Sentences* of Peter Lombard. The same commentary appears to be Erasmus' source for several of the further questions listed here. For details, see CWE 41 700.

[261]

2–9 **St John Chrysostom in the tenth homily on John's Gospel ... the same *hypostasis* embraced natures distinct from one another ...**] John Chrysostom *In Ioannem evangelistam homiliae* 11.2 (on the words of John 1:14, 'The Word became flesh and dwelt among us'). *Hypostasis* was the term adopted by Greek theologians in the fourth century to distinguish the three kinds of 'being' or 'nature' within the Trinity and was, from the start, the cause of considerable confusion to western theologians working in Latin. In the *Explanatio symboli* Erasmus reviewed the

324 Explanatory Notes

ancient 'spectral errors' that attempted to account for the relation of the human and divine in Christ, CWE 70 293–8.

13–14 **a certain man**] not identified

[262]

1–7 **In his fourth homily on Matthew, Chrysostom also shows ... Chrysostom says, 'What the omnipotent spirit of God has done is not incredible'**] Chrysostom *In Matthaeum evangelistam homiliae* 4.3 (on Matt 1:18: 'she was found to be with child of the Holy Spirit'). The citation from Chrysostom is paraphrastic, though Erasmus remains faithful to the tenor of the writer.

11–12 **that eternal nativity by which he is begotten outside of time**] The nativity 'outside time' implies a contrast with the 'nativity according to the flesh' mentioned just above. For the 'double nativity' of Christ, see the paraphrase on Acts 8:34–6 CWE 50 62.

[263]

8 **bachelors**] The 'bachelor' was a pupil-teacher. A student who had studied for several years, had received a licence to lecture on a chapter or a book, and had completed the lectures was a baccalaureate.

15–16 **the arguments with which one may either attack or defend what has been handed down to us**] A reference to the scholastic method of giving the arguments *pro* and *con* in the discussion of theological propositions.

[264]

1–4 **St Chrysostom ... in the first homily on Matthew ... warns us against the books of the philosophers**] Chrysostom *In Matthaeum evangelistam homiliae* 1.4–5, a passage whose central ideas are reflected throughout this paragraph.

7 **the good**] *to agathon*. For the Stoics, Academics, and Peripatetics, see note on 5/5–6. The Epicurean school was established by Epicurus (341–270 BC), who found the chief good in pleasure, which, properly understood, determined the nature of the virtues.

15–16 **raises so many complicated questions**] *Scirpos nectit*, literally, 'plaits rushes' – an image for intricacy in thought and expression.

[265]

1–2 **a certain theologian**] not identified

[266]

25 **... So far Chrysostom**] Chrysostom *In epistolas ad Timotheum homiliae* 1.2 (on 1:4)

[267]

13 **'mateologians'**] 'Mateologians': *mataeologi*, a Latin transliteration of the Greek word for 'empty talkers' in Titus 1:10, compounded from *mataios* and *logos* 'study or discourse of what is vain, empty or futile.' For its noun analogue *mataiologia* 'vain discussion,' see 1 Tim 1:6.

[268]

3 **the sacred discourses**] *contiones sacras*. In this paragraph the Latin word *contio* is used to designate both an address and an assembly. *Contio sacra* 'sacred discourse' means, quite simply, 'sermon'; see the colloquy 'The Sermon' CWE 40 940–53. In early Christianity, sermons were delivered in various settings, but preaching was customary during the liturgy of the word, after which catechumens were dismissed and the Eucharist (ie the 'sacrifice' as Erasmus here calls it) was celebrated by the faithful. The close bond between preaching and the Eucharist was loosened during the Middle Ages as a result of the paraparochial duties granted to the mendicant orders. On preaching and its contexts in the early sixteenth century, see the colloquy 'The Whole Duty of Youth' CWE 39 95–6 and 'The Well-to-Do Beggars' CWE 39 489–92, with CWE 67 96–101.

9 **theologast**] *theologaster* 'would-be theologian,' intended derisively

14–15 **as the Greek proverb has it, 'gaping like a wolf'**] *Adagia* II iii 58 CWE 33 167: 'said of anyone who hoped for something and made great efforts to get it, but was sent away frustrated.'

[269]

1–3 This is the teaching that James calls 'sensual' and 'devilish.' It is different from that which Paul, writing to Timothy, designates as 'sound teaching'] See James 3:15, where the writer speaks of *sapientia* 'wisdom' that is devilish, and 1 Tim 6:3 and 2 Tim 1:13 for 'sound words.' The precise expression *doctrina sana ... fideles sermones* 'sound teaching ... sincere discourse' is found in Titus 1:9. 'Effectual ... for urging,' 'comforting,' and 'confuting' may suggest 2 Tim 3:16. For the fundamental importance of the distinction between 'sincere' and 'sophistical' discourse in the *Ratio* and Erasmus' thinking, see 93–107 above.

17–24 whenever they each extol with extravagant praises their own saint ...] For a vivid and satirical account of the cult of saints, see the colloquy 'A Pilgrimage for Religion's Sake' CWE 40 624–8, but the sequel suggests that Erasmus has in mind here chiefly the founders of the monastic orders, such as St Francis and St Dominic. Erasmus elsewhere criticizes the custom of burial in the garb of the orders to avoid the pains of purgatory; see eg the colloquies 'The Funeral' CWE 40 764–79 and 'The Seraphic Funeral' CWE 40 999–1013.

[270]

3 a certain man] not identified

6 Catherine of Siena] Catherine of Siena (1347–1380), of the Third Order of the Dominicans, appears repeatedly in Erasmus' writings; see especially the colloquy 'The Apotheosis of Johann Reuchlin' CWE 39 246–52. For the story of Catherine with Jesus in the bedroom, see Ep 447:299–301 CWE 4 16 (dated Aug 1516).

7–8 Benedict, Francis, Bridget] Erasmus lists these founders of monastic communities chronologically: Benedict of Nursia (c 480–540) founded several monastic communities, most notably one at Monte Cassino; the Rule he established became the most influential of its kind in the Latin church. For other references to the Rule of St Francis of Assisi (1181/1182–1226), see Erasmus' colloquies, CWE 39 494 n78 and CWE 40 1020 n4). St Bridget of Sweden (c 1303–1373) founded the order of Brigittines, with double monasteries for men and women; see the colloquy 'The Old Men's Chat' CWE 39 457:30–41. On memorizing the Rules of St Benedict and St Francis, see also *Paraclesis* CWE 41 418.

16 **they frequently said their "hours" together**] The 'hours' are the eight liturgical hours of prayer: matins, lauds, prime, terce, sext, none, vespers, and compline.

27 **the entire octave**] The octave, technically the eighth day after a feast, came to include the celebration from the first day to the eighth day. During the Middle Ages, feasts with octaves honoured many saints.

[271]

5–6 **'But avoid the language of empty novelties'**] The citation combines two different translations given in the Vulgate for the Greek *kenophonia* (found here in 2 Tim 2:16 and also in 1 Tim 6:20): *novitates* 'novelties' (1 Tim 6:20) and *vaniloquia* 'vain babblings' (2 Tim 2:16). The paraphrases on these verses reflect the Vulgate translation: on 1 Tim 6:20 ('sophistic debates and novel dogmas') CWE 44 38 and on 2 Tim 2:16 ('meaningless verbal disputations') CWE 44 46.

[272]

14–15 **in Cambridge in England, and Louvain in Brabant**] Through the influence of John Fisher, bishop of Rochester, Erasmus had in 1511 taken up a lectureship in Greek created for him at Cambridge. Thereafter throughout his life he would repeatedly recreate the image of Cambridge as a flourishing centre for the humanities. For the foundation and development of the Trilingual College at Louvain, see note on **13/2**. In February, 1518, Erasmus wrote that Louvain was 'the place to which everyone should hurry who wants to get the three tongues' Ep 777:31–4 (1518).

[273]

3–4 **I once saw a good many of this sort at Paris**] Erasmus went to Paris in the autumn of 1495 and entered the Collège de Montague. His experience there is described, no doubt with some exaggeration, in the colloquy 'A Fish Diet' CWE 40 715–17. In Ep 64 CWE 1 135–8 he expresses his dislike of the lectures he attended.

7 *both kinds of studies*] The reference may be ambiguously to subject (both scholastic philosophy and the Scriptures) and also to method (both

328 Explanatory Notes

logical analysis and imaginative response as contrasting approaches to a text).

8–9 *Let him go where his abilities beckon – and good luck go with him*] Erasmus cites with slight modification Horace *Epistles* 2.2.37.

[274]

4–6 *a single pagan has been converted to faith in Christ or a single heretic has been refuted and changed*] Compare *Moria* CWE 27 128–9, where Erasmus satirically implies that scholastic theology has no power to convert 'heathen or heretic.'

[276]

14 **Durandus**] For Durandus (William Durand), see note on **32**/21–3.

15–16 **A theologian gets his name from the divine oracles ...**] 'Theologian': *theologus*; Erasmus plays on the derivation from the Greek *theos* and *logos* 'word of God.'

Conspectus of Church Fathers Cited in the *Ratio*

A striking feature of the *Ratio* is Erasmus' programmatic recourse to Christian writers of the early post-apostolic centuries – that is, to certain of the 'Church Fathers' – as sponsors for his literary-theological project. As well as quoting and synthesizing these ancient authorities in his New Testament *Annotations* and *Paraphrases*, Erasmus with his assistants and printer-publishers made a major contribution to the critical editing of their works. A selection of items from the Erasmian editions of St Jerome (1516, 1524–6, 1533–4) may be found in CWE 61, and a sampling of Erasmus' work on other fathers, Greek as well as Latin, will appear in CWE 62. For orientation, see den Boeft 'Erasmus and the Church Fathers'; Sider 'Erasmus and Ancient Christian Writers'; and, for individual fathers, the index of CWE 41.

The catalogue below provides a conspectus of the non-biblical, Greek and Latin Christian writers of the second through eighth centuries AD cited in the *Ratio*. Texts are listed in the form given in CWE 41.

Greek Church Fathers

Athanasius (c 300–373), bishop of Alexandria (328–73) **[255]**
Basil (ca 330–379), known as 'the Great,' bishop of Caesarea (370–9) in Cappadocia **[28, 255]**
Cyril (375–444), bishop of Alexandria (412–44) **[205, 255]**

– *Expositio sive commentarius in Iohannis Evangelium* **[205]**

Pseudo-Dionysius, writer of the fifth or sixth century AD [4, 233]

- *On Mystical Theology* [4]
- *Theological Institutes* [4]
- *On Symbolic Theology* [4]

Eusebius (c 260–c 340), bishop of Caesarea, a biblical scholar in the tradition of Origen and a prolific writer in several genres [22]

Gregory of Nazianzus (c 329–390), bishop of Constantinople (in 381) and, after 381, of Nazianzus in Cappadocia. His writings include nineteen thousand lines of poetry in classical Greek forms on Christian themes. [29, 255]

John Chrysostom (c 342–407), a distinguished preacher, first as a priest in Antioch (ordained 386), thereafter as bishop of Constantinople (398–404), was the author of many homilies on various books of the New Testament. His *Homilies* on Matthew (partly in the original Greek), John (in a Latin translation), and the Pastoral Epistles (also in Latin) are reflected in Erasmus' New Testament scholarship from the very first (1516) edition. [23, 28, 33, 201, 202, 205, 242, 255–7, 261–2, 264, 266, 273]

- *In Ioannem evangelistam homiliae* [205, 261]
- *In Mattheum evangelistam homiliae* [205, 252, 262, 264]
- *In epistolam secundam ad Timotheum homiliae* [242, 266]

Clement, bishop of Rome (fl c 96), presumably meant at 33

Origen (c 185–c 251) was born in Alexandria and active there as a teacher and scholar until c 233, when he went to Jerusalem and then Caesarea, where he spent the last years of his life and died, having suffered persecution under Decius. Already by 1516, Origen (in a Latin translation) was a chief source for Erasmus' annotations on Matthew and Romans. [23, 24–8, 188 note, 202, 204, 215, 228, 233, 240, 248, 254–7]

- *In Genesim homiliae* [24–8, 188 note, 204 with note, 233]
- *In epistolam ad Romanos* [204]
- *Commentarius in Matthaeum* [215]

Latin Church Fathers

Ambrose (c 339–397), bishop of Milan (374–97), author of exegetical works on the Old and New Testament, in which he shows a flair for allegorical interpretation. He was also traditionally but erroneously credited with a literal commentary on the Pauline Epistles, attributed by modern scholarship to an otherwise unidentfied 'Ambrosiaster' (ie pseudo-Ambrose) and signalled by an asterisk in the following list of references. [17, 20, 33, 48*, 139, 224–5, 228, 233, 242*, 255–6, 263]

- *Expositio evangelii secundum Lucam* [17, 20, 224–5, 228]
- *De spiritu sancto* [242]
- * *Commentarius in epistulam Pauli ad Corinthios* [48]
- * *Commentarius in epistolam Pauli ad Timotheum secundam* [242]

Augustine (354–430), bishop of Hippo in North Africa from 395, the most influential Christian theologian after St Paul, and a constant presence for Erasmus, who had been admitted as a young man to a religious order named after him. His *De doctrina christiana* provided a road-map for Christians' 'right use' (*usus iustus*) of the resources of their general culture and was a standard reference for biblical exegetes throughout the western Middle Ages; in book 3 of this manual, Augustine repurposed elements of the *Liber regularum* ('Book of Rules') of Tyconius (fl 370–90), a lay supporter of the Donatist faction in the African church [233 with note]. His own practice as a biblical exegete is represented by an immense legacy of homilies and commentaries, including expositions of all the Psalms (dubbed by Erasmus *Enarrationes in Psalmos*, by analogy with the *enarratio* or intepretation of poetic texts performed by ancient grammarians) and of the Gospel of John. [4, 90, 12, 14, 16–23, 29, 31, 33, 42, 45, 48, 57, 71, 138, 200–2, 204, 210–11, 223, 227, 233, 244–6, 248, 251–2, 255–6]

- *De doctrina christiana* [4, 9, 12, 14 note, 15, 16 note, 19–22, 29, 45, 71, 210–11, 223, 233, 251]
- *De civitate Dei* [16 note, 22–3]
- *Confessiones* [17 note, 30]
- *Locutiones in Heptateuchum* [17 note, 200]
- *Quaestiones in Heptateuchum* [17 note]
- *Contra Cresconium Donatistam* [17]
- *Contra Faustum Manichaeum* [20, 57]
- *Enarrationes in Psalmos* [42, 252]
- Epp [48, 204]
- *De fide et operibus* [48]
- *De coniugiis adulterinis* [48]
- *In Ioannis epistulam ad Parthos tractatus* [138]
- *De consensu evangelistarum* [201]
- *In Ioannis evangelium tractatus* [227, 244]
- *De baptismo contra Donatistas* [244]

Bede (c 673–735), 'the Venerable,' monk of Jarrow in Northumbria, whose prolific scholarly output included exegesis of Old and New Testament books in which he combined his own insights with material derived from a reading of Ambrose, Augustine, Jerome, and Gregory the Great (540–604), among others. [243]

– Bede *Homiliae genuinae* [243]

Cyprian (d 258), bishop of Carthage [33, 246, 254, 256, 263]

Damasus, bishop of Rome (366–84), from whom Jerome (see below) claimed a commission to revise the Latin version of the Gospels, wrote epigrams for inscriptions to memorialize martyrs at their shrines in and near Rome. [29]

Hilary (315–c 367), bishop of Poitiers from 353, was one of the first to attempt in Latin the defence and exposition of the Nicene formulation of the doctrine of the Trinity, more particularly of the Son's relation to the Father. He wrote commentaries on the Gospel of Matthew and on the Psalms. [17, 214, 228, 234, 255, 263]

– *Tractatus in Psalmos* [17, 214]
– *Commentarius in Matthaeum* [17]
– *De Trinitate* [234]

Isidore (c 560–636), bishop of Seville, author of many works that were standard references for centuries after him, including the encyclopedic *Etymologies* or *Origins* [22]

Jerome (c 347–420), by his own account and others' the most accomplished Latin writer on the Bible of the early Christian centuries, settled at Bethlehem in 386, where he produced a stream of commentaries, chiefly of the Old Testament prophetic books, and went about revising the current Latin version(s) of the Bible on the basis of the Greek and Hebrew texts. In later times he was credited with producing the commonly accepted or 'Vulgate' Latin translation of the Bible, though it is hard to know how much of that was in fact his work. Erasmus, who came early under Jerome's spell and fashioned his own intellectual persona partly in imitation of him, refused to hold him responsible for the error-ridden state of the Latin version of the New Testament as it had been transmitted, preferring (like Lorenzo Valla) to attribute it to an unknown translator. [14–17, 22, 28, 33, 200–2, 220, 226, 231, 240, 247, 255–9, 263]

– *Chronicle* [15 note]
– Epp [17, 231]

- *De situ et nominibus locorum Hebraeorum* [**22** note]
- *Commentarius in epistolam ad Titum* [**99**, **256** note]
- *Commentarius in Isaiam prophetam* [**220**]
- *Commentarius in evangelium Matthaei* [**226**]
- *Commentarius in Ieremiam prophetam* [**240**]
- *Adversus Iovinianum* [**241**]
- *De viris illustribus* [**254** note]

Juvencus, a Spanish presbyter, wrote (c 330) a life of Christ in Latin hexameters, paraphrasing the accounts in the Gospels. [**29**]

Novatian, presbyter at Rome (d 257/8) [**242**]

Paulinus (355–431), a native of Aquitaine in Gaul, became bishop of Nola (near Naples), where he wrote a series of poems in Latin hexameters in honour of the local saint, Felix, as well as a quantity of other poetry and letters (some of them in verse). [**29**]

Prudentius (c 348–after 405), from Spain, produced an ambitious suite of poems on Christian spiritual, theological, and apologetic themes, including a set of hymns to the martyrs. [**29**]

Tertullian (c 160–c 225), from Carthage in North Africa, prolific author of works of Christian theology, controversy, and edification in Latin, and some also in Greek. Without producing formal biblical exegesis, he engaged closely with texts of Scripture. [**32**, **67**, **220**, **254**]

- *De resurrectione mortuorum* [**32**]
- *Adversus Marcionem* [**67**, **220**]
- *De praescriptione haereticorum* [**240** note]

Bibliography

Primary Sources

The Adages of Erasmus. Selected by William Barker. Toronto: University of Toronto Press, 2001.
(St) Augustine. *On Christian Doctrine*. Trans. D.W. Robertson Jr. New York: Macmillan, 1958.
– *On Christian Teaching* [*De doctrina christiana*]. Trans. with an introduction and notes by R.P.H. Green. Oxford: Oxford University Press, 1997.
Cicero. *On the Orator* [*De oratore*]. Trans. E.W. Sutton and H. Rackham. 2 vols. Loeb Classical Library. Cambridge, MA: Harvard University Press, 1942.
Quintilian. *The Orator's Education* [*Institutio oratoria*]. Ed. Donald A. Russell. Loeb Classical Library. 5 vols. Cambridge, MA: Harvard University Press, 2001.

Secondary Sources

Arnold, Duane W.H., and Pamela Bright, eds. *De doctrina christiana: A Classic of Western Culture*. Notre Dame, IN: University of Notre Dame Press, 1995.
Baldwin, T.W. *William Shakspere's Small Latine & Lesse Greeke*. 2 vols. Urbana: University of Illinois Press, 1944.
Bataillon, Marcel. *Erasmo y España*. 2 vols. Mexico City: Fondo de Cultura Económica, 1966.
Bateman, John J. 'The Textual Travail of the *Tomus secundus* of the *Paraphrases*.' In Pabel and Vessey, eds., *Holy Scripture Speaks*. 213–63.
Bejczy, István. *Erasmus and the Middle Ages: The Historical Consciousness of a Christian Humanist*. Leiden: Brill, 2001.
Béné, Charles. *Érasme et saint Augustin, ou l'influence de saint Augustin sur l'humanisme d'Érasme*. Travaux d'Humanisme et de Renaissance 103. Geneva: Droz, 1969.

Bentley, Jerry H. 'Erasmus' *Annotationes in Novum Testamentum* and the Textual Criticism of the Gospels.' *Archiv für Reformationsgeschichte* 67 (1976): 33–53.
Bloemendal, Jan. 'Erasmus and His *Paraphrases on the New Testament*: What Kind of Enterprise?' ES 40 (2020): 34–54.
– 'Erasmus' *Paraphrases on the New Testament*: Introduction.' ES 36 (2016): 105–22.
Bolgar, R.R. *The Classical Heritage and Its Beneficiaries from the Carolingian Age to the End of the Renaissance*. Cambridge: Cambridge University Press, 1954.
Botley, Paul. *Latin Translation in the Renaissance: The Theory and Practice of Leonardo Bruni, Giannozzo Manetti and Desiderius Erasmus*. Cambridge: Cambridge University Press, 2004.
Boyle, Marjorie O'Rourke. *Erasmus on Language and Method in Theology*. Toronto: University of Toronto Press, 1977.
– *Rhetoric and Reform: Erasmus' Civil Dispute with Luther*. Cambridge, MA: Harvard University Press, 1983.
Brown, A.J. 'The Date of Erasmus' Latin Translation of the New Testament.' *Transactions of the Cambridge Bibliographical Society* 8 (1984): 351–80.
Catto, J.I. 'Theology after Wycliffism.' In J.I. Catto and T.A.R. Evans, eds., *Late Medieval Oxford*. Vol. 2 of The History of the University of Oxford. Oxford: Clarendon Press, 1992. 263–80.
Cave, Terence. *The Cornucopian Text: Problems of Writing in the French Renaissance*. Oxford: Clarendon Press, 1979.
– *Thinking with Literature: Towards a Cognitive Criticism*. Oxford: Oxford University Press, 2016.
Céard, Jean. 'Theory and Practices of Commentary in the Renaissance.' In J.R. Henderson, ed., *The Unfolding of Words: Commentary in the Age of Erasmus*. 3–23.
Chomarat, Jacques. *Grammaire et rhétorique chez Érasme*. 2 vols. Paris: 'Les Belles Lettres,' 1981.
Christ-von Wedel, Christine. *Erasmus of Rotterdam: Advocate of a New Christianity*. Toronto: University of Toronto Press, 2013.
Clark, Frederic. 'Reading the Life Cycle: History, Antiquity, and *Fides* in Lambarde's Perambulation and Beyond.' *Journal of the Warburg and Courtauld Institutes* 81 (2018 [2019]): 191–20.
Copeland, Rita. *Rhetoric, Hermeneutics, and Translation in the Middle Ages: Academic Traditions and Vernacular Texts*. Cambridge: Cambridge University Press, 1991.
Cottier, Jean-François. 'Erasmus's Paraphrases: A "New Kind of Commentary"?' In J.R. Henderson, ed., *The Unfolding of Words: Commentary in the Age of Erasmus*. 27–46.

Cummings, Brian. 'Encyclopaedic Erasmus.' *Renaissance Studies* 28 (2015): 183–205.
- 'Erasmus and the End of Grammar: Humanism, Scholasticism, and Literary Language.' *New Medieval Literatures* 11 (2009): 249–70.
- 'Erasmus and the Invention of Literature.' ERSY 33 (2013): 22–54.
- 'Erasmus on Literature and Knowledge.' In Subha Mukherji and Tim Stuart-Buttle, eds., *Literature, Belief and Knowledge in Early Modern England: Knowing Faith*. London: Palgrave Macmillan, 2018. 39–61.
- *The Literary Culture of the Reformation*. Oxford: Oxford University Press, 2002.

de Jonge, Henk Jan. 'Erasmus und die Glossa Ordinaria zum Neuen Testament.' *Nederlands Archief voor Kerkgeschiedenis* 56.1 (1975): 51–77.
- 'Novum Testamentum a nobis versum: The Essence of Erasmus' Edition of the New Testament.' *Journal of Theological Studies* New Series 35 (1984): 394–413.

de Lubac, Henri. *Medieval Exegesis: The Four Senses of Scripture*. Trans. Mark Sebanc. 3 vols. Grand Rapids: Eerdmans, 1998–2009.

den Boeft, Jan. 'Erasmus and the Church Fathers.' In Irena Backus, ed., *The Reception of the Church Fathers in the West: From the Carolingians to the Maurists*. 2 vols. Leiden: E.J. Brill, 1997. II 537–72.

Devereux, E.J. *Renaissance English Translations of Erasmus: A Bibliography to 1700*. Toronto: University of Toronto Press, 1983.

Dolfen, Christian. *Die Stellung des Erasmus von Rotterdam zur scholastischen Methode*. Osnabrück: Meinders und Elstermann, 1936.

Dresden, Sem. 'Érasme et les belles-lettres.' In Jean-Pierre Massaut, ed., *Colloque Érasmien de Liège: Commémoration du 450e anniversaire de la mort d'Érasme*. Bibliothèque de la Faculté de Philosophie et Lettres de l'Université de Liège 247. Paris: 'Les Belles Lettres,' 1987. 3–16.
- 'Présence d'Erasme.' In *Actes du Congrès Erasme organisé par la Municipalité de Rotterdam sous les auspices de l'Académie Royale Néerlandaise des Sciences et des Sciences Humaines*. Amsterdam: North-Holland Publishing Company, 1971. 1–13.

Eden, Kathy. 'The Erasmian *Parabola* and the Rhetoric of Plato's Poetics.' In Vladimir Brljak and Micha Lazarus, eds., *Poetics before Modernity*. Oxford: Oxford University Press, forthcoming.
- 'Erasmus on Dogs and Baths and Other Odious Comparisons.' ES 38 (2018): 1–20.
- *Friends Hold All Things in Common: Tradition, Intellectual Property, and the 'Adages' of Erasmus*. New Haven: Yale University Press, 2001.
- *Hermeneutics and the Rhetorical Tradition: Chapters in the Ancient Legacy and Its Humanist Reception*. New Haven: Yale University Press, 1997.

- *Poetic and Legal Fiction in the Aristotelian Tradition.* Princeton: Princeton University Press, 1986.
- *The Renaissance Rediscovery of Intimacy.* Chicago: University of Chicago Press, 2012.

Essary, Kirk. 'Annotating the Affections: The Philology of Feeling in Erasmus' New Testament Scholarship and Its Reception in Early Modern Dictionaries.' ES 37 (2017): 193–216.

Farge, James K. "Erasmus, the University of Paris, and the Profession of Theology." ERSY 19 (1999): 18–46.

Godin, André. *Érasme lecteur d'Origène.* Travaux d'Humanisme et Renaissance 190. Geneva: Droz, 1982.

Grafton, Anthony, and Lisa Jardine. *From Humanism to the Humanities: Education and the Liberal Arts in Fifteenth- and Sixteenth-Century Europe.* London: Duckworth, 1986.

Grant, John N. *Aldus Manutius: Humanism and the Latin Classics.* The I Tatti Renaissance Library. Cambridge, MA: Harvard University Press, 2017.

Grendler, Paul. 'How to Get a Degree in Fifteen Days: Erasmus' Doctorate of Theology from the University of Turin.' ERSY 18 (1998): 40–69.

Halporn, James W., and Mark Vessey, eds. *Cassiodorus: 'Institutions of Divine and Secular Learning' and 'On the Soul.'* Translated Texts for Historians 42. Liverpool: Liverpool University Press, 2004.

Henderson, Judith Rice, ed. *The Unfolding of Words: Commentary in the Age of Erasmus.* Toronto: University of Toronto Press, 2012.

Hoffmann, Manfred. *Rhetoric and Theology: The Hermeneutic of Erasmus.* Toronto: University of Toronto Press, 1994.

Jardine, Lisa. *Erasmus, Man of Letters: The Construction of Charisma in Print.* Princeton: Princeton University Press, 1993.

Kim, Sang-Yoon. 'Humanistic Commentary on Scripture in Zurich: Heinrich Bullinger's Commentary on 1 Corinthians (1534).' Unpublished PhD dissertation, Graduate Theological Union at Berkeley, 2015.

Lyon, Gregory. 'Baudouin, Flacius, and the Plan for the Magdeburg Centuries.' *Journal of the History of Ideas* 64 (2003): 253–72.

Mack, Peter. *A History of Renaissance Rhetoric 1380–1620.* Oxford: Oxford University Press, 2011.

- *Renaissance Argument: Valla and Agricola in the Traditions of Rhetoric and Dialectic.* Leiden: E.J. Brill, 1993.

Mann Phillips, Margaret. *The 'Adages' of Erasmus: A Study with Translations.* Cambridge: Cambridge University Press, 1964.

Mansfield, Bruce. *Erasmus in the Twentieth Century.* Toronto: University of Toronto Press, 2003.

Margolin, Jean-Claude. 'Duns Scot et Érasme.' In Margolin, *Érasme: Le prix des mots et de l'homme.* London: Variorum Reprints, 1986. 89–112.

McConica, James. *Erasmus*. Oxford: Oxford University Press, 1991.
McLuhan, Marshall. 'Erasmus: The Man and the Masks.' *Erasmus in English* 3 (1971): 7–10.
Michelson, Emily. *The Pulpit and the Press in Reformation Italy*. Cambridge, MA: Harvard University Press, 2013.
Monfasani, John. 'In Defense of Erasmus' Critics.' ES 39 (2019): 147–83.
Moss, Ann. *Printed Commonplace-Books and the Structuring of Renaissance Thought*. Oxford: Oxford University Press, 1996.
– *Renaissance Truth and the Latin Language Turn*. Oxford: Oxford University Press, 2003.
Muller, Richard A. *The Unaccommodated Calvin: Studies in the Foundation of a Theological Tradition*. New York: Oxford University Press, 2000.
Nauta, Lodi. 'Lorenzo Valla and the Rise of Humanist Dialectic.' In James Hankins, ed., *The Cambridge Companion to Renaissance Philosophy*. Cambridge: Cambridge University Press, 2007. 193–210.
Nellen, Henk, and Jan Bloemendal. 'Erasmus' Biblical Project: Some Thoughts and Observations on Its Scope, Its Impact in the Sixteenth Century and Reception in the Seventeenth and Eighteenth Centuries.' *Church History and Religious Culture* 96 (2016): 595–635.
Ocker, Christopher. 'The Bible in the Fifteenth Century.' In Miri Rubin and Walter Simons, eds., *Christianity in Western Europe, c. 1100–1500*. Vol. 3 of The Cambridge History of Christianity. Cambridge: Cambridge University Press, 2009. 472–93.
– *Biblical Poetics before Humanism and Reformation*. Cambridge: Cambridge University Press, 2002.
– 'The Four Senses of Scripture.' In Christine Helmer et al., eds., *Encyclopedia of the Bible and Its Reception*. 30 vols. Berlin: De Gruyter, 2009–. IX 551–6.
Pabel, Hilmar. *Herculean Labours: Erasmus and the Editing of Jerome's Letters in the Renaissance*. Brill: Leiden, 2008.
Pabel, Hilmar M., and Mark Vessey, eds. *Holy Scripture Speaks: The Production and Reception of Erasmus' Paraphrases on the New Testament*. Toronto: University of Toronto Press, 2002.
Payne, J.B. 'Toward the Hermeneutics of Erasmus.' In J. Coppens, ed., *Scrinium Erasmianum*. 2 vols. Leiden: E.J. Brill, 1969. II 13–49.
Piltz, Anders. *The World of Medieval Learning*. Trans. David Jones. Oxford: Blackwell, 1981.
Rice, Eugene F., Jr. *Saint Jerome in the Renaissance*. Baltimore: Johns Hopkins University Press, 1985.
Rist, John M. *The Mind of Aristotle: A Study in Philosophical Growth*. Toronto: University of Toronto Press, 1989.
Ross, Tricia. 'Anthropologia: An (Almost) Forgotten Early Modern History.' *Journal of the History of Ideas* 79.1 (2018): 1–22.

Rummel, Erika. *Erasmus' Annotations on the New Testament: From Philologist to Theologian*. Toronto: University of Toronto Press, 1986.
- *Erasmus and His Catholic Critics*. 2 vols. Nieuwkoop: De Graaf, 1989.
- *The Humanist-Scholastic Debate in the Renaissance and Reformation*. Cambridge, MA: Harvard University Press, 1995.
- 'Scholasticism and Biblical Humanism in Early Modern Europe.' In Rummel, ed., *Biblical Humanism and Scholasticism in the Age of Erasmus*. 1–14.

Rummel, Erika, ed. *Biblical Humanism and Scholasticism in the Age of Erasmus*. Leiden: Brill, 2008.

Saintsbury, George E.B. *A History of Criticism and Literary Taste in Europe from the Earliest Texts to the Present Day*. 3 vols. Edinburgh: Blackwood, 1900–4.
- *Loci Critici: Passages Illustrative of Critical Theory and Practice from Aristotle Downwards*. Boston, MA: Ginn, 1903.

Screech, M.A. *Ecstasy and the Praise of Folly*. London: Duckworth, 1980.

Seidel Menchi, Silvana. 'How to Domesticate the New Testament: Erasmus' Dilemmas (1516–1535).' In M. Wallraff et al., *Basel 1516: Erasmus' Edition of the New Testament*. 207–21.

Sider, Robert D. 'Erasmus and Ancient Christian Writers: The Search for Authenticity.' In John Petruccione, ed., *Nova & Vetera: Patristic Studies in Honor of Thomas Patrick Halton*. Washington, DC: Catholic University of America Press, 1998. 235–54.
- 'The Just and the Holy in Erasmus' New Testament Scholarship.' ERSY 11 (1991): 1–26.

Thomson, D.F.S., and H.C. Porter, eds. and trans. *Erasmus and Cambridge: The Cambridge Letters of Erasmus*. Toronto: University of Toronto Press, 1963.

Tilley, Maureen. 'Understanding Augustine Misunderstanding Tyconius.' *Studia Patristica* 27 (1993): 405–8.

Trapp, J.B. *Erasmus, Colet and More: The Early Tudor Humanists and Their Books*. The Panizzi Lectures 1990. London: British Library, 1991.

Vanautgaerden, Alexandre. *Érasme typographe: Humanisme et imprimerie au début du XVIe siècle*. Travaux d'Humanisme et Renaissance 503. Geneva: Droz, 2012.

van Gulik, Egbertus. *Erasmus and His Books*. Trans. J.C. Grayson. Ed. James K. McConica and Johannes Trapman. Toronto: University of Toronto Press, 2018.

van Poll-van de Lisdonck, Miekske. 'Die Annotationes in Novum Testamentum im Rahmen von Erasmus' Werken zur Bibel.' In M. Wallraff et al., *Basel 1516: Erasmus' Edition of the New Testament*. 175–86.

Veltri, Giuseppe. *Alienated Wisdom: Enquiry into Jewish Philosophy and Skepticism.* Berlin: de Gruyter, 2018.
Vessey, Mark. 'The Actor in the Story: Horizons of Interpretation in Erasmus's *Annotations on Luke*.' In J.R. Henderson, ed., *The Unfolding of Words: Commentary in the Age of Erasmus*. 55–69.
– 'Basel 1514: Erasmus's Critical Turn.' In Wallraff, Seidel Menchi, and von Greyerz, eds., *Basel 1516: Erasmus' Edition of the New Testament*. 3–26.
– 'Cities of the Mind: Renaissance Views of Early Christian Culture and the End of Antiquity.' In Philip Rousseau, ed., *A Companion to Late Antiquity*. Chichester: Wiley-Blackwell, 2009. 43–58.
– 'Erasmus (1515) between the Bible and the Fathers: Threshold of a Hermeneutic.' In Maria-Cristina Pitassi and Daniela Solfaroli Camillocci, eds., *Crossing Traditions: Essays on the Reformation and Intellectual History in Honour of Irena Backus*. Studies in Medieval and Reformation Traditions 212. Leiden: Brill, 2018. 133–48.
– 'Erasmus' Lucubrations and the Renaissance Life of Texts.' ERSY 24 (2004): 23–51.
– 'Erasmus's *Lucubrationes*: Genesis of a Literary Oeuvre.' In Stephen Partridge and Erik Kwakkel, eds., *Author, Reader, Book: Medieval Authorship in Theory and Practice*. Toronto: University of Toronto Press, 2012. 232–62.
– '"Nothing If Not Critical": G.E.B. Saintsbury, Erasmus, and the History of (English) Literature.' In Stephen Ryle, ed., *Erasmus and the Renaissance Republic of Letters: Proceedings of a Conference to Mark the Centenary of the Publication of the First Volume of Erasmi Epistolae by P.S. Allen, Corpus Christi College, Oxford, 5–7 September 2006*. Disputatio 24. Turnhout: Brepols, 2014. 427–55.
– '"Vera et Aeterna Monumenta": Jerome's Catalogue of Christian Writers and the Premises of Erasmian Humanism.' In Günter Frank, Thomas Leinkauf, and Markus Wriedt, eds., *Die Patristik in der frühen Neuzeit*. Melanchthon-Schriften der Stadt Bretten 10. Stuttgart/Bad Cannstatt: Fromann-Holzboog, 2006. 351–75.
Wallraff, Martin, Silvana Seidel Menchi, and Kaspar von Greyerz, eds. *Basel 1516: Erasmus' Edition of the New Testament*. Tübingen: Mohr Siebeck, 2016.
Waswo, Richard. *Language and Meaning in the Renaissance*. Princeton: Princeton University Press, 1987.
Weiss, J.M. '*Ecclesiastes* and Erasmus: The Mirror and the Image.' *Archiv für Reformationsgeschichte* 65 (1974): 83–108.
Wood, Rega. 'Richard Rufus' Significance in the Western Scientific Tradition.' In L. Honnefelder, R. Wood, M. Dreyer, and Marc-Aeilko Aris, eds., *Albertus Magnus and the Beginnings of the Medieval Reception of Aristotle in the Latin West*. Münster: Aschendorff, 2005. 455–89.

Worcester, Thomas, SJ. 'The Catholic Sermon.' In *Preachers and People in the Reformations and Early Modern Period*. Leiden, Boston, and Cologne: Brill, 2001. 3–33.

Zetzel, James E.G. *Critics, Compilers and Commentators: An Introduction to Roman Philology, 200 BCE–800 CE*. New York: Oxford University Press, 2018.

Concordance of Editions of the *Ratio*

The table below correlates the paragraphs of the present edition with the corresponding pages of CWE 41 (for the same English translation and more extensive annotation) and with the columns of LB V and pages of Holborn (for the Latin text). Where the text printed in LB V omits additions made by Erasmus in *1523*, the table shows a blank or, in more complex cases, a column number in square brackets; for explanation of these cases, the reader is referred to the textual notes in this edition and to the annotation in CWE 41.

	CWE 41	LB V	Holborn
1	488	75A	177:3
2	489	75B	177:14
3	489	75C	177:20
4	490	75D	178:7
5	491	76A	178:19
6	492	76B	179:2
7	493	76D	179:19
8	493	76E	179:35
9	494	77A	180:9
10	494	77B	180:19
11	495	77C	180:35
12	496	77E	181:15
13	496	77F	181:30
14	497	78A	182:10
15	498	78C	182:23
16	499	78D	183:8
17	499	78F	183:19
18	500	79B	184:15

	CWE 41	LB V	Holborn
19	501	79C	184:23
20	502	79F	185:19
21	502	80A	185:29
22	504	80B	186:12
23	505	80D	187:1
24	507	81A	188:1
25	508	81B	188:11
26	509	81E	189:2
27	509	81E	189:12
28	510	82A	189:26
29	511	82B	190:12
30	513	82E	191:7
31	514	83A	191:31
32	514	83B	192:6
33	516	83E	193:1
34	516	83F	193:9
35	517	84A	193:24
36	519	84D	194:27
37	520	84E	195:1
38	520	84F	195:15
39	521	85B	195:33
40	522	85D	196:12
41	523	85E	196:29
42	523	85F	197:5
43	525	86C	197:33
44	526	86D	198:21
45	527	86F	198:33
46	527	87A	199:13
47	529	87C	200:1
48	530	87D	200:20
49	532	88A	201:13
50	532	88B	201:20
51	532	88C	202:1
52	533	88C	202:7
53	534	88D	202:21
54	535	89A	203:10
55	536	89C	203:29
56	537	89D	204:10
57	538	89F	204:34
58	539	90C	205:24
59	540	90D	206:6
60	541	90E	206:17

Concordance of Editions of the *Ratio* 345

	CWE 41	LB V	Holborn
61	542	91A	206:37
62	543		207:8
63	544		207:21
64	544		207:36
65	545		208:14
66	546	91B	208:28
67	546	91C	209:1
68	548	91E	209:26
69	549		210:22
70	550	92B	210:33
71	550	92C	211:10
72	552	92D	211:28
73	553	93A	212:15
74	554	93B	212:33
75	554	93D	213:17
76	555	93E	213:29
77	556	94A	214:20
78	557	94C	215:3
79	558	94D	215:19
80	559	94E	215:32
81	559	94F	216:10
82	560	95A	216:21
83	561	95B	216:31
84	562	95D	217:17
85	563	95F	218:1
86	564	96B	218:22
87	564	96C	219:6
88	565	96C	219:10
89	565	96E	219:26
90	566	96F	220:11
91	568	97C	221:1
92	568	97D	221:16
93	570	97F	222:1
94	570	98A	222:13
95	571	98B	222:27
96	572	98C	223:6
97	573	98F	223:32
98	575	99B	224:21
99	575	99C	224:33
100	576	99E	225:21
101	577	100A	226:6
102	577	100B	226:18

	CWE 41	LB V	Holborn
103	578	100C	226:35
104	579	100E	227:28
105	581	101B	228:20
106	582	101C	229:3
107	583	101E	229:21
108	584	102A	230:11
109	584	102B	230:25
110	585	102C	231:4
111	587	102F	231:36
112	588	103C	232:28
113	589	103C	233:2
114	589	103E	233:16
115	590	104A	234:10
116	591	104B	234:23
117	592	104D	235:8
118	592	104E	235:25
119	593	104F	236:1
120	594	105A	236:13
121	594	105B	236:25
122	594	105C	236:36
123	596	105E	237:17
124	597	106A	238:1
125	597	106C	238:29
126	599	106F	239:23
127	600	107A	240:3
128	600	107B	240:17
129	601	107C	240:28
130	602	107E	241:11
131	603	108A	241:35
132	604	108C	242:22
133	605	108D	243:3
134	605	108E	243:14
135	606	109A	244:2
136	607	109B	244:10
137	607	109C	244:18
138	608	109D	245:1
139	609	109F	245:23
140	609	110A	246:2
141	611	110D	246:35
142	611	110E	247:8
143	612	110F	247:26
144	612	111A	247:35

	CWE 41	LB V	Holborn
145	613	111C	248:20
146	613	111D	249:1
147	614	111F	249:24
148	615	112C	250:16
149	616	112D	251:5
150	617	112F	251:24
151	617	113A	252:4
152	618	113B	252:16
153	619	113D	252:33
154	620	113E	253:16
155	621	113F	253:27
156	621	114A	254:1
157	622	114B	254:7
158	622	114B	254:14
159	622	114C	254:19
160	623	114C	254:22
161	623	114C	254:26
162	623	114D	254:35
163	623	114E	255:9
164	624	114F	255:14
165	624	114F	255:20
166	624	114F	255:24
167	625	115A	255:30
168	625	115A	256:1
169	625	115B	256:7
170	626	115C	256:15
171	626	115C	256:23
172	627	115D	256:32
173	627	115D	257:1
174	628	115E	257:8
175	628	115F	257:13
176	629	116A	257:26
177	629	116A	258:1
178	629	116B	258:7
179	630	116C	258:18
180	630	116C	258:21
181	631	116E	259:3
182	631	116E	259:7
183	632	116F	259:19
184	632	117A	259:28
185	632	117A	259:32
186	633	117C	260:10

	CWE 41	LB V	Holborn
187	634	117E	260:35
188	635	117F	261:9
189	635	118A	261:17
190	636	118B	261:31
191	636	118B	261:35
192	637	118C	262:12
193	638	118E	263:1
194	640	119B	263:29
195	641	119C	264:13
196	641	119E	264:30
197	642	119F	265:10
198	643	120B	265:33
199	644	120C	266:5
200	645	120D	266:19
201	648	121B	267:24
202	649	121C	268:5
203	649	121D	268:12
204	650	121F	269:3
205	652	122B	269:29
206	653	122D	270:15
207	654	122F	271:1
208	654	123A	271:10
209	654	123A	271:16
210	656	123C	271:33
211	656	123D	272:11
212	658	123E	272:32
213	659	124A	273:13
214	659	124B	273:24
215	660	124C	274:1
216	661	124E	274:24
217	662		275:3
218	663		275:13
219	663		275:29
220	663	[124E]	276:1
221	665		276:33
222	665		277:17
223	666	[125A]	277:31
224	667	125B	278:18
225	668	125C	278:33
226	669	125E	279:23
227	669	125F	279:35
228	671		280:23

	CWE 41	LB V	Holborn
229	672	[126B]	281:9
230	673	126B	282:3
231	674	[126D]	282:24
232	676	126E	283:3
233	677	127A	283:29
234	678	127D	284:28
235	679	127F	285:16
236	680	128A	285:28
237	680	128B	286:1
238	680	128B	286:6
239	682	128F	287:9
240	683	129A	287:19
241	684	129B	287:31
242	684	129C	288:8
243	686	129E	288:30
244	687	130A	289:21
245	688	130C	290:7
246	689	130D	290:27
247	690	130F	291:13
248	691	131B	292:1
249	692	131D	292:24
250	692	131E	292:33
251	693	131F	293:13
252	693	132B	293:26
253	694	132C	294:15
254	695	132E	295:1
255	695	133A	295:13
256	696	133B	295:26
257	697	133C	296:2
258	698	133C	296:12
259	698	133F	297:6
260	699	134A	297:22
261	700	134C	298:5
262	701	134D	298:19
263	702	134E	298:34
264	703	135A	299:18
265	703	135C	299:35
266	704	135C	300:8
267	705	135E	300:30
268	705	136A	301:10
269	706	136B	301:25
270	708		302:15

	CWE 41	LB V	Holborn
271	271	136D	303:11
272	710	136E	303:23
273	711	137A	303:37
274	711	137B	304:15
275	712	137C	304:28
276	712	138A	304:35
277	713	138B	305:16

Index of Rhetorical Terms and Literary-Critical Concepts

Bold numerals refer to paragraphs of the *Ratio verae theologiae*.

abutio, 90–1, **212**
accommodation, 82, 84–9, 92, **99**, 281
affectus, feelings, emotions, dispositions, 57–62, **10, 23, 104–21, 175**, 250, 258
allegory, 54–7, 75–7, 83, 88–92, 96, 99–100, **23, 45, 185–6, 189–98, 194, 216–33, 252**
ambiguity, 90–1, **211–12**
amplification, **23**, 258

collatio, comparison, 93–107, **29, 95, 116, 191–3, 232**, 260; *collatio locorum*, comparison of passages, 100–1, 105, **41, 247–50, 252**; *collatio studiorum*, 101, 105, **275** (meanings of, 106–7)
commonplaces. See *loci communes*
compendium, shortcut, 6, 25, 30–1, 41, **191**
context, 265, **41, 236**. *See also* historical sense
copia, rhetorical fluency, 51–2, 55, 60–1

difference of persons (*personae*), 42–4, **238**

difference of things or circumstances, **37–40, 238**
difference of times, **45–50, 238**

emphasis, 90–1, **212–15**
enargeia, vividness of expression, 60–1, 98, **10**
enarratio poetarum, interpretation of the poets, 98
enthymemes, 280, 299, **92, 193**
epagoge, induction, 99

fabula, 60, 94, 96, 98, 104; *fabula Christi*, drama of Christ, 60, 98, 104, **67–184**
fides narrationis, trustworthiness of the narrative, 104

heterosis, **201**, 302
historical sense, setting, interpretation, x–xi, xiii, 86–7, **19–20, 27, 37–50, 216–29, 234–6**, 259, 307–8. *See also* context
hyperbaton, 76, 90, **201, 210**
hyperbole, 82, 90–1, **202–7**, 303

imitatio (*mimesis*), imitation (of Christ), x, 50, 53, 57–62, 82–4, **104–29, 192**
irony, **209**

lectio, reading, 49, **10**, 250
lit(t)erae, letters, literature, 8–13, 34, 50–4; *bonae lit(t)erae*, 'good literature,' 13, 30, 48, 50–4, 97, 101n26, **29**, 260; (secular/ profane and) sacred/divine letters (*sacrae/divinae lit[t]erae*), ix, 35–6, 49 52–3, 55, 59, 61–2, 93, 98, 101
literal and allegorical senses, 54–7, **216–33, 223**, 308
loci communes, commonplaces, 33–4, 55, 77–8, **23, 247**, 258, 319
lucubrationes, synonym for 'literary works,' 26, 32, 35

metaphor, 33, 55–6, 89, 96–9, 260, 297, 310. *See also* similitudes
mimesis. See *imitatio*
mystical books, passages, and interpretation, 75, **8, 29, 187, 248**, 249, 319

parabola (parable), 94–100, **185–8, 192, 195, 229, 252**. See also *collatio*
persona(e), person(s), roles, 68, **42**, 265; difference of *personae*, **42–4, 238**; method of taking *personae*, 60, **44**
proverbs, **198**

riddles, **191, 194**

scopi, target points, xiii, 6, 86, 263, **35**
series narrationis, sequence of the narrative, **41**
simile, 94–5, **185**. See also *collatio*
similitudes, **186, 191–3**, 297–8
style, ix, 33, 83, 95
syllogisms, 102, 105, 107, **21, 29, 92, 96, 232, 259, 274, 276**, 280
synecdoche, 76, **201**, 302

types (in the Old Testament), 67, **69**, 271

varietas (*Christi*), diversity (in Christ), 60–1, **37–40, 72–96**
verba (words) and *res* (things), 33, 55, 69

General Index

Bold numerals refer to paragraphs of the *Ratio verae theologiae*.

Academics, school of philosophy, **29**, 260, **264**, 323, 324
Agricola, Rudolph, 54, 55, 77, **17**, 253
allegory. *See Index of Rhetorical Terms and Literary-Critical Concepts*
Ambrose, bishop of Milan, 33, 103–4, **17**, **20**, **33**, **48**, **139**, **224–5**, **228**, **233**, **242**, **255–6**, **263**, 254, 308, 309, 316, 321, 330–1; *De spiritu sancto*, **242**; *Expositio evangelii secundum Lucam*, **17**, **20**, **224–5**, **228**
Ambrosiaster (pseudo-Ambrose), 267, 316, 331
Ammonio, Andrea, 32
Anacreon, **30**, 261
Aquinas, Thomas, 54, 63–6, 68–9, **16**, **57**, **257**, 253, 261, 322
Aratus of Soli, **99**, 282
Aristophanes, 258, 322
Aristotle, 55, 58, 61, 71, 74, 94, **21**, **23**, **29**, **30**, **32**, **253**, **273**, 248, 253, 255, 258, 261, 269, 320
Athanasius, bishop of Alexandria, **255**, 329
Athenaeus, **21**, 256
Augustine, bishop of Hippo, x, 11–12, 47, 57, 62, 74, 90, 331; *Confessiones*, **30**, 253; *Contra Cresconium Donatistam*, **17**; *Contra Faustum Manichaeum*, **20**, **57**; *De baptismo contra Donatistas*, **244**, 317–18; *De civitate Dei*, **22–3**, 252; *De coniugiis adulterinis*, **48**; *De consensu evangelistarum*, **201**; *De doctrina Christiana*, x, 11, 14, 47, 55, 74–5, **4**, **9**, **12**, **15**, **19–22**, **29**, **45**, **71**, **210–11**, **223**, **233**, **251**, 251, 252, 331; *De fide et operibus*, **48**; *Enarrationes in Psalmos*, **42**, 252; *Epp*, **48**, **204**; *In Ioannis epistulam ad Parthos tractatus*, **138**; *In Ioannis evangelium tractatus*, **227**, **244**; *Locutiones in Heptateuchum*, **200–1**, 254, 301–2
Averroës (Ibn Rushd), **29**, **30**, 260, 261
Avicenna (Ibn Sina), **30**, 261

Bade, Josse, 32, 34
Bartolus of Sassoferrato, **32**, 262
Basil, bishop of Caesarea, 33, 45, **28**, **255**, 329
Béda, Noël, 60, 66
Bede, the Venerable, 73, **243**, 332
Benedict of Nursia, **270**, 326
Bernard of Clairvaux, **240**, 315

Blount, William, 22, 26, 31
Bricot, Thomas, **32**, 262
Bridget of Sweden, **270**, 326
Bullinger, Heinrich, 77–8
Busleyden, Gilles de, **13**
Busleyden, Jérôme de, **13**

Calvin, John, 78
Cassiodorus, 53
Catherine of Siena, **270**, 326
Cato the Elder, **17**, 253
Cebes, **231**, 311
centos, **240**
Chomarat, Jacques, 53
Chrysippus of Soli, 262, **32**
Chrysostom, John, 12, 49, 77, 90, **23**, **28**, **33**, **201**, **202**, **205**, **242**, **255**–**7**, **261**–**2**, **264**, **266**, **273**, 258, 321, 330; *In epistolam secundam ad Timotheum homiliae*, **242**, **266**; *In Ioannem evangelistam homiliae*, **205**, **261**; *In Mattheum evangelistam homiliae*, **205**, **252**, **262**, **264**
Church Fathers, i, 12, 15, 27, 30, 38–9, 41, 42, 46, 81, 90–1, 253, 265, 269, 322, 329–33. *See also entries for individual Church Fathers*
Cicero, xi, 11, 51, 53, 55, 59–62 64n6, 66, 75, 96, **30**, **212**, 253, 256, 260, 261, 269, 280, 310, 323
Clement, bishop of Rome, **33**, 262–3
Colet, John, 21, 22, 27, 30, 32, 48–9, 253, 265
Cresconius the Donatist, **18**, 254
Cromwell, Thomas, 50
Cyprian, bishop of Carthage, **33**, **246**, **254**, **256**, **263**, 319, 321, 332
Cyril, bishop of Alexandria, **205**, **255**, 303, 329

Damasus, bishop of Rome, **29**, 332
Dante Alighieri, 9–10

Demosthenes, **30**, 261
Derrida, Jacques, 12
dialectic, 70–2, 101–3, 105, 107, **19**, **21**, **24**, **34**, **96**, **227**, **232**, **253**, **259**, **267**
Diogenes Laertius, 262
Diomedes, grammarian, **210**, 304
Dioscorides, medical writer, **21**, 255
Donatists, **244–6**, 317–19
Donatus, Aelius, xi–xii, 97–8, 101, **27**, 259
Dorp, Martin, 38–9, 42, 44, 102n27, 103n29
Dresden, Sem, 12–14
Durand, William, **32**, **276**, 262, 328

Eberhard of Béthune, **22**, 257
Epicurus, **27**, **211**, 324
Erasmus, Desiderius: chronology of life and works, 17–18; complete oeuvre, 27–9; in Cambridge, 32, 34, 327; in England, 22, 30–2, 34, 37n42, 327; in Italy, 23–4, 26, 32; in Louvain, 38, 42, 44–5; in Paris, **273**, 327; knowledge of Greek, 23–5, 30–2, 35–7, 41; knowledge of Hebrew, 54; piety, understanding of, 27–8, 30, 81, 92
Erasmus, individual works
– *Adages*, ix, 3, 8, 9, 22–6, 34–5, 37, 247, 248, 249, 253, 269, 270, 271, 275, 276, 282, 283, 289, 293, 304, 314, 315, 325
– *Adagiorum chiliades*, 24–5, 31, 34
– *Adagiorum collectanea*, 22–3, 26
– allegories in Scripture, projected work on, 39, 100n24, 306–7, 313
– *Annotations on the New Testament*, ix, xii, 27, 58, 66–8, 77, 80–92, 249, 276, 321, 329
– *Antibarbari*, 14n18, 302
– *Apology against a Dialogue of Jacobus Latomus*, 63n1, 65

General Index 355

- *Apophthegmata*, 8, 9
- *Ciceronianus*, ix, xi
- *Clarification Concerning the Censures Published at Paris in the Name of the Faculty of Theology There*, 49n5
- *Colloquies*, 3, 8, 11, 45–6, 48–51, 69, 271
- *De bello Turcico / On the Turkish War*, 293
- *De copia / Foundations of the Abundant Style*, ix, 33–5, 37, 39, 51–2, 94–100, 105, **247**, 257, 276, 297–8, 302, 303, 306, 312, 319
- *De libero arbitrio / On Free Will*, 285, 286
- *De pueris instituendis / On Education for Children*, 253
- *De ratione studii / On the Method of Study*, ix, 32–3, 254, 256, 258, 260, 273, 319
- *De taedio Iesu / The Distress of Jesus*, 265, 294
- *Ecclesiastes / The Evangelical Preacher*, ix, xiv, 11, 64, 69, 297, 302, 303, 306, 307, 308, 313
- *Enchiridion militis Christiani / Handbook of the Christian Soldier*, ix, 3, 11, 27–8, 30–1, 38–9, 44–5, 56, 58, 101n26, 249, 250, 257, 258, 268, 271, 276, 282, 283, 287, 291, 294, 295, 300, 311–12, 320
- *Explanatio symboli / Explanation of the Creed*, 273
- *Expositions of the Psalms*, 92, 265, 276
- Handbook of the Christian Soldier. See *Enchiridion militis Christiani*
- *Hyperaspistes*, 66, 78n81
- *Institutio Christiani matrimonii / Institution of Christian Matrimony*, 270
- *Institutio principis christiani / Education of a Christian Prince*, 268, 282, 292
- Letters (Epp), 42–3, 62
- *Life of Jerome*, 319
- *Lucubrationes*, 27, 39–40
- *Lucubratiunculae*, 26–7, 38, 63
- *Methodus*, 4–7, 11, 14, 41–2, 46, 50, 54, 56, 58, 80–2, 254, 262–3, 265, 271, 313
- *Modus orandi Deum / On Praying to God*, 294
- *Moriae Encomium / Praise of Folly*, 3, 21–3, 26–8, 31, 34, 36–9, 46, 64, 66, 103n30, 249, 250, 268, 310, 311, 323, 328
- *Novum instrumentum*, 4, 21n1, 27, 37–9, 41–3, 80–1, **1**, 252
- *Novum Testamentum*, 6, 11–12, 46, 66–8, 80–92, 252
- *Parabolae sive Similia / Parallels*, 37, 96, **23**, **223**, 257, 285, 308
- *Paraclesis*, 28, 41, 54, 80, 83–4, 320, 326
- *Paraphrase on Acts*, 277
- *Paraphrase on Matthew*, 296
- *Paraphrase on Paul's Epistle to the Romans*, 44
- *Paraphrases on the New Testament*, 27, 80, 269, 285, 293, 329
- Praise of Folly. See *Moriae Encomium*
- *Ratio verae theologiae*. See separate entry below

Euripides, 31, 309
Eusebius, bishop of Caesarea, xii, **22**, 251, 257, 273, 330

figurative language in Scripture, 54–7, 75–6, 83, 88–92, **20**, **23–34**, **42**, **185–233**, 257–8. See also *Index of Rhetorical Terms and Literary-Critical Concepts*
Fisher, John, 327
Flacius (Matthias Flacius Illyricus), xiii
Francis of Assisi, **270**, 326

Froben, Johann, 29, 34, 36–9, 41–6, 49, 73, 113, 126n11

Galen, **30**, 261
Gerbel, Nikolaus, 39, 41–2
Gerson, Jean, 63, 64, 70, 73
Gillis, Pieter, 42, 59
Greek, utility of a knowledge of, **12–18**
Gregory, bishop of Nazianzus, **29**, **255**, 330

Hebrew, utility of a knowledge of, 54, 56, **12–18**
Hebrew idioms in Scripture, 76, **199–200**, 319
Henry VIII, king of England, 31, 32, 50, 65
Hesiod, **30**, 261
Hilary, bishop of Poitiers, **17**, **214**, **228**, **234**, **255**, **263**, 306, 314, 332; *Commentarius in Matthaeum*, **17**; *De Trinitate*, **234**; *Tractatus in Psalmos*, **17**, **214**
Hippocrates, **5**, **30**, 248, 261
Hispanus, Petrus, 262
Holcot, Robert, 60, 63, 71, **32**, 262
Homer, **30**, 257, 260, 261
Horace, 30, 31, **3**, **30**, 247, 257, 261, 320, 328
Hugh of St Cher, 63, 66, 73–4

Ibn Rushd. *See* Averroës
Ibn Sina. *See* Avicenna
Isidore of Seville, **22**, 257, 332

Jerome, ix, x, xii, 26, 33, 35–9, 42, 49, 56, 63, 66, 71, 73, **14–17**, **22**, **28**, **33**, **200–2**, **220**, **226**, **231**, **240**, **247**, **255–9**, **263**, 301, 316, 319, 332; *Adversus Iovinianum*, **241**; *Chronicle*, 251; *Commentarius in epistolam ad Titum*, **99**, 322; *Commentarius in evangelium Matthaei*, **226**; *Commentarius in Ieremiam prophetam*, **240**; *Commentarius in Isaiam prophetam*, **220**; *De situ et nominibus locorum Hebraeorum*, 257; *De viris illustribus*, xii, 321; Epp, **17**, **231**
Juvenal, 279
Juvencus, **29**, 333

Latin, need for a knowledge of, **12–18**
Latin idioms in Scripture, **199**, **208**, 250
Latomus, Jacob, 64–5, 77
liberal disciplines, value of a knowledge of, **19–22**
Lombard, Peter, 63, 68, **239**, 262, 315, 323
Lucan, **22**, 256
Lucian, 31, 42
Luther, Martin, 4–5, 28n18, 60, 65–6, 70, 72–4, 78, 101n26, 290, 292

Macrobius, **21**, 256
Magdeburg Centuries, xiii
Magnus, Albertus, 68, 253
Manutius, Aldus, 23–5, 32
Martens, Dirk, 38
Maternus, Julius Firmicus, **5**, 248
McLuhan, Marshall, 23
Melanchthon, Philipp, xiii, 72, 78
Menedemus of Eretrea, 285
Momigliano, Arnaldo, xiv
More, Thomas, 21, 22, 31, 42

Nicander of Colophon, **22**, 256
Nicholas of Lyra, 63, 64, 66, 72–4, 77
Novatian, **242**, 316–17

Ockham, William, 63, 67, 68, 71–2, **268**
Oecolampadius, Johannes, 53, 72

Oppian, 22, 256
Origen of Alexandria, xi, 12, 30, 33, 41, 56, 59, 77, 90, 97–8, **23**, **24–8**, **202**, **204**, **215**, **228**, **233**, **240**, **248**, **254–7**, 259, 298, 316, 319, 330; *Commentarius in epistolam Pauli ad Timotheum secundam*, **242**; *Commentarius in epistulam Pauli ad Corinthios*, **48**; *Commentarius in Matthaeum*, **215**; *In epistolam ad Romanos*, **204**, 303; *In Genesim homiliae*, **24–8**, **204**, **233**, 259, 298, 303; *Homilies on Genesis*, xii

Paul, the apostle, 30–1, 35, 44, 60, 62, 83–4, 86–9, 99–100, **6**, **23**, **29**, **36**, **48**, **50**, **53**, **56**, **97–102**, **113–17**, **120**, **130–50**, **196–7**, **212**, **230**, **267**, **271**, 274, 281, 285, 286, 321
Paulinus of Nola, **29**, 333
Pellikan, Konrad, 73–4
Peripatetics, school of philosophy, **5**, **36**, **264**, 248
philosophizing from Scripture, **75**, **122–84**, **232**, 312
philosophy of Christ, 28, 44–5, 60, 80, 82, 88, **32**, **35–6**, **56**, 262
Pindar, **30**, 261
Plato, x, 58, 94n6, 95, **30**, **70**, **227**, 248, 261, 270, 285, 297, 310, 312
Plautus, **258**, 322
Pliny the Elder, **21**, 256
poetry, 9–10, **23**, **29**
Poncher, Etienne, 250
Proba, 315
Proteus, Christ likened to, **72–7**, 276
Prudentius, **29**, 333
Pseudo-Dionysius, **4**, **233**, 248, 330; *On Mystical Theology*, 52, **4**; *On Symbolic Theology*, **4**; *Theological Institutes*, **4**
Pythagoras, **7**

Quintilian, x, 6, 11, 51, 55–7, 76, 77, 90, 93–5, 98, **23**, **210–12**, 257–8, 280, 297, 301, 304–5, 309

Rabanus Maurus, **231**, 311
Ratio verae theologiae: and Erasmus' *Annotations on the New Testament*, 80–92; as central to Erasmus' life's work, ix–x; concordance of editions, 343–50; in context of Erasmus' other works, 28; historical significance of, 6–7; literary premise of, 7–8; publishing history, 45–7; scheme of contents, 111–12; scope of, 5–6; shock value of, 4–6; structure of, 93–107. *See also entry for the 'Methodus' (precursor to the 'Ratio') under* Erasmus, individual works
Reuchlin, Johann, 12, 72–3, 310, 326
Rhenanus, Beatus, 9, 39, 45, 39, 45
rhetoric, i, x, 6, 8, 46, 53–5, 72, 75, 77, 79, 86–9, 98n21, 101–2, **19**, **23**, **29**, 280. *See also Index of Rhetorical Terms and Literary-Critical Concepts*
Robertson, D.W., Jr, 11

Saintsbury, G.E.B., 9–10
scholasticism, x, xiii, 37, 38, 60, 63–79, **32**, **57**, **60**, **63**, **259**, **260**, **262**, **263**, **275**, 250, 252, 255, 262, 322, 324. *See also entries for individual scholastic theologians*
Scotus, Duns, 66, 68–9, **57**, **253**, **257**, **263**, **265**, **273**, 261, 312, 320, 323
Seneca the Younger, **21**, **22**, **34**, **70**, 255–6, 263–5, 311
Septuagint, **17**, **18**, **200**, 252, 301

Sider, Robert D., 4n2, 6n5, 7, 37n42, 81–2
Sidney, Philip, 9–10
Socrates, 60, 61, 95, 97, 99, **70**, **185**, 248, 270, 285
Standish, Henry, 302
Stoics, 58, 59, **5**, **264**, 248, 262, 268

Tartaret, Peter, **32**, 262
Terence, xi, **27**, 252, 259
Tertullian, **32**, **67**, **220**, **254**, 321, 333; *Adversus Marcionem*, **67**, **220**; *De praescriptione haereticorum*, 315; *De resurrectione mortuorum*, **32**
Themistius, **30**, 261
Theocritus, **30**, 261
Theophrastus, **21**, **30**, 255, 261
Theophylact, Bulgarian bishop, **209**, 304
Thompson, Craig R., 11, 49, 64n6, 273
Titelmans, Frans, 59, 72, 74

tropes, 53, 55, 57, **23**, **185–233**, 257–8. *See also Index of Rhetorical Terms and Literary-Critical Concepts*
Turks, 64, 107, **54**, **157**, **197**, 269, 282
Tyconius the Donatist, **233**, 313

Ubaldis, Baldus degli, **32**, 262

Valla, Lorenzo, 31, 36, 38, 48, 63, 94, 252, 332
Villa Dei, Alexander de, 302
Virgil, **30**, **31**, 261, 322
Volz, Paul, 44, 54, 268, 314
Vulgate Bible, x, 36–8, 41, 58, 66–7, **16**, 247, 252, 289, 296, 302, 307, 332

Wimpfeling, Jakob, 37, 70

Xenophon, **30**, 261

Zeno, 248

www.ingramcontent.com/pod-product-compliance
Lightning Source LLC
Chambersburg PA
CBHW022210090526
44584CB00012BA/392